Air Pollution: Economic Modelling and Control Policies

Editor

Maria Llop

Departament d'Economia
Facultat de Ciències Econòmiques i Empresarials
Avgda. Universitat nº 1, Reus
Spain

CONTENTS

Foreword *i*

Preface *ii*

Contributors *iv*

CHAPTERS

1. **Determinant Sectors of CO_2 Emissions in Spain: An Input-Output Analysis Approach** 1
   V. Alcántara

2. **Measuring Sectoral Share of Green House Gases (Ghgs) Emissions from Fossil Fuel Consumption and Offering Solutions: The Case of Turkey** 13
   N. A. Bhutto and S. Cagatay

3. **Atmospheric Emissions and Structural Path Analysis in the Spanish Economy** 31
   I. Butnar, B. Gallego, M. Llop and F. Castells

4. **Energy Consumption and CO_2 Emissions in the Spanish Economy** 46
   M. A. Cardenete and P. D. Fuentes

5. **Hybrid IO Analysis of CO_2 Emissions: An Application to the Portuguese Economy** 65
   L. Cruz and E. Barata

6. **Compilation of Greek Regional Nameas and Emission Intensities for the Year 2005** 96
   C. Economidis, N. Stromplos and A. Sfetsos

7. **An Analysis of Primary Energy Requirements and Emissons Levels Using the Structural Decomposition Approach: The Spanish Case** 112
   A. I.Guerra and F. Sancho

8. **Measuring the Air Pollution of Tourism: An Input-Output Model for the Campania Region** 132
   M. Llop and S. Sabena

9. **Input-Output Table for Environmental Analysis of Japan: Construction and Application Study to Solar Power Satellites** 149
   S. Nakano and K. Asakura

Subject Index 175

FOREWORD

One of the most important problems facing the world this century is to preserve nature from the action of humans. In particular, humankind's use of production and consumption processes in which non-renewable material resources, like fossil fuels, are intensively used has given rise to air pollution emissions that lead to the greenhouse effect and climate change. These phenomena are so important that the world's leading governments have expressed their concerns in world summits in Kyoto and other cities (including the summit recently held in Copenhagen). During these summits, countries from all over the world have entered into agreements and negotiations to reduce the emissions of polluting gases and avoid climate change. Unfortunately not all countries have signed the agreements to reduce emissions among which are such leading players as the United States of America and China.

It should be pointed out that implementing the agreements made at these world conferences is not easy because the economic cost is sometimes very high. To reduce emissions a country can decrease its economic activity (which is very unlikely from a political point of view) or replace dirty economic activities with clean production and consumption processes. On the other hand, a clean atmosphere is a pure public good so no matter what countries do, they always benefit from the clean activities of other countries, which makes the problem more difficult to solve from a political point of view.

If we look at the problem from a purely economic perspective we should bear in mind the so-called Stern report, which makes an economic cost benefit analysis of the problem facing humankind. It first estimates the economic cost of doing nothing, and then compares it with the cost of taking steps to avoid climate change. The conclusion is that it pays to act today and not leave the current economic process unchanged. However, it is important to stress that not all countries are in the same economic situation so it is not clear which countries should pay for a clean environment when the benefits are for all. It is therefore important to analyse the specific situation of a particular country to make an individual balance of its situation.

This book, in the methodological tradition of Leontief, presents groups of first-class researchers and their recent studies on emissions in a variety of countries (Spain, Turkey, Portugal, Greece, Japan). They also construct data sets so that the situation in other countries can be estimated. However, they do not merely provide a number. They also identify those sectors of the economy that are responsible for the emissions so that specific policy recommendations can be implemented in an attempt to solve the problem. They also analyze the cost of substituting dirty economic activities for clean ones. Readers will benefit from all this information if they decide to read this book.

Antonio Manresa

(Departament de Teoria Econòmica
and Centre de Recerca en Economia del Benestar)
Universitat de Barcelona
SPAIN

PREFACE

In recent years, environmental pollution has received considerable attention from regulators, ecologists and economists who have integrated their ideas and concepts. Nowadays, it is generally accepted that environmental degradation is a multidisciplinary problem, and that environmental issues should be analysed by using multidisciplinary points of view to capture all the complexity involved.

This book contains several contributions that illustrate the state of the art of academic research and knowledge in the field of gas pollution and gas emissions. The layout of the book is an attempt to capture not only the environmental dimension of the problem, but also its economic and political implications. The research articles also cover different economies of application to show that the subject is of global interest.

The first chapter analyses the relationships between the productive structure of the Spanish economy and the associated CO_2 emissions, the most important of the greenhouse gases sent into the atmosphere. Important patterns of emissions are found which makes it possible to determine what the leading sectors in CO_2 emissions are.

The second chapter uses input-output techniques to estimate the Turkish greenhouse emissions for the immediate future and the effects of a reduction in pollution on the final demand of the economy. The chapter also analyses the impact of a substitution of natural gas completely for other fossil fuel types and illustrates that this substitution would lead to a significant reduction in greenhouse pollution.

The third chapter focuses on Spanish atmospheric pollution and macroeconomic data in an attempt to identify the main drivers of atmospheric pollution in Spain. The input paths of air pollution in the production system are identified by using Structural Path Analysis (SPA) in a generalised input-output framework. This methodology enables "hidden" sectors in the generation of pollution to be detected. The results show that the energy sectors, food processing industries, other manufacturing industries and transportation are the sectors with the highest emission intensities.

Chapter 4 analyses the emissions generated by energy in the Spanish economy. Particular attention is paid to final energy consumption and the demands that take most to satisfy in terms of emissions of pollutants into the atmosphere. The method used shows how the final demand of both the energy subsystem and complementary subsystem influences income generation and energy emissions.

Chapter 5 presents an extended environmental input–output model of interactions between the environment and the economy in Portugal and shows that it is possible to implement strategies that respect and promote a balanced management of the dynamics between energy supply, environmental protection and economic growth. The analysis presents the energy intensity coefficients by industry, as well as the energy requirements attributable to given final demand vectors. Then, the sources of Portuguese anthropogenic CO_2 emissions and the share of each sector in total emissions are identified and related to the use of fossil fuels.

Chapter 6 shows regional National Accounting Matrices with Environmental Accounts (NAMEA) for the five main Greek regions. The derived regional NAMEA tables are a valuable tool for examining environmental-economic indices such as direct emission intensity coefficients, direct and indirect emission intensity coefficients and the emission intensity factor of each of the components in the final demand of the Greek economy.

Chapter 7 applies Structural Decomposition Analysis to the Spanish economy and calculates how changes in efficiency gains, final demand, direct and indirect input/output requirements have affected energy use and emissions in recent years. The results show that the most energy intensive sectors have made the greatest contributions to energy efficiency gains. This is due not only to the reduction in their effective consumption of primary energy but also to the fact that their role as "key forward sectors" made these energy efficiency gains more effective. However, the notable growth in final demand has increased the strength of their push effects, offsetting the contribution of these improvements in energy efficiency. Finally, the contribution of indirect requirements dominates the contribution of direct requirements in most Energy sectors but the opposite is true in energy intensive sectors.

Chapter 8 describes a methodology for analysing the impacts of regional tourism and its associated environmental consequences. The methodology is implemented through an Input-Output model related to income generation by the tourism sector and the generation of emissions into the atmosphere. The model, which is applied to an area of high cultural value (the Italian region of Campania), is used not only to calculate the emission multipliers of regional activities, but also to simulate changes in tourism final demand and its subsequent effects on regional income and regional emissions.

Chapter 9 presents an Input-Output Table for the Environmental Analysis of Japan and its application study. Tables of energy inputs and CO_2 emissions are constructed with both economic and energy statistics. The analysis is completed by quantifying the CO_2 emission of new power generation technology (Solar Power Satellites) as an application study.

I would like to thank Professor Antonio Manresa, of the Universitat de Barcelona, for writing the foreword and Bentham Science Publishers, particularly Sara Moqeet, for their support and hard work. I would also like to thank Magda Lleixà, the administrative officer of the research group Quantitative, Urban and Regional Economics (QURE) at the Departament d'Economia of the Universitat Rovira i Virgili, for editing support.

Maria Llop

(Departament d'Economia and
Quantitative, Urban and Regional Economics)
Universitat Rovira i Virgili
SPAIN

CONTRIBUTORS

Vicent Alcántara	Associate Professor at Institut de Ciència i Tecnologia Ambiental (ICTA), Departament d'Economia Aplicada of the Universitat Autònoma de Barcelona (Spain)
Keiichiro Asakura	Associate Professor at the Faculty of Economics of the Ryutsu Keizai University (Japan)
Eduardo Barata	Assistant Professor at GEMF, Faculty of Economics of the University of Coimbra (Portugal)
Niaz Ahmed Bhutto	Associate Professor at Sukkur Institute of Business Administration (Pakistan)
Isabela Butnar	Research Assistant at the Departament d'Enginyeria Química of the Rovira i Virgili University (Spain)
Selim Cagatay	Associate Professor at Economics Department of Akdeniz University (Turkey)
M. Alejandro Cardenete	Associate Professor at Economics Department of the Pablo Olavide University (Spain)
Francesc Castells	Professor at Departament d'Enginyeria Química of the Rovira i Virgili University (Spain)
Luís Cruz	Assistant Professor at GEMF, Faculty of Economics of the University of Coimbra (Portugal)
Charalambos Economidis	Assistant Professor at Department of Public Administration of the Panteion University (Greece)
Patricia D. Fuentes Saguar	Assistant Professor at the Cepartment of Economics of the Pablo Olavide University (Spain)
Blanca Gallego	Research Fellow at the Integrated Sustainability Analysis Group of the University of Sydney (Australia). Currently Senior Research Fellow at the Institute of Heath Innovation of the University of New South Wales (Australia)
Ana-Isabel Guerra	Post-Doctoral Researcher at the Department of Applied Economics of the Universitat Autònoma de Barcelona (Spain)
Maria Llop	Associate Professor at the Departament d'Economia of the Rovira i Virgili University (Spain)
Satoshi Nakano	Research fellow at the Japan Institute for Labour Policy and Training, Keio Economic Observatory of the Keio University (Japan)
Simona Sabena	Post-Doctoral Researcher at the Politecnico di Torino University (Italy)
Ferran Sancho	Professor at the Department of Economics of the Universitat Autònoma de Barcelona (Spain)
Athanasios Sfetsos	Research Scientist in the Environmental Research Laboratory, INT-RP, NCSR of Demokritos (Greece)
Nikos Stromplos	Director of National Accounts in the National Statistical Service (Greece)

CHAPTER 1

Determinant Sectors of CO_2 Emissions in Spain: An Input-Output Analysis Approach

Vicent Alcántara

Departament d'Economia Aplicada and Institut de Ciència i Tecnologia Ambiental (ICTA), Universitat Autònoma de Barcelona, Bellaterra (Spain)

Abstract: The aim of this paper is to develop a first analysis of the relationships between the productive structure of the Spanish economy and CO_2 emissions, the most important of the greenhouse gases sent to the atmosphere. After presenting the methodology of interest, which allows a joint ex-post analysis of demand and supply multipliers, we arrive at some relevant findings that in turn permit a detailed study of the above mentioned relationships. Finally, the determinant sectors in the emission of this gas are established.

Keywords: Input-Output, CO_2 emissions, key sectors in emission, demand and supply multipliers.

INTRODUCTION

The evolution of CO_2 emissions in Spain has departed remarkably from the objective set by the European Guideline 2002/358/CE ratifying the Kyoto Protocol and limiting the increase of greenhouse gases[1] in Spain to 15% on average for the period 2008-2012 with respect to the 1990 emissions. According to information available on the UNFCCC (United Nations Framework Convention on Climate Change) website, the emissions of these gases, measured in CO_2-equivalent tons, increased by 50.4% between 1990 and 2004. On the other hand, Santamarta and Nieto (2007) estimated that for the six gases considered in the Protocol emissions in 2006 were 48,5% above the 1990 level. This represents a three-fold increase from the baseline, although a slight decrease was observed between 2005 and 2006.

It seems evident that the measures adopted in the past years to deal with the sharp increase in emissions were not enough. Among the measures implemented, the Plan Nacional de Asignación de Emisiones (in Spanish, National Programme of Emissions Allocation) is worth highlighting. In this programme, the compliance of which is guaranteed by the 2003/87/CE guideline on emission rights markets, certain sectors are required to control their CO_2 emissions by January 1st, 2005. However, one of the most important sectors responsible for the increase in emissions in the past years, namely the service sector, is not subject to this requirement. Transportation, commerce and other services, along with the domestic sector, are important diffusing emissions pockets that are not bounded by any sort of regulation or measure that limits their energy use or their emissions.

In light of the above, the need for an analysis of the relationships between these emissions and the Spanish economic structure is evident. The input-output (IO) analytical framework seems to be an adequate one for determining the importance of these relationships. It also allows a diagnosis of the responsibility of the different economic agents as part of a system. In this paper we will only analyse CO_2 emissions, which is the most important of the greenhouse gases.

Data for the present research come from the environmental accounts of the Instituto Nacional de Estadística – INE (the Spain Statistical Office), which include CO_2 emissions in 2000. The NAMEA (National Accounting Matrix including Environmental Accounts) system was used for this purpose[2]. Also, we use the 2000 symmetric OI table for Spain, which is elaborated by the INE.

The present research is structured as follows. In Section 2 we present the methodology followed by an application and findings. In order to make this paper more amenable, the results are presented in annexes to the Sections.

[1] Emissions measured in CO_2-equivalent tons using the IPCC conversion factor. The six gases considered are CO_2, N_2O, CH_4, HFCs, CFCs, y SF_4.
[2] For further details on the NAMEA environmental accounting system, please see Keuning, S.J. (1996) or Alcántara (2003). For an application and pilot project on atmospheric emissions, see Eurostat (2001).

Maria Llop (Ed)

However, we will give some previews of the sectoral environmental impact in this Section as this will allow a better understanding of the results presented in the following ones. Section 3 analyses the role played by the different types of final demand and their importance in CO_2 emissions in Spain. Applying the methodology laid out in Section 2, we determine in Section 4 the productive sectors that are the key determinants of these emissions in Spain. In Section 5 we make some concluding remarks.

METHODOLOGY AND EARLY FINDINGS

We define next the vectors as column vectors and transpose is as usual represented by (′), while diagonaliasation (i.e. expressing a vector as a diagonal matrix) is represented by (^). Vectors and matrices are in bold while scalars appear in normal character.

Let **c** (n x 1) be a vector of coefficients of direct emissions by sector. In our case, these are tons of CO_2 emissions per million of euros (see Annex **I**). So that,

ANNEX I

	Production branches	Direct emission CO_2 (kt)	%	Total emission (kt)	%	Emission coefficients (t/Meuros)
1	Agriculture, stock breeding and hunting	8296	3.34	5035	2.02	235.5
2	Silviculture and forestry	101	0.04	63	0.03	64.8
3	Fishing	3143	1.26	2606	1.05	1416.9
4	Anthracite, coal, lignite and peat	1078	0.43	8	0.00	934.1
5	Crude oil, natural gas, uranium and thorium	361	0.15	24	0.01	1925.3
6	Metal mineral extraction	176	0.07	37	0.01	932.7
7	Non-metal mineral extraction	495	0.20	380	0.15	198.4
8	Coking, refining and nuclear fuel	20300	8.16	12637	5.08	956.0
9	Electricity, gas, and vapour production and distribution	91048	36.61	25998	10.45	3882.8
10	Water collection, purification, and distribution	546	0.22	641	0.26	161.1
11	Food and beverages	5018	2.02	15167	6.10	75.8
12	Textile industry	1423	0.57	1286	0.52	149.1
13	Clothing industry and furriery	133	0.05	1643	0.66	15.9
14	19 leaher and shoe industry	121	0.05	1063	0.43	18.9
15	Wood and cork industry	445	0.18	350	0.14	51.0
16	Paper industry	2685	1.08	1608	0.65	266.0
17	Editing y graphic arts	198	0.08	909	0.37	14.3
18	Chemical industry	6890	2.77	8049	3.24	222.3
19	Plastic material and rubber industry	128	0.05	1160	0.47	9.7
20	Other non-metal mineral products	45041	18.11	11217	4.51	2203.5
21	Metallurgy	13353	5.37	6402	2.57	630.5
22	Metal products manufacture	396	0.16	2913	1.17	14.7
23	Machinery and mechanical equipment	312	0.13	3450	1.39	15.5
24	Office ware and informatics accessories	7	0.00	663	0.27	1.9
25	Machinery and electric material manufacture	98	0.04	2021	0.81	8.3
26	Electronics manufare	9	0.00	837	0.34	1.6
27	Medico-surgical and iprecision instruments	7	0.00	465	0.19	2.1

28	Motor vehicle and trailer manufacture	222	0.09	8239	3.31	4.8
29	Other transportation material manufacture	68	0.03	891	0.36	9.4
30	Furniture and other manufacturing industries	223	0.09	2455	0.99	16.8
31	Recycling	317	0.13	0	0.00	112.1
32	Construction	2654	1.07	42873	17.24	21.1
33	Vehicles and repair	5236	2.11	18317	7.37	47.3
34	Hostelery	2780	1.12	14264	5.74	38.3
35	Ground transportation	19477	7.83	10587	4.26	632.8
36	Ship transportation	2739	1.10	2230	0.90	1495.9
37	Air and spatial transportation	7404	2.98	6332	2.55	1275.6
38	Transport-related activities	1553	0.62	2529	1.02	60.3
39	Post office and telecommunications	232	0.09	1719	0.69	9.2
40	Financial intermediary	208	0.08	1523	0.61	5.1
41	Real estate and management services	567	0.23	9871	3.97	3.8
42	Education	743	0.30	3331	1.34	22.9
43	Health and social services	542	0.22	4482	1.80	12.5
44	Other services and social activities	915	0.37	5273	2.12	23.7
45	Public Administration	1004	0.40	7142	2.87	23.4
46	Households with domestic personnel	0	0.00	0	0.00	0.0
	Total production sectors	248692	100	248692	100	

$$\mathbf{c}'\mathbf{x} = \mathrm{E} \quad (1)$$

where **x** is production per sector, **c**, as we stated before, is a vector of coefficients that gives the amount of emissions per unit of output, and E is a scalar expressing the total amount of emissions.

By replacing **x** by its known value in the open Leontieff model, this yields:

$$e = \hat{c}(I - A)^{-1} y \quad (2)$$

where **e** is an (n x 1) vector of emissions by sector, **A** is a technical coefficients matrix, and **y** is the vector of final demand. The vector **e** represents the direct emissions by sector.

Consequently, the following matrix

$$\mathbf{F} = \hat{c}(\mathbf{I} - \mathbf{A})^{-1} \quad (3)$$

is a linear operator that converts increases in final demand into increases in the polluting emissions vector. If we pre-multiply the matrix **F** by **u**′, which is a unit row vector of appropriate dimension, this yields:

$$f' = u'F \quad (4)$$

where **f**′ is a (1 x n) vector of total direct and indirect unitary emissions generated by a unit of final demand. **f**′ represents the multiplier effect of the emissions accounted for by the different demands. In other words, this is the total polluting potential (or total pollution intensity) of the different sectors (see Annex **II**).

ANNEX II

		Total emissions multiplier			
		Unweighted		Weighted	
	Production branches	Demand	Supply	Demand	Supply
1	Agriculture, stock breeding and hunting	417.5	343.8	7.1	6.5
2	Silviculture and forestry	88.8	284.8	0.1	0.3
3	Fishing	1586.3	1434.5	3.7	1.6
4	Anthracite, coal, lignite and peat	1393.1	5297.9	0.0	3.3
5	Crude oil, natural gas, uranium and thorium	2442.5	3617.0	0.0	0.3
6	Metal mineral extraction	1265.0	1523.9	0.1	0.1
7	Non-metal mineral extraction	721.8	1044.7	0.5	1.0
8	Coking, refining and nuclear fuel	1165.1	1510.1	17.8	21.4
9	Electricity, gas, and vapour production and distribution	4854.3	5005.4	36.5	57.8
10	Water collection, purification, and distribution	403.1	349.8	0.9	0.5
11	Food and beverages	418.5	142.9	21.3	2.4
12	Textile industry	406.5	234.7	1.8	1.1
13	Clothing industry and furriery	244.2	53.0	2.3	0.2
14	19 leaher and shoe industry	226.4	36.7	1.5	0.1
15	Wood and cork industry	322.3	270.9	0.5	1.0
16	Paper industry	631.7	527.1	2.3	2.5
17	Editing y graphic arts	294.5	162.9	1.3	1.0
18	Chemical industry	523.2	427.5	11.3	6.9
19	Plastic material and rubber industry	285.7	177.6	1.6	1.1
20	Other non-metal mineral products	2880.1	2480.8	15.8	18.3
21	Metallurgy	1037.2	809.0	9.0	6.9
22	Metal products manufacture	427.5	307.3	4.1	3.6
23	Machinery and mechanical equipment	265.4	198.5	4.8	1.9
24	Office ware and informatics accessories	216.6	47.1	0.9	0.1
25	Machinery and electric material manufacture	371.7	127.6	2.8	0.6
26	Electronics manufare	201.4	23.0	1.2	0.1
27	Medico-surgical and iprecision instruments	160.6	12.4	0.7	0.0
28	Motor vehicle and trailer manufacture	226.3	36.5	11.6	0.9
29	Other transportation material manufacture	174.8	153.5	1.3	0.5
30	Furniture and other manufacturing industries	242.4	56.5	3.5	0.3
31	Recycling	604.4	912.0	0.0	0.2
32	Construction	523.0	69.9	60.3	3.2
33	Vehicles and repair	240.0	162.4	25.7	9.5
34	Hostelry	211.1	61.0	20.0	2.3
35	Ground transportation	870.2	994.5	14.9	15.3
36	Ship transportation	1749.1	1656.5	3.1	1.4
37	Air and spatial transportation	1498.8	1390.6	8.9	4.4

38	Transport-related activities	361.5	526.1	3.6	5.3
39	Post office and telecommunications	206.3	196.6	2.4	2.6
40	Financial intermediary	81.5	173.1	2.1	4.2
41	Real estate and management services	126.7	163.1	13.9	13.9
42	Education	107.8	44.7	4.7	1.1
43	Health and social services	112.7	26.0	6.3	0.7
44	Other services and social activities	177.0	60.9	7.4	1.2
45	Public Administration	166.2	23.4	10.0	0.7
46	Households with domestic personnel	0.0	0.0	0.0	0.0
	Weighted average multipliers			7.6	4.5

Reminder:

Household emissions: 55.292 kt.

Economy total emissions 303.984 kt.

Source of annexes: Author´s own calculations based on information from INE. See the text.

Total direct and indirect emissions by sector would be given by the following expression:

$$\varepsilon' = \hat{c}(\mathbf{I}-\mathbf{A})^{-1}\hat{y} = u'F\hat{y} \qquad \textbf{(5)}$$

The results from computing (5) are presented in Annex **I** as total emission.

To illustrate the importance of certain sectors we aggregated the productive branches considered for the study into a small number of sectors that can be depicted from Graph **1** below.

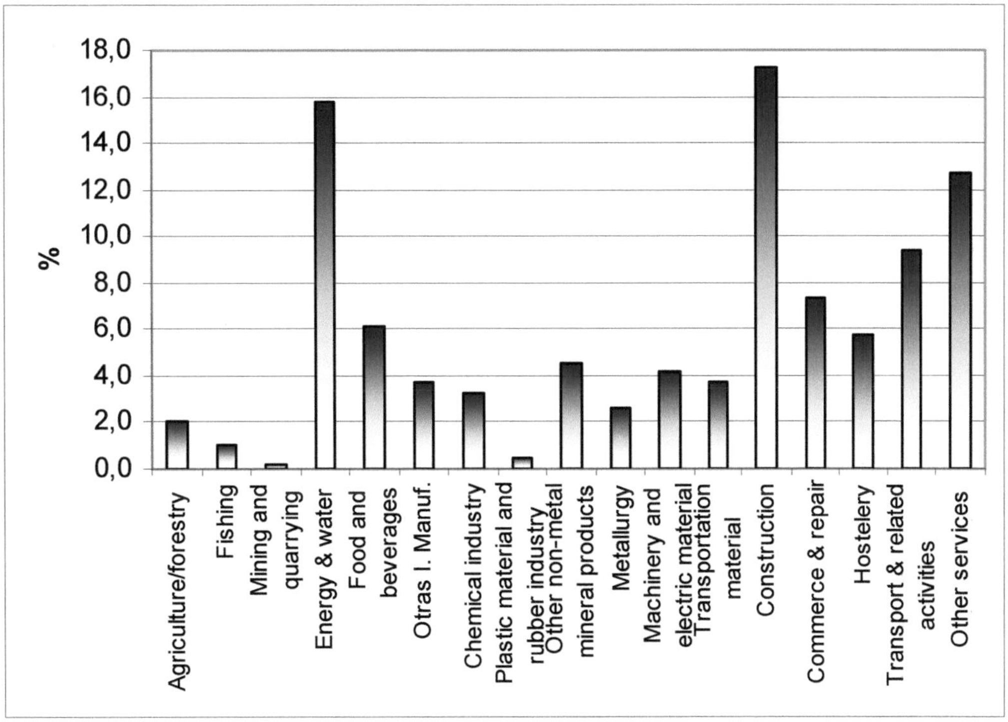

Source: Author´s own elaboration from the information in Annex I.

Graph 1: Distribution of total emission by sector

As can be seen, the construction sector is the most important one from the point of view of direct and indirect emission generated in order to meet this sector´s demand. It represents 17,2% of emissions of the entire production process. If in Annex **I** we account for this sector direct emission, it can be observed that its direct emissions are relatively low, with 1,1% of total emission. The role of the construction sector is determined by its pull effect on highly polluting productive sectors that are its suppliers of productive inputs. Alcántara (2007) pointed out this fact and called for the need of a detailed analysis of this sector in the design of environmental policies to reduce the emissions of greenhouse gases.

The second most important sector is Energy and Water. It is constituted by branches 8, 9, and 10 of Annex **1** and represents 15,8% of productive emissions.

TOTAL EMISSIONS BY TYPE OF FINAL DEMAND

Now we can decompose vector **y** into a set of vectors representing the final demand for the different types of sectors. We are used to thinking in terms of private consumption, gross capital accumulation, etc., as variables of final demand in an economic space. If we adopt this classification we can be observe the impact that different categories in which total demand is divided have on total pollution. If we decompose the final demand of each sector into h components (k = 1, 2, …k, …h), we can associate a matrix **H** with the final demand vector **y**, and the characteristic element of **H,** H_{ik}, would represent the final demand of category k from sector i. We can thus posit

$$\varepsilon^{y}{}' = \hat{c}(\mathbf{I}-\mathbf{A})^{-1}\mathbf{H} = u'\mathbf{F}\mathbf{H} \quad \mathbf{(6)}$$

as a vector, the generic element of which, $\varepsilon^{y}{}'$, represents total pollution, which in our case is CO_2 generated to meet the final demand of category k.

The total direct and indirect relative impact of each category of final demand that we get by calculating (6) is given in Graph **2** below.

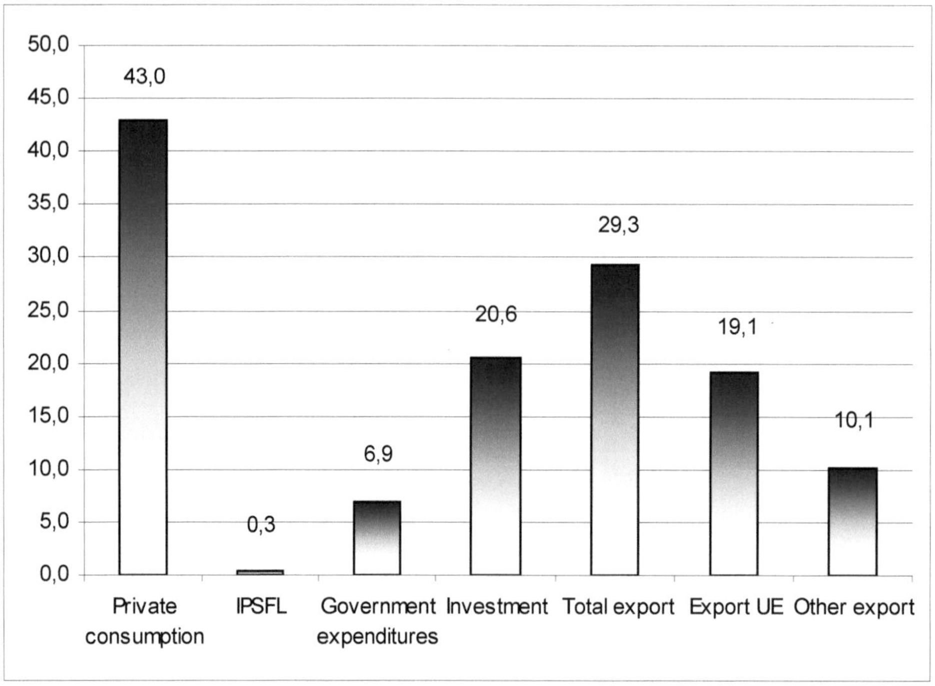

Source: Author´s own elaboration. See text

Graph 2: CO_2 emissions contribution by type of final demand

It is evident that final domestic consumption, represented by private consumption, non-profit private organisations (IPSFL), and government expenditures, has the highest contribution. It represents approximately 50% of the emissions that all sectors generate to meet this demand. We should add to this the direct emission from consumption that in 2000 reached 55,292 kt of CO_2. The implications from this analysis are that the life style and consumption pattern in our society are the basis for the emissions of one of the most important greenhouse gases. It should be pointed that of the 303,984 kt CO_2 emitted to the atmosphere in 2000, the productive processes to meet the final demand of the different branches of production are responsible for 248,692 kt. This represents approximately 82% of total emission, of which 50% is to meet domestic consumption. Accounting for the fact that 18% of total emission corresponds to direct emission caused by this consumption just to keep consumers´ good going[3], it is no exaggeration if we conclude that about 59% of total emission comes from final domestic demand.

DETERMINANT SECTORS IN CO_2 EMISSIONS

The technique for establishing the determinant sectors allows a first approximation to analyse the role played by the different productive sectors of the economy. Rasmussen´s indicators technique is perhaps the most widely used and in some sense it allows identifying "determinant industries".[4] This approach has been subjected to criticism and Rasmussen (1956: 132-144) himself pointed out some of them. Skolka (1986), cited in Pulido and Fontela (1993: 133), is perhaps one of the main detractors of this technique. The criticisims are made extensive in Chenery and Wanatabe (1958) and Hirschman (1958). In any case, we believe that the complaints about this technique would be well-grounded only with respect to the indicators used to measure the backward and forward linkages but never with regard to those that are essential to the entire IO analysis, particularly when studying the vertically integrated effects.[5]

In the following pages we will develop an analysis by sector of CO_2 emissions in Spain. The other methodology proposed is based on the criticism of Jones (1976), which we extend to environmental impacts in this paper.

When we explained equation (4) we said that the vector **f**´ represented the multiplier effect of emissions caused by the expansion of different demands. In this literature, this vector represents the so-called *backward linkages*. These are pull effects (i.e. emission) due to the expansion of final demand. Under such a definition, these pull effects are similar to those in Rasmussen and Hirschman. Those coefficients represent the total pollution potential form the demand side.

As an emission-provoking measure that any given sector would receive from the entire economy, from a conventional perspective one could propose:

$$f^* = F\,u \tag{7}$$

where **f*** is an (n x 1) vector arising from the sum of the rows of matrix **F**, and represents the so-called *forward linkages* in the literature. It is usually interpreted as the importance of the different productive sectors from the supply side. Nevertheless, as is put by Jones (1958), this approach is not symmetrical with respect to the computation of the mentioned backward linkages. The author proposes the use of Gosh´s (1958) inverse in establishing the supply multipliers.[6]

Following the proposed alternative to establish the *forward linkages* we would have:

From the Leontieff´s inverse, the establishment of Gosh´s inverse is straightforward (Miller, R.A. and Blair, P.D., 2009):

---

[3] We should remember that in line with the NAMEA system the emissions corresponding to private transportation are included in this 18%.

[4] Rasmussen himself sustains that it is not possible to define "determinant industry" in a unique way since this will depend on the problem at hand. After setting the criterion for establishing the determinant industry with respect to employment and imports he concludes: "Other definitions of determinant industry, suiting other problems, can be considered; however, these observations suffice to attract our attention on the importance of the IO model."

[5] In reference to the analysis from a vertical integration perspective, see Alcántara (1995) and (1999), and Sánchez Chóliz and Duarte (2003).

[6] A heated theoretical debate started with respect to Leroy P. Jones´ proposition, which added to the already important discussion around A. Gosh´s model. A good synthesis can be found in M. Lenzen (2003). The latter author shows how Gosh´s inverse can be used to establish "ex-post" the determinant sector. We build on this work as a justification of our take on this issue.

$$(I-D)^{-1} = \hat{x}^{-1}(I-A)^{-1}\hat{x} \quad \textbf{(8)}$$

where **D** is the distribution coefficients matrix. The characteristic element of this matrix $D_{ij} = X_{ij}/x_i$ reflects the proportion of that part of the production of sector *i* used in sector *j* represents in the production of *i.* thus, the Gosh model is given by:

$$x' = v'(I-D)^{-1} \quad \textbf{(9)}$$

where the (n x 1) vector expresses the monetary value of the primary inputs used in the production of the *n* sectors of production. As in the demand model, we can now connect the emissions vector as follows:

$$e' = v'(I-D)^{-1}\hat{c} \quad \textbf{(10)}$$

and the matrix,

$$G = (\mathbf{I}-D)^{-1}\hat{c} \quad \textbf{(11)}$$

is now, as in the demand model before, a linear operator that transforms added values, or their increments, into emissions.

It is clear that if we post-multiply the matrix **G** by an appropriate dimension unit vector:

$$\eta = Gu \quad \textbf{(12)}$$

we obtain a vector, the characteristic element of which, η_i, represents the total direct and indirect emission due to the expansion of primary inputs necessary for increasing sector *i* supply. This is thus a set of emissions multipliers from a supply perspective.[7] (See Annex **II**).

As we pointed out before, the same potential wrong conclusions that can be made about the demand multipliers when the weight of the different sectors is no accounted for are also applicable to the supply multipliers. Accordingly, we re-express the multipliers given by equations (7) and (12) the following way:

From the vectors of final demand and primary inputs we defined two distribution vectors of both variables $\tilde{\mathbf{y}}$, $\tilde{\mathbf{v}}$, such that: $\sum_i \tilde{y} = 1$ y $\sum_i \tilde{v} = 1$. So that the demand and supply multipliers can be redefined as follows:

$$\mu_y^{'} = c'(I-A)^{-1}\hat{\tilde{y}} \quad \textbf{(13)}$$

where $\mu_y^{'}$ is a (1 x n) demand-weighted emission multipliers vector.

If we proceed as previously,

$$\mu_v = \hat{\tilde{v}}(I-D)^{-1}c \quad \textbf{(14)}$$

[7] The reader interested in the difference between $\boldsymbol{\eta}$ and the conventional multiplier $\mathbf{f}^*$ can consult Lenzen´s paper and the reference therein.

once the weighted emission multipliers determined, the average multiplier is set by:

$$\mu = \frac{\mu_y^{'} u}{n} = \frac{\mu_v^{'} u}{n} \quad (15)$$

The results using information for Spain in the previous equations are given in Annex **II**.

Comparing emission multipliers by sector for both demand and supply with the average multiplier allows the following classification by sector:

	$\mu_{v,i}/\mu > 1$	$\mu_{v,i}/\mu < 1$
$\mu_{y,i}/\mu > 1$	A: Determinant emission sectors	B: Demand push sectors
$\mu_{y,i}/\mu < 1$	C: Supply push sectors	D: Remaining sectors

If apply the data from Annex **II** to these criteria we get the results shown in Table **1**. As can be seen, the determinant production branches represented 81,2% of direct emission from all the production branches in 2000. If we include households direct emissions this represents 66,4% of total emission. On the other hand, these determinant production branches reached 41,4% of production emission from the point of view of demand, while this percentage is 72,1 from the supply side. This large difference should not be surprising. What this is telling us is that, albeit the pull effects of these determinant branches to other production branches to meet the former´s final demand are significant, this is mainly due to the fact that these sectors are providers of other branches. So, their pollution is induced by the production of other sectors, hence the importance of taking into account their direct emission.

The most important production branch is electricity and gas production and distribution, with the highest impact indices, from both a demand and supply point of view. From a supply perspective, the importance of this production branch is evident. The reason is that 85,2% of its production goes to demand from other sectors and the rest to its own final demand. If we account for the important role of this energy sector in the economy and its relevance in total CO_2 emissions, it is surely a good candidate for close scrutiny.

Nevertheless, we should bear in mind that ground transportation, which includes road transportation, does not account for private transportation nor firms′ own means of transportation in the NAMEA system. That is why it only ranks fifth as a determinant emission sector. Had we have more detailed information ground transportation would be beyond doubt the most important determinant emission sector in the present paper. This was pointed out in a recent research (see Alcántara, 2007).

Table 1: Classification by sector taking into account weighted CO_2 emission coefficients

			Demand		Supply	
Code	**Production sectors**	**Direct emission**	**Total emission (direct + indirect)**	**Demand impact index** $\mu_{y,i}/\mu$	**Total emission (direct + indirect)**	**Supply impact index** $\mu_{v,i}/\mu$
	Group A: Determinant sectors					
9	Electricity, gas, and vapour production and distribution	91048	25998	4.809	69075	12.777
33	Commerce, sale and repair of vehicles	5236	18317	3.388	25610	4.737
8	Coking plants, refining and nuclear fuels	20300	12637	2.338	21892	4.049
20	Other mineral non-metal products	45041	11217	2.075	18267	3.379
35	Ground transportation	19477	10587	1.958	16557	3.063
41	Real estate and management services	567	9871	1.826	11364	2.102

18	Chemical industry	6890	8049	1.489	8231	1.523
21	Metallurgy	13353	6402	1.184	8214	1.519
	Total	201912	103077		179210	
	%	81.2	41.4		72.1	
	Group B: Demand determinant sectors					
32	Construction	2654	42873	7.930	3841.3	0.711
11	Food and beverages	5018	15167	2.805	2916.0	0.539
34	Hostelry	2780	14264	2.638	2735.8	0.506
28	Motor vehicles and trailer manufacturing plants	222	8239	1.524	1065.8	0.197
45	Public administration	1004	7142	1.321	810.0	0.150
37	Air transportation	7404	6332	1.171	5239.3	0.969
	Total	19082	94017		16608	
	%	7.7	37.8		6.7	
	Group C: Supply determinant sector					
1	Agriculture, stock breeding and hunting	8296	5035	0.931	7708	1.426
38	Transportation-related activities	1553	2529	0.468	6366	1.177
	Total	9849	7565		36737	
	%	4.0	3.0		14.8	
	Group D: Remaining sectors					
	Other sectors	17849	44033		16137	
	%	7.2	17.7		6.5	
		248692	248692		248692	

Source: Author´s own elaboration based on information in Annex II.

The second most important sector after production and distribution of electricity and gas is the branch commerce, sale and repair of vehicles. Demand and supply impact indexes in this branch are much closer. This is attributable the branch´s own characteristics. An interesting remark from this result is that, from a pollution standpoint an apparently innocuous branch of activity turns out to be the most important emission sector. The same applies to Real Estate and management services.

The third most important sector for its impacts is coking plants and petroleum derivatives. Here also, the supply impact index (4,049) shows the greater influence of the rest of the sectors on this branch than the pull effects (2,338) the latter has on the former.

The data from the Table for the remaining branches are self-indicating, therefore there is no necessity to spend time discussing them.

In relation to group B, the direct emissions of the branches we deemed determinant from a demand standpoint represents a relatively small percentage (7,7) of total emissions of the production sectors. From a supply standpoint, their emissions are also low, with 6,7%. As is evident, these branches stand out because of the emissions pull effects from other branches that provide them with inputs to meet their final demand. It not strange that total direct and indirect emissions of these branches represents 37,8% of total production emissions. This percentage is very close to those of group A, which we considered determinant.

Two points are worth highlighting in this group. First is the role of Construction, which represents 45,2% of the emission induced by this group. Albeit with a low level of direct emission, both its direct and indirect role in total emission of all the production branches are 17,2%, which is almost one fifth of all emissions in Spain for the year 2000. Note that its demand impact index (7,930) is the highest of all the production branches. From a supply standpoint, we could in this respect conclude that the role it plays is as relevant as that of electricity and gas production and distribution.

The other point worth highlighting is the service sector, such as hostelry, the public administration itself, and air transportation. As to hostelry, its demand impact index (2,638) is greater than that of the Chemical industry and metallurgy.

We cannot end the discussion on this group without pointing out the importance of the Food, beverages, and tobacco branch. Its demand impact index (2,805) is greater than those of petroleum and non-metal mineral products. It is true that the latter are more important polluters from a supply point of view, but it is useful to make this comparison as it allows de-mythify certain production branches that, despite not being direct polluters, are able to trigger emission in other important branches. Some of these finding were evident already in 1995 (Alcántara and Padilla, 2003).

With respect to group C, among the determinant sectors from a supply standpoint, the importance of direct emission of agriculture is worth noting. Note that the production impact index (1,426) is closer to that of the Chemical industry and metallurgy. It is evident that this situation is in line with the mechanisation of the agricultural sector in Spain.

CONCLUSIONS

With the use of the analytical tool developed we arrived at some important results. First, it becomes clear that among the forty six production branches analysed only eight are determinant in the emissions of CO_2, both from the standpoint of their final demand and their supply (or their production if you wish). The design of policies to control the emissions on these branches of production could help reduce a part of the 80% of emissions in Spain. Of course we must stress that the operation of many industries depends on these activities, therefore the importance of the demand analysis and its pull effects. The question to beg is which demands are indispensable to cover certain need and to what extent certain other could be substituted.

In the last case, it would be good to consider the role of the service sector in CO_2 emissions. There exists the wrong belief that the service sector is not very harmful the to environment. But that sector is composed of many activities, and, as we just saw, some of them have serious impacts on the environment. And not only the transportation sector for which, due to lack of information, we could not show the full impact in the emissions we analysed, but also for other remarkable ones such as the Commerce, sale and repair of vehicles, Hostelry, and Real estate management services, the responsibility of which is quite high. Maybe we should abandon altogether the idea that a service-based economy is dematerialised.

The same applies to her activities such as the construction industry, production and distribution of electricity and gas, and even agriculture.

In any event, the results obtained reinforce the idea that the expansion of the service sector and the increase of energy efficiency and the ensuing dematerialisation of the economy usually accompany economic growth should be completely discarded. Although the industrial production processes are more directly linked to energy consumption, the responsibility lies in the end on the sectors demanding their inputs and therefore pulling the emissions they generate.

ACKNOWLEDGEMENTS

The author acknowledges financial support for this research from the following projects: ECO2009-10003 (Ministerio de Ciencia e Innovación), 2009SGR-600 and XREPP (DGR).

REFERENCES

Alcántara, V. (2003). *Propuesta de cuentas ambientales para Catalunya*, Institut d'estadistica de Catalunya (IDESCAT) www.idescat.es.

Alcántara, V., Padilla, E. (2003). ""Key" sectors in final energy consumption: an input-output application to the Spanish case", *Energy Policy* 31, 1673-1678.

Alcántara, V. (1999). "Análisis de impactos ambientales desde una perspectiva input - output" in Ricaldi, T. (1999).

Alcántara, V. (1995). *Economía y contaminación atmosférica: hacia un nuevo enfoque desde el análisis input-output*. Doctoral Thesis, Universitat de Barcelona.

Eurostat (2001). *Nameas for Air Emissions – Results of Pilot Studies*. Eurostat, European Commission. European Communities, Luxemburg.

Haan, M.de., Keuning, S.J. (1996). "Taking the environment into account. The NAMEA approach", *Review of Income and Wealth* 42 (2), 131-148.

Miller, R.A., Blair, P.D., (2009). *Input–Output: foundations and extensions*. 2nd edition, Cambridge University Press, UK.

Pulido, A., Fontela, E., (1993). *Análisis input–output (Modelos, datos y aplicaciones)*. Pirámide, Madrid.

Rasmusen, P., (1956). *Studies in Intersectoral relations*. North-Holland Publishing Company, Amsterdam.

Ricaldi, T. (1999). *La economía ecológica: una nueva mirada a la ecología humana*. Ed. CESU (UMSS)- UNESCO.

Sánchez Chóliz, J., Duarte, R. (2003). "Analysing pollution by vertically integrated coefficients, with an application to the water sector in Aragon", *Cambridge Journal of Economics*, 27, 433-448.

Skolka, J. (1986). "Input–Output multipliers and linkages". Eighth International Conference on Input–Output Techniques. Sapporo, Japan.

CHAPTER 2

Measuring Sectoral Share of Green House Gases (GHGs) Emissions from Fossil Fuel Consumption and Offering Solutions: The Case of Turkey

Niaz Ahmed Bhutto[a,*] and Selim Cagatay[b]

[a]Sukkur Institute of Business Administration, Pakistan. Sukkur Institute of Business Administration, Airport Road Sukkur 65200 Sindh, Pakistan and [b]Economics Department of Akdeniz University, Turkey. Akdeniz University, Department of Economics, Director of Centre for Economic Research on Mediterranean Countries Akdeniz University, 07058-Antalya Turkey.

Abstract: Bringing balance among social, economic and environmental goals has remained hot issue for high income countries' planning policies since last four decades. Doubtlessly, Turkey has also not remained behind in joining the hands in bringing clean and green environment in the world along with other nations of the world. Turkey has ratified Kyoto Protocol is 2009 and Turkey has not been given any reduction target of GHGs emissions but if Turkey morally reduces GHGs emissions by 10 or 5 percent subject to the level of 2009 GHGs emissions by the year 2012; by how much such reductions will cause decrease in final demand, employees' compensation and total output of sectors is the central investigation of this study. Using input-output techniques, this study has estimated GHGs emissions for the year 2012 from fossil fuel consumption and results suggest that all GHGs emissions have increased by 22.5 percent from 2009 levels. This study has developed a new technique that uses GHGs emissions target as exogenous variable and solves for final demand which is endogenous variable. The opportunity cost of reducing GHGs emissions by 10 and 5 percent in 2012 is the giving up of 8.12 and 4.08 percent of final demand, employees' compensation and total output of sectors respectively. Substitution of natural gas completely for other fossil fuel types reduces GHGs emissions so significantly in 2012 that Turkey can pursue her sustainable development goals.

Keywords: GHGs Emissions, Kyoto Protocol and Natural Gas Substitution.

INTRODUCTION

Turkey has been experiencing a fragile economy for the last 50 years which is quite vulnerable to international economic developments. The population of the country had an average annual growth rate of about 2.4 percent until the new millennium and since then it had slowed down to about 1.5 percent. In spite of this high population growth, the increase in per capita income was mostly below the population growth over the same period but per capita energy use has increased with an average annual figure of about 2 percent (Joberta and Karanfil, 2007).

The Turkish economy has preferred a rather planned economy until 1980 with the aim of capital accumulation through the implementation of import substitution policy. To adopt and support the strategy of import substitution, import restrictions and tight monetary policy was in place to keep the domestic currency overvalued. However, during this protectionist period production efficiency did not increase much and the demand for energy has grown very largely, but neither domestic energy production nor energy imports was enough to supply the required energy in the economy. Moreover, the two severe energy crises of the period in the world have not only increased the energy supply problem of Turkey but also put huge pressure on trade deficit, external debt and inflation of the country.

By 1980's the economy decided to follow export-led growth strategy first to reduce external debt and inflation and second to follow the new liberalization trend in the world. The new economic policies aimed at encouraging exports and foreign direct investments with a rather loose monetary policy which was accompanied by liberalization in the domestic markets, privatization and full capital account liberalization. The new growth strategy adopted in early 1980's was quite successful for a while and restored the growth again without experiencing any recession until mid 1990's. In this period, government liberalized the energy market and increasing energy requirements were satisfied

[*]**Address Correspondence to Niaz Ahmed Bhutto:** Sukkur Institute of Business Administration, Pakistan. Sukkur Institute of Business Administration, Airport Road Sukkur 65200 Sindh, Pakistan. Mobile No. 00 92 (334) 2727989. Fax: 00 92 (71) 5632465. Email: niazbhutto@gmail.com

Maria Llop (Ed)

via imports, but domestic energy investments decreased largely at the same period. By mid 1990's Turkey became not only an energy importer but energy import-dependent country as well by total imported energy exceeding the national energy production (Joberta and Karanfil, 2007). Total energy production and consumption in this period increased by 70 and 415 percent respectively and share of domestic energy production in total energy consumption decrease from 77 percent in 1970 to 31 percent in 2002 (Energy Statistics, 2003).

The economy apparently moved to a more unstable equilibrium with these neo-liberal reforms particularly due to the dependency of the growth on the short-term capital inflows. The Turkish economy witnessed the biggest economic crises of her recent history in year 2000 and 2001, which made it clear that macroeconomic stability should be achieved with a new reform program. In the same period, the "Eighth Five-Year Development Plan" of Turkey changed her approach towards energy market and environment, and government spent considerable efforts to address energy security, energy efficiency and environmental protection, in a sustainable manner (IEA, 2005). Intensifying research on energy technologies to satisfy increasing energy demand, to maintain energy security and to reduce import dependence constituted the main objectives. Currently, The Ministry of Energy and Natural Resources, The General Directorate of Energy Affairs and The Energy Market Regulatory Authority are mainly the responsible institutions for implementation of energy policies and regulation of the energy market.

In Turkey the share of the fossil resources in total energy consumption is more than 80 percent and the main fossil resources are petroleum and coal (Energy Statistics, 2003). Natural gas use has increased only in 1990's. As Turkey has a significant coal potential, about 90% of this reserve is low-calorie lignite and it is mostly used in thermal power plants. On the other hand, Turkey has very limited oil and natural gas resources. About 12 percent of total primary energy consumption in Turkey is renewable and Turkey has considerable reserves of renewable energy resources which are mainly hydro, biomass, wind, geothermal, and solar. Until 1990's the housing sector had the highest energy consumption, but by 1990's the housing sector lost its significance and share of industry increased (about 30 percent) parallel to the economic growth. The agricultural sector had a slightly increasing trend; however, its consumption has been the lowest (about 4 percent) compared to the other sectors. Energy transformation for the production of the electricity is also increasing year by year. This sector constitutes a significant portion in the total consumption (about 25 percent). It is observed that the thermo-power plants produce the majority of the electricity (about 74 percent) while the share of hydraulic plants is about 26 percent (Say and Yücel, 2006).

Turkey has been obviously a net energy importer when the domestic energy production and consumption figures of the past and present are considered. Foreign dependency ratio of domestic energy consumption has been increasing. For example, while this ratio was about 60 percent in 1995, it reached 74 percent ten years after. If the energy sector is approached from another angle, imports of crude petroleum, natural gas and petroleum products constitute more than 35 percent of Turkey's foreign trade deficit. In countries like Turkey where there are limited foreign currency reserves and high budget deficit and foreign debt, increasing cost of energy imports may play crucial rule in driving the country to economic crises. Moreover, increasing energy bill puts downward pressure on export performance of countries like Turkey.

Another angle to approach the energy sector in Turkey is the change in greenhouse gas emission that contribute to global warming and which is mostly sourced by energy sector. United Nations Framework Convention on Climate Change, which was declared in Rio de Janerio in 1992, has been signed by more than 170 countries and European Union as of today. This convention was one of the first and serious attempts to control world-wide greenhouse gas emissions and Turkey has also signed it. While the Convention proposed the reduction of greenhouse gas emissions in year 2000 to 1990 levels, Turkey increased her emissions about 65 percent over the same period. Finally, Turkey ratified the Kyoto Protocol in 2009; Turkey has to reduce her emissions, although this reduction is not an official obligation (UNFCCC, 2009). Turkey has to develop policies towards using the "flexibility" alternatives introduced by the Kyoto Protocol such as emission trading, joint implementation and clean development mechanism.

Turkey's recent developments regarding the energy sector can create the tools to achieve a better operating market and structure for energy sub-sectors, to anticipate the future developments however, country's vulnerability to international developments and particularly to energy prices should also be taken into account.

Basing on the above this study attempts to find the way out for meeting the social, economic and environmental goals. The second part of the chapter is about the estimation of GHGs emissions from fossil fuel consumption for the year 2009. In third part of the chapter, a policy scenario is developed for reducing GHGs emissions under two targets and measuring the impact of these reductions on the final demand, employees' compensation and total output of the sectors. An alternative method is also developed to reduce GHGs emissions without too much decrease in social and economic goals. The fourth part concludes the chapter and makes the recommendation based on the findings of the chapter.

ESTIMATION OF GHGS FROM FOSSIL FUEL CONSUMPTION BY USING INPUT-OUTPUT MODEL

Turkish economy is mostly driven by fossil fuel consumption for energy systems like most economies and fossil fuel consumption is the major source of GHGs emissions in the country. The agriculture focused input-output table and the agriculture focused environmental input-output table of Turkey for the year 1998 have been taken from the Bhutto (2007).

The input-output (I-O) analysis simply measures the magnitudes of direct and indirect variation in total production caused by changes in the final demand. The solution procedure of the model is summarized through the equations 1 to 5. Given X as the vector of total production (equation 1), it is equal to sum of Ax and Y (final demand vector), where Ax represents the matrix of intermediate demand and A is the matrix of technical coefficients $[a_{ij}]$ found as in equation 2. In equation 2, x_{ij} is the sale of $_i^{th}$ sector to sector $_j$ and X_j is the total outlay of sector $_j$.

$$X = Ax + Y \tag{1}$$

$$a_{ij} = \frac{x_{ij}}{X_j} \tag{2}$$

Rearranging equation (1) and simplifying it results in equation 4, in which $(I - A)$ is required to be a non-singular matrix in order to find a solution for *X*. Then by using the Leontief inverse $(I - A)^{-1}$ total industrial output can be obtained by solving equation 5 with respect to exogenous changes in *Y* by calculating both direct and indirect effects in the chain of inter-industries linkages.

$$X - Ax = Y \tag{3}$$

$$X(I - A) = Y \tag{4}$$

$$X = (I - A)^{-1} Y \tag{5}$$

The I-O model can be used to trace the environmental discharges in an economy, as firstly introduced and used in Leontief (1970). To incorporate environment into input-output analysis equation 6 is introduced.

$$E_i = \hat{R}_i X \tag{6}$$

where E_i is the vector of environmental burden of category *i* and $\hat{R}_i$ is the diagonal matrix of environmental discharges of type *i* per monetary unit of sector's output. In order to solve for E_i, simply *X* in equation 5 is substituted into equation 6. As a result, economic data can be linked with resource use (such as energy and ore consumption) and/or environmental impact categories (such as greenhouse gas emissions, toxic discharges, ozone depletion potential, hazardous or non-hazardous waste), as in equation 7.

$$E_i = \hat{R}_i (I - A)^{-1} Y \tag{7}$$

In order to estimate the GHGs emissions for the year 2009 when turkey ratified the Kyoto protocol, final demand is needed. To obtain final demand for all 33 sectors of agriculture focused input-output table for the year 2009, real growth rates have been used with the base year of 1998. The growth rates are given in Table **1**.

Table 1: Real growth rates (1998 prices)

Year	Real Growth Rates (1998 Prices)
1999	-3.4
2000	6.8
2001	-5.7
2002	6.2
2003	5.3
2004	9.4
2005	8.4
2006	6.9
2007	4.7
2008	0.9
2009	-8.4

Source: TURKSTAT (Various Years).

Tables **2** and **3** reveal the results of GHGs emissions from fossil fuel consumption for the year 2009. The total CO2, N20, CH4, CO, SOx, NOx and NMVOC emissions were 248,531.66, 2.51, 5.75, 2,731.92, 2,835.49, 1,043.53, and 502.44 thousand Tons. Energy production and distribution sector produces almost highest shares 45.15, 52.52, 34.84, 0.88, 53.79, 31.35, and 1.30 percent in total emissions of CO2, N20, CH4, CO, SOx, NOx and NMVOC with 112,202.89, 1.32, 2.00, 24.06, 1,525.28, 327.12, and 6.55 thousand Tons emissions respectively. Whereas, the transport sector is taking the second position in the emissions of GHGs by contributing 17.57, 12.38, 27.21, 90.36, 14.16, 42.33, and 92.22 percent in total emissions of CO2, N20, CH4, CO, SOx, NOx and NMVOC with 43,675.79, 0.31, 1.56, 2,468.52, 401.59, 441.77, and 463.36 thousand Tons emissions respectively.

The other industries that contribute significantly are manufacture of coke, refined petroleum prod, basic chemicals, and others and manufacture of ferrous, non-ferrous metals, and others. The share of agriculture sector is very minor, even less than half of the share of the services sector.

Table 2: GHGs emissions in 1000tons in 2009 from fossil fuel

Sectors	CO2	N2O	CH4	CO	SOx	NOx	NMVOC
Growing of cereals and other crops n.e.c.	4,459.70	0.03	0.16	31.96	40.76	40.74	6.42
Wheat	880.01	0.01	0.03	6.31	8.04	8.04	1.27
Maize	153.75	0.00	0.01	1.10	1.41	1.40	0.22
Sunflower	193.86	0.00	0.01	1.39	1.77	1.77	0.28
Cotton	119.89	0.00	0.00	0.86	1.10	1.10	0.17
Growing of vegetables, horticultural specialties and nursery products	163.01	0.00	0.01	1.17	1.49	1.49	0.23
Growing of fruit, nuts, beverage and spice crops	173.56	0.00	0.01	1.24	1.59	1.59	0.25
Farming of animals	55.82	0.00	0.00	0.40	0.51	0.51	0.08
Agricultural and animal husbandry service activities, except veterinary activities	15.33	0.00	0.00	0.11	0.14	0.14	0.02
Forestry, logging and related service activities	233.10	0.00	0.01	3.03	2.97	1.26	0.39
Fishing	491.90	0.00	0.02	3.76	4.64	4.34	0.72
Mining and quarrying [08-12]	1,294.10	0.01	0.05	0.20	11.92	3.64	0.09
Production, processing and preserving of meat and meat products	99.38	0.00	0.00	0.09	1.36	0.27	0.01
Processing and preserving of fish and fish products	10.63	0.00	0.00	0.00	0.10	0.03	0.00
Processing and preserving of fruit and vegetables	191.75	0.00	0.01	0.03	1.70	0.50	0.01

Manufacture of vegetable and animal oils and fats	432.35	0.00	0.01	0.38	5.42	1.21	0.06
Manufacture of dairy products	76.71	0.00	0.00	0.02	0.75	0.20	0.01
Manufacture of grain mill products, starches and starch products	6.95	0.00	0.00	0.00	0.06	0.02	0.00
Manufacture of prepared animal feeds	7.00	0.00	0.00	0.01	0.12	0.02	0.00
Manufacture of bakery products	115.01	0.00	0.00	0.05	0.75	0.29	0.01
Manufacture of sugar	3,258.89	0.04	0.05	3.99	48.03	9.49	0.56
Manufacture of cocoa, chocolate, sugar confert.& other food products n.e.c.	857.78	0.01	0.02	0.66	7.97	2.40	0.11
Manufacture of alcoholic, soft drinks and mineral waters[23-24]	192.44	0.00	0.01	0.04	1.51	0.50	0.01
Manufacture of tobacco products	55.78	0.00	0.00	0.02	0.40	0.15	0.00
Manufacture of textiles [26-32]	3,112.07	0.02	0.08	1.53	20.34	8.28	0.29
Wood, furniture, paper, publishing [33-37, 67]	3,425.41	0.03	0.12	0.84	29.71	9.16	0.26
Manufacture of fertilizers, pesticides, other agro-chemicals, paints, and varnishes [40-41]	2,668.38	0.01	0.07	1.18	9.64	7.14	0.23
Manufacture of coke, refined petroleum prod, basic chemicals, rubber, plastics, glass, ceramic prod., non-metallic minerals, etc. [38-39, 42-49]	25,399.19	0.23	0.63	16.03	262.00	66.68	2.79
Manufacture of ferrous, non-ferrous metals, various machinery, vehicles, etc. [50-66, 68]	25,305.37	0.31	0.41	28.90	240.10	73.42	4.12
Energy production and distribution [69-70]	112,202.89	1.32	2.00	24.06	1,525.28	327.12	6.55
Water and Construction [71-72]	4,207.71	0.03	0.15	1.06	35.50	11.68	0.33
Transport [73, 78-81]	43,675.79	0.31	1.56	2,468.52	401.59	441.77	463.36
Services [74-77, 82-97]	14,996.15	0.14	0.33	132.99	166.81	17.20	13.56
Total	248,531.66	2.51	5.75	2,731.92	2,835.49	1,043.53	502.44

Source: Author's Calculations.

Table 3: GHGs emissions in % in 2009 from fossil fuel

Sectors	**CO2**	**N2O**	**CH4**	**CO**	**SOx**	**NOx**	**NMVOC**
Growing of cereals and other crops n.e.c.	1.79	1.25	2.84	1.17	1.44	3.90	1.28
Wheat	0.35	0.25	0.56	0.23	0.28	0.77	0.25
Maize	0.06	0.04	0.10	0.04	0.05	0.13	0.04
Sunflower	0.08	0.05	0.12	0.05	0.06	0.17	0.06
Cotton	0.05	0.03	0.08	0.03	0.04	0.10	0.03
Growing of vegetables, horticultural specialties and nursery products	0.07	0.05	0.10	0.04	0.05	0.14	0.05
Growing of fruit, nuts, beverage and spice crops	0.07	0.05	0.11	0.05	0.06	0.15	0.05
Farming of animals	0.02	0.02	0.04	0.01	0.02	0.05	0.02
Agricultural and animal husbandry service activities, except veterinary activities	0.01	0.00	0.01	0.00	0.00	0.01	0.00
Forestry, logging and related service activities	0.09	0.10	0.10	0.11	0.10	0.12	0.08
Fishing	0.20	0.14	0.30	0.14	0.16	0.42	0.14
Mining and quarrying [08-12]	0.52	0.37	0.82	0.01	0.42	0.35	0.02
Production, processing and preserving of meat and meat products	0.04	0.04	0.03	0.00	0.05	0.03	0.00
Processing and preserving of fish and fish products	0.00	0.00	0.00	0.00	0.00	0.00	0.00
Processing and preserving of fruit and vegetables	0.08	0.06	0.13	0.00	0.06	0.05	0.00
Manufacture of vegetable and animal oils and fats	0.17	0.18	0.16	0.01	0.19	0.12	0.01
Manufacture of dairy products	0.03	0.02	0.05	0.00	0.03	0.02	0.00
Manufacture of grain mill products, starches and starch	0.00	0.00	0.00	0.00	0.00	0.00	0.00

products							
Manufacture of prepared animal feeds	0.00	0.00	0.00	0.00	0.00	0.00	0.00
Manufacture of bakery products	0.05	0.02	0.05	0.00	0.03	0.03	0.00
Manufacture of sugar	1.31	1.67	0.84	0.15	1.69	0.91	0.11
Manufacture of cocoa, chocolate, sugar confert.& other food products n.e.c.	0.35	0.35	0.36	0.02	0.28	0.23	0.02
Manufacture of alcoholic, soft drinks and mineral waters[23-24]	0.08	0.05	0.11	0.00	0.05	0.05	0.00
Manufacture of tobacco products	0.02	0.01	0.03	0.00	0.01	0.01	0.00
Manufacture of textiles [26-32]	1.25	0.72	1.35	0.06	0.72	0.79	0.06
Wood, furniture, paper, publishing [33-37, 67]	1.38	1.02	2.13	0.03	1.05	0.88	0.05
Manufacture of fertilizers, pesticides, other agro-chemicals, paints, and varnishes [40-41]	1.07	0.44	1.13	0.04	0.34	0.68	0.05
Manufacture of coke, refined petroleum prod, basic chemicals, rubber, plastics, glass, ceramic prod., non-metallic minerals, etc. [38-39, 42-49]	10.22	9.12	10.98	0.59	9.24	6.39	0.56
Manufacture of ferrous, non-ferrous metals, various machinery, vehicles, etc. [50-66, 68]	10.18	12.21	7.13	1.06	8.47	7.04	0.82
Energy production and distribution [69-70]	45.15	52.52	34.84	0.88	53.79	31.35	1.30
Water and Construction [71-72]	1.69	1.12	2.53	0.04	1.25	1.12	0.07
Transport [73, 78-81]	17.57	12.38	27.21	90.36	14.16	42.33	92.22
Services [74-77, 82-97]	6.03	5.74	5.76	4.87	5.88	1.65	2.70
Total	100.00	100.00	100.00	100.00	100.00	100.00	100.00

Source: Author's Calculations.

POLICY ANALYSIS

Turkey has ratified Kyoto Protocol in 2009 after the immense pressure of EU and other OECD countries, though Turkey has not been given any target of reduction of GHGs emissions but Turkey has emphasized on the adoption of clean development plans – that is shift from traditional development to modern development plans that run under the umbrella of sustainable development. Morally, Turkey has to decrease emissions of GHGs along with the other countries that have ratified the Kyoto Protocol.

To know the change in GHGs emissions between the 2009 and 2012, we first need to estimate the GHGs emissions for the year 2012 by using the Leontief Inverse method (see equation 7). For this, the final demand for the year 2012 is estimated using the growth rate of 7 percent from 2010 to 2012[1]. The major GHG CO2 increased from 248531.66 to 304461.96 thousand Tons. All GHGs have increased by 22.5 percent; the results are summarized in Table **4**[2].

Table 4: Inter-industries GHGs emissions in 1000 tons

Year	CO2	N2O	CH4	CO	SOx	NOx	NMVOC
2009	248531.66	2.51	5.75	2731.92	2835.49	1043.53	502.44
2012	304461.96	3.08	7.04	3346.72	3473.59	1278.37	615.51

If Turkey decreases the GHGs emissions then what will be the possible impact of such change on the growing economy of Turkey is the key question. To answer this question, certain policy scenario has been developed in this study. In this policy scenario, it is assumed that the base year will be 2009 and therefore no significant change in industry-wise production technology is assumed till the commitment period 2012. If Turkey takes the targets of 5 and 10 percent reduction in GHGs emissions subject to the levels of 2009 inter-industries in the commitment period

[1] The target growth rate of Turkey under 9th Development Plan (2007-2013) is 7 percent.

[2] The results of GHGs emissions under the target growth rate of 7 percent for the year 2012 are given in appendix 2.

2012, by how much of these reductions will affect the values of final demand, employee's compensation and total output of all sectors.

To find out the cost of reduction of GHGs emissions in terms of final demand, employee's compensation and total output of all sectors, we have to reintroduce the equation 6 from section 2.

$$E_i = \hat{R}_i X \quad (6)$$

$$X = \frac{E_i}{\hat{R}_i} \quad (8)$$

As we know:

$$X(I - A) = Y \quad (4)$$

Put the value of X from equation 8 into equation 4.

$$Y = (I - A)\hat{R}_i^{-1} E_i \quad (9)$$

By using equation 9, Y can be solved given the exogenous environmental discharges of type i. The employee's compensation and total output of all sectors are calculated by using simply Leontief Inverse method by using the final demand obtained in equation 9 under two targets.

In order to find out the cost of reduction of GHGs emissions in terms of final demand, employee's compensation and total output of all sectors, we need to first find out the final demand, employee's compensation and total output of all sectors if Turkey grows on its targeted growth rate. The results are given in Table **5**.

Table 5: Final demand, employees' compensation and total output (Millions TL)

	Final Demand (Y)	Employees Income	Total Output Xi
2012	112047286984.89	21029973481	173303174471.1
Policy Target 10 %	-9146396248	-1716672270	-14146701338
Policy Target 5 %	-4573198124	-858336135.2	-7073350669

Source: Author's Calculations.

If Turkey reduces the GHGs emissions by 10 percent subject to the base level of 2009 GHGs emissions, then Turkey will have to give up 9146396248, 1716672270 & 14146701338 millions of TL of final demand, employees' compensation and total output of all sectors respectively and this makes 8.12 percent reduction subject to the base level of 2012. On the contrary, if Turkey reduces the GHGs emissions by 5 percent subject to the base level of 2009 GHGs emissions, it will have to give up 4573198124, 858336135.2 & 7073350669 millions of TL of final demand, employees' compensation and total output of all sectors respectively and this makes 4.08 percent reduction subject to the base level of 2012.

Turkey is a developing country and its people need higher growth rates in real output, more employment opportunities rather than attainment of environmental goals. Currently economic and social goals weigh more importance in the country's development plans than improvement in environmental targets at the economic and social cost.

Natural gas is one of the types of fossil fuel that produces the least emissions of GHGs among all other fossil fuel types and one more advantage of using natural gas is that it is cost efficient. This study has developed one policy scenario that if natural gas is substituted completely in place of other fuel types, what will be the size of GHGs emissions in 2012 with projected final demand and change with respect to results of GHGs emissions from fossil fuel consumption in 2012.

In this policy scenario, we assume that prices and technology will not change till the period 2012; and all fuel types are perfect substitutes to each other. In Table **6** prices (Millions of TL per Ton) of fuels and net calorific values (NCVs) TJ/Gg are given.

Table 6: Prices and net calorific values of fuels

Fuel Type	Prices Millions TL per Ton	NCVs TJ/Gg
Lignite	10.90	11.9
Sulphur	12.00	40.2
Coke powder	13.72	25.0
Hard coal	14.16	26.7
Petroleum coke	16.62	32.5
Coking coal	21.23	28.2
Fuel oil	31.64	40.4
Natural gas	40.83	48.0
LPG	88.36	47.3
Diesel oil	129.54	43.0
Kerosene	151.20	43.8
Gasoline	202.66	44.3

Source: (TURKSTAT, 2001) and (IPCC, 2006).

Lignite has the minimum price 10.9 Million TL per Ton and minimum NCV 11.9 TJ/Gg; natural gas has the maximum NCV 48 TJ/Gg and price 40.83 Million TL per Ton; and gasoline has the maximum price 202.66 Million TL per Ton with the NCV of 44.3. The rankings of emissions (Kgs/Ton) for three direct GHGs - CO_2, CH_4 and N_2O are given in Table 7. In terms of CO_2 emissions, lignite has the lowest emissions 1201.9 Kgs/Ton, natural gas 2692.8 Kgs/Ton and highest emissions by diesel oil 3186.3 Kgs/Ton. For CH_4, again lignite has the lowest emissions 0.0119 Kgs/Ton, natural gas 0.048 Kgs/Ton and highest value 0.1329 Kgs/Ton goes to gasoline. In case of N_2O, LPG has the lowest emissions 0.0047 Kgs/Ton, natural gas has the second lowest emissions 0.0048 Kgs/Ton and coking coal has the highest emissions 0.0432 Kgs/Ton.

Table 7: Rankings of emissions in ascending order for three GHGs

Fuel Type	CO2 Emissions Kgs per Ton	Fuel Type	CH4 Emissions Kgs per Ton	Fuel Type	N2O Emissions Kgs per Ton
Lignite	1201.9	Lignite	0.0119	LPG	0.00473
Coke powder	2449.165	Coke powder	0.025	Natural gas	0.0048
Hard coal	2624.61	Hard coal	0.0267	Lignite	0.01785
Coking coal	2667.72	Coking coal	0.0282	Petroleum coke	0.0195
Natural gas	2692.8	LPG	0.0473	Sulphur	0.02412
Sulphur	2946.66	Natural gas	0.048	Fuel oil	0.02424
LPG	2984.63	Petroleum coke	0.0975	Diesel oil	0.0258
Gasoline	3069.99	Sulphur	0.1206	Kerosene	0.02628
Fuel oil	3126.96	Fuel oil	0.1212	Gasoline	0.02658
Kerosene	3149.22	Diesel oil	0.129	Coke powder	0.0375
Petroleum coke	3168.75	Kerosene	0.1314	Hard coal	0.04005
Diesel oil	3186.3	Gasoline	0.1329	Coking coal	0.0423

Source: Author's Calculations.

Here question arises, when lignite has the lowest emissions per Ton in two main GHGs (CO_2 and CH_4), as well as, the advantage of the minimum price per Ton, then, why natural gas has been chosen as a substitution for fuel types that are mentioned in the above tables. This is the one side of the picture, on the other side of the picture; we see the NCV (the useful calorific value or heating value in boiler plant) which is one of the significant factors (emissions and prices of natural gas per Ton) that made us choose natural gas as substitute for other fuel types. In simple words, lignite has the lowest NCV 11.9 TJ/Gg, in order to produce as much as heat that 1 Gg of natural gas (NCV 48 TJ/Gg) produces, more than 4Gg of lignite would be needed that would mean four times more emissions and more costly too. If natural gas is substituted for LPG, diesel oil, kerosene, gasoline and lignite, it will reduce costs significantly. But in terms of GHGs emissions minimization, natural gas will decrease emissions compared to all other fuel types mentioned in the above tables.

Substitution of natural gas for other fuel types takes place in the following manner:

Transform all the fuels into energy units (TJ) by simply multiplying quantity of fuels expressed in 1000 Tons with their net calorific values (NCVs).

Divide each fuel type expressed in energy units TJ (step 1) with the NCV of natural gas 48 TJ/Gg that will give us the quantities of natural gas (1000 Tons) equivalent to correspondent fuel types.

The following Table **8** reveals the mechanism described in above 2 steps. The 4th column of Table **8** is obtained multiplying column 2 with column 3 and 5th column is obtained by dividing column 4 with the NCV of natural gas 48 TJ/Gg.

Table 8: Conversion of fuel types into natural gas in manufacturing industries

Energy Type	Quantity in 1000 Tons	NCVs TJ/Gg	Energy Type in TJ	NG Equivalent in 1000 Tons
Natural gas	2667.632	48.0	128046.30	2667.632
Fuel oil	3780.943	40.4	152750.10	3182.294
LPG	362.545	47.3	17148.38	357.258
Kerosene	6.866	43.8	300.73	6.265
Sulphur	144.705	40.2	5817.14	121.190
Diesel oil	129.533	43.0	5569.92	116.040
Gasoline	18.634	44.3	825.49	17.198
Petroleum coke	1443.449	32.5	46912.09	977.335
Coking Coal	828.289	28.2	23357.75	486.619
Coke Powder	419.814	25.0	10495.35	218.653
Hard coal	4891.877	26.7	130613.10	2721.107
Lignite	5050.529	11.9	58081.08	1210.023

Source: Author's Calculations.

A 100 percent substitution of natural gas in 2012 produces incredible results useful in current policy priorities. In terms of CO2, overall reduction is 30.31 percent in which highest reduction 42 percent takes place in manufacture of prepared animals feed sector, manufacture of sugar 38 percent, manufacture of ferrous, non-ferrous metals, various machinery, vehicles, etc sectors 35.24, energy production and distribution sectors 34.46 percent, transport sectors 21.38 percent, agriculture sectors on average above 21 percent and manufacture of fertilizers, pesticides, other agro-chemicals, paints, and varnishes sectors 9.67 percent. The results are given in Table **9**.

Table 9: Percentage change in GHGs emissions from natural gas substitution completely subject to the level of 2012 emissions from fossil fuel

Sectors	CO2	N2O	CH4	CO	SOx	NOx	NMVOC
Growing of cereals and other crops n.e.c.	-21.16	-80.00	-61.54	-55.88	-99.99	-19.23	-95.12
Wheat	-21.16	-80.00	-61.54	-55.88	-99.99	-19.23	-95.12
Maize	-21.16	-80.00	-61.54	-55.88	-99.99	-19.23	-95.12

Sunflower	-21.16	-80.00	-61.54	-55.88	-99.99	-19.23	-95.12
Cotton	-21.16	-80.00	-61.54	-55.88	-99.99	-19.23	-95.12
Growing of vegetables, horticultural specialties and nursery products	-21.16	-80.0	-61.54	-55.88	-99.99	-19.23	-95.12
Growing of fruit, nuts, beverage and spice crops	-21.16	-80.0	-61.54	-55.88	-99.99	-19.23	-95.12
Farming of animals	-21.16	-80.00	-61.44	-55.97	-99.99	-19.11	-95.11
Agricultural and animal husbandry service activities, except veterinary activities	-21.16	-80.00	-61.54	-55.88	-99.99	-19.23	-95.12
Forestry, logging and related service activities	-31.59	-88.52	-49.82	-78.88	-99.99	18.31	-96.39
Fishing	-22.03	-81.03	-60.89	-59.11	-99.99	-17.34	-95.24
Mining and quarrying [08-12]	-21.38	-80.28	-61.27	167.31	-99.99	-25.26	-2.44
Production, processing and preserving of meat and meat products	-31.35	-87.62	-37.18	-58.36	-99.99	-33.26	-54.52
Processing and preserving of fish and fish products	-11.71	-13.78	-6.01	2.18	-99.99	-1.05	0.00
Processing and preserving of fruit and vegetables	-26.39	-82.32	-65.06	163.14	-99.99	-23.69	-0.05
Manufacture of vegetable and animal oils and fats	-31.62	-88.24	-42.10	-58.02	-99.99	-34.53	-54.92
Manufacture of dairy products	-27.38	-83.60	-63.61	59.95	-99.99	-25.56	-13.49
Manufacture of grain mill products, starches and starch products	-27.33	-83.29	-66.60	198.33	-99.99	-24.95	0.00
Manufacture of prepared animal feeds	-42.06	-92.62	-24.33	-76.47	-99.99	-47.17	-71.57
Manufacture of bakery products	-13.33	-60.58	-33.42	9.51	-99.99	-9.40	-5.70
Manufacture of sugar	-38.27	-91.46	-25.74	-72.96	-99.99	-43.22	-67.85
Manufacture of cocoa, chocolate, sugar confert.& other food products n.e.c.	-30.61	-87.80	-48.14	-52.02	-99.99	-33.47	-51.11
Manufacture of alcoholic, soft drinks and mineral waters[23-24]	-22.98	-79.68	-59.86	79.26	-99.99	-20.78	-3.96
Manufacture of tobacco products	-18.53	-76.98	-55.62	55.70	-99.99	-18.29	-4.31
Manufacture of textiles [26-32]	-17.20	-74.42	-40.88	-9.66	-99.99	-16.64	-20.20
Wood, furniture, paper, publishing [33-37, 67]	-23.10	-81.59	-61.48	68.21	-99.99	-22.94	-8.66
Manufacture of fertilizers, pesticides, other agro-chemicals, paints, and varnishes [40-41]	-9.69	-61.05	-33.91	9.84	-99.99	-9.57	-5.75
Manufacture of coke, refined petroleum prod, basic chemicals, rubber, plastics, glass, ceramic prod., non-metallic minerals, etc. [38-39, 42-49]	-32.39	-86.62	-51.37	-42.61	-99.99	-31.02	-45.09
Manufacture of ferrous, non-ferrous metals, various machinery, vehicles, etc. [50-66, 68]	-35.25	-90.46	-28.54	-69.62	-99.99	-40.22	-64.52
Energy production and distribution [69-70]	-34.46	-90.07	-34.52	8.97	-99.99	-39.89	0.00
Water and Construction [71-72]	-19.60	-78.50	-58.50	72.98	-99.99	-23.34	-9.34
Transport [73, 78-81]	-21.38	-80.33	-60.85	-90.08	-99.99	-16.87	-99.34
Services [74-77, 82-97]	-27.74	-86.61	-41.68	-92.74	-99.99	-43.85	-92.88
Total	-30.31	-87.71	-46.24	-87.96	-99.99	-27.58	-96.93

Source: Author's Calculations

Natural gas substitution has shown overall reduction of 87.71 percent in N2O emissions in which manufacture of prepared animals feeds sector 92.62 percent, manufacture of sugar 91.46 percent, energy production and distribution sectors 90 percent, transport sectors 80.33 percent, agriculture sectors on average 80 percent reduce respectively. CH4 has shown an overall reduction of 46.24 better than CO2 reductions. Manufacture of grain mill products, starches and starch products sector has shown a great response in reducing the emissions of CH4 by 66.60 percent, processing and preserving of fruit and vegetables takes the second position and reduces CH4 by 65 percent, manufacture of dairy products with 65 percent, transport sector 60 percent, energy production and distribution sectors 34.51 and agriculture sectors on average above 61 percent.

Natural gas substitution has produced much better results in four indirect GHGs compared to three GHGs. In SOx, the results are unbelievable - 99.99 percent overall and sectoral reductions; in CO, overall reduction is 87.96 percent but in some sectors CO emissions have increased with the natural gas substitution. Manufacture of grain mill products, starches and starch products sectors and mining and quarrying sectors have shown great increase 198.33 and 167.3 percent respectively. But many sectors have shown significant reductions in CO whose shares in total emissions of CO in 2012 emissions table from natural gas substitution are very high i.e. transport and water and construction sectors are prominent. Increase in CO emissions in some sectors whose shares in total CO emissions are very low (0.0008 percent for manufacture of grain mill products, starches and starch products sectors and 0.165 percent for mining and quarrying sectors) cannot affect the overall reduction of CO from the natural gas substitution.

NOx has produced the lowest reductions 27.58 percent overall and main contributors are services, energy production and distribution, transport and agriculture sectors. NMVOC has shown overall reduction of 96.93 percent in which transport sector and agriculture sectors have contributed 99.34 and 95.12 percent reduction respectively, whereas, energy production and distribution and manufacture of grain mill products, starches and starch products sectors have no role in reducing the emissions. In all seven gases, NOx has produced the lowest reductions 27.58 percent overall and main contributors are services, energy production and distribution, transport and agriculture.

CONCLUSION AND RECOMMENDATIONS

Massive use of fossil fuel consumption has caused rapid economic growth in the world in the past two centuries. This economic growth has been achieved at the cost of climate change, acid rain, damage to eco-system from the extraction of fossil fuels and impact of oil spills on marine eco-system. Among these problems climate change is at the top of concern in the world agenda. Climate change results from combustion of fossil fuels which accounts for 80 % of emissions. According to current estimates of IPCC, average temperature will rise by 1^0 to 6^0 C by 2100. This rise in world temperature can result in dry regions becoming even drier and humid regions even more humid and lead to cause extreme weathers such as, hurricanes, floods and droughts.

This serious problem drew the attention of almost all the developed countries and some developing countries and ultimately brought some progress in bringing the nations of the world together on common platform and paved the way for the formation of UNFCCC and Kyoto Protocol. Turkey is already Annex I Party to UNFCCC, and she has also ratified Kyoto Protocol in 2009. Though Turkey has not been given any target of reduction of GHGs emissions, it morally faces the pressure to reduce anthropogenic carbon dioxide equivalent of the GHGs emissions by certain level.

The main objective of this study is to estimate GHGs emissions from fossil fuel consumption for 2009 and 2012 using input-output techniques. This study has simulated policy scenario of estimating the cost of reducing GHGs emissions in terms of final demand, employees' compensation and total output of sectors under 10 and 5 percent targets of reduction of GHGs emissions subject to the level of 2009 emissions. This policy scenario further extends by incorporating the estimation of GHGs emissions from natural gas substitution completely for the year 2012.

This study finds that in 2009, the total sectoral CO2, N20, CH4, CO, SOx, NOx and NMVOC emissions were 248,531.66, 2.51, 5.75, 2,731.92, 2,835.49, 1,043.53, and 502.44 thousand Tons respectively. Energy production and distribution, transport, manufacture of coke, refined petroleum products, basic chemicals, and others and manufacture of ferrous, non-ferrous metals, and others were the main sectors contributing GHGs emissions significantly. The share of agriculture sector was very minor, even less than half of the share of the services sector. All GHGs have increased by 22.5 percent in the year 2012 from fossil fuel consumption if Turkey grows on average with 7 percent.

The opportunity cost of reducing GHGs emissions by 10 and 5 percent subject to the level of 2009 GHGs emissions in 2012 is to give up final demand, employees' compensation and total output of sectors by 8.12 and 4.08 percent respectively. The substitution of natural gas completely for other fossil fuel types solves the problem of reducing GHGs emissions even Turkey grows with the 7 percent from 2010 to 2012. The overall reduction in CO2, N20, CH4, CO, SOx, NOx and NMVOC are 30.31, 87.71, 46.24, 87.96, 99.99, 27.58 & 96.93 percent respectively.

This research has discovered the possible implications of implementations of above three policies on the three pillars of sustainable development – environmental, economic and social – in Turkey and this research has given the solution that minimizes the economic and social cost of environmental sustainability. This research paves the guidelines for the policy makers and decision bodies in Turkey and tries to draw their attention on the findings so that necessary steps may be taken from now on to the path of sustainable development in Turkey.

Natural gas substitution puts the baseline for framing future policy frameworks for sustainable development of Turkey. This study strongly recommends natural gas substitution should be given first priority in the future policies for clean development-development with the least cost of environmental damage of Turkey.

The opportunity costs of reducing GHGs emissions are very high in terms of economic and social goals of Turkey. Shifting to natural gas use in the industries that have relatively high shares in total emissions may be a solution as natural gas produces much less emissions compared to others. However, in that case, the rising import bill and its impact on trade account and on production cost has to be taken into account as Turkey is a big net-importer in natural gas. In addition, net natural gas exporter countries have the price setting power and have the freedom to totally or partially restrict supply, as seen in the previous years. In Turkey, the share of renewable energy in total energy production is very less; Turkey has to take very crucial steps to develop and boost renewable energy sources as they are totally environmental friendly technologies. Turkey has to develop new set of policies by considering the above recommendations that will lead Turkey to meet the environmental targets without getting much cost in economic and social goals of sustainable development.

REFERENCES

Bhutto, N. A. (2007). Building Environmental Input-Output Model for Turkey with Special Focus on Agri-Food Sectors. Unpublished Ph.D. dissertation, Hacettepe University, Department of Economics, Ankara, Turkey.

Energy Statistics, (2003). In: Altaş, M., Özkan, F., Çelebi, E. (Eds.), Ninth Turkey Energy Congress, 24–27 September. World Energy Council Turkish National Committee, İstanbul.

Intergovernmental Panel on Climate Change. (2006). 2006 IPCC Guidelines for National Greenhouse Gas Inventories. Retrieved in July 2009 from http://www.ipcc-nggip.iges.or.jp.

International Energy Agency, (2005). Energy Policies of IEA Countries: Turkey 2005 Review. Paris. Retrieved in July 2009 from http://iea.org/textbase/nppdf /free /200/ turkey 2005.pdf.

Joberta, T. and Karanfil, F., (2007). "Sectoral energy consumption by source and economic growth in Turkey", *Energy Policy* 35, 5447–5456.

Leontief, W. (1970). The dynamic inverse In Carter, A.P., Brody, A. (Eds), *Contributions to Input-Output Analysis*, North-Holland Publishing, Amsterdam, 17-46.

Say, N.P. and Yücel, M., (2006). "Energy consumption and CO2 emissions in Turkey: Empirical analysis and future projection based on an economic growth", *Energy Policy* 34, 3870–3876.

Turkish Institute of Statistics (TURKSTAT) (2001). "Energy Consumption in the Manufacturing Industry (Establishments with 500 Tons of Oil Equivalent or More Energy Consumption) 1998." Ankara.

Turkish Institute of Statistics (TURKSTAT) (2009). Growth Rate of Expenditure on the Gross Domestic Product (at 1998 prices), 1998-2009 Retrieved in November 2009 from http:// www.turkstat.gov.tr/ VeriBilgi.do? tb_id =55&ust_id=16.

APPENDIX 1

Full Disaggregated Version of Agriculture Focused

Input-output Tables

01 Growing of cereals and other crops n.e.c.

1.1 Wheat
1.2 Maize
1.3 Sunflower
1.4 Cotton

02 Growing of vegetables, horticultural specialties and nursery products

03 Growing of fruit, nuts, beverage and spice crops

04 Farming of animals

05 Agricultural and animal husbandry service activities, except veterinary activities

06 Forestry, logging and related service activities

07 Fishing

08 Mining of coal and lignite

09 Extraction of crude petroleum and natural gas

10 Mining of metal ores

11 Quarrying of stone, sand and clay

12 Mining and quarrying n.e.c.

13 Production, processing and preserving of meat and meat products

14 Processing and preserving of fish and fish products

15 Processing and preserving of fruit and vegetables

16 Manufacture of vegetable and animal oils and fats

17 Manufacture of dairy products

18 Manufacture of grain mill products, starches and starch products

19 Manufacture of prepared animal feeds

20 Manufacture of bakery products

21 Manufacture of sugar

22 Manufacture of cocoa, chocolate, sugar confert. & other food products n.e.c.

23 Manufacture of alcoholic beverages

24 Manufacture of soft drinks; production of mineral waters

25 Manufacture of tobacco products

26 Manufacture of textiles

27 Manufacture of other textiles

28 Manufacture of knitted and crocheted fabrics and articles

29 Manufacture of wearing apparel, except fur apparel

30 Dressing and dyeing of fur; manufacture of articles of fur

31 Tanning and dressing of leather; man.of luggage, handbags, saddlery and harness

32 Manufacture of footwear
33 Sawmilling and planning of wood
34 Manufacture of wood and of products of wood and cork
35 Manufacture of paper and paper products
36 Publishing
37 Printing and service activities related to printing
38 Manufacture of coke, refined petroleum products
39 Manufacture of basic chemicals, plastics & synthetics rubber
40 Manufacture of fertilizers and nitrogen compounds
41 Manufacture of pesticides, other agro-chemicals and paints, varnishes
42 Manufacture of pharmaceuticals, medicinal chemicals &botanical products
43 Manufacture of cleaning materials, cosmetics & man-made fibers
44 Manufacture of rubber products
45 Manufacture of plastic products
46 Manufacture of glass and glass products
47 Manufacture of ceramic products
48 Manufacture of cement, lime and plaster related articles these items
49 Cutting and finishing of stone and man. of non-metallic mineral products n.e.c.
50 Manufacture of basic iron and steel
51 Manufacture of basic precious and non-ferrous metals
52 Casting of metals
53 Manufacture of fabricated metal products, tanks, reservoirs &steam generators
54 Manufacture of other fabricated metal products; metal working service activities
55 Manufacture of general purpose machinery
56 Manufacture of special purpose machinery
57 Manufacture of domestic appliances n.e.c.
58 Manufacture of office, accounting and computing machinery
59 Manufacture of electrical machinery and apparatus n.e.c.
60 Manufacture of radio, television and communication equipment and apparatus
61 Manufacture of medical, precision and optical instruments, watches and clocks
62 Manufacture of motor vehicles, trailers and semi-trailers
63 Building and repairing of ships, pleasure and sporting boats
64 Manufacture of railway and tramway locomotives and rolling stock
65 Manufacture of aircraft and spacecraft
66 Manufacture of transport equipment n.e.c.
67 Manufacture of furniture
68 Manufacturing n.e.c.
69 Production, collection and distribution of electricity

70 Manufacture of gas; distribution of gaseous fuels through mains
71 Collection, purification and distribution of water
72 Construction
73 Sale, maintenance and repair of motor vehicles, motorcycles; retail sale of fuel
74 Wholesale trade and commission trade, except of motor vehicles and motorcycles
75 Retail trade, except of motor vehicles and motorcycles; repair of personnel &household goods
76 Hotels; camping sites and other provision of short-stay accommodation
77 Restaurants, bars and canteens
78 Transport via railways
79 Land transport; transport via pipelines
80 Water transport
81 Air transport
82 Supporting and auxiliary transport activities; activities of travel agencies
83 Post and telecommnications
84 Financial intermediation, except insurance and pension funding
85 Insurance and pension funding, except compulsory social security
86 Real estate activities
87 Renting of machinery and equip. without operator and of personal & household goods
88 Computer and related activities
89 Research and development
90 Other business activities
91 Education
92 Health and social work
93 Activities of membership organizations n.e.c
94 Recreational, cultural and sporting activities
95 Other service activities
96 Public services
97 Ownership of dwelling

Aggregated Version of Agricultural Focused Input-Output Tables

1 Growing of cereals and other crops n.e.c.
2 Wheat
3 Maize
4 Sunflower
5 Cotton
6 Growing of vegetables, horticultural specialties and nursery products
7 Growing of fruit, nuts, beverage and spice crops
8 Farming of animals

9 Agricultural and animal husbandry service activities, except veterinary activities

10 Forestry, logging and related service activities

11 Fishing

12 Mining and quarrying [08-12]

13 Production, processing and preserving of meat and meat products

14 Processing and preserving of fish and fish products

15 Processing and preserving of fruit and vegetables

16 Manufacture of vegetable and animal oils and fats

17 Manufacture of dairy products

18 Manufacture of grain mill products, starches and starch products

19 Manufacture of prepared animal feeds

20 Manufacture of bakery products

21 Manufacture of sugar

22 Manufacture of cocoa, chocolate, sugar confert. & other food products n.e.c.

23 Manufacture of alcoholic, soft drinks and mineral waters [23-24]

24 Manufacture of tobacco products

25 Manufacture of textiles [26-32]

26 Wood, furniture, paper, publishing [33-37, 67]

27 Manufacture of fertilizers, pesticides, other agro-chemicals, paints, and varnishes [40-41]

28 Manufacture of coke, refined petroleum prod., basic chemicals, rubber, plastics, glass, ceramic prod., non-metallic minerals, etc. [38-39, 42-49]

29 Manufacture of ferrous, non-ferrous metals, various machinery, vehicles, etc. [50-66, 68]

30 Energy production and distribution [69-70]

31 Water and Construction [71-72]

32 Transport [73, 78-81]

33 Services [74-77, 82-97]

APPENDIX 2

GHGs Emissions in 1000 Tons in 2012 from Fossil Fuels

Sectors	CO2	N2O	CH4	CO	SOx	NOx	NMVOC
Growing of cereals and other crops n.e.c.	5,463.32	0.04	0.20	39.16	49.93	49.90	7.87
Wheat	1,078.05	0.01	0.04	7.73	9.85	9.85	1.55
Maize	188.35	0.00	0.01	1.35	1.72	1.72	0.27
Sunflower	237.49	0.00	0.01	1.70	2.17	2.17	0.34
Cotton	146.87	0.00	0.01	1.05	1.34	1.34	0.21
Growing of vegetables, horticultural specialties and nursery products	199.70	0.00	0.01	1.43	1.83	1.82	0.29
Growing of fruit, nuts, beverage and spice crops	212.62	0.00	0.01	1.52	1.94	1.94	0.31
Farming of animals	68.38	0.00	0.00	0.49	0.62	0.62	0.10
Agricultural and animal husbandry service activities, except veterinary activities	18.78	0.00	0.00	0.13	0.17	0.17	0.03
Forestry, logging and related service activities	285.56	0.00	0.01	3.71	3.64	1.55	0.48
Fishing	602.59	0.00	0.02	4.61	5.69	5.32	0.88
Mining and quarrying [08-12]	1,585.33	0.01	0.06	0.25	14.60	4.46	0.11
Production, processing and preserving of meat and meat products	121.75	0.00	0.00	0.11	1.67	0.34	0.02
Processing and preserving of fish and fish products	13.02	0.00	0.00	0.01	0.12	0.03	0.00
Processing and preserving of fruit and vegetables	234.90	0.00	0.01	0.04	2.08	0.61	0.02
Manufacture of vegetable and animal oils and fats	529.65	0.01	0.01	0.46	6.64	1.48	0.07
Manufacture of dairy products	93.97	0.00	0.00	0.02	0.92	0.25	0.01
Manufacture of grain mill products, starches and starch products	8.52	0.00	0.00	0.00	0.08	0.02	0.00
Manufacture of prepared animal feeds	8.58	0.00	0.00	0.01	0.15	0.03	0.00
Manufacture of bakery products	140.89	0.00	0.00	0.06	0.92	0.36	0.01
Manufacture of sugar	3,992.28	0.05	0.06	4.88	58.84	11.63	0.68
Manufacture of cocoa, chocolate, sugar confert.& other food products n.e.c.	1,050.81	0.01	0.03	0.81	9.76	2.94	0.13
Manufacture of alcoholic, soft drinks and mineral waters[23-24]	235.75	0.00	0.01	0.05	1.85	0.61	0.02
Manufacture of tobacco products	68.33	0.00	0.00	0.02	0.49	0.18	0.01
Manufacture of textiles [26-32]	3,812.41	0.02	0.10	1.87	24.91	10.14	0.35
Wood, furniture, paper, publishing [33-37, 67]	4,196.28	0.03	0.15	1.03	36.39	11.22	0.32
Manufacture of fertilizers, pesticides, other agro-chemicals, paints, and varnishes [40-41]	3,268.88	0.01	0.08	1.44	11.81	8.74	0.28
Manufacture of coke, refined petroleum prod, basic chemicals, rubber, plastics, glass, ceramic prod., non-metallic minerals, etc. [38-39, 42-49]	31,115.10	0.28	0.77	19.64	320.96	81.69	3.42
Manufacture of ferrous, non-ferrous metals, various machinery, vehicles, etc. [50-66, 68]	31,000.16	0.38	0.50	35.40	294.13	89.94	5.05
Energy production and distribution [69-70]	137,453.37	1.62	2.45	29.47	1,868.53	400.73	8.03
Water and Construction [71-72]	5,154.63	0.03	0.18	1.29	43.49	14.31	0.41
Transport [73, 78-81]	53,504.72	0.38	1.92	3,024.05	491.97	541.18	567.64
Services [74-77, 82-97]	18,370.93	0.18	0.41	162.92	204.35	21.07	16.61
Total	304461.96	3.08	7.04	3346.72	3473.59	1278.37	615.51

Source: AuSource: Author's Calculations.

APPENDIX 3

GHGs Emissions in 1000 Tons in 2012 from Natural Gas

Sectors	CO2	N2O	CH4	CO	SOx	NOx	NMVOC
Growing of cereals and other crops n.e.c.	4,307.09	0.01	0.08	17.27	0.0007	40.31	0.38
Wheat	849.90	0.00	0.02	3.41	0.0001	7.95	0.08
Maize	148.49	0.00	0.00	0.60	0.0000	1.39	0.01
Sunflower	187.23	0.00	0.00	0.75	0.0000	1.75	0.02
Cotton	115.79	0.00	0.00	0.46	0.0000	1.08	0.01
Growing of vegetables, horticultural specialties and nursery products	157.43	0.00	0.00	0.63	0.0000	1.47	0.01
Growing of fruit, nuts, beverage and spice crops	167.62	0.00	0.00	0.67	0.0000	1.57	0.01
Farming of animals	53.91	0.00	0.00	0.22	0.0000	0.50	0.00
Agricultural and animal husbandry service activities, except veterinary activities	14.81	0.00	0.00	0.06	0.0000	0.14	0.00
Forestry, logging and related service activities	195.36	0.00	0.00	0.78	0.0000	1.83	0.02
Fishing	469.85	0.00	0.01	1.88	0.0001	4.40	0.04
Mining and quarrying [08-12]	1,246.32	0.00	0.02	0.67	0.0002	3.33	0.11
Production, processing and preserving of meat and meat products	83.58	0.00	0.00	0.04	0.0000	0.22	0.01
Processing and preserving of fish and fish products	11.50	0.00	0.00	0.01	0.0000	0.03	0.00
Processing and preserving of fruit and vegetables	172.92	0.00	0.00	0.09	0.0000	0.46	0.02
Manufacture of vegetable and animal oils and fats	362.18	0.00	0.01	0.19	0.0001	0.97	0.03
Manufacture of dairy products	68.24	0.00	0.00	0.04	0.0000	0.18	0.01
Manufacture of grain mill products, starches and starch products	6.19	0.00	0.00	0.00	0.0000	0.02	0.00
Manufacture of prepared animal feeds	4.97	0.00	0.00	0.00	0.0000	0.01	0.00
Manufacture of bakery products	122.11	0.00	0.00	0.07	0.0000	0.33	0.01
Manufacture of sugar	2,464.47	0.00	0.04	1.32	0.0004	6.60	0.22
Manufacture of cocoa, chocolate, sugar confert.& other food products n.e.c.	729.15	0.00	0.01	0.39	0.0001	1.95	0.07
Manufacture of alcoholic, soft drinks and mineral waters[23-24]	181.57	0.00	0.00	0.10	0.0000	0.49	0.02
Manufacture of tobacco products	55.67	0.00	0.00	0.03	0.0000	0.15	0.00
Manufacture of textiles [26-32]	3,156.85	0.01	0.06	1.69	0.0005	8.46	0.28
Wood, furniture, paper, publishing [33-37, 67]	3,226.78	0.01	0.06	1.73	0.0006	8.64	0.29
Manufacture of fertilizers, pesticides, other agro-chemicals, paints, and varnishes [40-41]	2,952.06	0.01	0.05	1.58	0.0005	7.91	0.26
Manufacture of coke, refined petroleum prod, basic chemicals, rubber, plastics, glass, ceramic prod., non-metallic minerals, etc. [38-39, 42-49]	21,036.36	0.04	0.38	11.27	0.0036	56.35	1.88
Manufacture of ferrous, non-ferrous metals, various machinery, vehicles, etc. [50-66, 68]	20,073.86	0.04	0.36	10.75	0.0034	53.77	1.79
Energy production and distribution [69-70]	90,085.60	0.16	1.61	32.12	0.0154	240.87	8.03
Water and Construction [71-72]	4,144.49	0.01	0.07	2.24	0.0007	10.97	0.37
Transport [73, 78-81]	42,064.13	0.07	0.75	299.92	0.0072	449.88	3.75
Services [74-77, 82-97]	13,274.62	0.02	0.24	11.83	0.0023	11.83	1.18
Total	212,191.09	0.38	3.78	402.82	0.0363	925.82	18.92

Source: AuSource: Author's Calculations.

CHAPTER 3

Atmospheric Emissions and Structural Path Analysis in the Spanish Economy

Isabela Butnar[*,a], Blanca Gallego[b], Maria Llop[c] and Francesc Castells[d]

[a]Departament d'Enginyeria Química, Universitat Rovira i Virgili, Campus Sescelades, 43007 Tarragona, Spain; [b]ISA, School of Physics, A28, The University of Sydney, NSW 2006, Australia; [c]Departament d'Economia, Universitat Rovira i Virgili, Avgda. Universitat n° 1, 43204 Reus, Spain and [d]Departament d'Enginyeria Química, Universitat Rovira i Virgili, Campus Sescelades, 43007 Tarragona, Spain

Abstract: The objective of this paper is to integrate Spanish atmospheric pollution and macro-economic data in order to identify the main drivers of atmospheric pollution in Spain. This paper uses data from the Satellite Atmospheric Emissions Accounts as well as the 2002 input-output tables both published by the Spanish National Statistics Institute. The identification and analysis of the input paths of air pollution in the Spanish production system is performed using Structural Path Analysis (SPA) in a generalised input-output framework. This methodology allows for the detection of "hidden" sectors in the generation of pollution. Our results rank the energetic sectors, food processing industries, other manufacturing industries and transportation as the sectors with the highest emission intensities. Our results also show the production layers contribution in each pollutant, identifying fluorocarbons and ammonia as the substances with higher up-stream sources.

Keywords: Structural Path Analysis, Input-Output analysis, atmospheric emissions, Spain.

INTRODUCTION

The production and consumption of goods and services causes the emission of pollutants to the atmosphere. It has long been recognised that these substances have major impacts on our health and environment and must therefore be monitored and managed. Air pollution includes the emission of substances of global concern such as greenhouse gases as well as substances which have a more localised effect but are toxic to human health and the environment. In many cases, air pollution abatement strategies have dual benefits of improved public health and climate protection (Griffiths and Rao, 2009). Under the Kyoto Protocol on climate change, the European Union established cuts for most of its members, pledging an overall reduction of 8% of greenhouse gases (GHG) emissions between 1990 and 2012. A "burden-sharing" agreement between EU governments established differentiated emissions limits for each Member State. These limits are expressed in terms of percentages by which Member States must reduce, or in some cases may hold or increase, their emissions compared with 1990, the base year level. Spain was allowed to increase its emissions by 15% above their base-level values. To ensure that this limit is not exceeded, on November 2006 the Spanish National Allocation Plan for Emissions Rights came out, establishing quotas for the country's main industries through the period 2008-2010. The highest emissions quotas were granted to the electrical energy sector (35.40%) and the cement industry (19%) from the total allowed CO_2 emissions. Other measures to decrease the emission of GHG included promoting efficient energy use and clean energy sources, supporting cleaner technologies, and making the public more sensitive to the problem of global warming.

In order to assist air pollution reduction at a national level, it is important to identify the polluting industries and to describe and quantify their emissions as detailed as possible. Furthermore, it is important to consider not only the direct or on site emissions, but also the emissions "embodied" or "enclosed" in the products or services that an industry buys for its functioning. This is precisely the aim of this paper, to determine the direct and indirect emissions associated with the activity of each sector in the Spanish economy in order to detect the key sectors and supply chains that play an important role in the generation of air pollution. This information will help decision-making for further emission reduction measures in Spain.

In this work, we employ a generalised input-output (IO) model supplemented by a detailed analysis of the "embodied" emissions using an analytical tool, which has not been applied before to the study of the Spanish

[*]**Address correspondence to Isabela Butnar:** Departament d'Enginyeria Química, Universitat Rovira i Virgili, Campus Sescelades, 43007 Tarragona, Spain; Tel: +34 977 55 8553; Fax: +34 977 55 9621; E-mail: isabela.butnar@urv.cat.

Maria Llop (Ed)

production factors, namely Structural Path Analysis (SPA). The use of IO techniques to study environmental problems is not new for Spain, the first application dates from 1980 when Pajuelo (1980) proposed an extended Leontief model to analyze the role of the economy in atmospheric pollution. The extended Leontief model included new rows and columns to account for the atmospheric pollutants as part of the production processes. In the field of water consumption, Duarte *et al.* (2002) and Sánchez-Chóliz and Duarte (2003) used a traditional IO model, but considered water needs as inputs in the model. To detect key sectors in the consumption of water, the transfer of water between economic sectors and the relationships between water use and income generation these authors used a particular methodology based on linkage analysis. Combining Structural Decomposition Analysis with the previous method, Sánchez-Chóliz and Duarte (2004) investigated the connection between water use and technical changes in the economy or changes in the final demand. A different approach to the estimation of sectoral water consumption was suggested by Velázquez (2006) who proposes a new model by combining the Leontief model with the Proops' energy model. This method allows for predictions of the impact that new water consumption regulations would have on the regional economy of Andalusia.

An important contribution to the study of atmospheric pollution and primary energy consumption was made by Alcántara and Roca (1995). They proposed a different input-output model based on the Organisation for Economic Co-operation and Development's (OECD's) energy balance sheets combined with information on energy consumption by type and by economic sector. This permitted them to explain primary energy demands and CO_2 emissions during the decade 1980-1990. Recently, Alcántara and Padilla (2009) have improved this model and applied it to the study of greenhouse gas emissions associated with the services sector in the Spanish economy. Anton Valero *et al.* (1993) constructed the energy input-output tables of the Spanish economy and study CO_2 emissions under different scenarios of economic development. The calculation of total atmospheric emissions using IO multipliers has been performed by various authors. Cadarso and Fernández-Bolaños (2002) computed the emissions multipliers for the Spanish economy for the period 1980-1995 and the total emissions related to each component of the final demand for 11 kinds of pollutants. They analysed the temporal evolution of the emissions and recommended to pay attention to private consumption which, according to their results, was responsible for the main part of the total emissions. Manresa and Sancho (2004) calculated the energy requirements and CO_2 emissions for the Catalan economy using social accounting matrix (SAM) multipliers. In their work, the simple IO multipliers were discussed as a particular case of SAM multipliers. Although the results obtained using the SAM multipliers were more comprehensive, since they reflected amplified inter-sectoral links, the authors recommended the use of the simple IO multipliers to detect and isolate the effects due only to the productive sectors links. Sánchez-Chóliz *et al.* (2005) used the SAM multipliers calculated for 1999 to estimate seven water pollution and atmospheric emissions footprints of the Spanish population. Associating the estimated footprints with households' income, they found that the *per capita* pollution (an approximation to the ecological footprint) is strongly dependent on the income levels and rises in line with them. On the other side, Roca and Serrano (2007) used Structural Path Analysis and IO multipliers to analyse the relationship between atmospheric pollution and income growth and found that for pollutants, such as NH_3, CH_4 and N_2O, the income growth is associated to a decrease in emission intensities. However, they considered this de-linking as weak as it is due to changes in the structure of final demand (decrease of food-products demand over the analysed period: 1995-2000). Argüelles *et al.* (2006) calculated the direct, indirect and induced greenhouse gas emissions in Asturias for 1995. They compared the results obtained by considering households exogenous as a whole versus endogenizing part of the household consumption, and identified the sectors more affected by the Kyoto Protocol implementation in Asturias.

The present work applies Structural Path Analysis (SPA) to the Spanish economy in order to identify the key economic sectors and inter-industry linkages that play a role in given production factors. In particular, to illustrate this methodology, we apply it to the study of atmospheric pollution in Spain, although it can be easily adapted to other production factors such as water consumption and pollution, land-use, natural resource consumption, etc., depending on the availability of data and user interests. Atmospheric emissions by unit of final consumption are estimated using a generalised IO model through the calculation of IO multipliers for 11 kinds of atmospheric pollutants. SPA is applied through a decomposition of the IO multipliers into economic paths along the supply chain. If the previous applications of IO techniques to environmental problems made possible the evaluation of the emissions of each economic sector, our study goes deeper providing also information on the indirect polluting sectors and the paths through which the generation of pollution is propagated. Only knowing both, the direct and the indirect polluting sectors, a good decision-making can be made.

The Spanish National Institute of Statistics provides both the economic and the environmental data used in our calculations, namely the IO tables for the year 2002 (the last year for each are compiled both IO data and data on emissions) and the Satellite Atmospheric Emissions Accounts for the same year (INE, 2006, 2009). The modifications we brought to the original data to fit in the methodology are explained in Section 2.2. The remaining of the paper is organized as follows. In Section 2.1, we present the generalised IO model and the SPA methodology employed in this study. Section 3.1 contains the results of their application to the Spanish economic sectors as direct and indirect polluters. The results are presented in detailed by emission type. Section 3.2 summarises and discusses the main results and Section 4 draws some conclusions.

METHODOLOGY

Generalized Input-Output Model and Structural Path Analysis

Input-output analysis is a top-down economic technique that traces the monetary flows throughout an economic system for a particular period of time, connecting the gross outputs of economic sectors with primary inputs and final demand. In particular, the gross output x_i of an economic sector i can be expressed as the sum of the sector's final demand y_i plus all its inter-industry sales:

$$x_i = y_i + \sum_j z_{ij} \quad \textbf{(1)}$$

Here, z_{ij} represents the monetary transaction from industry i to industry j. In the input-output formalism, a matrix of direct requirements A is defined as the inter-industry flows a_{ij} from an industry i to an industry j per gross output of sector j, $a_{ij} = z_{ij}x_j^{-1}$. Using this definition in equation (1), the connection between the gross output (endogenous to the system) and the final demand (exogenous to the system) in a given economy is uniquely determined by the matrix of direct requirements of the system through the relation:

$$x = (I - A)^{-1} y \quad \textbf{(2)}$$

where I is the identity matrix. The matrix $(I - A)^{-1}$, usually named the Leontief inverse or the matrix of total requirements, is also known as the matrix of "IO multipliers" as it captures the extent to which the total output of a sector is amplified through a change in the final demand. Furthermore, the Leontief inverse can be decomposed into the contributions coming from each layer of the supply chain by using its series expansion:

$$(I - A)^{-1} = I + A + A^2 + A^3 + \ldots \quad \textbf{(3)}$$

Here, each element A^l represents the contribution to the gross output from the layer l of production, with the first element (l=0) representing the effect on gross output due to direct purchases from final demand (for an introduction and further details on the IO theory see Miller and Blair (2009).

If the relation between the output of each economic sector and the environmental impact of that sector's activity is known, and assumed linear, a vector of direct impact coefficients v is defined, where each element v_i represents the environmental impact (e.g. tones of CO_2 or Mega litres of water used) associated with one euro's worth of industry i's output. These production impacts can then be distributed across final demand using the Leontief model,

$$m = v(I - A)^{-1} \quad \textbf{(4)}$$

The resulting environmental multipliers, m, express the total "content" or "embodiment" of environmental factors per monetary unit of final consumption supplied by the production sectors.

In order to analyse in detail the structure of the sectoral contributions to a given multiplier, the total factor multipliers can be decomposed by using the series expansion of the Leontief inverse,

$$m = v(I - A)^{-1} = v + vA + vA^2 + vA^3 + \ldots \quad \textbf{(5)}$$

In particular, following Lenzen (2002), the multiplier associated with the final demand of industry i can be written as follows:

$$m_i = v_i + \sum_{j=1}^{n} v_j A_{ji} + \sum_{j=1}^{n}\sum_{k=1}^{n} v_j A_{jk} A_{ki} + \sum_{j=1}^{n}\sum_{k=1}^{n}\sum_{l=1}^{n} v_j A_{jk} A_{kl} A_{li} + \ldots \quad \textbf{(6)}$$

where n is the total number of industries of the economic system under consideration. Each element of this series expansion represents a set of paths (each consisting on a sequence of purchases) from the "polluting" industry j (the industry directly responsible for the environmental impact) to the final demand of industry i. The first term, v_i, is the direct impact coefficient that takes place in industry i; the next term contains n first order paths $v_j A_{ji}$ between industries j and i; the n^2 second order paths $v_j A_{jk} A_{ki}$ connect industries j and i via industry k and so on. This analysis is known as structural path analysis. Although the order of these indirect effects is infinite, each term of the series expansion becomes smaller with each round of purchases and the series eventually converges. Here, we analyse only the first 5 layers of suppliers.

Data Sources

The economic and atmospheric pollution data used in this paper come from the Spanish National Institute of Statistics. We have chosen to work with data from 2002 as it is the last year for which the Spanish Institute of Statistics (INE) provides both economic and environmental data.

The economic data comprises the make and use tables (INE, 2009). The use table (matrix U) is given as flows of 118 commodities into 75 industries or economic sectors, while the make (or supply) table (matrix S) is given as 118 commodities produced by 75 industries. The transactions in both make and use tables are expressed in basic prices. The commodity classification follows the National Classification of Products (CNAP-96). The industry classification follows the National Classification of Economic Activities (CNAE93-Rev.1).

We have aggregated both the make and the use matrices into 73 industrial sectors (see Annex I), considering homogenous sectors as reported by INE. The assumption of homogeneity implies that each activity in a homogenous aggregated sector j requires the same inputs per unit of output from the aggregate sector i. In other words, the homogeneous sectors are considered to produce only primary products, the secondary production being ignored.

The 73-industry-by-73-industry direct requirements matrix A, used in our IO model can be computed from the make and use tables following the equation: $A = D^t B$ (see e.g. Miller and Blair, 2009), where D^t stands for the transpose of the share matrix D and B is the matrix of technical coefficients in commodity-by-industry terms. Each element of the share matrix d_{ij} represents the fraction of commodity i produced by the industry j and is derived from the make matrix through: $d_{ij} = s_{ij} / \sum_i s_{ij}$. Meanwhile, each element of the matrix B, b_{ij} is the flow of commodity i to industry j per unit of industry j's output: $b_{ij} = u_{ij} * (x_j)^{-1}$.

The environmental data comes from the Satellite Atmospheric Emissions Accounts (INE, 2006) and consists of emissions of 12 atmospheric pollutants released by 47 domestic economic sectors. The atmospheric pollutants are: sulphur oxides (SO_x), nitrogen oxides (NO_x), no methane volatile organic compounds (NMVOC), methane (CH_4), carbon monoxide (CO), carbon dioxide (CO_2), nitrous oxide (N_2O), ammonia (NH_3), particulate matter (PM10), sulphur hexafluoride (SF_6), hydro-flour carbonates (HFC) and perfluorocarbonates (PFC).

The division of the Spanish economy into 47 sectors in this environmental matrix follows NACE-Rev 1 classification (EUROSTAT, 1993). While this classification is a standard of the European Union, the CNAE-93 industry classification used in the economic tables is a standard national classification that has been elaborated from the NACE Rev.1. Both classifications have, therefore, compatible structures. This similarity allowed us to bring the emissions matrix to the same disaggregation level as the matrix of direct requirements. To further disaggregate the emission data by industry, we used supplementary pollution data published in the Spanish National Inventory of Atmospheric Emissions (EIONET, 2005).

RESULTS AND DISCUSSION

Based on the 73-sectors IO tables described above and 12 vectors of atmospheric emissions, we determine the main direct and indirect polluting sectors in the Spanish economy and their interdependencies. We perform two types of analyses. First, we analyse each atmospheric pollutant, focusing on the identification of its direct and indirect emitting sectors and the paths through which pollution is transmitted (Section 3.1). Secondly, we make a global analysis of the economy, showing which few sectors are responsible for most of the atmospheric pollution in Spain (Section 3.2).

Fig. **1** shows the contribution from each layer of suppliers to the total multipliers of the 12 atmospheric pollutants under consideration. The multipliers have been normalized by the values of their respective direct emissions.

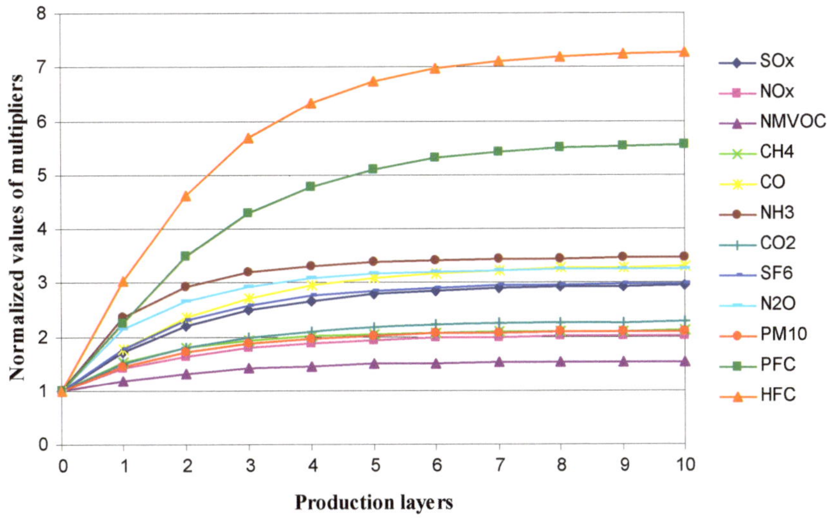

Figure 1: Contribution from production layers to the total multipliers

As expected, indirect effects become increasingly less important as we move up the supply chain, and become mostly negligible after the fifth layer. For some gases, such as HFC and PFC, indirect emissions are very significant, with the first three or four layers of suppliers making an important contribution. For other pollutants, like NMVOC and CH_4 or CO_2 most of the emissions can be attributed to on-site sources.

Input Paths of Atmospheric Pollution

In what follows, we analyse the most important input paths of atmospheric pollution. For simplicity we take into consideration only the first five production layers. The results of this decomposition are shown in tables **1** to **6**, where the top 20 input paths appear ranked by their contribution to the total multiplier. Each input path is described by: the path value in its corresponding physical units per euro of final demand (column 2), the path order (column 3), the industries participating in the supply chain (column 4) and the path coverage (the contribution in % to the total multiplier of the industry supplying the final demand – column 5). For example, the seventh row in Table **1** refers to 8.13 grams of SO_x per euro of final demand of industry 9, standing for Electricity production and distribution, that are embedded in its purchase from industry 4, Anthracite, coal, lignite and peat extraction. The path is of 1st order and represents 13% of the total SO_x multiplier of sector 9.

SOx Emissions

Sulphur oxides emissions, which are the most important contributors to acid rain, result from the combustion of fossil fuels that contain sulphur impurities, gasoline extraction from oil, and metals extraction from ore. Common sources of SO_x include thermal power plants, petroleum refineries, cement manufacturing, and metal processing facilities, as well as locomotives, large ships, and some non-road diesel equipment that burn high sulphur fuel. Because of its petrochemical plants and the traditional use of coal for firing power plants, Spain is one of the main sulphur oxides emitters in Europe. Over the period 1990-2003, the use of alternative fuels for power plants and other pollution prevention actions, resulted in a 28.35% decrease of sulphur oxides emissions. In spite of this effort, in 2002 Spanish emissions were of 1.52 Mt SO_x, representing 18.86% from the total SO_x emissions of the EU27. The major input paths of SOx emissions (see Table **1**) are associated with on-site emissions from the sectors: Electricity production and distribution (9), Manufacture of cement, lime and plaster (25), Maritime Transport (48), Petroleum crude and natural gas extraction (5), and Anthracite, coal, lignite and peat extraction (4). Together they are responsible for 78.8% of the national direct SO_x emissions. Most of the important first order paths emerge from sectors 4 and 5, due to extraction of fuels (coal, petroleum, natural gas) consumption by the processing sectors 8 (Coke refinement and nuclear fuels), 9 (Electricity production and distribution), and 10 (Production and distribution of gas, steam and hot water).

Table 1: Top 20 paths for SO_x and NO_x emissions in Spanish economy

Paths for the SO_x emissions					Paths for the NO_x emissions				
Rank	Path Value (g/€)	Path order	Sectors	% from the total multiplier	Rank	Path Value (g/€)	Path order	Sectors	% from the total multiplier
1	47.66	0	9	75%	1	27.69	0	25	89%
2	21.63	0	25	77%	2	23.78	0	48	90%
3	15.02	0	48	74%	3	17.28	0	3	92%
4	14.56	0	5	77%	4	14.47	0	6	86%
5	13.10	0	4	65%	5	14.40	0	9	74%
6	9.63	1	5 10	74%	6	4.64	0	1	72%
7	8.13	1	4 9	13%	7	4.22	0	47	68%
8	8.19	1	5 8	36%	8	4.07	1	25 28	57%
9	7.54	0	8	33%	9	3.90	0	49	64%
10	6.91	0	27	62%	10	3.80	0	26	58%
11	3.76	0	26	42%	11	2.76	0	8	40%
12	3.48	1	8 4	17%	12	2.69	0	5	60%
13	3.18	1	25 28	36%	13	2.46	1	8 9	12%
14	2.87	1	9 46	57%	14	2.44	0	27	53%
15	2.32	1	25 25	8%	15	2.40	0	10	43%
16	2.00	1	9 7	33%	16	2.28	1	1 12	48%
17	1.72	0	29	26%	17	2.12	0	4	44%
18	1.41	1	26 26	16%	18	2.04	0	2	86%
19	1.39	2	9 9 9	2%	19	1.78	1	9 10	32%
20	1.38	1	9 28	15%	20	1.57	1	1 13	36%

NO_x Emissions

Nitrogen oxides, or NO_x, is the generic term for a group of highly reactive, acidifying gases, all of which contain nitrogen and oxygen in varying amounts. Nitrogen oxides also contribute to stratospheric ozone layer depletion and to global warming. NO_x forms when fuel is burned at high temperatures in a combustion process. Therefore, the primary sources of NO_x are motor vehicles, electric utilities, and other industrial, commercial, and residential equipment that burns fuels. The total amount of NO_x released in Spain in 2002 was 1.21 Mt, 20% more than in 1990. Resulting from our analysis, there are various direct emitters of NO_x (see Table **1**), the most important being Manufacture of cement, lime and plaster (25), Maritime Transport (48), Fishing (3), Extraction of metallic ores (6), and Electricity production and distribution (9), due to their burning of fuel and oil. Interesting first order NO_x emissions are those embedded in the products the food processing industries (12 to 16) purchase from Agriculture, livestock and hunting (1). The main contributor to the agricultural NO_x emissions is the combustion of fuel in farm equipment.

NMVOC Emissions (No Methane Volatile Organic Compounds)

No Methane Volatile Organic Compounds are organic compounds of anthropogenic nature, other than methane, that are capable of producing photochemical oxidants by reactions with nitrogen oxides in the presence of sunlight. The main VOC of interest are those with eight or less carbon atoms per molecule as these are the most reactive in the atmosphere. They are precursors of ground level ozone formation. In most areas, domestic home heating and motor vehicles are estimated to be the main contributors to VOC emissions. Other sources include housekeeping and maintenance products, and building and furnishing materials, such as solvents, paints, and glues. They also appear in agricultural burns, gasoline pumps, and forestall fires. In Spain, the most important on site polluter is the Forestry sector and forestry operation (2) with a contribution of 43% to the total national NMVOC emissions, which in 2002 totalized 1.90 Mt. As Table **2** shows, there are important input paths of NMVOC pollution that generate from sector 2; e.g., the most important NMVOC emissions from the Wood and cork industry (20) and Paper industry (21) are due to the use of wood supplied by the Forestry and forestry operation sector (2). Following Table **2**, another important on site polluting sector is Agriculture, livestock and hunting (1), its direct emissions totalizing 16% of the national NMVOC emissions.

Table 2: Top 20 paths for NMVOC and CH_4 emissions in Spanish economy

Paths for the NMVOC emissions					Paths for the CH_4 emissions				
Rank	**Path Value (g/€)**	**Path order**	**Sectors**	**% from the total multiplier**	**Rank**	**Path Value (g/€)**	**Path order**	**Sectors**	**% from the total multiplier**
1	501.82	0	**2**	99%	1	46.53	0	**4**	98%
2	36.90	1	**2 20**	63%	2	28.66	0	**1**	86%
3	21.31	1	**2 21**	66%	3	14.05	1	**1 12**	73%
4	12.46	2	**2 20 20**	21%	4	12.14	0	**66**	94%
5	5.91	2	**2 21 21**	17%	5	10.78	0	**70**	79%
6	7.48	0	**1**	70%	6	9.67	1	**1 13**	67%
7	5.13	2	**2 20 38**	38%	7	8.64	0	**72**	91%
8	3.67	1	**1 12**	44%	8	8.48	1	**1 14**	62%
9	2.56	0	**23**	37%	9	7.72	0	**71**	73%
10	2.52	1	**1 13**	33%	10	7.66	0	**68**	91%
11	2.21	1	**1 14**	28%	11	7.38	0	**69**	86%
12	2.19	0	**6**	32%	12	7.07	1	**1 16**	74%
13	2.11	0	**10**	57%	13	5.65	0	**67**	44%
14	1.91	0	**48**	46%	14	5.21	0	**10**	56%
15	1.85	1	**1 16**	30%	15	4.82	0	**5**	81%
16	1.82	1	**2 24**	31%	16	4.38	1	**4 9**	65%
17	1.69	0	**22**	16%	17	4.77	1	**67 67**	37%
18	1.40	0	**41**	39%	18	3.19	1	**70 10**	34%
19	1.37	0	**47**	47%	19	2.76	1	**1 15**	47%
20	1.34	0	**19**	22%	20	2.71	1	**5 8**	59%

CH_4 Emissions

Methane is a potent greenhouse gas; it traps over 21 times more heat per molecule than carbon dioxide. Anthropogenic sources of CH_4 include landfills, natural gas and petroleum systems, agricultural activities, coal mining, stationary and mobile combustion, wastewater treatment, and certain industrial processes. In 2002, the Spanish emissions of methane were 32.4% higher compared to 1990's level (EEA, 2007), manly due to agriculture activities, manure management, landfill sites and mining. The results presented in Table **2** rank Anthracite, coal, lignite and peat extraction (4), Agriculture, livestock and hunting (1), and the services sectors Other community, social and personal service activities (66) which include activities of waste management, and Recreational, cultural and sporting activities (70), as having the greatest on site intensities. It is important to note however that in terms of total amounts of emissions, Agriculture (1) is the largest CH_4 on-site polluting sector in Spain, releasing almost 66% from the total national CH_4 emissions. However, its high monetary output places its CH_4 intensity in the 2nd position in Table **2**. Note as well the significant first and higher order paths emerging from the use of agricultural products (mostly from cattle and sheep farming) in the food manufacturing industries (12 to 16). In addition to the polluting effects of the tracks transporting feedstuffs, cattle and meat products, cattle contribute directly to the enhanced greenhouse effect because of the methane they produce. On average, CH_4 emissions of grazing animals in temperate regions are 76.8 kg/head/yr for dairy cattle and 67.5kg for beef cattle (IPCC, 2001b). Cattle manure also emits CH_4 and N_2O during its storage and use as fertilizer.

CO Emissions

CO contributes to the formation of ground-level ozone (smog) and indirectly increases global warming by being oxidized to carbon dioxide or by reacting with hydroxyl radicals, which otherwise would destroy methane. Carbon monoxide is created when carbon-containing fuels are burned incompletely. Direct sources of CO include industrial processes, transportation activities, biomass burning and biogenic activity (both in soils and oceans). Over the period 1990-2002, the total Spanish emissions of CO decreased by 29.6% (EEA, 2007). The main decrease was registered in the transport sectors (46 to 50) that lowered their CO emissions by 45.7% from 1990 (EEA, 2007), emitting 1.28 Mt in 2002. The reduction of CO emissions in spite of the increasing number of vehicles is explained by an increased efficiency of the new cars engines, the improved catalysts these use and by the increasing use of alternative fuels. Following our results presented in Table **3**, the biggest CO emission intensity corresponds to Metallurgy (29) and Manufacture of cement, lime and plaster (25) that emit respectively 48.4% and 2.8% of the direct CO emissions. Its small monetary output places sector 25 on the 2nd position, while the really CO polluting sectors – transport sectors (46 to 50) occupy lower positions due to their higher monetary outputs. Note the important indirect intensities of the manufacturing industries (30 to 38) because of the embodiment of CO emissions in the products they buy from Metallurgy (29).

Table 3: Top 20 paths for CO and CO_2 emissions in Spanish economy

Paths for the CO emissions					**Paths for the CO_2 emissions**				
Rank	**Path Value (g/€)**	**Path order**	**Sectors**	**% from the total multiplier**	**Rank**	**Path Value (kg/€)**	**Path order**	**Sectors**	**% from the total multiplier**
1	19.62	0	**29**	80%	1	11.11	0	**25**	92%
2	7.61	0	**25**	83%	2	4.35	0	**9**	74%
3	6.14	1	**29 30**	68%	3	1.63	1	**25 28**	67%
4	4.94	0	**6**	62%	4	1.45	0	**48**	69%
5	4.18	0	**1**	75%	5	1.20	0	**27**	68%
6	3.44	1	**29 33**	52%	6	1.06	0	**8**	44%
7	3.26	0	**2**	93%	7	1.00	0	**3**	74%
8	3.09	0	**48**	69%	8	0.99	0	**6**	62%
9	3.09	0	**47**	73%	9	0.97	0	**49**	61%
10	2.60	2	**29 30 39**	41%	10	0.96	0	**5**	65%
11	2.15	0	**49**	62%	11	0.88	0	**26**	55%
12	2.06	0	**10**	59%	12	0.81	0	**4**	51%
13	2.05	1	**1 12**	54%	13	0.74	1	**8 9**	13%
14	1.99	1	**29 31**	38%	14	0.64	0	**47**	52%
15	1.84	1	**29 36**	33%	15	0.63	1	**5 10**	41%
16	1.71	1	**6 29**	7%	16	0.62	0	**29**	44%
17	1.41	1	**1 13**	44%	17	0.54	1	**8 8**	23%
18	1.35	1	**29 38**	39%	18	0.51	0	**10**	34%
19	1.29	1	**29 37**	32%	19	0.32	1	**8 4**	20%
20	1.24	1	**1 14**	39%	20	0.30	1	**9 25**	2%

CO_2 Emissions

With 82.2% of the total net greenhouse gas emissions coming from CO_2 emissions, CO_2 contributes the largest share to the anthropogenic greenhouse effect. Carbon dioxide is released to the atmosphere when fossil fuels (oil, natural gas, and coal), solid waste, and wood and wood products are burned. Following the data published by the European Environment Agency, the total Spanish CO_2 emissions increased by 44.6% from 1990 (EEA, 2009). This increase represents almost 20% more then the Kyoto target established for Spain for 2012. The main industrial sectors contributing to the release of CO_2 are the manufacturing sectors and the production of electricity sector. Transport intensities are also significant in Spain (see Table **3**). The top on-site CO_2 intensities come from the manufacturing industries (25 to 28), Electricity production and distribution (9), and the transport sectors (46 to 50). The high CO_2 intensity of Manufacture of cement (25) is explained by a relatively low industry output combined with a high emission factor of 0.540 tCO_2/t clinker used in Spain (the IPCC default is of 0.507 tCO_2/t clinker).

N_2O Emissions

Nitrous oxide is a persistent greenhouse gas that results from the use of N-fertilizers and from some industrial processes at high temperatures (e.g. nylon and plastic production, adipic acid production). In Spain, Agriculture (1) is the largest source of nitrous oxide emissions, primarily from fertilizer application and land conversion to agricultural use (91%) and also from manure management (8%). Emissions of N_2O from agricultural sources in

2002 were estimated at 50.4 kt, representing 74.1% of the national emissions. The results we present in Table **4** indicate also important direct intensities from the services sectors (66 to 72), Chemical Industry (23) and Manufacture of cement, lime and plaster (25). The food manufacturing sectors (12 to 16) have important indirect intensities because of their purchases from Agriculture (1), especially meat and milk.

Table 4: Top 20 paths for N_2O and NH_3 emissions in Spanish economy

Paths for the N_2O emissions					Paths for the NH_3 emissions				
Rank	Path Value (g/€)	Path order	Sectors	% from the total multiplier	Rank	Path Value (g/€)	Path order	Sectors	% from the total multiplier
1	1.28	0	**1**	86%	1	8.62	0	**1**	87%
2	0.63	1	**1 12**	73%	2	4.22	1	**1 12**	75%
3	0.43	1	**1 13**	68%	3	2.91	1	**1 13**	70%
4	0.38	1	**1 14**	63%	4	2.55	1	**1 14**	65%
5	0.32	1	**1 16**	77%	5	2.13	1	**1 16**	80%
6	0.18	0	**23**	62%	6	0.83	1	**1 15**	56%
7	0.12	0	**25**	79%	7	0.63	0	**66**	90%
8	0.12	1	**1 15**	50%	8	0.61	1	**23 1**	6%
9	0.11	0	**66**	82%	9	0.56	0	**70**	53%
10	0.09	0	**70**	52%	10	0.52	2	**1 14 14**	13%
11	0.09	1	**23 1**	6%	11	0.51	2	**1 12 12**	9%
12	0.08	0	**9**	64%	12	0.45	0	**72**	83%
13	0.08	2	**1 14 14**	13%	13	0.41	0	**23**	60%
14	0.08	2	**23 12 12**	9%	14	0.40	1	**1 17**	50%
15	0.08	0	**72**	72%	15	0.40	0	**71**	59%
16	0.07	0	**71**	55%	16	0.39	0	**68**	84%
17	0.07	0	**68**	76%	17	0.38	0	**69**	73%
18	0.06	0	**69**	63%	18	0.35	2	**1 14 1**	4%
19	0.06	0	**64**	58%	19	0.33	2	**1 13 13**	8%
20	0.06	1	**1 17**	35%	20	0.29	0	**67**	41%

NH_3 Emissions

Ammonia, one of the major agents of acid rain, comes mostly from manure, both before mucking out and when the manure is stored or spread. Manure and urine from livestock and pasture also emit ammonia into the atmosphere. Smaller quantities of ammonia are emitted from agricultural land treated with commercial fertilizer. Altogether, agriculture accounts for about 90% of Spanish's direct ammonia emissions, which in 2002 totalized 340 kt. Note the important (hidden) "indirect" intensities expressed by higher order paths deriving from Agriculture, e.g. emissions from the food processing sectors (12 to 16), (see Table **4**). These emissions represent almost 50% of the total Spanish ammonia emissions and are due to the use of agricultural products as raw materials for the food processing industries.

PM10 Emissions

PM10 stands for particulate matter (liquid or solid) with aerodynamic diameter less than 10µm. The chemical composition of particulates varies widely as they can originate from a variety of sources, such as diesel cars, woodstoves, power plants, etc. or they can form into the air when gaseous pollutants such as SO_2 and NO_x react in the air forming fine particles. Following MMA (2009), the main factors which contributed to the PM10 pollution in Spain were the "dieseling" of automobiles and the reduced precipitations that can not remove the urban dust. As this type of pollution is manly found in cities, it affects a large part of the population. PM10 is known to cause acute pulmonary inflammation and exert oxidative stress on cells in the lung and has been linked to adverse health effects in many epidemiological studies.[1] Following INE (2006), the main direct PM10 polluters are the sectors of Agriculture (1) with a share of 36.47% from the national emissions in 2002, followed by the Electricity production and distribution (9) with 15.36%, the transport sectors (46 to 50) with 9.25% and Manufacture of cement, lime and

[1] http://www.who.int/topics/air_pollution/en/

plaster (25) with 7.4%. Our results, presented in Table **5**, confirm the main direct polluters and draw attention on the indirect PM10 emissions of the food industries (12 to 16) due, once more to their purchase of agricultural products.

SF_6, HFC and PFC Emissions

Fluorocarbon gases, fluorocarbons (HFC), perfluorocarbon (PFC), and sulphur hexafluoride (SF_6), are potent industrial greenhouse gases with no natural sources, and deliberately manufactured, mostly for use in refrigeration and air conditioning. During the period 1995-2000, the SF_6 and HFC emissions increased faster than other greenhouse gases by 109% and 425.4% respectively, while PFC emissions decreased by 51.5% (MMA, 2006). However, between 2000 and 2002, the HFC emissions dropped below 1990's level, SF6 kept constant and PFCs continue to decrease. The most significant group are the HFCs, widely promoted from the early 1990s by the chemical industry as a substitute for their chlorine-containing gases CFCs and HCFCs. After 2001, HFCs decreased considerably mainly due to their recovery in certain industrial processes. Each of the three groups of fluorocarbon gases has mainly one industry responsible for all the direct emissions: HFCs are emitted by the Chemical Industry (23), SF_6 by the Manufacture of machinery and electrical material (33), and PFC by Metallurgy (29) manly during the aluminium production. All the second and third order paths are derived from these three sectors (see Tables **5** and **6**).

Table 5: Top 20 paths for PM10 and SF_6 emissions in Spanish economy

Paths for the PM10 emissions					Paths for the SF_6 emissions				
Rank	**Path Value (g/€)**	**Path order**	**Sectors**	**% from the total multiplier**	**Rank**	**Path Value (mg/€)**	**Path order**	**Sectors**	**% from the total multiplier**
1	3.61	0	**25**	90%	1	0.80	0	**33**	83%
2	2.98	0	**6**	91%	2	0.12	1	**33 34**	55%
3	2.10	0	**48**	87%	3	0.12	1	**1 33**	13%
4	1.86	0	**4**	86%	4	0.09	1	**33 35**	54%
5	1.79	0	**27**	87%	5	0.06	1	**33 32**	47%
6	1.53	0	**1**	82%	6	0.05	1	**33 31**	67%
7	1.14	0	**9**	63%	7	0.03	2	**33 34 34**	14%
8	0.75	1	**1 12**	65%	8	0.02	1	**33 37**	43%
9	0.53	1	**25 28**	59%	9	0.02	1	**33 40**	45%
10	0.52	1	**1 13**	56%	10	0.02	1	**33 36**	37%
11	0.45	1	**1 14**	52%	11	0.02	1	**33 11**	47%
12	0.43	0	**29**	40%	12	0.02	1	**33 9**	51%
13	0.40	0	**5**	65%	13	0.02	2	**33 34 35**	11%
14	0.38	1	**1 16**	62%	14	0.02	2	**33 32 32**	14%
15	0.36	0	**8**	40%	15	0.01	1	**33 52**	41%
16	0.28	0	**39**	40%	16	0.01	1	**33 38**	45%
17	0.26	1	**5 10**	45%	17	0.01	2	**33 31 6**	42%
18	0.26	0	**47**	52%	18	0.01	2	**33 33 31**	10%
19	0.24	1	**39 29**	22%	19	0.01	2	**33 36 36**	15%
20	0.24	0	**26**	45%	20	0.01	2	**33 40 40**	14%

Summary and Discussion of the Results

In Section 3.1 we analysed each atmospheric pollutant, determining its main direct and indirect sources and the chains through which pollution generation is "transmitted". In this section we resume and reorganize these results, focusing on each economic sector, analysing its emissions and contributions to the total national. For an easier national analysis, we group together the acid gases (SO_x, NO_x and NH_3) and the greenhouse gases (CO_2, CH_4, N_2O, SF_6, HFC and PFC), reporting their intensities as gSO_2-eq./€ and $kgCO_2$-eq./€ respectively, based on their acidification and global warming potentials considered by INE (2006) and IPCC (2001a). Also, we grouped together some economic sectors, such as: extractive sectors (comprising the sectors from 4 to 8), energetic sectors (9 and 10), food industries (12 to 16), manufacturing industries (25 to 28 and 30 to 38), transport (46 to 50) and services (51 to 73). Fig. **2** gives an overview of the direct emissions intensities of the Spanish economic sectors in 2002. The results are presented as percentages from the total direct emissions.

Table 6: Top 20 paths for fluoro compounds emissions in the Spanish economy

Paths for the HFC emissions					Paths for the PFC emissions				
Rank	**Path value (mg/€)**	**Path order**	**Sectors**	**% from the total multiplier**	**Rank**	**Path value (mg/€)**	**Path order**	**Sectors**	**% from the total multiplier**
1	3.25	0	**23**	70%	1	1.30	0	**29**	83%
2	0.91	1	**23 23**	20%	2	0.41	1	**29 30**	74%
3	0.61	1	**23 24**	52%	3	0.23	1	**29 33**	57%
4	0.44	1	**23 17**	46%	4	0.17	2	**29 30 39**	51%
5	0.30	1	**23 65**	61%	5	0.13	1	**29 31**	43%
6	0.25	2	**23 23 23**	5%	6	0.12	1	**29 36**	37%
7	0.25	1	**23 11**	53%	7	0.11	1	**1 29**	7%
8	0.24	1	**23 7**	52%	8	0.09	1	**29 38**	48%
9	0.22	1	**23 26**	48%	9	0.09	1	**29 37**	37%
10	0.21	1	**23 6**	46%	10	0.08	1	**29 32**	31%
11	0.21	1	**23 21**	40%	11	0.06	1	**1 39**	17%
12	0.20	1	**23 64**	56%	12	0.06	2	**29 30 31**	18%
13	0.17	1	**23 29**	37%	13	0.05	2	**29 36 36**	15%
14	0.17	1	**23 27**	44%	14	0.05	1	**29 22**	52%
15	0.17	2	**23 23 24**	15%	15	0.04	1	**29 34**	21%
16	0.17	1	**23 1**	48%	16	0.04	1	**29 28**	33%
17	0.17	2	**23 17 18**	33%	17	0.04	1	**29 6**	25%
18	0.14	1	**23 4**	46%	18	0.04	2	**29 29 30**	6%
19	0.13	1	**23 20**	32%	19	0.04	2	**29 33 33**	9%
20	0.12	1	**23 28**	34%	20	0.03	2	**29 33 34**	16%

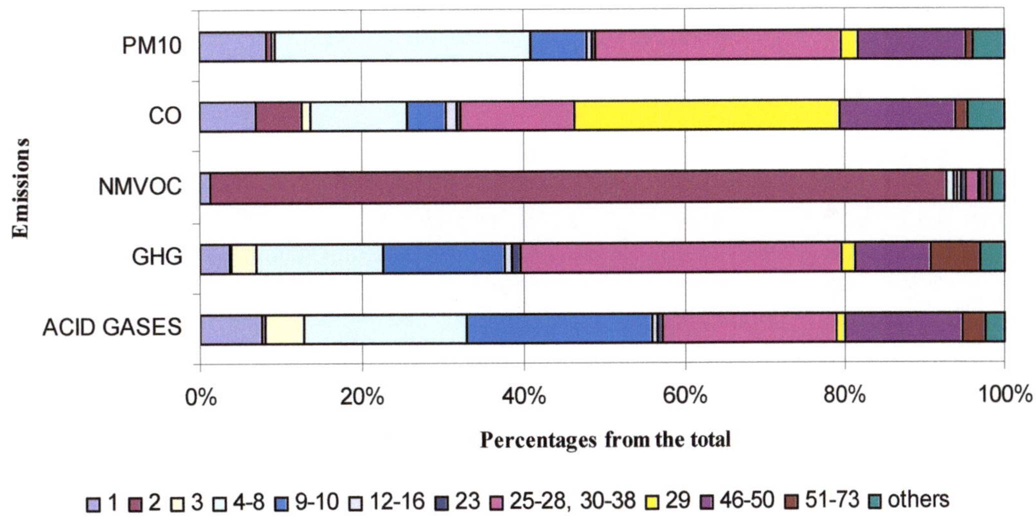

Figure 2: Direct emissions intensities (2002) of grouped sectors.

Fig. **2** reveals that the main contributors to the direct Spanish emissions are the group of manufacturing industries (25 to 28 and 30 to 38), extractive industries (4 to 8), energetic sectors (9 and 10), Agriculture (1) and the transportation sectors (45 to 49). However, in terms of total emissions (sum of direct and indirect emissions) this ranking changes (see Fig. **3**), and other sectors, or group of sectors, occupy top positions because of their important indirect emissions.

In this classification, the contribution of Agriculture (1), extractive industries (4 to 8), and energetic sectors (9 and 10) decreases while groups of sectors such as the food industries (12 to 16), manufacturing industries (25 to 28 and 30 to 38) and services sectors are more visible in the national pollution stage, due to their significant input of intermediate consumption.

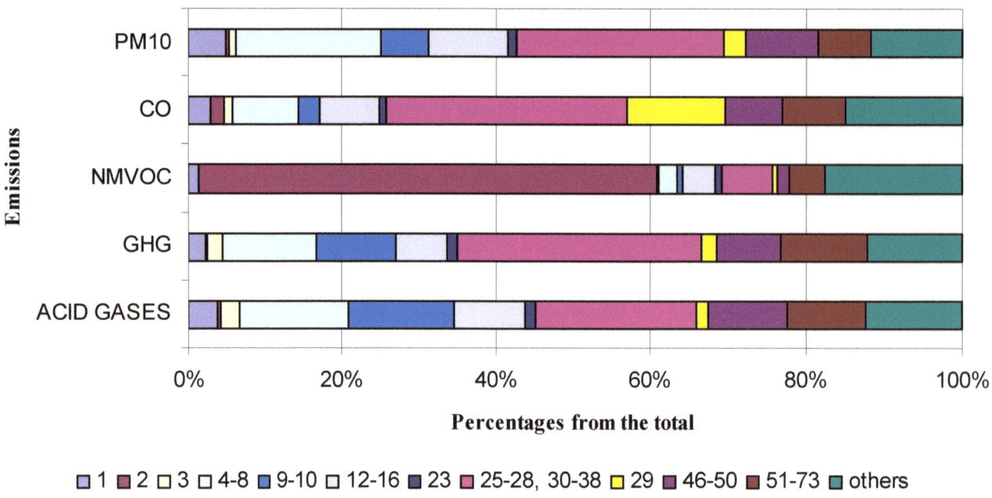

Figure 3: Total emissions intensities (2002) of grouped sectors.

This type of results provides an overview of the major (direct and indirect) polluting sectors in an economy. However, for an efficient decision making at the national level, these results are too aggregated and difficult to translate into concrete actions. Therefore, in order to inform policy-making we suggest complementing these generic results with data as that presented in Tables **1** to **6**, which allow understanding the mechanism of pollution creation and propagation in the economy. For instance, according to the aggregated data presented in Fig. **2**, the group of food industries (12 to 16) has a small contribution to the national direct emissions. However, in Fig. **3** we can see they are one of the most polluting groups in terms of their contribution to the total national emissions. This is explained by the important indirect emissions associated with the activity of food processing industries, in other words, due to their significant input of intermediate consumption, in this case, from the Agriculture (1) sector.

When interpreting these results it is important to keep in mind that we have calculated the amount of pollutants embedded in the Spanish commodities that are delivered to the final demand. In other words, we did not calculate the impacts associated with the production of economic sectors, but with the products or services these sectors sell to the final demand. This means that sectors with a small final demand will have important intensities of emissions, although they could have a small contribution to the total emissions. Similarly, sectors with an important final demand will have small intensities although they may have big contributions to total emissions. To see the difference between using one or the other approaches (intensities vs. total embodiments of pollution), let us consider the direct emissions of the above grouped sectors in terms of acid gases, greenhouse gases, CO, NMVOC and PM10 in Fig. **4**.

Comparing Fig. **2** (direct emissions intensities) to Fig. **4** (direct emissions), we see the increased contribution of Agriculture (1), energetic sectors (9 and 10), and manufacturing industries (25 to 28 and 30 to 38) over the others in terms of direct sectoral emissions. The explanation of this change is the high final demands of sectors 1 and 9, implying smaller intensities of emission.

The method we have presented here has some limitations that should be considered. The linearity of the IO model to calculate the environmental burdens (linear inter-industry interactions, proportionality between the production and the emission of a productive sector), the estimations at national level, data availability and data quality are some of the issues that should be considered when using these results. Some pollutants have effects at local level (CO, NMVOC), so local policies for their reduction would be more effective. The aggregation of data used for calculations may lead to under/overestimations, e.g., sector 67 standing for Other community, social and personal service activities; no market, includes all the services of waste collection, treatment and disposal indifferently of the waste type, collection or applied treatment. Another limitation is the exclusion of imports in our estimations. For the Spanish economy, in which the imports for sectors such as Coke, refinement and nuclear fuels (8), Chemical industry (23), Manufacture of motor vehicles and trailers (36) or Construction (40) are important, the national GHC balances can be considerably influenced by the inclusion of imports or exclusion of exports.

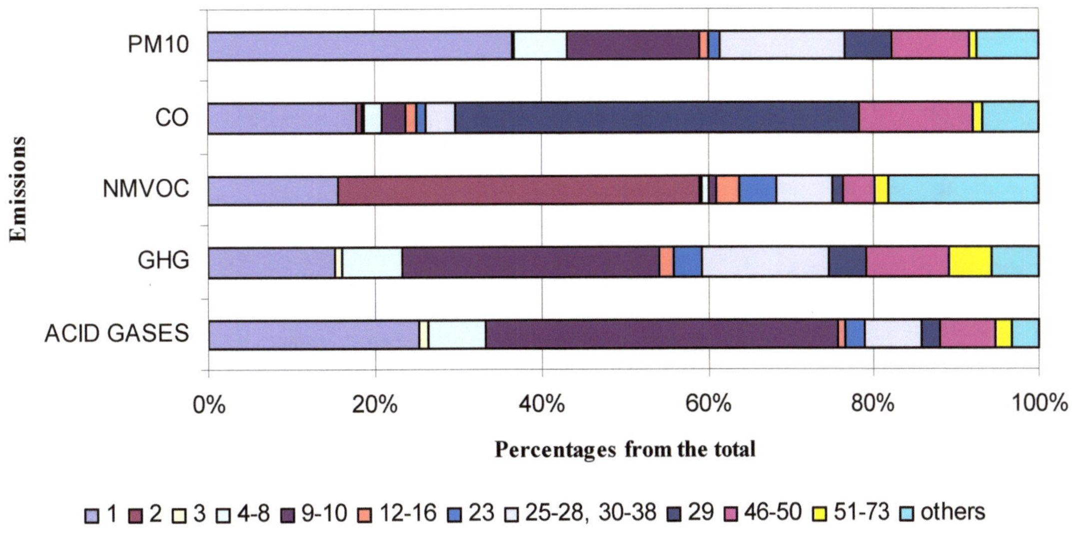

Figure 4: Direct emissions (2002) of grouped sectors.

The generalized IO model used in this work to calculate the sectoral burdens is superior to those used in previous Spanish studies because of its higher level of industrial disaggregation. Specifically we use 73 sectors versus the 17 used in Anton Valero *et al.* (1993), Cadarso and Fernández-Bolaños (2002) and Velázquez (2006) and the 56 sectors used in Sánchez-Chóliz and Duarte (2004). Higher disaggregation permits a more accurate identification of key responsible polluting industries. Further improvements may be brought by increasing the number of industries in the national classification and better than that, by making the analysis at local or regional levels, particularly in the presence of heterogeneous regional economies.

CONCLUSIONS

This paper calculates the direct and indirect atmospheric emissions associated with the activities of the Spanish economy and detects key sectors and important input paths of air pollution generation in Spain. The incorporation of the embedded emissions associated with the delivery of a good or service is essential to assist pollution abatement policies since it identifies otherwise hidden pollution drivers. This is particularly true when considering the reduction of HFC, PFC and NH_3 emissions, which are driven by the manufacturing sectors. For other pollutants such as NMVOC and CH_4, most of the emissions can be attributed to on-site sources.

The analysis presented in this paper reallocates pollution emissions from the on-site producer to the sectors delivering to final demand following a standard Leontief approach. Knowledge of the final demanders' profile such as household composition and income can be easily incorporated to this model to analyse the contribution of the various groups of Spanish consumers to the generation of pollution. An analysis of this type for a group of selected environmental burdens can be found in Sánchez-Chóliz *et al.* (2005). It is important to notice that when seeking to describe the effect of producing entities on production factors, the classical Leontief model is incomplete because it only accounts for the fraction of industrial output that is delivered into final demand. In order to take into account full industrial outputs while conserving the desirable accounting properties of the classical input-output framework, the introduction of shared producer-consumer responsibility is required, see Gallego and Lenzen (2005) and Lenzen *et al.* (2006).

ACKNOWLEDGMENTS

This work was supported by the Spanish Ministry of Education (grants AP2001-232, SEJ2007-66318) and by the *Generalitat de Catalunya* (grants SGR2009-230 and SGR2009-322). We wish to express our thanks to Vincent Bourdette and Dan Libotean for their help in the computer programming of multipliers decomposition.

Table A1: Numbers assigned to the economic sectors specified in Spanish IO classification

No.	Sector name	No.	Sector name
1	Agriculture, livestock and hunting	41	Sale, maintenance and repair of motor vehicles and motorcycles; retail sale of automotive fuel
2	Forestry and forestry operation	42	Wholesale trade and commission trade, except of motor vehicles and motorcycles
3	Fishing	43	Retail trade, except of motor vehicles and motorcycles; repair of personal and household goods
4	Anthracite, coal, lignite and peat	44	Accommodation
5	Petroleum crude and natural gas Extraction. Uranium and thorium ores extraction	45	Catering
6	Extraction of metallic ores	46	Railway transport
7	Extraction of non-metallic ores	47	Other land transport; transport via pipelines
8	Coke, refinement and nuclear fuels	48	Maritime transport
9	Electricity production and distribution	49	Air and space transport
10	Production and distribution of gas, steam and hot water	50	Activities annexed to transport
11	Collection, treatment and water distribution	51	Travel agencies activities
12	Production, processing and preserving of meat and meat products	52	Post and communications
13	Manufacture of dairy products	53	Financial intermediation, except insurance and pension funding
14	Manufacture of other food products	54	Insurance and pension funding, except compulsory social security
15	Manufacture of beverages	55	Activities auxiliary to financial intermediation
16	Manufacture of tobacco products	56	Real estate activities
17	Textile industry	57	Renting of machinery and equipment without operator and of personal and household goods
18	Clothing and furs industry	58	Computer and related activities
19	Leather and footwear industry	59	Research and development
20	Wood and cork industry	60	Other business activities
21	Paper industry	61	Public Administration
22	Publishing and graphic arts	62	Education; market
23	Chemical industry	63	Education; no market
24	Rubber and plastic materials industry	64	Health and social services; market
25	Manufacture of cement, lime and plaster	65	Health and social services; no market
26	Manufacture of glass and glass products	66	Other community, social and personal service activities; market
27	Manufacture of ceramic tiles and flags	67	Other community, social and personal service activities; no market
28	Manufacture of other non-metallic mineral products	68	Other service activities; market
29	Metallurgy	69	Other service activities; no market
30	Manufacture of metallic products	70	Recreational, cultural and sporting activities; market
31	Machinery and mechanical equipment	71	Recreational, cultural and sporting activities; no market
32	Office machines and computers	72	Personal service activities
33	Manufacture of machinery and electrical material	73	Private households with employed persons
34	Manufacture of electronic material		
35	Medico-surgical and precision instruments		
36	Manufacture of motor vehicles and trailers		
37	Manufacture of other transport material		
38	Furniture and other manufacturing industries		
39	Recycling		
40	Construction		

REFERENCES

Alcántara, V., Roca, J. (1995). "Energy and CO_2 emissions in Spain: Methodology of analysis and some results for 1980-90". *Energy Economics*. 17 (3), 221-230.

Alcántara, V., Padilla, E. (2009). "Input–output subsystems and pollution: An application to the service sector and CO_2 emissions in Spain". *Ecological Economics*. 68, 905-914.

Argüelles M., Benavides C., Junquera B. (2006). "The impact of economic activity in Asturias on greenhouse gas emissions: Consequences for environmental policy within the Kyoto Protocol framework". *Journal of Environmental Management*. 81 (3), 249-264.

Anton Valero, V., de Bustos Guadaño A., Manzanedo del Hoyo L., Sierra Ludwig V., (1993). "La emisión de CO2 y su problemática comunitaria. Un método de estimación general". Ministerio de Economía y Hacienda, Instituto de Estudios Fiscales, Madrid

Cadarso, M. A., Fernández-Bolaños A. (2002). "Patterns of growth and consumption and their influence on the environment in Spain". Fourteenth International Conference on Input-Output Techniques. Montréal, Canada.

Duarte, R., Sánchez-Chóliz J., Bielsa J. (2002). "Water use in Spanish economy: an input-output approach". *Ecological Economics*. 43, 71-85.

EEA (2007). "National emissions reported to the Convention on Long-range Transboundary Air Pollution (LRTAP Convention)" European Environment Agency, Copenhagen K, Denmark.

EEA (2009). "National emissions reported to the UNFCCC and to the EU Greenhouse Gas Monitoring Mechanism". European Environment Agency, Copenhagen K, Denmark.

EIONET (2005). "National inventory of atmospheric emissions for Spain". European Environment Information and Observation Network (EIONET).

EUROSTAT (1993). "NACE Rev.1", Council Regulation. Eurostat, Luxemburg

Gallego, B., Lenzen M. (2005). "A consistent input-output formulation of shared producer and consumer responsibility". *Economic Systems Research*. 17 (4), 365-391.

Griffiths, J., Rao M. (2009). "Editorials, Public health benefits of strategies to reduce greenhouse gas emissions. What's good for the climate is good for health". BMJ 2009;339:b4952

INE (2006). *Cuentas satélite sobre emisiones atmosféricas. Serie 1990 y 1995-2003*. Instituto Nacional de Estadística, Madrid

INE (2009). *Marco input-output. Serie 2000-2006*. Instituto Nacional de Estadística, España, Madrid

IPCC (2001a). *Climate Change 2001: The Scientific Basis. Intergovernmental Panel on Climate Change*, Cambridge, UK: Cambridge University Press.

IPCC (2001b). *Climate Change 2001*. Working group III: Mitigation. Intergovernmental Panel on Climate Change, Cambridge, UK: Cambridge University Press.

Lenzen, M. (2002). "A guide for compiling inventories in hybrid life-cycle inventories: some australian results". *Journal of Cleaner Production*. 10, 545-572.

Lenzen, M., Murray J., Sack F., Wiedmann T. (2006). "Shared producer and consumer responsibility – theory and practice". *ISA Research Paper* 01-06, Integrated Sustainability Group, Sydney University, Sydney

Manresa, A., Sancho F. (2004). "Energy intensities and CO2 emissions in Catalonia: a SAM analysis" *International Journal of Environment, Workplace, and Employment*. 1 (1), 91-106.

Miller, R. E., Blair P. D. (2009). *Input-Output Analysis: Foundations and Extensions*. 2nd edition. Cambridge University Press, UK.

MMA (2006). *Perfil ambiental de España, 2005*. Ministerio de Medio Ambiente, y Medio Rural y Marino.

MMA (2009). *Inventario de Emisiones a la Atmósfera de España. Edición 2009* [serie 1990-2007]. Emisiones a la atmósfera de partículas. Dirección General de Calidad y Evaluación Ambiental. Ministerio de Medio Ambiente, y Medio Rural y Marino.

Pajuelo, A. (1980). "Equilibrio general vs. Análisis parcial en el análisis I-O económico-ambiental". *Revista del Instituto de Estudios Económicos*. 3, 3-57.

Roca, J., M. Serrano (2007). I"ncome growth and atmospheric pollution in Spain: An input–output approach". *Ecological Economics*. 63, 230-242.

Sánchez-Chóliz, J., Duarte R. (2003). "Analysing pollution by way of vertically integrated coefficients, with an application to the water sector in Aragon". *Cambridge Journal of Economics*. 27 (3), 433-448.

Sánchez-Chóliz, J., Duarte R. (2004). "CO_2 emissions embodied in international trade: evidence for Spain". *Energy Policy*. 32, 1999-2005.

Sánchez-Chóliz, J., Duarte R., Mainar A. (2005). "Ecological impact of household activity in Spain: a new approximation to ecological footprints". Fifteenth International Input-Output Conference. Beijing, China P.R.

Velázquez, E. (2006). "··An input-output model of water consumption: Analysing intersectoral water relationships in Andalusia". *Ecological Economics*. 56 (2), 226-240.

CHAPTER 4

Energy Consumption and CO_2 Emissions in the Spanish Economy

M. Alejandro Cardenete and Patricia D. Fuentes Saguar*

Departamento de Economía. Universidad Pablo Olavide, Carretera de Utrera, Km.1, 41013, Seville, (SPAIN)

Abstract: In this paper we set out to examine the energy generated emissions from a different viewpoint, focusing on final energy consumption and trying to ascertain which demands are the most costly to satisfy in terms of emissions of pollutants to the atmosphere. To do this, we apply an additive multiplier decomposition methodology to the Spanish Social Accounting Matrix for the year 2000 that we have developed. This way, we can disaggregate the Spanish energy sector's revenue-generating process into different effects depending on the source of the demand. To gain a better understanding of the behaviours of the different branches of the economy, we divide Spanish productive activities into two groups, which we call subsystems (energy subsystem and complementary subsystem). We then apply the multiplier decomposition methodology to each one separately. This way, we can identify the influence that the final demand of each of these groups has on income generation and energy sector emissions in the Spanish economy. The results confirm that some branches of the services sector are the most costly in terms of CO_2 emissions.

Keywords: CO2 emissions, energy, social accounting matrices, multipliers decomposition methodology, subsystems analysis.

INTRODUCTION

There is no question today about how important the energy sector is for any country or region from both the economic and the environmental viewpoints. Thanks to their strategic importance, energy commodities have been the centre of attention of a great deal of research undertaken from different angles with the aim of reducing energy dependency, guaranteeing supply and reducing the emissions of pollutants to the atmosphere.

Nevertheless, energy and emissions studies appear to focus primarily on investigating energy sector itself and the use to which energy is put by other sectors, and tend to hold the sectors that use most energy, like transport or electricity sectors, responsible for emissions. In Spain, energy studies (Alcántara and Roca (1995) or Labeaga and Labandeira (2002)) have employed the Input-Output model to estimate energy intensities and CO2 emissions. Manresa and Sancho (2004) first employed a SAM model to calculate energy intensities in Catalonia, a Spanish region, and have estimated final arbitrary demand impacts. In the same way, Cardenete et alia (2008) analyze Andalusian energy sector using a SAM model for year 2000.

The approach taken in the research presented here is different. We focus on analysing how much energy (and, consequently, how many emissions) is necessary to satisfy final demand in each branch. This way, we will be able to find out which are the directly and indirectly most pollutant final demands.

To do this we will use a multiplier decomposition methodology borrowed from Alcántara and Padilla (2009), using a model based on the Spanish Social Accounting Matrix[1] for the year 2000 (SAMES00) that we have developed. Thanks to this methodology, we can separate the emissions generated by the branches of the economy into different effects depending on what demands their output is to satisfy. Tools like these are potentially very useful for application in energy studies.

SAM models, as we will see in next sections, are specified numerically using a social accounting matrix (SAM). The concept was first introduced by Stone (1962) as a useful tool to present national accounts and Pyatt and Round (1979) propose the fix-price multiplier set up that has been extensively employed since then. Kehoe, Manresa, Polo and Sancho (1988) constructed the first SAM of the Spanish economy.

*Address correspondence to M. Alejandro Cardenete: Departamento de Economía. Universidad Pablo Olavide, Carretera de Utrera, Km.1, 41013, Seville (SPAIN); Email: macardenete@upo.es.

[1] Cardenete and Fuentes (2009).

The paper is structured as follows. In Section 2 we will briefly discuss the SAMES00, followed by the methodology used. In Section 3 we present the application of the methodology to the Spanish economy and end with a discussion of the key results. In Section 4 we highlight some conclusions.

SOCIAL ACCOUNTING MATRIX FOR THE SPANISH ECONOMY IN THE YEAR 2000

The statistical support or database underlying models such as are presented here are Social Accounting Matrices (SAM). SAMs are useful on the one hand for describing an economic reality. On the other hand, they are a database for building models. For this reason, we start by presenting the Spanish social accounting matrix for the year 2000 (SAMES2000), which we use as statistical support for our model.

A SAM is a matrix representation of the interrelationships within a particular economy at any time. Social accounting matrices originate from the attempt to integrate social statistics in an input-output table of the interdependence among the productive sectors. It is an extension of these models represented in matrix form.

As already mentioned above, social accounting matrices serve two purposes. On the one hand, they offer a snapshot of the situation of an economy at a point in time, as they describe an economic reality, providing additional information about a particular sector or a country's or a region's productive structure. On the other, they are very useful as a database for building models (linear SAM models and Computable General Equilibrium –CGE- models) that rate the socioeconomic impact of different economic policies.

SAM models are specified by means of equations that use the observable SAM data to explain endogenous variables based on exogenous variables, as in the Leontief model. In the Leontief model, the endogenous accounts are necessarily the productive sectors, which are explained by exogenous final demand and the multiplier matrix reflecting the productive structure of the economy.

On top of the fact that they contain more information, SAMs are more flexible than input-output tables, as they are square matrices. Thus determining which accounts are endogenous is confined, technically speaking, to setting at least one account aside as exogenous. Despite this flexibility, deciding which accounts are exogenous is not an arbitrary choice; it is determined by both the analysis to be conducted and by the economic reality itself, as there are variables that are determined outside the productive system, as is usually the case with public sector and foreign sector.

Based on these models it is possible to run linear simulations of the effect that an improvement in efficiency modifying the productive structure or the variation of any of the exogenous variables could have on an economy. On the other hand, using the right size and unit vectors, this type of technology can convert the model's monetary units into other units as required by the proposed analysis. Finally, the information that the matrices contain can be manipulated to some extent; for example, by applying multiplier decomposition methodologies that increase the descriptive information that they provide.

Each account in the SAM are represented by a row and a column. By convention, the rows show the source of the income of the different accounts and the columns indicate the destination of the same income in the form of expenditure. The values entered in the cells are monetary. Therefore, each non-zero value in a cell represents a transaction or money flow between two accounts accounted for by a single record, signifying expenditure in the case of the column and income in the case of the row.

SAMs have a flexible structure and can assume different forms depending on their purpose. For example, sector accounts can be more or less disaggregated (if the goal is to analyse a particular sector), consumers or taxes can be disaggregated by types (if the aim is to assess social or taxation policies), the foreign sector account can be separated into different areas, possibly at the regional level to assess interregional relationships, or the number of accounts in the intermediate consumption matrix can be duplicated making a distinction between activities and products, using the Use and Make Tables of the Input-Output Framework and thereby providing for secondary production. There are, however, matrices where the order of the accounts is determined by part of the system to be highlighted[2].

---

[2] For example, De Miguel and Manresa (2004) present a SAM for Extremadura where the first accounts are the factors of production and the consumer household groups.

In short, the level of disaggregation and the order of the different accounts should be implemented depending on the model to be built using the SAM and its application, stressing the accounts that are to be analysed or depending on whether it is designed for a regional, sectoral or fiscal analysis, etc. Although, as already mentioned, SAMs are very flexible; there is a basic, what we might call *standard*, structure (see, Fig. **1**, for example). Nevertheless, a SAM has to conform to certain rules for it to be meaningful in its own right and useful as a database.

During the construction of a SAM, we should never forget that, on the one hand, it must be consistent with national accounts and, on the other, it must conform to certain identities, such as the total sum of each row (uses) must be the same as the total of each column (resources), as account expenditure (column) must be covered by income (row). On the other hand, the accounts should be disaggregated in manner that they are homogeneous and clearly separable from each other.

The meaning of the basic SAM structure is as follows. The productive system generates revenue from the sale of its products (both to the productive activities for intermediate consumption and to final demand) that it uses to pay for the factors of production. This revenue is the value added and represents income of institutional sectors. The institutional sectors spend their revenue on the productive sectors and on the payment of the institutional sectors themselves. This generates revenue for both and, through this revenue, increases production needs, thereby starting another cycle.

The SAM that we present here is at basic prices. This has advantages over SAMs at purchasers' prices, such as purer multipliers and trade and transport accounts with more meaningful content. The decision to use a SAM at basic prices is justified for the analyses proposed here, as if we accounted for the amounts in the SAM at purchasers' prices, they would include trade and transport margins. This would distort the sectoral distribution of the CO_2 emissions with which we are concerned here.

Fig. **1** shows the SAMES00 structure. The content of the matrix is clearly divided into four submatrices: the intermediate consumption matrix, the primary factors matrix, the final demand matrix and the closure matrix.

The **Intermediate Consumption submatrix**, at the top left of the SAM, is composed of the rows and columns of the productive sectors (27x27). It contains all the intersectorial relations, that is, each sector's expenditure on and income from intermediate consumption in other sectors. Each non-zero cell *ij* represents a flow, that is, an expenditure on *inputs* by sector *j* in sector *i*, and, conversely, the income that sector *i* receives from sales to sector *j*. The intermediate consumption matrix at basic prices was calculated directly from the symmetric input-output table at basic prices.

The **Primary Factors submatrix**, which sets out payments by factors used by each productive activity, was taken primarily from the 2000 Spanish Input-Output framework (MIOES00). All the cells are zero except for the ones containing resource payments by sectors. This matrix was based on the Symmetric Table at basic prices. The first accounts in this matrix, located at the bottom left of the SAM, are Labour and Capital (28 and 29). Capital payment is taken from the symmetric input-output table at basic prices (gross operating surplus), as well as from the labour account (28) and employers' social security contributions (32), using the weights of the contributions over employee pay taken from the Use Table, as, in this table, they are disaggregated, whereas the Symmetric Table contains is a single row for total employee pay. After calculating the weights, this row of the Symmetric Table is separated into two accounts: Wages (28) and employers' social security contributions (32).

This account is followed by indirect net taxes from subsidies. The information offered by the Spanish National Statistics Office (INE) does not disaggregate indirect taxes on products and imports (it only disaggregates total taxes paid by sectors on their purchases of intermediate consumption). For this reason, a number of calculations have to be made to separate these headings. Of the taxes on products, we extract tariffs, applied to imports, and VAT, applied to production in each sector. They appear in another two separate accounts (34 and 35). To do this, we use the average rates of both taxes for the year 1995. The net indirect tax account (33) is the sum of taxes on products (except VAT and tariffs) sold by a branch, taken from the Make Table, and the net indirect taxes on output (Symmetric Table).

Finally, the primary factors matrix contains the imports account (39), taken directly from the Make table.

<table>
<tr><th></th><th>Productive Activities</th><th>Primary Factors</th><th>Saving/Invest-ment</th><th>Institutional Sectors</th><th>Foreign Sector</th></tr>
<tr><td>Productive Activities
(1) … (27)</td><td>Intermediate Consumption</td><td colspan="4">Final Demand</td></tr>
<tr><td>Primary Factors:
(28) Labour
(29) Capital</td><td rowspan="4">Primary Factors</td><td rowspan="4" colspan="4">1. Closure submatrix</td></tr>
<tr><td>Saving/Investment:
(31) FBK</td></tr>
<tr><td>Institutional Sectors:
▪ Households
(30) Consumption
▪ Government
(32) Employers' social security contributions
(33) Net indirect taxes
(34) VAT
(35) Tariffs
(36) Employees' social security contributions
(37) IRPF
(38) Public Sector</td></tr>
<tr><td>Foreign Sector:
(39) Imports/Exports</td></tr>
</table>

Source: Own elaboration.

Figure 1: Structure of the SAMES00

The **Final Demand submatrix** (non-zero accounts from 28 to 39), situated at the top right of the SAM, provides information about the final uses of the goods and services, meaning that all except the cells of the columns of the final demand components are zero.

The values are at basic prices and are all taken directly from the Use Table at basic prices (which should be equal to the Symmetric Table).

The accounts in the final demand matrix are Consumption (30), reflecting household and private consumption, Saving/Investment (31), composed of gross fixed capital formation and variations in stock, Public Sector (38), which mirrors public sector consumption and is composed of the collective consumption expenditure and individual consumption expenditure of the public administrations and non-profit institutions serving households[3]; and, finally, Exports (39).

The **Closure submatrix** was filled in from the INE National Accounts. It is this matrix that enables the circular flow of revenue by presenting the relationships between the factors matrix and the final uses. It is also the matrix that is, statistically speaking, hardest to build.

Households receive their revenue from labour (30, 28), which is obtained from employee pay after discounting employers' social security contributions, and from the gross operating profit (30, 29), taken from the symmetric input-output table at basic prices. The final component of revenue is the transfers to households (30/ 38), which are taken from the INE National Accounts. The Transfers to the rest of the world (30, 39) are used as a balance of purchases by non-residents on the domestic market less purchases by residents on the foreign market, as this is interpreted as a net transfer received by the domestic consumer[4].

[3] We followed the earlier ESA (European System Account) methodology, as the new approach includes NPISH (Non-Profit Institutions Serving Households) expenditure on private consumption, which would distort our results. As it is added to the public sector account as expenditure, we have to adjust income to the operations in the public saving cell.

[4] Cardenete and Sancho (2006).

The use to which households put their revenue is divided into consumption and direct taxes paid by households[5]. Personal income tax (37,30) is taken from the INE National Accounts, 2000 base year. This account covers not only personal income tax, but also all direct taxes. The Employees' social security contributions account (36, 30) is deduced from the National Accounts as the difference after deducting employers' social security contributions from total social security contributions.

Private saving (31, 30) is taken from the income uses national accounting identity[6], as shown in Table **1**. The cells related to indirect taxes are taken directly from the totals of the SAM rows, as well as from employers' social security contributions.

Table 1: Income source and uses (Million of euros)

	Accounts	**Cells**	**Value**
1	Gross wages and salaries (Labour)	30/ 28	247,209
2	Gross Operating Surplus (Capital)	30/ 29	255,488
3	Transfers	30/ 38	83,430
4	**Sum of revenue**	**(1+2+3)**	**586,127**
5	Consumption	1-27/ 30	363,813
6	Employees' social security	36/ 30	16,179
7	Direct taxes	37/ 30	64,002
8	**SAVING**	**(4-5-6-7)**	**142,133**
9	**Sum of revenue uses**	**(4)**	**586,127**

Source: Own elaboration.

The Foreign Sector data are taken from the INE's Foreign balance (31, 39). The figure used is the difference between net exports and imports, which is equal to the figure for the Rest of the world account in the National Accounts for the year 2000. For the foreign sector net transfers we use the net balance between the domestic expenditure of non-residents and the foreign expenditure of residents, as mentioned above. Public sector income is shown as the sum of direct and indirect taxes (38, 32:37).

Public saving (31, 38) is the only cell extracted from the SAM itself, as it is the account balance deduced by applying Walras' law, the result of which is checked against the National Accounts (Table **1**).

Sector disaggregation is conditioned by the SAMES00 being used as a database for analysing the energy sector. Consequently, the accounts of this sector are disaggregated (3, 4, 6, 7, 8).

ADDITIVE MULTIPLIER DECOMPOSITION METHODOLOGY BASED ON SUBSYSTEM ANALYSIS

The additive accounting multiplier decomposition methodology[7] based on the SAMES00 can disaggregate the output of the subsystems (i.e. groupings of productive sectors) into different effects. Based on a classification of institutions as n endogenous and m exogenous, the income of endogenous institutions satisfies

$$y_n = A_{nn} y_n + A_{nm} y_m = A_{nn} y_n + d_n \quad \textbf{(1)}$$

where y_n and y_m denote the vector of income of endogenous and exogenous institutions, respectively; A_{nn} and A_{nm} are two $n \times n$ and $n \times m$ matrices defined by the expenditure coefficients of endogenous and exogenous institutions,

[5] We assign these taxes to the consumption column because they are not generated by just labour.
[6] This cell contains all national saving except public sector saving.
[7] There are other ways of decomposing additive and multiplicative accounting multipliers (Polo, Roland-Host and Sancho, 1990) that are equally as capable of disaggregating an economy's revenue generation process.

respectively, destined for endogenous institutions; and $d_n = A_{nm}y_m$ is the vector of the exogenous income destined for the endogenous institutions. As in the Leontief model, the income of endogenous institutions can be obtained as

$$y_n = (I - A_{nn})^{-1} d_n = M_{nn} d_n \quad \textbf{(2)}$$

where M_n is the generalized multipliers matrix. Substituting (2) into (1), we get

$$y_n = A_{nn} M_{nn} d_n + d_n \quad \textbf{(3)}$$

Following Alcántara and Padilla (2009)[8], if we denote the subsystem of endogenous accounts under analysis by *s* and the complementary subset by *r*, and partition the expenditure and multiplier matrices,

$$A_{nn} = \begin{pmatrix} A_{ss} & A_{sr} \\ A_{rs} & A_{rr} \end{pmatrix} = \begin{pmatrix} A_{ss} & 0 \\ 0 & A_{rr} \end{pmatrix} + \begin{pmatrix} 0 & A_{sr} \\ A_{rs} & 0 \end{pmatrix} \quad \textbf{(4a)}$$

$$M_n = \begin{pmatrix} M_{ss} & M_{sr} \\ M_{rs} & M_{rr} \end{pmatrix} \quad \textbf{(4b)}$$

Equation (3) can be rewritten as

$$\begin{pmatrix} y_s \\ y_r \end{pmatrix} = \left[\begin{pmatrix} A_{ss} & 0 \\ 0 & A_{rr} \end{pmatrix} + \begin{pmatrix} 0 & A_{sr} \\ A_{rs} & 0 \end{pmatrix} \right] \begin{pmatrix} M_{ss} & M_{sr} \\ M_{rs} & M_{rr} \end{pmatrix} \begin{pmatrix} d_s \\ d_r \end{pmatrix} + \begin{pmatrix} d_s \\ d_r \end{pmatrix} \quad \textbf{(5)}$$

where y_s and y_r are the column vectors of the accounts included or otherwise, respectively, in subsystem *s*, and d_s and d_r are the vectors of exogenous income destined for subsystem *s* or the complementary subsystem *r*, respectively. Supposing that exogenous income destined for the complementary subsystem *r* is zero, $d_r = 0$, we get the following system of equations:

$$\begin{aligned} y_s &= A_{ss} M_{ss} d_s + A_{sr} M_{rs} d_s + d_s \\ y_r &= A_{rr} M_{rs} d_s + A_{rs} M_{ss} d_s \end{aligned} \quad . \quad \textbf{(6)}$$

This system provides the revenue of the institutions when the demand targeting the complementary subsystem *r* is zero.

The revenue of the institutions included in the subsystem *s* (first equation in (6)) is decomposed into three summands:

- $A_{ss}M_{ss}d_s$ represents the revenue generated within the actual subsystem *s* when it receives exogenous revenue d_s. It is called own effect (OE) and denoted y_s^{OE}.
- $A_{sr}M_{rs}d_s$ represents revenue generated in subsystem *s* due to the increase in revenue generated in the complementary subsystem *r* to satisfy the exogenous demand d_s. It is called the feedback effect (FBE) and is denoted y_s^{FBE}.
- d_s represents the direct revenue of subsystem *s* when the exogenous revenue is d_s. It is called the scale effect (SCE) and is denoted y_s^{SCE}.

[8] Whereas Alcántara and Padilla (2009) analyse the services subsystem, we look at the Spanish energy sector.

The second equation in (6) provides the revenue generated in the complementary subsystem r when the exogenous revenue is d_s. The second term, $A_{rs}M_{ss}d_s$, represents the revenue induced in the complementary subsystem *r* by the revenue generated in the institutions *s*; and the first term, $A_{rr}M_{rs}d_s$ reflects the revenue induced in subsystem *r* by the generation of revenue in its institutions induced by the exogenous revenue destined for the institutions in *s*. The sum of both terms of this equation is called the spill-over effect (SOE) and is denoted y_r^{SOE}.

An Estimate of Sectorial CO_2 Emissions

To link the above analysis with CO_2 emissions, we need a vector that converts the monetary units of the model into emission units. To do this, we use the vector c_e of emissions per unit of each energy commodity used, that we can see in next section. Multiplying this vector by the submatrix A_{nn}^E (Rows of energy branches of the A_{nn} matrix), we get a vector of unit emissions[9] for each institution,

$$c_n = c'_e \; A_{nn}^E \tag{7}$$

where c_e' is the transpose of the vector c_e. By dividing this vector c_n into two, one for the institutions in subsystem r (c_r), and another for subsystem *s* (c_s), we get a breakdown of total CO_2 emissions,

$$E^T = c'_s\, y_s + c'_r\, y_r \tag{8}$$

generated to satisfy the vector of final demand d_s by the four above-mentioned effects:

- Emissions associated with the own effect:

$$E^{OE} = c'_s\, y_s^{OE} = c'_s\, A_{ss}M_{ss}d_s \tag{9}$$

- Emissions associated with the feedback effect:

$$E^{FBE} = c'_s\, y_s^{FBE} = c'_s\, A_{sr}M_{rss}d_s \tag{10}$$

- Emissions associated with the scale effect:

$$y_s^{SCE} = c'_s\, d_s \tag{11}$$

- Emissions associated with the spill-over effect:

$$E_s^{SOE} = c'_r\, y_r = c'_r\left(A_{rr}M_{rs}d_s + A_{rs}M_{ss}d_s\right) \tag{12}$$

To get the emissions by branches, we have to diagonalize vector *d* ($\hat{d}$), whereby, for scale effect emissions, we get the vector em_S^{SCE} (*1 x s*),

$$em_S{}'^{\,SCE} = c_S{}' \cdot \hat{d}_S \tag{13}$$

where these are the emissions generated by each branch of subsystem *s* to produce the units destined to satisfy its final demand.

We get the spill-over effect in terms of emissions by calculating the vector em_S^{SOE} (*1 x R*),

[9] In this analysis we consider only the emissions generated by energy consumption, being the main source of emissions, and ignore other sources such as wood burning, that represent a small percentage of the total.

$$em_S{}'^{SOE} = c_r{}' \cdot (A_{rr} \cdot M_{rs} + A_{rs} \cdot M_{ss}) \cdot \hat{d}_S \quad \textbf{(14)}$$

This vector is composed of emissions generated by the other productive branches to produce what each branch of subsystem *s* demands to be able to satisfy its final demand.

To get the emissions generated by the output of the analysed subsystem destined to meet the needs of each branch of the subsystem for own inputs to satisfy its final demand (emissions due to the own effect), we calculate the vector em_S^{OE} $(1 \times s)$:

$$em_S{}'^{OE} = c_S{}' \cdot A_{SS} \cdot M_{SS} \cdot \hat{d}_S \quad \textbf{(15)}$$

In this case, the results suggest that the final demand of each branch of the subsystem has a pull effect on the emissions that it generates.

Similarly, we calculate the emissions due to FBE,

$$em_S{}'^{FBE} = c_S{}' \cdot A_{sr} \cdot M_{rs} \cdot \hat{d}_S \quad \textbf{(16)}$$

where each element of this vector represents the emissions generated by the subsystem as a whole to produce what the other branches belonging to *r* need to be able to produce what each branch of subsystem *s* demands to satisfy its final demand.

Therefore, the total effect (EM_{TE}) in terms of emissions generated directly or indirectly to satisfy the final demand of subsystem *s* would be:

$$EM_{TE} = EM_{SCE} + EM_{OEP} + EM_{FBE} + EM_{SOE} \quad \textbf{(17)}$$

And the total effect in terms of emissions due to the final demand of each of the branches of *s* would be the vector em_S^{TE} $(1 \times s)$:

$$em_S^{TE} = em_S^{SCE} + em_S^{OE} + em_S^{FBE} + em_S^{SOE} \quad \textbf{(18)}$$

Moreover, we can use Equation (5) again, this time making the vector d_S zero to get the sales made by subsystem *s* to the other sectors to enable them to satisfy their own final demands. Following the same procedure as in the last section, we would get for the other branches[10],

$$A_{ss} \cdot M_{sr} \cdot d_r + A_{sr} \cdot M_{rr} \cdot d_r + 0 = y_s \quad \textbf{(19)}$$

If we multiply this expression by the vector of emissions, we will have the emissions generated by sales to other sectors to satisfy their demand, which we will denote sales effect (SE),

$$EM_{SE} = c_S{}' \cdot y_s \quad \textbf{(20)}$$

And the emissions for each branch of the subsystem by sales to other sectors would be

$$em_S{}'^{SE} = c_S{}' \cdot \hat{y}_s \quad \textbf{(21)}$$

In a SAM analysis such as this, the emissions due to the sales effect account for the influence of the endogenized accounts, as we will see later. This means that these emissions are closer than in the Input-Output Model to the direct emissions, called EM_{DE}, generated by each productive subsystem, which we calculate by multiplying the unit emissions generated per unit output by each subsystem by production.

[10] Note that this expression reflects the spill-over effect for branches of *r* in the same way as the second equation of (6) does for the branches of *s*.

$$EM_{DE} = c_S' \cdot y_s \quad (22)$$

Application and Results

To conduct this analysis we separate the productive activities of the Spanish economy into two groups. The first, which we call the energy subsystem, is composed of the five energy accounts in the SAMES00 (Coal (3), Oil and Natural Gas (4), Oil Refining (6), Electrical Energy (7), and Manufactured Gas (8)). The second group, which we call the complementary subsystem, would be composed of the remaining 22 accounts corresponding to the non-energy-producing activities.

In the following, we apply the multiplier decomposition methodology, presented above, to the SAMES00 using a SAM model (considering the Labour (29), Capital (30) and Consumption (31) accounts as endogenous) for the energy subsystem. This outputs the production for each branch destined to satisfy the final demand [11] of the energy subsystem divided into the different effects forming what we term the total effect.

Table 2: c_e emissions' vector (Kt CO_2/ 1000€)

	Coal	*Oil and natural gas*	*Oil refining*	*Electricity*	*Manufactured gas and water steam*
Intermediate uses	46.40	0.00	8.08	0.00	7.25
Final uses	27.25	0.00	4.53	0.00	3.17

Source: Manresa and Sancho (2004), INE and own elaboration.

We transform these results into CO_2 emissions as explained in the last section, using the vector c_e of emissions per unit of each energy commodity used (Table 2), separated into emissions generated from Intermediate uses and emissions generated from Final uses. This way, as shown in the next table, we get the emissions generated to satisfy the final demand of the subsystem.

Table 3: Total and direct CO_2 emissions generated by the Spanish energy system (2000) based on the SAM* model

	Coal	Oil and Natural Gas	Oil Refining	Electricity	Manufactured Gas	Total
EM_{OE}	-0.46	0.57	905.11	147.37	-4.64	1,047.95
EM_{FBE}	-0.14	0.31	230.22	17.19	-5.70	241.89
EM_{SCE}	-0.29	1.12	4,167.61	633.59	-4.19	4,797.83
EM_{SOE}	-0.23	0.49	403.05	25.63	-8.13	420.81
$\mathbf{EM_{TE}}$	-1.12	2.48	5,705.99	823.78	-22.65	6,508.48
*%EM_{TE}/EM_{SEC}***	*-0.0005%*	*0.0010%*	*2.3496%*	*0.3392%*	*-0.0093%*	*2.6801%*
EM_{SE}	342.77	85.37	15,644.95	98,888.52	142.66	115,104.27
$\mathbf{EM_{DE}}$	347.41	105.89	20,288.08	100,311.23	139.33	121,191.93
*%EM_{DE}/EM_{SEC}***	*0.14%*	*0.04%*	*8.35%*	*41.31%*	*0.06%*	*49.91%*

(*) Expressed in kilotonnes (kt) of CO_2.
(**)Spanish economy sectorial emissions (EM_{SEC}): 242,845.

Source: Own Elaboration

Table **3** shows the different effects making up the EM_{TE} for each branch and for the energy subsystem. This table contains the emissions due to the own effect (EM_{OE}), that is, emissions generated by the subsystem s (energy), and its branches, to produce what the subsystem requires of itself to satisfy its final demand. This is followed by the feedback effect (EM_{FBE}), that is, emissions generated by the branches of the energy subsystem to produce what this

[11] Remember at this point that the final demand of this model does not include private consumption, which is converted into an endogenous account.

subsystem needs to sell to other sectors for them to produce what the energy subsystem demands from them to satisfy its final demand. The scale effect (EM_{SCE}), which is the emissions generated by the energy subsystem and each of its branches to produce what it is to sell directly to its final demand. And, finally, the spill-over effect (EM_{SOE}), that is, the emissions generated by the other sectors to output what the energy subsystem demands from them to be able to satisfy its final demand.

On the other hand, we present the emissions due to sales made by the branches of the energy subsystem to the other sectors r (EM_{SE}) in order to satisfy the final demands of r, and the emissions generated directly by the energy subsystem due to production, which we call the direct effect (EM_{DE}). Finally, we present both the EM_{TE} and the EM_{DE}, for each branch of the energy subsystem, as a ratio of the total sectoral emissions (which we call EM_{SEC}) of the Spanish economy.

These ratios are also illustrated as percentages in Fig. **1** to give a clearer and fuller view of the results and make the detailed analysis that follows easier to understand and follow.

Clearly, EM_{DE} are, generally, greater than EM_{TE}. This indicates that these are branches that absorb more emissions from other sectors and are characterized by high emissions per sales to other sectors (EM_{SE}) and low values for emissions due to the spill-over effect. On the other hand, the high emissions due to the scale effect and own effect, were to be expected. They are explained by the high use of the energy commodities by both the productive system and the final demand.

As Table **3** shows, the emissions generated directly by the energy subsystem (2) in its production process (EM_{DE}) account for almost 50% of total emissions by productive activities, where this subsystem ranks well above the rest of the economy. This is explained primarily by the EM_{SE}. The value of EM_{SE} in this model amounts to almost 90% of this subsystem's direct emissions, as this sector absorbs all the emissions generated by the energy needs of the other branches of the Spanish economy to satisfy their final demands.

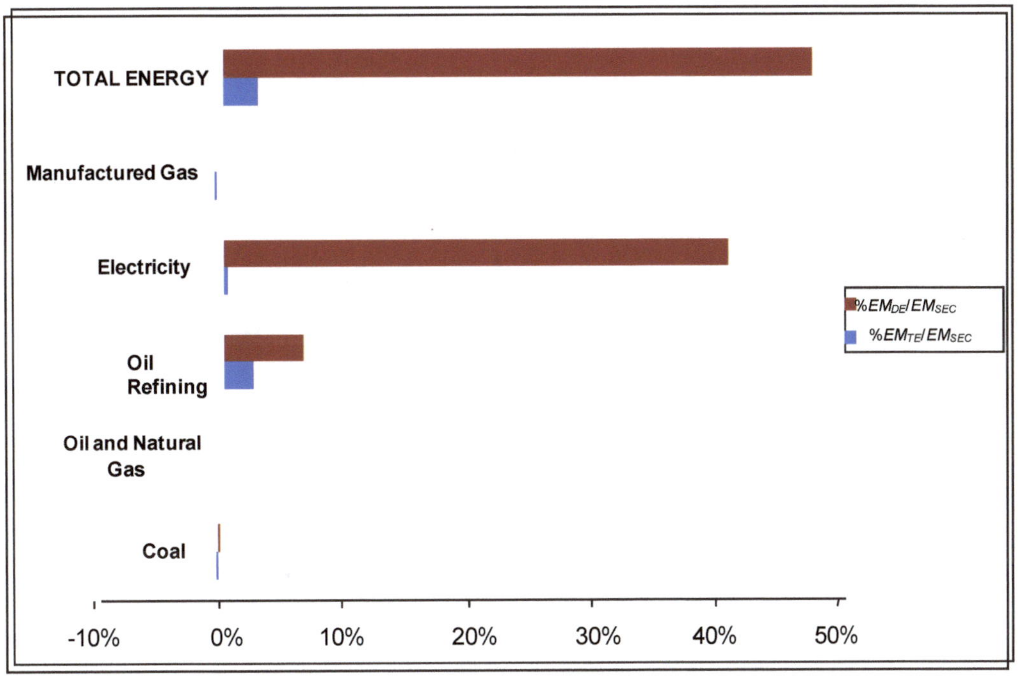

Figure 2: Direct and total emissions of the Spanish economy's energy subsystem over sectorial emissions (%)

Source: Own Elaboration

Additionally, we find that the emissions due to the energy final demand (EM_{TE}) account for 2.68% of sectoral emissions, of which just over 70% correspond to EM_{SCE}, that is, to output destined for the energy final demand.

In relation to the branches of this subsystem, we find that the electricity sector ranks top, with direct emissions accounting for over 41% of the emissions of the productive activities. This is the branch of the Spanish economy that releases most emissions into the atmosphere[12]. This is explained by the high emissions generated by sales to other sectors (EM_{SE}, which account for 40% of total emissions in the Spanish productive system).

However, the EM_{TE} of this branch account for just 0.34% of sectoral emissions. This is explained partly by the model, as we have endogenized private consumption, meaning that final demand (exogenous accounts) does not include consumption, and, therefore, the emissions due to the scale effect are less than we would get with an input-output model, as are emissions due to own effect, as the demand they have to satisfy is lower. The values of the other effects, especially the spill-over and feedback effects, for the electricity branch are very low.

The EM_{TE} of the Oil refining branch (7), which accounts for direct emissions amounting to 8.35% of sectoral emissions, are ranked top in terms of emissions generated by this subsystem, at 2.35%. This shows just how important the final demand of this sector is in terms of emissions. This is likely to be due to exports (where 35% of the output of this sector is destined for this use), as sales to other sectors include private transport[13], which explains its high value, outranking even total emissions.

Note that the way that this model has been defined by removing private consumption from the exogenous accounts means that the Investment account sometimes plays a bigger role in the exogenous accounts total and that, as this account is sometimes negative[14], the results may be negative. This is the case of Coal (3) and Manufactured Gas (8). In the first case, direct emissions account for 0.14% of sectoral emissions and its EM_{TE} offer values of just under zero, which could be interpreted as a divestment in the sector resulting in a slight reduction of emissions. Noteworthy are the emissions generated by sales to other sectors, as most of this branch's output destined, as inputs, for the energy branches, especially the electricity sector, whereas its final uses have decreased in importance. The second case is Manufactured Gas (8). One of the most noteworthy results of the analysis of this subsystem is the low level of emissions of the Gas branch (9), accounting for less than 0.1% of direct emissions over total sectoral emissions. Finally, another interesting point is that EM_{SOE} accounts, in all cases, for a very small percentage of sectoral emissions, as expected.

To complete this analysis, let us detail the results of this exercise presented in Table **4**. This table shows the emissions due to both the total effect and the direct effect, weighted, in the first case, against the final demand of each subsystem branch and, in the second, against the domestic output of each branch of the subsystem. The aim here is to fine-tune the results, as, in some cases, they are due to a greater weight in the economy and, in others, to sizeable price differences.

Table 4: Total and direct unit emissions of the Spanish energy subsystem for 2000

	Coal	**Oil and Natural Gas**	**Oil Refining**	**Electricity**	**Manufactured Gas**	**Total energy**
EM_{TE}/D**	0.66	0.02	1.04	6.62	0.20	1.15
EM_{DE}/Y_d*	0.30	0.56	0.96	5.12	0.04	2.63

***** Y_d**: Domestic production.***

**** D: Final demand.***

Source: Own Production.

The values for EM_{TE}/D indicate the emissions generated by the system as a whole to be able to satisfy a unit of the system's final demand, whereas EM_{DE}/Y_d are emissions generated by the subsystem per unit output.

---

[12] One of the reasons for electricity sector being the biggest polluter of the Spanish economy is the use of a high percentage of coal production, this being the energy commodity that generates most emissions when consumed.

[13] Note that Private Consumption is endogenized and that in Spain's input-output framework for the year 2000, and therefore in the SAMES00, private transport is allocated to the Oil Refining row and the Private consumption column.

[14] Due to the direction of the variations of stock.

Here we find that, as expected, the energy subsystem ranks top in terms of direct emissions, and has relatively low total effect emissions. This means that most of the emissions generated by this subsystem are derived from satisfying the final demand of the complementary subsystem. As regards its branches, electrical energy emissions are the highest ranking for both ratios, where they are higher in the case of total effect over domestic demand. The next highest ranked branch is oil refining, albeit at a considerable distance.

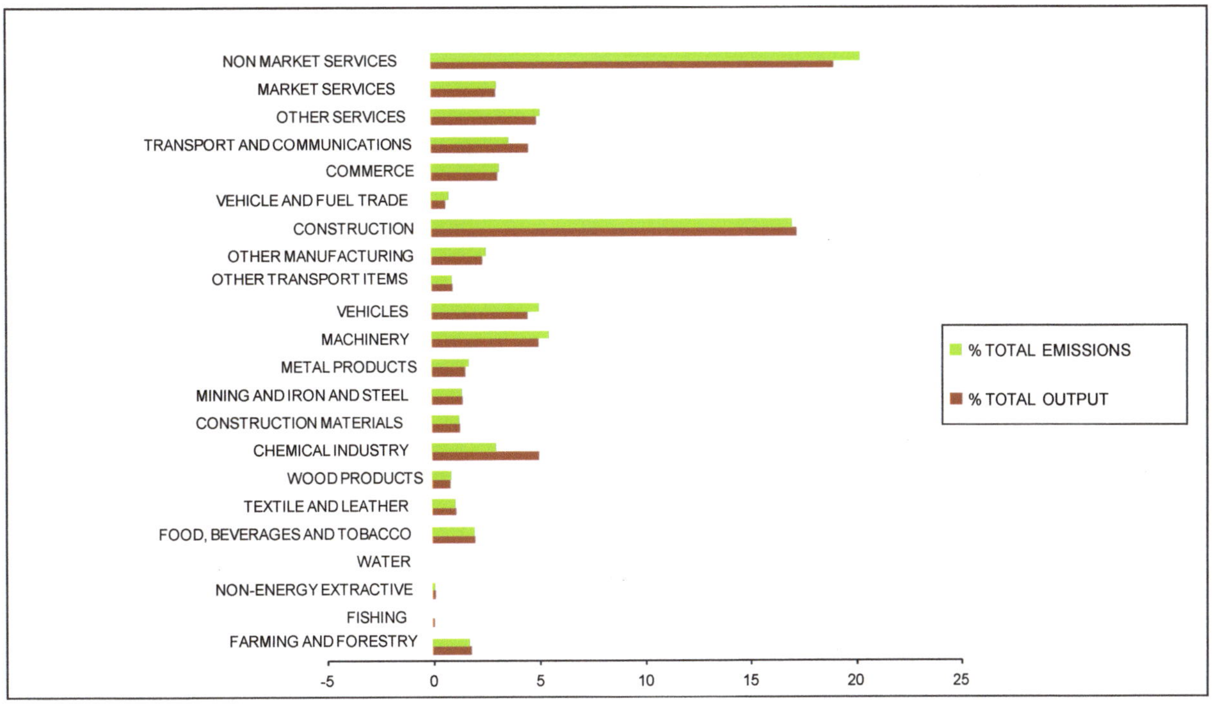

Figure 3: Production and emissions of the Spanish energy sector due to the final demand of the other sectors (%)

Source: Own Elaboration

Now we disaggregate the effect of sales to other sectors to determine which demands are the ones that generate greater emissions in Spanish energy sector production. Fig. **3** illustrates output and emissions generated by the Spanish energy sector derived from the final demands of the complementary subsystem that they are destined to satisfy.

In the first place, two sectors rank above the others in terms of both output and emissions. Starting with the sector that generates most emissions and output in the energy sector, we have the Non-Market Services sector (27), which, as we pointed out earlier, is another example of the high indirect emissions generated by services sector.

Construction (21) is another sector that generates high emissions in the energy subsystem. In this case, the value of subsystem output is slightly higher than for emissions. The most likely explanation is the use of less pollutant energy commodities than in the case of the Non-Market Services sector (27).

Other branches, like vehicles, machinery, the chemical industry and other branches of the services sector, have a slight edge in terms of output and emissions over the others.

CONCLUSIONS

The growing awareness about the consequences of climate change has spread to all agents, especially since the Stern Review (2006). This makes it increasingly necessary to conduct economic studies including environment-related issues that can provide some clues as to and help to define the direction that tax, environmental or economic policies should take if we are to reduce emissions or increase energy efficiency levels.

As such models require a consistent database, we have had to build the Social Accounting Matrix of the Spanish economy for the year 2000, which we presented in Section 1. Apart from its descriptiveness, this matrix provides statistical support for applying the methodology that we developed in the remainder of the paper.

In Section 3 we developed an additive multiplier decomposition methodology (Alcántara and Padilla, 2009) based on the SAMES00. Thanks to this methodology, we have been able, based on the SAM model linked to a vector of emissions per unit expenditure, to extend the information about CO_2 emissions. This way, apart from identifying the emissions that each branch generates in its productive process, we were able to ascertain what indirect emissions the Spanish energy system generates to satisfy the final demand of each branch of the economy.

This additive methodology involves separating the emissions generated by the Spanish energy sector into different effects, identifying which demands are responsible for the output in each case. This way, we get a total effect that is defined as the direct and indirect emissions generated across the system to satisfy the final demand of each branch of the energy system.

As expected, it is the energy subsystem itself that obviously generates most direct emissions, as the energy sectors have the biggest energy intensities and ranks high on direct emissions due to the high energy needs of it production process.

Comparing the results of this total effect against the direct emissions for each of the branches of the Spanish energy subsystem, we find that the sector that generates the highest levels of direct emissions over emissions due to the total effect is Electricity (7), responsible for almost half of total sectoral emissions, and the most pollutant branch of the Spanish productive system. This sector has a sizeable system emissions absorption effect.

About the Total effect emissions, it is remarkable the low emissions in all branches, being the unique significant value that from Oil refining representing almost the 90% of the emissions of the energy subsystem.

The results obtained in this study reveal how the productive activity of the Spanish energy sector, and within it the branches of electricity and Oil refining products, is responsible for nearly half of all emissions to the atmosphere generated by productive activities. However, this outcome is tempered when we analyze what demand will meet this energy production. The final energy demand is responsible for a low 2.7% of total emissions, while more expensive to satisfy demands in terms of pollutants in the atmosphere are those of the service sector and construction, being the main energy source used by these very electricity followed by Oil refining.

From the estimates that can be detached when formulating energy policies would be desirable to enhance these cleaner energy sources, whether primary or secondary. In the particular case of electricity, we would recommend a replacement of the primary energy sources used in more polluting than the production process, such as coal, with other, less polluting, whether renewable or non-renewable. Finally, the high use some areas of production make electricity or refining, and environmental consequences this has, indicate that emissions reductions should not come only from the energy production system, but a more responsible use of energy by the other activities and may establish mechanisms such as enhanced energy plans recently, to prevent the waste of energy and allow greater efficiency in their use.

Models such as the one presented here also have their limitations. One such limitation worth mentioning is the shortage of data or parameter specification. As mentioned earlier, however, they are of great interest to authorities as tools for simulating different scenarios on which to sound out the effect of specific policies, as they can output *ex ante* information on the possible effects of a particular policy and *ex post* information for assessing the impact of such measures.

ACKNOWLEDGEMENTS

We want to thank financial support from Foundation Escuela de Organización Industrial from the Spanish Ministry of Industry, Commerce and Tourism, Research Projects 2009.

REFERENCES

Alcántara, V. and Padilla, E. (2009). "Input-output subsystems and pollution: an application to the service sector and CO_2 emissions in Spain", *Ecological Economics,* 68(3), p. 905-914.

Alcántara, V. and Roca, J. (1995). "Energy and CO_2 emissions in Spain: methodology of analysis and some results for 1980-90", *Energy Economics* 17(3), p. 221-230.

Cardenete, M. A. and Fuentes-Saguar, P. D. (2009). *El sector energético español a través de un modelo de crecimiento sostenible*. Madrid: Fundación Escuela de Organización Industrial. Ministerio de Industria, Comercio y Turismo.

Cardenete, M. A. and Fuentes-Saguar, P. D. (2010). Análisis económico de la Central Nuclear de Almaraz, en *Realidad Económica del Sector Nuclear en España, Un Análisis Empírico de la Central Nuclear de Almaraz*. Servicio de Publicaciones de la Universidad de Extremadura.

Cardenete, M. A., Fuentes-Saguar, P. D. and Polo, C. (2008). "Análisis de intensidades energéticas y emisiones de CO_2 a partir de la Matriz de contabilidad social de Andalucía para el año 2.000", *Revista de Economía Agraria y Recursos Naturales*, 8(2), p. 31-48.

Cardenete, M. A. and Sancho, F. (2006). "Elaboración de una matriz de contabilidad social a través del método de entropía cruzada: España 1995", *Estadística Española*, 48(161), p. 67-100.

EC (2002). Council Decision of 25 April 2002 concerning the approval, on behalf of the European Community, of the Kyoto Protocol to the United Nations Framework Convention on Climate Change and the joint fulfilment of commitments thereunder.

De Miguel, F. J. and Manresa, A. (2004). "Modelos SAM lineales y distribución de la renta: una aplicación para la economía extremeña". *Estudios de Economía Aplicada*, 22(3), p. 577-603.

Heimler, A. (1991). "Linkages and vertical integration in the Chinese economy", *Review of Economics and Statistics*, 73, p.261-267.

Hewings, G.J.D., Sonis, M., Guo, J., Israilevich, P.R. and Schindler, G.R. (1997). "The Hollowing-Out process in the Chicago economy, 1975-2011", *Geographical Analysis*, 30, p.217-233.

Kehoe, T.J., Manresa, A., Polo, C. and Sancho, F. (1988). "Una Matriz de Contabilidad Social de la Economía española", *Estadística Española*, 30(117), p. 5-33.

Labandeira, X., and Labeaga, J. M. (2002). "Estimation and Control of Spanish Energy-Related CO2 Emissions: an Input-Output Approach", *Energy Policy* 30(7), p. 597-611.

Leontief, W. (1966). *Input-Output Economics*. New York: Oxford University Press.

Manresa, A. and Sancho, F. (2004). "Energy intensities and CO2 emissions in Catalonia: a SAM analysis", *International Journal Environment. Workplace and Employment*, 1(1), p. 91-106.

Nieto, J. and Santamarta, J. (2003). Las Emisiones de Gases de Efecto Invernadero en España. CC.OO. Madrid.

Nieto, J. and Santamarta, J. (2007). Evolución de las Emisiones de Gases de Efecto Invernadero en España (1990-2006). CC.OO. Madrid.

Polo, C., Roland-Host, D. and Sancho F. (1990). "Distribución de la renta en un modelo SAM de la economía española", *Estadística Española*, 32 (125), p. 537-567.

Pyatt, G. and Round, J. (1979). "Accounting and Fixed Price Multipliers in a Social Accounting Framework", *Economic Journal*, 89, p. 850-873.

Sánchez Chóliz, J. and Duarte, R. (2003). "Analysing pollution by vertically integrated coefficients, with an application to the water sector in Aragon", *Cambridge Journal of Economics*, 27, p. 433-448.

Stern, N. (2006). *Stern review: The economics of Climate Change*. Cambridge University Press, New York.

Stone, R. (1962). A Social Accounting Matrix for 1960. *A Programme for Growth*. Edit. Chapman and Hall Lid. London.

ANNEX

	1	2	3	4	5	6	7	8	9	10
1	2960	9	0	0	0	1	5	0	0	21143
2	0	0	0	0	0	0	0	0	0	235
3	1	0	0	0	6	17	1727	0	0	0
4	0	0	0	7	0	12788	1	2637	0	0
5	1	6	1	0	20	8	1	0	0	18
6	529	98	42	10	133	2392	1852	17	72	105
7	270	7	77	6	133	294	3244	11	62	494
8	2	8	0	4	7	25	724	1	4	135
9	261	5	1	0	18	38	29	0	6	136
10	4865	129	0	0	0	0	3	0	0	14454
11	23	52	7	2	0	1	1	0	11	112
12	136	17	58	0	24	10	14	0	2	1586
13	1522	17	47	4	195	157	23	1	301	553
14	8	1	5	0	18	8	9	0	0	943
15	0	0	9	4	19	19	3	0	0	7
16	442	29	18	18	131	107	430	0	38	1137
17	318	6	51	6	144	158	604	2	511	378
18	3	2	1	1	1	2	1	0	2	19
19	4	143	8	0	6	2	0	0	0	27
20	224	28	11	4	29	51	79	2	90	992
21	211	1	5	1	57	50	191	6	60	226
22	265	6	6	6	32	91	46	3	138	113
23	1422	80	1	1	64	27	696	0	17	2558
24	510	193	56	5	368	964	397	19	86	3524
25	600	84	45	18	170	885	1142	110	371	4447
26	339	31	23	20	62	172	366	16	50	1338
27	0	0	0	0	0	0	0	0	0	0
28	2807	587	428	26	399	353	1244	120	653	6498
29	20039	595	87	37	459	1983	6436	823	659	5695
30	0	0	0	0	0	0	0	0	0	0
31	0	0	0	0	0	0	0	0	0	0
32	379	91	169	8	129	135	462	43	236	2067
33	-1374	-11	-1	1	57	487	-139	45	13	-2808
34	15	2	1	0	2	10	3	0	7	27
35	7	0	0	0	0	2	0	0	0	86
36	0	0	0	0	0	0	0	0	0	0
37	0	0	0	0	0	0	0	0	0	0
38	0	0	0	0	0	0	0	0	0	0
39	5413	780	879	15450	1701	5533	119	0	0	10991
TOTAL RESOURCES	42199	2998	2033	15637	4384	26767	19711	3857	3389	77233

Table 1: Spanish social accounting matrix for 2000 – million euros at basic prices (SAMES00)

	11	12	13	14	15	16	17	18	19	20
1	583	1195	92	1	0	2	14	0	0	89
2	0	0	1	0	0	0	0	0	0	0
3	0	0	19	4	206	2	7	0	0	0
4	0	0	16	0	0	0	0	0	0	0
5	2	17	343	731	1461	47	23	0	0	11
6	29	80	2687	233	218	69	109	27	37	83
7	224	414	376	567	485	413	498	407	55	581
8	103	150	277	358	177	71	52	52	7	81
9	34	17	52	24	12	36	38	19	7	33
10	428	39	186	0	0	0	8	0	0	3
11	8701	37	153	44	48	26	97	609	36	650
12	173	6340	461	347	63	232	328	101	47	6113
13	1407	967	9547	824	1252	771	901	644	162	3344
14	2	15	147	1782	84	123	434	349	35	106
15	16	37	49	338	2132	8482	4616	4768	472	1968
16	166	299	111	543	1485	1847	3418	1663	405	2404
17	301	387	673	1060	843	996	10441	2213	685	999
18	11	2	7	20	5	35	196	18836	99	46
19	0	3	0	3	2	12	24	1	1506	10
20	444	307	751	178	2805	274	1615	3003	464	4663
21	47	64	60	175	33	93	146	54	7	76
22	62	55	272	124	98	63	154	692	32	168
23	1408	970	510	662	859	773	1253	161	162	1639
24	1168	1045	1997	2759	1367	1112	1475	1452	200	1839
25	1567	915	2939	1581	1105	1470	3867	2188	642	3237
26	336	159	583	478	213	322	518	242	92	512
27	0	0	0	0	0	0	0	0	0	0
28	3858	2350	3485	3249	2183	4977	7332	4254	1354	7302
29	2407	2281	3896	3221	3489	3021	4598	3113	439	5069
30	0	0	0	0	0	0	0	0	0	0
31	0	0	0	0	0	0	0	0	0	0
32	1058	711	1204	991	617	1587	2293	1303	394	2091
33	-269	-43	80	135	-95	46	79	24	-130	33
34	7	4	22	11	7	4	8	15	3	22
35	60	4	3	0	24	7	44	33	17	12
36	0	0	0	0	0	0	0	0	0	0
37	0	0	0	0	0	0	0	0	0	0
38	0	0	0	0	0	0	0	0	0	0
39	9224	5888	18632	2033	9299	3943	40806	29754	3940	8686
TOTAL RESOURCES	33557	24709	49628	22474	30477	30855	85391	75977	11169	51870

Table 1: Spanish social accounting matrix for 2000 – million euros at basic prices (SAMES00) (Cont'd)

	21	22	23	24	25	26	27	28	29	30
1	401	3	983	21	530	53	95	0	0	5848
2	0	0	558	2	0	18	11	0	0	1943
3	0	3	3	4	6	3	19	0	0	8
4	0	0	0	20	3	1	0	0	0	0
5	1073	0	18	16	10	19	2	0	0	13
6	461	94	935	4186	245	378	595	0	0	5556
7	318	324	1849	1248	915	683	1238	0	0	4396
8	35	15	341	40	79	81	196	0	0	951
9	43	32	344	109	78	209	217	0	0	1593
10	1	16	12239	104	262	392	411	0	0	34241
11	68	57	993	195	453	170	334	0	0	13641
12	2284	45	632	487	780	288	377	0	0	230
13	1377	402	1372	422	1226	1349	1297	0	0	4033
14	13435	108	259	256	82	72	86	0	0	266
15	1225	1	25	10	100	1	5	0	0	1
16	7105	279	221	284	420	373	118	0	0	133
17	6259	236	1080	2297	1596	1170	1858	0	0	4984
18	3	4146	34	509	129	133	93	0	0	12550
19	8	58	28	876	74	58	507	0	0	698
20	1794	239	1222	1051	8619	1068	1174	0	0	9244
21	28035	122	1853	691	1551	8450	1271	0	0	3177
22	842	1725	659	1879	274	471	209	0	0	10618
23	4484	322	5966	2476	2181	1125	2780	0	0	116696
24	2531	761	7621	20252	6140	2052	2514	0	0	20590
25	3841	2127	11219	6422	23454	10181	6318	0	0	32222
26	3288	975	8760	2773	4998	5189	2113	0	0	73208
27	0	0	0	0	0	0	0	0	0	6975
28	24150	4824	41613	13064	38961	21847	49291	0	0	0
29	14913	3944	49658	23866	29567	56665	8528	0	0	0
30	0	0	0	0	0	0	0	247209	255488	0
31	0	0	0	0	0	0	0	0	0	169310
32	6418	1219	8490	3741	10167	4319	14646	0	0	0
33	1055	205	1996	2141	557	3585	317	0	0	0
34	24	10	65	79	1023	1144	2619	0	0	0
35	22	11	53	3	6	17	16	0	0	0
36	0	0	0	0	0	0	0	0	0	16179
37	0	0	0	0	0	0	0	0	0	64002
38	0	0	0	0	0	0	0	0	0	0
39	18	0	1564	6880	16773	1146	0	0	0	0
TOTAL RESOURCES	125511	22302	162650	96402	151258	122708	99253	247209	255488	613304

Table 1: Spanish social accounting matrix for 2000 – million euros at basic prices (SAMES00) (Cont'd)

	31	32	33	34	35	36	37	38	39	TOTAL USES
1	946	0	0	0	0	0	0	0	7224	42199
2	0	0	0	0	0	0	0	0	230	2998
3	-3	0	0	0	0	0	0	0	1	2033
4	161	0	0	0	0	0	0	0	4	15637
5	8	0	0	0	0	0	0	0	536	4384
6	247	0	0	0	0	0	0	0	5252	26767
7	0	0	0	0	0	0	0	0	125	19711
8	-116	0	0	0	0	0	0	0	0	3857
9	-2	0	0	0	0	0	0	0	0	3389
10	419	0	0	0	0	0	0	0	9032	77233
11	239	0	0	0	0	0	0	0	6797	33557
12	212	0	0	0	0	0	0	0	3323	24709
13	210	0	0	0	0	0	0	4631	10672	49628
14	127	0	0	0	0	0	0	0	3719	22474
15	98	0	0	0	0	0	0	0	6073	30477
16	3719	0	0	0	0	0	0	0	3513	30855
17	25306	0	0	0	0	0	0	82	19749	85391
18	10077	0	0	0	0	0	0	0	29019	75977
19	3343	0	0	0	0	0	0	43	3727	11169
20	3734	0	0	0	0	0	0	0	7713	51870
21	78791	0	0	0	0	0	0	0	9	125511
22	1727	0	0	0	0	0	0	0	1473	22302
23	2747	0	0	0	0	0	0	2222	8388	162650
24	166	0	0	0	0	0	0	989	12251	96402
25	13225	0	0	0	0	0	0	1067	13800	151258
26	8645	0	0	0	0	0	0	6739	147	122708
27	0	0	0	0	0	0	0	92277	0	99253
28	0	0	0	0	0	0	0	0	0	247209
29	0	0	0	0	0	0	0	0	0	255488
30	0	0	0	0	0	0	0	83430	27177	613304
31	0	0	0	0	0	0	0	-34784	19498	154024
32	0	0	0	0	0	0	0	0	0	64967
33	0	0	0	0	0	0	0	0	0	5987
34	0	0	0	0	0	0	0	0	0	5134
35	0	0	0	0	0	0	0	0	0	426
36	0	0	0	0	0	0	0	0	0	16179
37	0	0	0	0	0	0	0	0	0	64002
38	0	64967	5987	5134	426	16179	64002	0	0	156695
39	0	0	0	0	0	0	0	0	0	199450
TOTAL RESOURCES	154024	64967	5987	5134	426	16179	64002	156695	199450	

Source: Own elaboration.

Table 2: SAMES00 Accounts

1	Farming and Forestry
2	Fishing and related activities
3	Coal
4	Oil and Natural Gas
5	Non-energy extractive
6	Oil Refining
7	Production and distribution of electricity
8	Production and distribution of gas, steam and hot water
9	Collection, purification and distribution of water
10	Food, beverages and tobacco
11	Textiles & Leather
12	Woods products
13	Chemical
14	Mining and iron and steel industry
15	Metal products
16	Machinery
17	Vehicles
18	Construction materials
19	Other transport elements
20	Other manufacturing
21	Construction
22	Vehicle and fuel trade
23	Commerce
24	Transport and Communications
25	Other services
26	Market Services
27	Non-market Services
28	Labour
29	Capital
30	Consumption
31	FBK
32	Employers' social security contributions
33	Net indiret taxes
34	VAT
35	Tariffs
36	Employees' social security contributions
37	IRPF
38	Public Sector
39	Imports/ Exports

CHAPTER 5

Hybrid IO Analysis of CO_2 Emissions: An Application to the Portuguese Economy

Luís Cruz* and Eduardo Barata

GEMF – Faculty of Economics, University of Coimbra (Portugal)

Abstract: Since the late 1980s, global climate change issues gained an ever-growing attention. The seriousness of the greenhouse effect is now widely recognized as one of the hottest topics in the world agenda. This poses important challenges. For one, global warming is a serious threat, pushing a shift of our mindset from economic growth to more eclectic approaches towards the sustainability of the resources base. Second, we lack effective mechanisms for decision making and policy implementation that encompass the complex interactions between environmental and economic activities.

The Leontief input-output model has been applied for macro environmental analysis since the 1970s. Using data for the Portuguese economy, this paper explores an extended environmental input–output model to study environment and economy interactions in order to support strategies that respect and promote a balanced management of the dynamics between energy supply, environmental protection and economic growth.

Thus, from the empirical analysis of primary energy flows, sets of energy intensity coefficients by industry, as well as the energy requirements attributable to given vectors of final demand, are estimated. Then, sources of anthropogenic CO_2 Portuguese emissions and the share of sectors in total emissions are identified, relating this pollution with the use of fossil fuels. Besides, 'CO2 responsibility', which takes into account the CO_2 content of imports, is estimated. The sectoral CO_2 emissions and CO_2 responsibilities are compared and these two notions are linked to foreign trade. Accordingly, a summary of the key lessons learned and a discussion of their policy relevance will be offered.

Keywords: Hybrid I-O Analysis; Energy Intensities; CO_2 Emissions; CO_2 Responsibility; Portugal.

INTRODUCTION

The continuous search for a balanced management amid the implicit opportunity costs of three critical goals - availability of energy, environmental protection and economic growth - has guided the energy policy in the European Union (EU) and elsewhere in the last decades. Additionally, energy policy decisions cannot ignore the Kyoto Protocol's commitments.

Under the Kyoto Protocol and the flexibility mechanisms designed to allow the signatory countries a more efficient (and cost effective) approach to reduce greenhouse gases (GHG) emissions (the Joint Implementation, the Clean Development Mechanism, and Emissions Trading), in January of 2005 was launched one of the most ambitious multilateral initiatives in the environmental policy history: the European Union CO_2 emissions trading scheme (ETS). This is the first major global scheme of its kind, covering about 12000 installations, which represents almost half of the EU anthropogenic CO_2 emissions, with major evidence for energy activities (combustion installations with a rated thermal input exceeding 20 MW, mineral oil refineries, coke ovens), production and processing of ferrous metals, mineral industry (cement clinker, glass and ceramic bricks) and pulp, paper and board activities (van Asselt and Biermann, 2007).

During the first phase of the ETS program (relating the period 2005-07), the various Member-States were called to establish their National Allocation Plans (NAPs), i.e., to define the total amounts of CO_2 emission licenses to be allocated (at no cost) to their companies, which could then be sold or bought in the market. This initial phase was designed to familiarise European firms with emissions trading and to promote learning by doing. A dominant feature of this process is that both cap-setting and allocation are highly decentralized, negotiated processes. However, the

***Address correspondence to Luís Cruz:** GEMF – Faculty of Economics, University of Coimbra (Portugal)

Maria Llop (Ed)

initial high degree of autonomy for Member States has also increased complexity, administrative burdens and transaction costs. Therefore, concerning Phase 2 of NAPs (covering the period 2008-12) some major improvements were introduced. NAPs 2 are far more stringent than NAPs 1, and take into account that, considering the results achieved, they are simply too modest when compared with the magnitude of the challenge. Moreover the EU ETS effectiveness (in delivering emission reductions), efficiency (at least cost), and equity (with acceptable distributional consequences) remain topics of an ongoing debate.

The present research recognizes that the companies already explicitly enclosed within the ETS are major generators of CO_2 emissions and other GHG emissions due to fossil fuel burning in their production processes. However, one should not ignore that the raw materials and others inputs used by these companies, as well as their corresponding processes of distribution, use and residuals deposition, will involve many other companies, of the same or other economies, that also generate CO_2. That is, CO_2 emissions occur, directly and indirectly, in different phases and multiple industries of the economies. As such, with this research it is intended to explore the multi-sector nature of the production processes regarding the implementation of the mechanisms to estimate and control CO_2 emissions. An abundant literature with various recent developments (see, for example: Cruz, 2009; Hayami and Nakamura, 2007; Tunc et al., 2007; Llop, 2007; Su et al., 2010) has contributed to argue that Input-Output (I-O) models are fairly adequate to proceed with this ambitious analysis.

This paper will begin by presenting a brief outline of the basic I-O model, and then there will be succinctly discussed the core aspects of its extensions for the consideration of environmental and energy issues. Then, there will be presented the data sets for the Portuguese empirical model. Next, energy and CO_2 intensity coefficients by industry will be estimated, as well as the energy requirements and the level of CO_2 emissions derived from fossil fuel use attributable to given sets of final demand. Finally, the study's main conclusions will be presented and the limitations and needs for future research discussed.

THE I-O FRAMEWORK

In an I-O approach the economic structure is defined in terms of sectors. It can be said that the relative simplicity of such a systematic connection of a set of economic variables provides a modelling framework suitable for calculating economic impacts (over all of the economy) of several human activities.

The basic principle of I-O analysis states that each sector's production process can be represented by a vector of structural coefficients that describes the relationship between the inputs absorbed and the outputs produced[1]. This is represented through the basic equation of the Leontief static model (in matrix form)[2]:

$$\mathbf{x} = (\mathbf{I}-\mathbf{A})^{-1}\mathbf{y} \qquad \textbf{(1)}$$

where **x** is the vector of total outputs for ach sector, **A** is the matrix of the technological coefficients (a_{ij}) and **y** is the vector of final demand. This expression is the fundamental matrix representation of I-O analysis, and the inverse matrix $(\mathbf{I}-\mathbf{A})^{-1}$ is known as the 'Leontief inverse matrix' (or also as the 'multiplier matrix'), whose elements are denoted by α_{ij}, representing the total amount of commodity *i* required both directly and indirectly to deliver one unit of final demand of commodity *j*.

By decomposing equation (1) (which can be seen as the result of an iterative process that shows the progressive adjustments of output to final demand and input requirements), one can separate out the direct from the indirect requirements for production, which are necessary to satisfy a certain vector of final demand commodities:

$$\mathbf{x} = \mathbf{y} + \mathbf{A}\mathbf{y} + \mathbf{A}^2\mathbf{y} + \ldots + \mathbf{A}^n\mathbf{y} + \ldots \qquad \textbf{(2)}$$

[1] General assumptions of the basic I-O model are: homogeneity (i.e. each sector or industry produces a single product) and linear production functions (which implies proportionality of inputs with outputs in each sector and excludes both the possibility of economies or diseconomies of scale, and of substitution between production factors).

[2] Notational conventions: upper case bold letters are used to denote matrices, and lower case italic letters with subscript indices to denote its elements; lower case bold letters are used to denote vectors, and upper case italic letters with subscript indices to denote its elements; and lower case italic letters are used to denote scalars.

So, we can decompose the total demand for the *n* goods produced in the economy as follows:

- **y** is required for final demand. This is the direct effect.
- **Ay** is the production necessary to allow the production of a final demand vector, **y**. This is the 'first-round indirect effect'.
- $\mathbf{A}^2\mathbf{y} = \mathbf{A}(\mathbf{Ay})$ is needed to produce the goods **Ay**. This is the 'second-round indirect effect'.
- $\mathbf{A}^t\mathbf{y} = \mathbf{A}(\mathbf{A}^{t-1}\mathbf{y})$ is needed to produce the goods $\mathbf{A}^{t-1}\mathbf{y}$. This is the '$t^{th}$-round indirect effect'.

Clearly, the total indirect effects (or intermediate demand) are the sum of the first-round, second-round, etc. (Proops *et al.,* 1996).

EXTENSIONS OF THE BASIC MODEL TO ACCOUNT FOR ENERGY-ECONOMY-ENVIRONMENT INTERACTIONS

Having established the basic I-O framework, it is time to move on to discuss some extensions of this technique, in order to make explicit the link between the level of economic activity in a country, its corresponding impact on the environment, and/or the corresponding energy interactions.

Extensions of the application of I-O models to the examination of interactions between economic activity and environmental issues date back to the late 1960s and early 1970s[3]. These studies can be considered as benchmarks of an approach that would be further developed by some energy analysts during the 1970s and the 1980s, extending the use of I-O analysis to consider energy-economy interactions[4].

But, over time, the modelling approaches have become more and more complex, to allow, for example, the consideration of global environmental issues such as the greenhouse effect and the 'resulting' climate change problem. This has led to the development of numerous theoretical models and empirical studies that combine both perspectives, making it hard to distinguish between environment and energy models, and therefore it become usual to talk about 'energy-economy-environment' models (Faucheaux and Levarlet, 1999).

Thus, it is not surprising that also the I-O models have been extended to deal with both environmental and energy issues. Therefore, in this section, it is intended to illustrate some of the potentialities of the energy-economy-environment models, applying the I-O technique to the structural analysis of energy requirements and CO_2 emissions by economies, relating this pollution with the use of fossil fuels. This will be done using an approach very similar to the one used by Cruz (2002) and Proops *et al.* (1993).

To start, it is important to note that we need to introduce two kinds of distinctions into the analysis:

1. The division of the fossil fuel use, and the corresponding pollution emissions, in what concerns to energy directly demanded by household consumers (for lighting, cooking, heating/cooling, transport, etc.), and energy (directly and indirectly) demanded by industrial and agricultural producers of goods to 'power' the production processes. The former will be designated as 'direct consumption demand' and the latter as (direct plus indirect) 'production demand'.
2. The distinction between various forms of primary (fossil) fuels[5], namely solid (coal), liquid (oil) and gaseous (natural gas), since they have different pollution emissions per unit mass, and per unit of energy delivered.

---

[3] Detailed surveys of environmental I-O models, with many references, including theoretical extensions and applications are provided, for example, by: Barata (2009), Cruz *et al.* (2005), Hawdon and Pearson (1995), Miller and Blair (2009).
[4] A detailed survey of energy I-O analysis is presented, for example, by Miller and Blair (2009); additional contributes and references can be seen in Cruz (2002).
[5] Applying an I-O approach to fuel use, as it is the case, 'only primary fuels need be consider directly', since the use of secondary fuels is 'dealt with automatically within the interindustry demand structure' (Gay and Proops, 1993). This means that the manufacture of secondary fuels (such as, e.g. electricity or gasoline) should be ignored in the main calculation of CO_2 emissions so that double counting is avoided (IPCC, 2006).

Lets consider: matrix $\mathbf{C}_{3xn}$, whose generic element (c_{fi}) represents the (physical) quantity of fuel *f* used by sector *i* per unit of total output (i.e. the 'energy intensities corresponding to direct production demand'); matrix $\mathbf{P}_{3xn}$, which has only three non-zero elements, one for each fuel type, expressing the (physical) quantity of fossil fuel use per unit of final demand (i.e. the 'energy intensities corresponding to direct consumption demand'); and a diagonal matrix $\mathbf{H}_{nxn}$, with only three non-zero elements, which are the ratios of the sum of 'final consumption of households' and 'collective consumption', to total final demand, for the three fossil fuel sectors[6]. Accordingly, in this model total (primary) energy requirements by an economy (given by the 3-vector **f**) can be considered as the sum of the production energy requirements (given by the 3-vector $[\mathbf{f}_{ind}=\mathbf{C}(\mathbf{I}-\mathbf{A})^{-1}\mathbf{y}]$), and final demand energy requirements (given by the 3-vector $[\mathbf{f}_{dem}=\mathbf{PHy}]$), i.e.:

$$\mathbf{f} = \mathbf{f}_{ind} + \mathbf{f}_{dem} = \mathbf{C}(\mathbf{I}-\mathbf{A})^{-1}\mathbf{y} + \mathbf{PHy} \qquad (3)$$ [7]

Moreover, anthropogenic CO_2 emissions are produced when carbon-based fuels are burned. Therefore, after adjusting primary energy figures, it is possible to estimate CO_2 emissions from fuel combustion, by considering the carbon contents of each type of fuel. For this purpose, conversion factors from primary energy to CO_2 were applied. These conversion factors were calculated following the IPCC's default methodology to make countries' GHG emissions inventories (IPCC, 2006), and were arranged in a vector of CO_2 emission per unit (tonnes of oil equivalent - toe) of fuel burnt (vector **e**). Accordingly, it is assumed that each toe of coal, oil and natural gas burnt generates 3.88, 3.04 and 2.34 tonnes of CO_2, respectively[8].

Considering **e'** as the transpose of vector $\mathbf{e}_{3x1}$, whose generic element (e_f) represents the amount of CO_2 emission per unit of fuel *f*, total CO_2 emissions by an economy (given by the scalar *c*) can be considered as the sum of the production CO_2 emissions $[c_{ind} = \mathbf{e'C}(\mathbf{I}-\mathbf{A})^{-1}\mathbf{y}]$ and final demand CO_2 emissions $[c_{dem} = \mathbf{e'PHy}]$[9], that is:

$$c = c_{ind} + c_{dem} = \mathbf{e'C}(\mathbf{I}-\mathbf{A})^{-1}\mathbf{y} + \mathbf{e'PHy} \Leftrightarrow c = [\mathbf{e'C}(\mathbf{I}-\mathbf{A})^{-1} + \mathbf{e'PH}]\,\mathbf{y} \qquad (4)$$ [10].

Moreover, as will be shown, according to the 'components' of the (total) final demand considered, it will be possible to distinguish energy requirements and CO_2 emissions attributable to the domestic consumption of goods and services produced in a country, from that attributable to exports, as well as to estimate the levels of energy and CO_2 emissions 'embodied' in the country's imports. It will then be possible to estimate primary energy and CO_2 emissions 'embodied' in a country's international trade, as well as the country's 'responsibility' for CO_2 emissions and the CO_2 emissions produced by the country's economy.

Usually, total final demand for goods and services produced in a country[11] (given by the *n*-vector **y**) has four main components: 'household consumption', 'government consumption', 'investment' ('changes in stocks' plus 'gross fixed capital formation'), and 'exports'. The first three categories constitute the domestic final demand (given by the *n*-vector $\mathbf{y}_{dom}$), while the last one represents foreign demand, for goods and services produced in the country under consideration (given by the *n*-vector $\mathbf{y}_{exp}$). Additionally, lets consider a diagonal matrix $\mathbf{Z}_{nxn}$, with only three non-zero elements, which are the ratios of the sum of 'final consumption of households' and 'collective consumption', to domestic final demand, for the three fossil fuel sectors.

Accordingly, equations (3) and (4), representing total primary energy requirements by an economy, as well as the corresponding total CO_2 emissions, respectively, can be rewritten as:

---

[6] The final demand for fossil fuels corresponding to investment is not used (burnt), and consequently do not correspond to CO_2 emissions. Furthermore, the final demand for fossil fuels corresponding to exports, as these fuels leave the country concerned, are used elsewhere and therefore does not corresponds to domestic CO_2 emissions. Thus, as interest is directed towards only those fuels which were burnt (Proops *et al.*, 1993), there is need to consider only the final consumption ('final consumption of households' plus 'collective consumption'). Accordingly, we can 'modify' the final demand vector (**y**) to 'exclude' the investment and export components, by premultiplying it by a suitable scaling matrix, $\mathbf{H}_{nxn}$, and therefore using a modified final demand vector (**Hy**).

[7] This expression is also the result of some considerations, namely: *n* activity sectors; three types of fossil fuels: natural gas, coal and oil; and the assumption that the use of fossil fuels by any sector remains proportional to the total output from that sector.

[8] These figures clearly show that the amounts of CO_2 emitted directly depend on the fuel, with more CO_2 being emitted per unit of energy content for coal than for oil and for natural gas.

[9] For reasons of completeness, other minor sources of CO_2 emissions – other then fossil-fuel burning – should have been included in the analysis. Proops et al. (1993) do this in their analysis. However, in this specific study, and because of a lack of detailed information for Portugal, the production of CO_2 emissions from non-fuel sources will not be covered.

[10] If we use $\hat{\mathbf{e}}$ (where $\hat{\mathbf{e}}$ is a (3x3) matrix, with the vector **e** on the diagonal) instead of **e'**, the fuel sources fundamentally responsible for CO_2 emissions are explicitly identified, since a vector of pollution intensities for each of the fuels combusted in the economy is estimated. If we use **e'**, as is the case here, then the scalar of pollution obtained represents pollution intensities for the total fuels burnt.

[11] It is important to recall that what is considered in the I-O table is the domestic output by sector (i.e., imports are excluded); therefore, the energy requirements (and consequent CO_2 emissions) correspond to goods and services produced in the country.

$$\mathbf{f} = \mathbf{f}_{\mathbf{dom}} + \mathbf{f}_{\mathbf{exp}} = [\mathbf{C}(\mathbf{I}\text{-}\mathbf{A})^{-1}\mathbf{y}_{\mathbf{dom}} + \mathbf{PZy}_{\mathbf{dom}}] + [\mathbf{C}(\mathbf{I}\text{-}\mathbf{A})^{-1}\mathbf{y}_{\mathbf{exp}}], \quad (5)$$

and

$$c = c_{dom} + c_{exp} = [\mathbf{e}'\mathbf{C}(\mathbf{I}\text{-}\mathbf{A})^{-1}\mathbf{y}_{\mathbf{dom}} + \mathbf{e}'\mathbf{PZy}_{\mathbf{dom}}] + [\mathbf{e}'\mathbf{C}(\mathbf{I}\text{-}\mathbf{A})^{-1}\mathbf{y}_{\mathbf{exp}}]. \quad (6)$$ [12]

Equation (6) can be interpreted as follows. The term ($\mathbf{e}'\mathbf{C}(\mathbf{I}\text{-}\mathbf{A})^{-1}\mathbf{y}_{\mathbf{dom}}$) corresponds to the CO_2 emissions attributable to fossil fuel use for producing goods and services for domestic final demand. The term ($\mathbf{e}'\mathbf{PZy}_{\mathbf{dom}}$) corresponds to the CO_2 emissions attributable directly to (domestic) households. Finally, the term ($\mathbf{e}'\mathbf{C}(\mathbf{I}\text{-}\mathbf{A})^{-1}\mathbf{y}_{\mathbf{exp}}$) represents the CO_2 emissions attributable to the (domestic) production of goods and services to export[13].

However, if one intends to determine only the CO_2 emissions for which one country is 'responsible', the country's emissions attributable to exports should not be considered, and the CO_2 emissions taking place in foreign countries, but resulting from the satisfaction of the country's imports, should be added on (Gay and Proops, 1993: 130).

Regarding an accurate calculation of CO_2 emissions because of imports, the task is not so straightforward as for exports, since new energy intensity coefficients should be estimated based on I-O tables of the relevant countries from which the imports come. Evidently, this would be a major task, if not operationally impossible. However, as Machado et al. (2001) remark, if the aim is to assess the energy 'saved' by a country, by importing non-primary energy goods, then the appropriate energy intensity coefficients to be used in assessing the energy embodied in imports are the same estimated for domestic industrial production.

Therefore, considering that **B** is the imports coefficient matrix, and that $\mathbf{y}_{\mathbf{imp}}$ represents the country's (final demand) imports vector[14], total energy 'embodied' in a country's imports (given by the 3-vector $\mathbf{f}_{\mathbf{imp}}$) will be given by

$$\mathbf{f}_{\mathbf{imp}} = \mathbf{C}(\mathbf{I}\text{-}\mathbf{A})^{-1}\mathbf{B}(\mathbf{I}\text{-}\mathbf{A})^{-1}\mathbf{y}_{\mathbf{dom}} + \mathbf{C}(\mathbf{I}\text{-}\mathbf{A})^{-1}\mathbf{y}_{\mathbf{imp}} \quad (7)$$

Thus, the level of CO_2 emissions that occurs in foreign countries in order to meet the domestic and the imported final demand of a country is given by:

$$c_{imp} = \mathbf{e}'\mathbf{C}(\mathbf{I}\text{-}\mathbf{A})^{-1}\mathbf{B}(\mathbf{I}\text{-}\mathbf{A})^{-1}\mathbf{y}_{\mathbf{dom}} + \mathbf{e}'\mathbf{C}(\mathbf{I}\text{-}\mathbf{A})^{-1}\mathbf{y}_{\mathbf{imp}} \quad (8)$$ [15]

Finally, combining the results achieved above concerning CO_2 emissions, it is also possible to determine:

- the country's 'responsibility' for CO_2 emissions (given by the scalar c_{resp}), i.e. the CO_2 emissions attributable to consumption by one country's residents, whether arising from domestic or from foreign goods and services; as well as

$$c_{resp} = \mathbf{e}'\mathbf{C}(\mathbf{I}\text{-}\mathbf{A})^{-1}\mathbf{y}_{\mathbf{dom}} + \mathbf{e}'\mathbf{PZy}_{\mathbf{dom}} + \mathbf{e}'\mathbf{C}(\mathbf{I}\text{-}\mathbf{A})^{-1}\mathbf{B}(\mathbf{I}\text{-}\mathbf{A})^{-1}\mathbf{y}_{\mathbf{dom}} + \mathbf{e}'\mathbf{C}(\mathbf{I}\text{-}\mathbf{A})^{-1}\mathbf{y}_{\mathbf{imp}} \quad (9)$$

---

[12] The reader will note that the terms ($\mathbf{PHy}_{\mathbf{exp}}$) and ($\mathbf{e}'\mathbf{PHy}_{\mathbf{exp}}$) (implicit in equations (3) and (4), respectively) have been suppressed, as this would have no sensible interpretation. Moreover, the reader will also note that terms of the type ($\mathbf{PHy}_{\mathbf{dom}}$) and ($\mathbf{e}'\mathbf{PHy}_{\mathbf{dom}}$) do not 'come out', but instead there appear the terms ($\mathbf{PZy}_{\mathbf{dom}}$) and ($\mathbf{e}'\mathbf{PZy}_{\mathbf{dom}}$), respectively. This change, from matrix **H** to matrix **Z**, can be understood through the analysis of their own definitions. Indeed, as explained concerning final demand energy requirements (equation (3)), the final demand vector (**y**) was 'modified' to 'exclude' the investment and export components, by premultiplying it by the (nxn) scaling matrix **H**, and therefore using a modified final demand vector (**Hy**). Therefore, as what is now under consideration is the domestic final demand vector ($\mathbf{y}_{\mathbf{dom}}$) (that does not include exports), only the investment component needs to be excluded. This can be done by premultiplying the domestic final demand vector ($\mathbf{y}_{\mathbf{imp}}$) by a suitable scaling matrix, **Z**, and therefore using a modified final demand vector ($\mathbf{Zy}_{\mathbf{dom}}$).

[13] Of course, the interpretation of equation (5) is similar, but concerning energy requirements instead of CO_2 emissions.

[14] Concerning the (intermediate demand) imports coefficients matrix (**B**), it is achieved by dividing the imports used to satisfy the intermediate demand of the country's sectors by the domestic total inputs (=total outputs) by industry. Concerning the imported direct final demand, as interest is directed towards only those fuels which are burnt, only its domestic final consumption is considered. Therefore, the final demand vector ($\mathbf{y}_{\mathbf{imp}}$) considered in the study includes only the imported final demand components: 'final consumption of households' plus 'collective consumption'. A detailed analysis of the calculation of CO_2 attributable to imports can be found in Proops *et al.* (1993).

[15] The first term corresponds to foreign CO_2 emissions attributable to one country's imports that will be used as intermediate consumption, i.e., attributable to imported products that will be introduced in the country's production processes in order to satisfy domestic final demand (which is given by vector $\mathbf{y}_{\mathbf{dom}}$). The second term corresponds to foreign CO_2 emissions that occur to meet the country's imported final demand (imports for direct final consumption, which is given by vector $\mathbf{y}_{\mathbf{imp}}$).

- the CO_2 emissions produced by the country's economy (given by the scalar c_{emis}), i.e. the CO_2 emissions attributable to the production made in the country's economy, whether demanded by national or by foreign final consumers and industries.

$$c_{emis} = \mathbf{e'C(I\text{-}A)^{-1}y_{dom}} + \mathbf{e'PZy_{dom}} + \mathbf{e'C(I\text{-}A)^{-1}y_{exp}} \qquad \mathbf{(10)}$$ [16]

THE PORTUGUESE CASE

In this section, there will be presented an I-O empirical application of the energy-economy-environment interactions for Portugal, namely concerning the energy intensities and CO_2 emissions derived from fossil fuels use, according to the modelling approach described above.

Used Data

Portuguese National Accounts and the I-O Table

A number of adjustments needs to be made to the way figures are presented by the Portuguese system of economic accounts, published by the National Institute of Statistics (INE), to achieve a valuation of the supply and use flows as consistently and homogenously as possible, and obtain the I-O tables that are the basis for the empirical analysis to be performed in this work. However, Portuguese national accounts have not been producing the 'auxiliary' data to perform the required treatments, surveyed with a breakdown of all interindustry transactions (by industries and by products) and of final uses by product. Thus we will use the most recent symmetric (product by product) I-O table at basic prices available for Portugal, produced by Dias (2009), for 2005[17], as the basis for the analysis performed in this study.

It is also important to mention that in order to be able to explore alternative scenarios (in future work), namely concerning eventual impacts of changes in electricity generation, or impacts of changes in the use of different transport modes, we disaggregated sectors 40 and 60 (according to the classification of the economic activities proposed by the System of European Accounts - SEA95) as follows:

40 - Electricity, gas, steam and hot water supply

  40101A - Production of electricity from fossil fuels

  40101B - Production of electricity from renewable sources

  40102 - Distribution and trade of Electricity

  402 – Manufacture, distribution and trade of gas

60 - Land transport and transport via pipeline services

  601 – Transport via railways

  602 – Other land transports

  603 - Transport via pipelines

This disaggregation was performed according to more disaggregated data from supply and use tables for 2005 (INE, 2009). However, as there is no official data for some of the sub-sectors (with exception of information regarding the disaggregation of the natural gas sector, by Dias, 2009), we have assumed that the proportion of each sub-sector in relation to the total of the sector presented in the supply and use tables would be acceptable to disaggregate the corresponding values in the symmetric I-O table (Dias, 2009).

Moreover, to perform the disaggregation of sector 401, following Proops et al. (1993), it is assumed that: the two generating sectors (40101A and 40101B) sell all of their output to the distribution sector (40102)[18]; the fuel inputs to

---

[16] This representation of the total CO_2 emissions produced by an economy is no more than the rewriting of the expression used in equation (6). Alternatively, one can represent CO_2 emissions produced by the country's economy considering its dependence on total final demand, which is no more than the expression used in equation (4).

[17] Of course, the absence of more up-to-date data may constitute a drawback to providing useful information for practical policy decisions. However, the basic economic structure of the economy changes relatively slowly over time and therefore, for many aspects, the table(s) will be relevant over a reasonable period of time (Miller and Blair, 2009).

[18] This means that the two electricity-generating sectors have zero final demand.

electricity are attributed entirely to fossil fuel generation[19], and all other inputs are split between the two generating sectors in proportion to their total output; and all purchases of electricity by the remaining sectors and by final demand are supplied by electricity distribution.

This resulted in the use of a *(61x61)* product-by-product I-O table, for Portugal, in 2005. From this table was derived the matrix **A**, by dividing inter-industry flows by the total inputs by industry at basic prices, as usual. It was also from this table that were derived the matrices **H** and **Z**, as well as the various vectors according to the different components of final demand considered, i.e.: $\mathbf{y}$, $\mathbf{y}_{\mathbf{dom}}$, $\mathbf{y}_{\mathbf{exp}}$, and $\mathbf{y}_{\mathbf{imp}}$.

The Physical Quantities of Primary Fossil Fuels used in the Portuguese Economy

To perform the study there is also the need to consider the (physical) quantities of primary fossil fuels used by each industry per unit of total output, as well as the quantities of fossil fuels used per unit of final demand. However, such data was generally not directly available in the appropriate, or consistent, form. Therefore, there was need to make some assumptions and estimations in order to make consistent the different data sources, namely the I-O table (provided by Dias, 2009) and the energy balance statistics (supplied by the Portuguese Directorate General of Energy and Geology – DGEG, 2010).

According to the 'Energy Balance' statistics for 2005 (DGEG, 2010), and excluding the value of fuels consumption for final use as raw materials, it was considered that total use of energy, to distribute by the 61 sectors and by final consumption, was of 14,059,369 and 3,761,084 tonnes of oil equivalent (toe) of oil and natural gas, respectively. These values were considered as credible totals of domestic energy use (by type of fuel) and it was from these, combined with monetary data from the symmetric I-O table, that were derived the physical quantities of oil and gas used by each of the 61 sectors and by final consumers in 2005[20]. Then, dividing these values by the corresponding element of the total input vector or by the final demand vector, it was possible to determine the primary energy intensities (or requirements) per unit of total output by sector (matrix $\mathbf{C}_{2x63}$) and per unit of final demand (matrix $\mathbf{P}_{2x63}$).

Assessment of Primary Energy Requirements

In this section there will first be determined (both by sector and in aggregated terms) the primary energy intensities per unit of total output and per unit of final demand, in terms of toe/million of Euro, and then the corresponding energy requirements will be estimated[21].

Before the presentation of the main results, it is important to note that the numbers which were estimated through the performance of this study are not exact, but carry some degree of inaccuracy with them. This is not only because of the level of (in)accuracy on the data used as 'inputs' to the model, but also because of the several assumptions made in its construction. Therefore, they should be considered as rough estimates of the energy requirements and CO_2 emissions, mainly to give us a broad idea of the amounts involved and on the inter-industrial distribution.

Primary Energy Intensities

Table **1** (see Appendix) contains the basic data on fuel use (for convenience of presentation, the elements of the matrices are presented in transposed form).

The highest energy intensity for oil is found in sectors 602-Other land transport and 40101A-Production of electricity from fossil fuels, mainly because of direct production demand. Sectors 40102-Distribution and trade of electricity and 23-Manufacture of coke, refined petroleum products also present relatively high energy intensities. As expected, other sectors that offer transport services (61-Water transport, 601-Transport via railways, and 62-Air transport) are also high ranking (namely 6th, 7th and 8th) for oil intensity use. For natural gas the highest intensities

---

[19] Which means that electricity generation through renewable sources and the distribution side of electricity are recorded as using no fossil fuel at all, which is clearly an underestimation (Gay and Proops, 1993).

[20] It is important to note that, as presented in Section 3, the use of coal (as a fossil fuel), which according to the 'Energy Balance' statistics was of 3,348.835 toe in 2005, should also have been considered in this analysis. However, the nil value for this sector's total input in the symmetric I-O table (Dias, 2009) means that it is not technically possible to find a 'production technology' for the coal sector, and it justifies the elimination of this sector from the symmetric I-O table. Accordingly, the estimation of energy requirements and CO_2 emissions will be made considering only two primary energy sources: oil and natural gas. Consequently, matrices **C** and **P** are of dimension (2x61), and vector **e** is a 2-vector.

[21] It is important to note that sectors 10–Mining of coal and lignite and 12-Mining of uranium and thorium presented nil value in all of the cells of the I-O table for 2005, reason why they were not considered in the model.

are found in sectors 40101A-Production of electricity from fossil fuels, 40102-Distribution and trade of electricity, and 402-Manufacture, distribution and trade of gas. The first results mainly from direct production demand, while the second derives from indirect production demand and the third results from the importance of natural gas consumption directly by final consumers. Sector 26-Manufacture of other non-metallic mineral products also presents relatively high energy intensities for both fuels. On the other hand, the smallest energy intensity coefficients were generally registered in the services sectors.

Comparing direct and indirect energy intensities corresponding to production demand, it can be seen that concerning the use of gas there are several sectors that do not present values for direct energy intensity. Concerning the use of oil, there are figures for direct intensities for almost all the sectors, although they are almost negligible for the services sectors. Therefore, it is clear that, generally speaking, the indirect production energy intensities are typically larger than the direct ones. This result clearly emphasizes the importance of the use of an inter-sectoral analysis.

Primary Energy Requirements Corresponding to Domestic Consumption

Following equation (5), multiplying the primary energy intensities presented above by the domestic final demand vector, one achieves the primary energy requirements of the economy to satisfy domestic consumption, which are shown in Table **2** (see Appendix). It was estimated that the consumption by the Portuguese of domestic production in 2005 required the use of $9{,}052.3 \times 10^3$ toe of oil and $2{,}736.5 \times 10^3$ toe of natural gas.

Of this, sectors 40102-Distribution and trade of electricity, 45-Construction, 55-Hotels and restaurants, 52-Retail trade and 75-Public administration and defence, are the ones that clearly require more natural gas. Indeed, the satisfaction of final demand for the production of sector 40102-Distribution and trade of electricity alone is ultimately responsible for 34.1%, and together with 45-Construction (14.2%) for almost half, of total natural gas requirements. Moreover, it is also important to emphasize that the natural gas requirements of all these sectors correspond almost entirely to indirect production demand. This result is clear evidence of the 'value-added' that the I-O technique may bring to policy analysis, as an approach that takes economic interrelations into account, as on a first 'thought' one might have excluded these sectors from the 'list' of those for whose production is required the use of natural gas.

On the other hand, the satisfaction of final demand for the products from sectors 602-Other land transport (16.5%), 45-Construction (14.6%), 40102-Distribution and trade of electricity (10.1%), 85-Health and social work (6.6%), and 51-Wholesale trade and commission trade (6.3%) are responsible for more than half of oil needs. Here, in opposition to what happens for natural gas, the 'responsibility' for oil requirements does not have a so clear 'pattern'. Indeed, if for the first sector the main 'guilt' is attributable to the sector's direct production demand (as fuels are inputs directly required for the production of transport services), for the second is mainly attributable to the sector's indirect production demand, but with some 'contribution' of the direct production demand. Moreover, for the third the 'guilt' is totally attributable to the sector's indirect production demand (as it is assumed that Distribution and trade of electricity does not directly require oil, but the production of this sector requires inputs from other sectors whose production directly or indirectly requires primary fuels).

Relating these results with those from Table **1**, one can notice that the sectors that are more highly energy intensive are not necessarily the ones whose total production requires more energy. This is explained by what might be called the 'scale effect' of the final demand (corresponding to the fact that total energy requirements of any sector are given by the product of the intensity per unit of final demand and the level of final demand)[22].

Assessment of CO_2 Emissions

In this section there will first be calculated the CO_2 intensities corresponding to the primary energy intensities presented in the previous section, in terms of tonnes of CO_2/million Euro. Subsequently, there will be reported the total CO_2 emissions for a given structure of Portuguese final consumption, both in aggregate and disaggregated to 61 sectors.

---

[22] Indeed, sector 45-Construction and sectors, 51-Wholesale trade and commission trade, 52-Retail trade, 55-Hotels and restaurants, 75-Public administration and defence, for example, which were generally seen to have relatively low energy-intensities, require important amounts of fuels; this happens because these sectors account for important shares of the transactions made in the Portuguese economy. Conversely, for example, sectors such as 26-Manufacture of other non-metallic mineral products, and 21-Manufacture of pulp, paper and paper products are quite fuel-intensive, but they do not account for significant amounts of fuels because their final demand is not very considerable (this indicates that most of the energy required in making their products will be recorded as indirect energy requirements for other sector(s)).

CO_2 Intensities

As derives from the methodology proposed in Section 3, particularly from equation (4), it is possible to estimate CO_2 intensities corresponding to direct and to indirect production demand, as well as to direct consumption demand (for fossil fuels). The figures estimated, expressed in terms of tonnes of CO_2 emitted per million Euro of final demand, for each sector, can be found in Table **3** (again, for convenience of presentation, in transpose form - see Appendix).

Concerning total CO_2 intensities, sectors 40101A-Production of electricity from fossil fuels, 602-Other land transport, 40102-Distribution and trade of electricity and 26-Manufacture of other non-metallic mineral products, are (unsurprisingly) the ones that appear in the upper ranking. The total CO_2 intensity of these sectors (except sector 40102-Distribution and trade of electricity) is dominated (in 97.7, 86 and 64.3%, respectively) by the intensities corresponding to direct production demand. However, for the great majority of the remaining sectors the CO_2 intensities correspond mainly to indirect production demand.

CO_2 Emissions Corresponding to Domestic Consumption

As derives from equation (4), multiplying the CO_2 intensities determined above by the domestic final demand figures, one achieves the corresponding tonnes of CO_2 emitted by each sector. The results obtained are reported in Table **4** (see Appendix). According to the estimation made through the model, the production of CO_2 emissions by the consumption of domestic production by the residents in Portugal was, in 2005, of $33{,}910.9\text{x}10^3$ tonnes. The estimation of this total value for CO_2 emissions, although similar to the ones estimated by alternative methods, should be highlighted mainly because of the way it was obtained, namely the fact that it can be decomposed according to the sectors considered.

The top five sectors 'responsible' for those CO_2 emissions are 40102-Distribution and trade of electricity (14.7%), 45-Construction (14.6%), 602-Other land transport (13.4%), 85- Health and social work (6.0%), and 15-Manufacture of food products and beverage (5.7%). This means that the final demand for the products of these five sectors account for more than half of total CO_2 emissions attributable to production in the Portuguese economy.

Moreover, as the CO_2 emissions by sector 602-Other land transport is largely connected with freight and passengers transport, and as the production of CO_2 emissions by sector 23-Manufacture of coke, refined petroleum products, is extensively associated with the use of private cars, one can say that (personal and public) transport (of passengers and goods) was 'responsible' for almost one-sixth of all the emissions that occurred in Portugal in 2005.

Another key result is the significant importance of the indirect production demand (of fuels) for production (by industries) in the generation of CO_2 emissions. Indeed, more than two-thirds (72.2%) of the CO_2 emissions are attributable to indirect demand, while only 26.2 per cent of the emissions are attributable to direct demand for fossil fuels by industries; the remaining 1.6% are directly attributable to household demand for fossil fuels (mainly associated with fuel use in private cars, and at a much smaller scale with the use of cooking and heating equipment). Accordingly, it is noticeable that the great majority of industries are 'responsible' for much more CO_2 production indirectly than directly[23]. Again, this type of result clearly reinforces the importance of using an approach that considers inter-industrial relations when analysing CO_2 emissions.

Similarly to what was observed in relation to energy requirements, relating these results with those concerning CO_2 intensities (comparing results from tables 3 and 4), one can notice that sectors that are more highly CO_2 intensive are not necessarily the ones whose production generates more CO_2 emissions, again explained by the 'scale effect' of the final demand (corresponding to the fact that total CO_2 emissions of any sector are given by the product of the intensity per unit of final demand and the level of final demand).

Analysis of Energy and CO_2 'Embodied' in a Country's International Trade

The study performed above concentrates on the appraisal of energy requirements and corresponding CO_2 emissions attributable to the (final and intermediate) consumption by the Portuguese of goods and services produced in

[23] Unsurprisingly, among the exceptions, i.e. the sectors that have a significant (direct) production element, one can find, e.g.: 05-Fishing, fish farming and related service activities, 26-Manufacture of other non-metallic mineral products, and sectors that offer transport services (602-Other land transport, 61-Water transport, and 62-Air transport).

Portugal. However, the reality is that Portugal is an open economy, and GHG emissions and climate change are global phenomena, with transboundary effects. Therefore, it is important to analyse what happens to energy use and CO_2 emissions in what concerns to Portuguese imports and exports of non-primary energy goods and services.

As described above, taking some simplifying assumptions, it is possible to estimate the energy and CO_2 'embodied' in the Portuguese international trade (see Table **5**, presented in the Appendix), which can be analysed both at aggregated and at disaggregated levels. It can be said that it was estimated that in 2005 there were $4{,}442.9 \times 10^3$ toe of oil and 867.7×10^3 toe of natural gas 'embodied' in Portuguese exports. The sectors that contributed the most to these energy requirements were: 602-Other land transport, 26- Manufacture of other non-metallic mineral products, 62-Air transport, 23-Manufacture of coke, refined petroleum products, 17-Manufacture of textiles, and 21-Manufacture of pulp, paper and paper products. While for the generality of these sectors the energy-intensity is relatively high, it is important to mention that the last two (i.e. 17 and 21) are sectors near the middle of the energy-intensities' ranking; but its significance in terms of energy 'embodied' in exports is not at all surprising, mainly because of the 'scale effect', as they are traditionally very important sectors in Portuguese exports.

Moreover, it was estimated that $3{,}112.4 \times 10^3$ toe of oil and 238.3×10^3 toe of natural gas were 'embodied' in Portuguese imports, which can be interpreted as the quantities of energy that were 'saved' by Portugal because it imported the corresponding goods and services instead of producing them in Portugal. In terms of ranking, it is worthwhile to mention sectors 24-Manufacture of chemicals and chemical products and 15-Manufacture of food products and beverages.

Thus, it can be said that in 2005 Portugal faced a positive 'primary energy trade balance' (for both oil and natural gas). In other words, one can say that the amount of primary energy 'embodied' in Portuguese exports was greater than the amount of primary energy that was 'saved' by Portugal because it imported the corresponding goods and services instead of producing them in Portugal. This result can represent an unfavourable situation, particularly taking into account the strong external energy dependence of the Portuguese economy.

Concerning CO_2 emissions, the main results obtained are in accordance to the ones found for energy requirements. Indeed, for example the sectors which contributed the most to CO_2 emissions attributable to Portuguese exports were: 602-Other land transport, 26-Manufacture of other non-metallic mineral products, 62-Air transport, 23-Manufacture of coke, refined petroleum products, 24- Manufacture of chemicals and chemical products, and 17-Manufacture of textiles. The estimated CO_2 emissions attributable to Portuguese exports were of $15{,}532.5 \times 10^3$ tonnes.

The top three sectors in terms of 'responsibility' for foreign CO_2 emissions in order to satisfy the final demand of the Portuguese were 15-Manufacture of food products and beverages, 34-Manufacture of motor vehicles, trailers and semi-trailers, and 45-Construction, not because of their CO_2-intensity, but mainly for the reason that their final demand by the Portuguese was high. It is also important to note that about 60.2% of the $10{,}117.1 \times 10^3$ tonnes of CO_2 emitted in foreign countries in order to satisfy Portuguese final demand are attributed to imported goods and services that were used in further production (and not to be directly used by final consumers).

Therefore, in 2005, the difference between the emissions that occurred in Portugal to satisfy foreign final demand and the emissions that occurred in foreign countries to satisfy Portuguese final demand was of $5{,}415.4 \times 10^3$ tonnes, which means that Portugal faced a positive 'CO_2 emissions trade balance'. In other words, one can say that CO_2 emissions released in Portuguese territory to satisfy the final demand of non-residents for goods and services produced in Portugal (exports) are greater than the CO_2 emissions that were not emitted in Portuguese territory because residents imported the corresponding goods and services (instead of producing them in Portugal).

As for the 'primary energy trade balance', the sectors which most contributed for this result in the 'CO_2 emissions trade balance' were 602-Other land transport, 26-Manufacture of other non-metallic mineral products and 62-Air transport.

To sum up, one can say that, according to the estimations, in 2005 total exports of goods and services produced in Portugal 'embodied' more energy and CO_2 than total imports made by residents in Portugal.

The Country's 'Responsibility' for CO_2 Emissions *versus* CO_2 Emissions Produced by the Country's Economy

Finally, combining the results achieved in the two previous sections, as shown in Table **6** (see Appendix), it is also possible to determine:

- the country's 'responsibility' for CO_2 emissions (c_{resp} – as results from equation (9)), and
- the CO_2 emissions produced by the country's economy (c_{emis} – as results from equation (10)).

In 2005, 49,443.4x10^3 tonnes of CO_2 were emitted on Portuguese territory, derived from the use of fossil fuels[24]. This figure corresponds to the CO_2 emissions that were produced by the Portuguese economy in 2005, in order to satisfy the (domestic and foreign) final demand for goods and services domestically produced. Of these, 68.6% occurred in order to satisfy the final demand by the residents, while the remaining 31.4% resulted from the satisfaction of the foreign final demand (exports).

It is important to highlight that the five sectors that contributed the most to this amount of CO_2 emissions (602-Other land transport, 40102-Distribution and trade of electricity, 45-Construction, 15-Manufacture of food products and beverages, and 51- Wholesale trade) account for almost half of total CO_2 emissions attributable to production in the Portuguese economy. Moreover, as the production of CO_2 emissions to satisfy the final demand for 602-Other land transport is mostly connected with freight and passengers transport, and as the CO_2 emissions by sector 23-Manufacture of coke, refined petroleum products are importantly associated with the use of private cars, one can say that transports are 'responsible' for around one-fifth of all the emissions that occurred to satisfy the final demand in 2005.

Concerning the CO_2 emissions whose 'responsibility' is attributed to the consumption of the residents in Portugal[25], whether of goods and services domestically produced or imported, the amount estimated was of 44.028x10^3. To be illustrative, one can say, in a simplified way, that from these CO_2 emissions that occurred throughout the world because of the consumption of residents in Portugal, only 77% were released in Portuguese territory, while the remaining 23% were released in foreign countries.

Thus, incorporating the flows of international trade in the analysis, one can notice that, in 2005, the CO_2 emissions 'released in Portuguese territory' (i.e. attributable to the satisfaction of both domestic and foreign final demand for goods and services produced in Portugal) were (slightly) higher than the ones that were 'released throughout the world' to satisfy the final demand of the residents in Portugal.

This type of analysis can be of great importance in the context of the Kyoto Protocol, as it draws attention to the possibility that some countries may be tempted to reduce their GHG emissions 'artificially', mostly by stopping producing certain (energy and CO_2 intensive) goods to import them from other countries[26] (Machado et al., 2001: 410). On a first approach one can admit that such kind of attitude can eventually attenuate the problem at the internal level, but the result might be the same at the global level (i.e., the CO_2 emissions produced by the world economy will be similar). However, this will not be true if the imports of those goods and services become from countries where they are produced with more efficient technologies (in terms of energy requirements and/or making use of 'cleaner' fuels).

---

[24] This figure is slightly lower (-0,19%) than alternative estimates made by IA (2007) (*Instituto do Ambiente* - body of the Portuguese Ministry of Environment), following the 'IPCC Guidelines' (IPCC, 2006), which reports that the total production of CO_2 derived from oil and natural gas combustion (Reference Approach), in 2005, was of 49,537.1x10^3 tonnes of CO_2. Moreover, according to IA (2007), there were generated 12,633.6x10^3 tonnes of CO_2 as result of the use of coal. Thus, this figure for CO_2 emissions resulting from coal combustion can be considered as a good estimate of the emissions which we have not accounted for in this study (indeed, as mentioned before, for reasons of application of the I-O technique to the Portuguese data it was not possible to incorporate in this analysis the sectoral assessment of coal requirements and corresponding CO_2 emissions).

[25] The top sectors in terms of contribution to these emissions were the same mentioned above for the emissions of CO_2 produced by the Portuguese economy in 2005 (although not exactly by the same order).

[26] Conversely, the results achieved in this work illustrate the circumstance that Portugal might be penalised in terms of its efforts to reduce CO_2 emissions, required to accomplish the Kyoto Protocol's requirements, relatively to what might be considered its 'ecological responsibility' (since Portugal is 'responsible' for less CO_2 emissions than it actually emits).

POLICY RELEVANCE

In this study, an extensive I-O analysis was used to investigate energy flows and CO_2 emissions in the Portuguese economy, for 2005. The approach adopted allowed the distinction between the 'direct consumption demand' (by final consumers), and the (direct and indirect) 'production demand' (by industries) for primary energy fuels.

One of the key results found was the significant importance of the indirect production demand for fuels in the production of CO_2. Indeed, it was seen that more than two-thirds of the CO_2 emissions are attributable to indirect demand for fossil fuels to satisfy the domestic final demand for goods and services produced in Portugal. These results 'indicate how crucial it is to use an approach which takes economic interrelations into account when analysing CO_2 production' (Gay and Proops, 1993), and therefore show that the analysis here performed has clear policy relevance.

Indeed, it appears that there is significant general awareness about the CO_2 emissions that occur from direct energy use in households and private cars, as well as about the CO_2 emitted directly in energy industries and by the transport sectors[27]. Thus, it looks almost 'natural' that important reductions in CO_2 emissions in Portugal can be achieved by focusing policies on transport and on the production and use of electricity.

However, the major importance of industries' indirect production demand for fuels, and consequently the fact that the great majority of direct consumption is 'responsible' for much more CO_2 production indirectly than directly is generally ignored by producers, consumers and policy-makers. For example, the results of this approach indicate the singular importance associated with the flows of energy and CO_2 emissions explained by the final demand for the production of sector 45-Construction. However, until now the authorities did not gave it special attention. Indeed, if we observe, for example, the sectors included in ETS, it becomes evident the absence of this sector, since the scheme consider the sectors which are 'responsible' for emissions according to direct use of fuels in their production activity (as, e.g., the industries of glass, cement and ceramics).

The study here performed also revealed that the sectors that are more highly energy (or CO_2) intensive are not necessarily the ones whose production requires more energy (or which produce more CO_2 emissions), which is explained by what might be called as the 'scale effect' of the final demand. At this level, it is important to highlight, e.g., that sectors 26-Manufacture of other non-metallic mineral products and 21-Manufacture of pulp, paper and paper products, which represent an important part of the economic units included in the ETS, where there included considering their 'apparent' energy intensity, but the analysis made in this study indicates that in terms of responsibility for emissions they only assume relevance in Portugal when considering the final demand by non-residents (i.e., only considering the 'scale effect' of exports).

Moreover, as shown, according to the 'components' of the (total) final demand considered, it is possible to discuss the flows of energy and CO_2 emissions associated with international trade. The analysis of such flows also alert us for the possibility, in a near future, of a possible confront with logics of international specialization where one of the dimensions taken into account results from 'comparative advantage' in terms of energy efficiency and CO_2 emissions.

Therefore, the analysis performed here may help policy-makers in dealing with the problem of CO_2 emissions as they are better informed about the root causes of some outcomes. Thus, it is possible to claim that one of the key accomplishments of the use of this type of modelling, which integrates economic, energy and environmental interactions in an I-O framework, is that it allows the analysis of how energy, and therefore CO_2 emissions, are related to industrial production, and ultimately to final demand, making it a tool particularly important for (*ex ante*[28] and/or *ex post*) policy analysis purposes.

[27] For example, it was not surprising the estimation that, in a broad sense, transports were 'responsible' for about 15% of all the emissions that occurred in 2005 in order to satisfy domestic demand. These findings mean that the reductions in the final demand for these sector's outputs are the ones that would be most worthwhile for reducing Portuguese CO_2 emissions.

[28] Indeed, both the model and the database are formulated in terms of detailed technical parameters, on a multi-sector basis, that can be directly evaluated by technical experts and readily changed in order to explore the consequences of alternative scenarios (see Cruz, 2002).

LIMITATIONS AND PROPOSALS FOR FUTURE RESEARCH

The empirical exercise performed in this research presents, as any other study of this nature, important limitations, which should be weighed in terms of the methodology used (see Miller and Blair, 2009, for an exhaustive analysis of this methodology's limitations) and of the hypothesis taken in the process of data treatment. These limitations do not invalidate the results achieved, but should be reflected in their interpretation, namely in processes directed towards helping policy-makers in the definition and adoption of specific policy measures.

It is also relevant to mention that the information generated by the analysis undertaken was vast. However, only some of it is shown in the tables presented. This was a deliberate approach, as there is the need to condense information, so that it can be comprehended and thus allow policy conclusions to be drawn. Nevertheless, it is also worthwhile to note that the full potential of the data set was not exploited; indeed, many areas of further work remain, and there are several extensions to the model that should be explored in later stages of the research.

Indeed, in future work some scenarios should be performed in order to obtain a broad idea of the consequences (in terms of amounts of reductions in energy requirements and CO_2 emissions) of:

- recent national policy measures to promote non-fossil-fuel electricity generation;
- switching to a mix of fuel inputs with lower CO_2 emissions (inter-fuel substitution), namely concerning an increasing penetration of natural gas use in industries;
- changes in the technologies used for specific purposes (energy efficiency);
- modification in the structure of inter-industry relations, as well as in the structure and in the level of the final demand.

Finally, it will also be important to perform the analysis for different years and to study the reasons behind the changes which might have occurred, namely through techniques of structural decomposition analysis. Also, it can particularly relevant to present contributes that allow us to become aware not only of the reactions of the sectors included in NAPs 2, but also to identify the weak and strong points, the threats and the opportunities, that this process may bring to the Portuguese economy, with the goal of anticipate potential (positive and negative) changes throughout the current (and eventually of a third) trading period.

REFERENCES

Barata, E. (2009). Economy-Waste-Environment Input-Output Model: Effects of Portuguese Production and Consumption, in: S. Suh (ed.) *Handbook of Input-Output Economics in Industrial Ecology*, Eco-Efficiency in Industry and Science, 23 (27), pp. 561-5601 (Springer).

Cruz, L. (2002). A Portuguese Energy-Economy-Environment I-O Model: Policy Applications, PhD Thesis (SPIRE, Keele University, UK).

Cruz, L., J. Proops, and P. Safanov (2005). I-O Models, in: J. Proops and P. Safanov (eds.) Modelling in Ecological Economics (3), pp. 36-57 (Edward Elgar, Cheltenham-UK).

Cruz, L. (2009). Application of IO Energy Analysis for CO_2 Emissions by the Portuguese Economy, in: S. Suh (ed.) Handbook of Input-Output Economics in Industrial Ecology, Eco-Efficiency in Industry and Science, 23 (25), pp. 507-532 (Springer).

DGEG (2010). *Estatíticas - Balanços Energéticos 2004-2005* (Direcção Geral de Energia e Geologia, Lisboa) *(portuguese only).*

Dias, A. (2009). *Sistema de Matrizes Input-Output para Portugal, 2005, com desagregação do sector do gás natural*, Doc. Trab. nº 4/2009 (Departamento de Prospectiva e Planeamento e Relações Internacionais, Lisboa) *(portuguese only).*

Faucheaux, S. and F. Levarlet (1999). Energy-economy-environment models, in: J. van den Bergh (ed.), *Handbook of Environmental and Resource Economics*, (73), pp. 1123-1145 (Edward Elgar, Cheltenham-UK).

Gay, P. and J. Proops (1993). Carbon-dioxide production by the UK economy: an I-O assessment, *Applied Energy*, 44, pp. 113-130.

Hayami, H., and M. Nakamura (2007). Greenhouse gas emissions in Canada and Japan: Sector-specific estimates and managerial and economic implications, *Journal of Environmental Management*, 85 (2), pp. 371-392.

Hawdon, D. and P. Pearson (1995). I-O simulations of energy, environment, economy interactions in the UK, *Energy Economics*, 17 (1), pp. 73-86.

IA (2007). *Portuguese National Inventory Report on Greenhouse Gases, 1990-2005, Submitted under the UNFCCC* (Instituto do Ambiente, Amadora).

INE (2009). *Contas Nacionais – Quadro de Recursos e Empregos - 2005* (Instituto Nacional de Estatística, Lisboa) *(portuguese only)*.

IPCC (2006). *2006 IPCC Guidelines for National Greenhouse Gas Inventories*, Prepared by the National Greenhouse Inventory Programme, Eggleston H.S., Buendia L., Miwa K., Ngara T. e Tanabe K. (eds). (IGES, Japan).

Llop, M. (2007). Economic structure and pollution intensity within the environmental input–output framework, *Energy Policy*, 35(6), pp. 3410-3417.

Machado, G., R. Schaeffer, and E. Worrell (2001). Energy and carbon embodied in the international trade of Brazil: an input–output approach, *Ecological Economics*, 39(3), pp. 409-424.

Miller, R. and P. Blair (2009). *I-O analysis: foundations and extensions*, 2nd Edition (Cambridge University Press, New York).

Proops, J., M. Faber and G. Wagenhals (1993). *Reducing CO_2 emissions – a comparative I-O study for Germany and the UK* (Springer-Verlag, Heidelberg, Germany).

Proops, J., P. Gay, S. Speck and T. Schröder (1996). The lifetime pollution implications of various types of electricity generation, *Energy Policy*, 24 (3), pp. 229-237.

Tunc, G., S. Turut-Asik and E. Akbostanci (2007). CO_2 emissions *vs.* CO_2 responsibility: An input-output approach for the Turkish economy, *Energy Policy*, 35(2), pp. 855-868.

Su, B., H. Huang, B. Ang, P. Zhou (2010). Input–output analysis of CO_2 emissions embodied in trade: The effects of sector aggregation, *Energy Economics*, 32(1), pp. 166-175.

van Asselt, H. and F. Biermann (2007). European emissions trading and the international competitiveness of energy-intensive industries: a legal and political evaluation of possible supporting measures, *Energy Policy*, 35(1), pp. 497-506.

APPENDIX

Table 1: Primary energy intensities

Table 1. Primary energy intensities		Corresponding to Direct Production demand		Corresponding to Indirect Production demand		Corresponding to Total Production demand		Corresponding to Direct Consumption Demand		Corresponding to Final Demand			
		C		C (A+A^2+...)		C(I-A)$^{-1}$		P		Total Primary Energy Intensity		Tt. Primary Energy Intens.' Rank	
	unit: *toe / million €*	(1) Oil	(2) Natural gas	(3) Oil	(4) Natural gas	(5) Oil	(6) Natural gas	(7) Oil	(8) Nat. gas	(9) Oil	(10) Natural gas	Oil	Natural gas
01	Agriculture, hunting and related service activities	33.6	0.5	56.3	17.8	89.8	18.3			89.8	18.3	14	22
02	Forestry, logging and related service activities	19.1		8.6	2.0	27.7	2.0			27.7	2.0	46	59
05	Fishing, fish farming and related service activities	128.4		42.7	9.5	171.1	9.5			171.1	9.5	10	35
13	Mining of metal ores	13.0	10.2	67.9	33.4	80.9	43.6			80.9	43.6	18	9
14	Other mining and quarrying	63.9	5.2	200.0	28.6	263.9	33.8			263.9	33.8	9	13
15	Manufacture of food products and beverages	13.2	1.7	75.6	14.8	88.8	16.4			88.8	16.4	15	26
16	Manufacture of tobacco products	0.0	0.0	27.8	5.6	27.9	5.7			27.9	5.7	44	48
17	Manufacture of textiles	22.8	33.1	47.7	24.0	70.5	57.2			70.5	57.2	21	6
18	Manufacture of wearing apparel; dressing and dyeing of fur	1.1	1.5	46.3	20.5	47.4	22.0			47.4	22.0	31	19
19	Tanning and dressing of leather; manufacture of luggage, handbags, saddlery, harness and footwear	0.9	1.3	35.1	9.3	36.0	10.5			36.0	10.5	38	33
20	Manufacture of wood and of products of wood and cork, except furniture; manufacture of articles of straw and plaiting materials	2.6	1.9	73.4	11.3	76.0	13.2			76.0	13.2	20	29
21	Manufacture of pulp, paper and paper products	13.3	18.4	97.4	27.6	110.8	46.0			110.8	46.0	11	8
22	Publishing, printing and reproduction of recorded media	0.1	1.4	35.3	9.6	35.4	11.0			35.4	11.0	40	31
23	Manufacture of coke, refined petroleum products and nuclear fuel	228.4		11.8	1.1	240.3	1.1	148.6		388.8	1.1	4	60
24	Manufacture of chemicals and chemical products	28.1	9.5	63.0	12.7	91.1	22.1			91.1	22.1	13	18
25	Manufacture of rubber and plastic products	0.5	3.9	58.9	18.4	59.4	22.3			59.4	22.3	24	17
26	Manufacture of other non-metallic mineral products	202.8	113.6	130.2	40.1	332.9	153.7			332.9	153.7	5	4
27	Manufacture of basic metals	8.7	17.4	58.1	23.9	66.8	41.3			66.8	41.3	22	11
28	Manufacture of fabricated metal products, except machinery and equipment	2.8	3.2	47.6	14.1	50.4	17.3			50.4	17.3	30	25
29	Manufacture of machinery and equipment n.e.c.	12.1	15.7	41.3	12.5	53.4	28.3			53.4	28.3	29	15
30	Manufacture of office machinery and computers	0.1		17.9	4.8	18.0	4.8			18.0	4.8	52	51

31	Manufacture of electrical machinery and apparatus n.e.c.	0.1	0.1	57.7	9.3	57.8	9.4			57.8	9.4	26	36
32	Manufacture of radio, television and communication equipment and apparatus	0.0	0.0	18.6	3.9	18.6	4.0			18.6	4.0	51	53
33	Manufacture of medical, precision and optical instruments, watches and clocks	0.1	0.1	40.5	8.3	40.6	8.4			40.6	8.4	36	39
34	Manufacture of motor vehicles, trailers and semi-trailers	0.0	0.1	27.7	8.1	27.8	8.2			27.8	8.2	45	41
35	Manufacture of other transport equipment	0.1	0.1	25.8	9.0	25.9	9.1			25.9	9.1	47	37
36	Manufacture of furniture; manufacturing n.e.c.	4.1	3.0	52.8	14.3	56.9	17.3			56.9	17.3	27	24
37	Recycling	0.8		83.7	18.2	84.5	18.2			84.5	18.2	17	23
40101 A	Production of electricity from fossil fuels	931.8	968.8	30.7	11.1	962.5	979.9			962.5	979.9	2	1
40101 B	Production of electricity from renewable sources			10.7	2.9	10.7	2.9			10.7	2.9	57	56
40102	Distribution and trade of Electricity			500.4	508.5	500.4	508.5			500.4	508.5	3	2
402	Manufacture, Distribution and trade of gas		32.8	35.9	7.0	35.9	39.8		154.6	35.9	194.4	39	3
41	Collection, purification and distribution of water			41.8	29.5	41.8	29.5			41.8	29.5	35	14
45	Construction	9.7	0.2	68.4	22.7	78.1	22.9			78.1	22.9	19	16
50	Sale, maintenance and repair of motor vehicles and motorcycles; retail sale of automotive fuel	6.0	0.1	40.7	7.3	46.7	7.4			46.7	7.4	32	43
51	Wholesale trade and commission trade, except of motor vehicles and motorcycles	14.4	0.0	71.2	8.6	85.6	8.6			85.6	8.6	16	38
52	Retail trade, except of motor vehicles and motorcycles; repair of personal and household goods	6.0	0.0	52.3	18.5	58.3	18.5			58.3	18.5	25	21
55	Hotels and restaurants	3.2	4.0	43.4	17.0	46.6	21.0			46.6	21.0	33	20
601	Transport via railways	164.1	0.4	162.2	126.8	326.2	127.2			326.2	127.2	7	5
602	Other land transport	1228.3	2.1	195.3	5.8	1423.6	7.9			1423. 6	7.9	1	42
603	Transport via pipelines			11.9	3.4	11.9	3.4			11.9	3.4	55	54
61	Water transport	267.2		63.5	7.3	330.7	7.3			330.7	7.3	6	45
62	Air transport	255.6		48.9	10.9	304.4	10.9			304.4	10.9	8	32
63	Supporting and auxiliary transport activities; activities of travel agencies	13.4		40.1	14.4	53.5	14.4			53.5	14.4	28	27
64	Post and telecommunications	1.3		18.9	5.7	20.2	5.7			20.2	5.7	50	47
65	Financial intermediation, except insurance and pension funding	0.0		11.5	5.0	11.6	5.0			11.6	5.0	56	50
66	Insurance and pension funding, except compulsory social security	0.4		6.1	2.6	6.5	2.6			6.5	2.6	60	58
67	Activities auxiliary to financial intermediation	0.1		8.8	2.9	8.9	2.9			8.9	2.9	59	57
70	Real estate activities	1.0	0.1	9.5	4.3	10.5	4.4			10.5	4.4	58	52
71	Renting of machinery and equipment without operator	9.8		22.1	3.2	32.0	3.2			32.0	3.2	41	55

	and of personal and household goods												
72	Computer and related activities	2.3		18.7	8.3	21.0	8.3			21.0	8.3	49	40
73	Research and development	2.6	43.9	13.3	4.7	15.9	48.5			15.9	48.5	53	7
74	Other business activities	3.9		18.3	5.4	22.2	5.4			22.2	5.4	48	49
75	Public administration and defence; compulsory social security	10.0		26.4	9.8	36.4	9.8			36.4	9.8	37	34
80	Education	2.4	0.7	12.7	6.6	15.1	7.3			15.1	7.3	54	44
85	Health and social work	22.3	0.6	22.6	6.6	44.9	7.2			44.9	7.2	34	46
90	Sewage and refuse disposal, sanitation and similar activities	16.8	0.6	43.4	12.1	60.2	12.7			60.2	12.7	23	30
91	Activities of membership organizations n.e.c.	11.0	8.2	87.7	35.4	98.6	43.5			98.6	43.5	12	10
92	Recreational, cultural and sporting activities	2.9	0.7	25.2	12.7	28.1	13.3			28.1	13.3	43	28
93	Other service activities	7.1	23.0	21.5	11.5	28.6	34.5			28.6	34.5	42	12
95	Activities of households as employers of domestic staff											61	61

Table 2: Primary energy requirements corresponding to domestic consumption

Table 2. Primary Energy Requirements corresponding to domestic consumption		**Energy Requirements by Direct Production Demand**		**Energy Requirements by Indirect Production Demand**		**Energy Requirements by Total Production demand**		**Energy Requirements by Direct Consumpt. Demand**		**Energy Requirements by Final Demand**					
(y_{dom} = Final consumption of households + Collective consumption + Gross fixed capital formation + Change in stocks)		**C y_{dom}**		**$C(A+A^2+...)y_{dom}$**		**$C(I-A)^{-1}y_{dom}$**		**PZy_{dom}**		**Total Primary Energy Requirements**		**Tt. Prim. Energy Requir.' Rank.**		**% Distrib. of Energy Req. by Industry**	
	unit: *10^3 toe*	**(1) Oil**	**(2) Natural gas**	**(3) Oil**	**(4) Natural gas**	**(5) Oil**	**(6) Natural gas**	**(7) Oil**	**(8) Natural gas**	**(9) Oil**	**(10) Natural gas**	**Oil**	**Natural gas**	**Oil**	**Natural gas**
01	Agriculture, hunting and related service activities	46.7	0.7	78.4	24.8	125.1	25.5			125.1	25.5	14	18	1.4	0.9
02	Forestry, logging and related service activities	1.2		0.5	0.1	1.7	0.1			1.7	0.1	52	53	0.0	0.0
05	Fishing, fish farming and related service activities	44.5		14.8	3.3	59.3	3.3			59.3	3.3	21	40	0.7	0.1
13	Mining of metal ores											56	56	0.0	0.0
14	Other mining and quarrying	0.1	0.0	0.3	0.0	0.4	0.1			0.4	0.1	54	54	0.0	0.0
15	Manufacture of food products and beverages	82.3	10.4	470.5	91.8	552.7	102.3			552.7	102.3	6	6	6.1	3.7
16	Manufacture of tobacco products	0.0	0.0	7.4	1.5	7.5	1.5			7.5	1.5	45	44	0.1	0.1
17	Manufacture of textiles	8.5	12.3	17.7	8.9	26.2	21.2			26.2	21.2	29	20	0.3	0.8
18	Manufacture of wearing apparel; dressing and dyeing of fur	1.5	2.1	62.7	27.7	64.2	29.8			64.2	29.8	19	14	0.7	1.1
19	Tanning and dressing of leather; manufacture of luggage, handbags, saddlery, harness and	0.4	0.6	17.3	4.6	17.8	5.2			17.8	5.2	35	35	0.2	0.2

	footwear														
20	Manufacture of wood and of products of wood and cork, except furniture; manufacture of articles of straw and plaiting materials	0.2	0.1	5.5	0.9	5.7	1.0			5.7	1.0	48	47	0.1	0.0
21	Manufacture of pulp, paper and paper products	1.2	1.7	8.8	2.5	10.0	4.2			10.0	4.2	38	37	0.1	0.2
22	Publishing, printing and reproduction of recorded media	0.1	0.9	22.2	6.1	22.3	6.9			22.3	6.9	32	33	0.2	0.3
23	Manufacture of coke, refined petroleum products and nuclear fuel	220.4		11.4	1.1	231.9	1.1	150.3		382.2	1.1	10	46	4.2	0.0
24	Manufacture of chemicals and chemical products	24.5	8.2	54.8	11.0	79.2	19.2			79.2	19.2	17	22	0.9	0.7
25	Manufacture of rubber and plastic products	0.1	0.9	13.2	4.1	13.3	5.0			13.3	5.0	37	36	0.1	0.2
26	Manufacture of other non-metallic mineral products	27.6	15.4	17.7	5.4	45.2	20.9			45.2	20.9	25	21	0.5	0.8
27	Manufacture of basic metals											56	56	0.0	0.0
28	Manufacture of fabricated metal products, except machinery and equipment	1.2	1.3	19.7	5.8	20.9	7.2			20.9	7.2	33	32	0.2	0.3
29	Manufacture of machinery and equipment n.e.c.	11.5	15.0	39.4	12.0	50.9	26.9			50.9	26.9	23	17	0.6	1.0
30	Manufacture of office machinery and computers	0.0		3.4	0.9	3.5	0.9			3.5	0.9	51	50	0.0	0.0
31	Manufacture of electrical machinery and apparatus n.e.c.	0.0	0.0	6.7	1.1	6.8	1.1			6.8	1.1	47	45	0.1	0.0
32	Manufacture of radio, television and communication equipment and apparatus	0.0	0.0	4.4	0.9	4.5	1.0			4.5	1.0	49	48	0.0	0.0
33	Manufacture of medical, precision and optical instruments, watches and clocks	0.0	0.0	9.7	2.0	9.7	2.0			9.7	2.0	40	43	0.1	0.1
34	Manufacture of motor vehicles, trailers and semi-trailers	0.0	0.0	7.4	2.2	7.4	2.2			7.4	2.2	46	42	0.1	0.1
35	Manufacture of other transport equipment	0.0	0.0	8.0	2.8	8.0	2.8			8.0	2.8	44	41	0.1	0.1
36	Manufacture of furniture; manufacturing n.e.c.	5.1	3.8	65.3	17.7	70.4	21.5			70.4	21.5	18	19	0.8	0.8
37	Recycling											56	56	0.0	0.0
40101A	Production of electricity from fossil fuels											56	56	0.0	0.0
40101B	Production of electricity from renewable sources											56	56	0.0	0.0
40102	Distribution and trade of Electricity			918.5	933.4	918.5	933.4			918.5	933.4	3	1	10.1	34.1
402	Manufacture, Distribution and trade of gas		9.1	9.9	1.9	9.9	11.0		42.8	9.9	53.8	39	11	0.1	2.0
41	Collection, purification and distribution of water			14.5	10.3	14.5	10.3			14.5	10.3	36	27	0.2	0.4
45	Construction	163.7	3.5	1160.9	385.8	1324.6	389.3			1324.6	389.3	2	2	14.6	14.2
50	Sale, maintenance and repair of motor vehicles and motorcycles; retail sale of automotive fuel	24.9	0.6	170.2	30.6	195.1	31.1			195.1	31.1	11	13	2.2	1.1
51	Wholesale trade and commission trade, except	95.4	0.3	470.8	56.8	566.2	57.1			566.2	57.1	5	10	6.3	2.1

	of motor vehicles and motorcycles														
52	Retail trade, except of motor vehicles and motorcycles; repair of personal and household goods	50.4	0.2	442.1	156.2	492.5	156.4			492.5	156.4	8	4	5.4	5.7
55	Hotels and restaurants	28.8	36.0	391.2	153.5	420.0	189.4			420.0	189.4	9	3	4.6	6.9
601	Transport via railways	12.2	0.0	12.0	9.4	24.2	9.5			24.2	9.5	31	28	0.3	0.3
602	Other land transport	1289.0	2.2	204.9	6.0	1493.9	8.3			1493.9	8.3	1	29	16.5	0.3
603	Transport via pipelines			0.0	0.0	0.0	0.0			0.0	0.0	55	55	0.0	0.0
61	Water transport	7.8		1.9	0.2	9.7	0.2			9.7	0.2	41	51	0.1	0.0
62	Air transport	80.8		15.5	3.5	96.3	3.5			96.3	3.5	16	38	1.1	0.1
63	Supporting and auxiliary transport activities; activities of travel agencies	11.8		35.3	12.7	47.1	12.7			47.1	12.7	24	25	0.5	0.5
64	Post and telecommunications	3.6		52.0	15.7	55.6	15.7			55.6	15.7	22	23	0.6	0.6
65	Financial intermediation, except insurance and pension funding	0.1		27.2	11.8	27.3	11.8			27.3	11.8	28	26	0.3	0.4
66	Insurance and pension funding, except compulsory social security	0.5		7.8	3.3	8.3	3.3			8.3	3.3	43	39	0.1	0.1
67	Activities auxiliary to financial intermediation	0.0		0.5	0.2	0.5	0.2			0.5	0.2	53	52	0.0	0.0
70	Real estate activities	11.6	0.7	111.6	50.7	123.2	51.4			123.2	51.4	15	12	1.4	1.9
71	Renting of machinery and equipment without operator and of personal and household goods	2.9		6.5	0.9	9.3	0.9			9.3	0.9	42	49	0.1	0.0
72	Computer and related activities	2.2		17.9	7.9	20.1	7.9			20.1	7.9	34	30	0.2	0.3
73	Research and development	0.7	12.0	3.6	1.3	4.3	13.2			4.3	13.2	50	24	0.0	0.5
74	Other business activities	5.2		24.5	7.2	29.7	7.2			29.7	7.2	26	31	0.3	0.3
75	Public administration and defence; compulsory social security	140.3		369.8	137.3	510.2	137.3			510.2	137.3	7	5	5.6	5.0
80	Education	24.0	7.3	129.7	67.5	153.6	74.8			153.6	74.8	13	9	1.7	2.7
85	Health and social work	295.9	8.4	300.3	87.3	596.2	95.7			596.2	95.7	4	7	6.6	3.5
90	Sewage and refuse disposal, sanitation and similar activities	8.2	0.3	21.2	5.9	29.5	6.2			29.5	6.2	27	34	0.3	0.2
91	Activities of membership organizations n.e.c.	21.1	15.7	168.5	68.0	189.6	83.7			189.6	83.7	12	8	2.1	3.1
92	Recreational, cultural and sporting activities	6.5	1.5	56.1	28.3	62.6	29.8			62.6	29.8	20	15	0.7	1.1
93	Other service activities	6.1	19.7	18.4	9.8	24.5	29.5			24.5	29.5	30	16	0.3	1.1
95	Activities of households as employers of domestic staff											56	56	0.0	0.0
	Total	2,770.8	190.9	6,131.2	2,502.7	8,902.0	2,693.7	150.3	42.8	9,052.3	2,736.5			100	100

Table 3: CO_2 Intensities

Table 3. CO_2 intensities		Corresponding to Direct Prod. Demand		Corresponding to Indirect Prod. Demand		Corresponding to Total Prod. Demand	Corresponding to Direct Cons. Demand		Corresponding to Final Demand	
		e'C		e'C(A+A^2+...)		e'C (I-A)$^{-1}$	e'P		Total CO_2 Intensity	Tt. CO_2 Intensit.' Ranking
	unit: *tonnes of CO_2/ million €*	(1)	(1)/(5) %	(2)=(3)-(1)	(2)/(5) %	(3)	(4)	(4)/(5) %	(5)=(3)+(4)	
01	Agriculture, hunting and related service activities	103.2	32.7	212.8	67.3	315.9			315.9	17
02	Forestry, logging and related service activities	58.1	65.5	30.7	34.5	88.8			88.8	48
05	Fishing, fish farming and related service activities	390.3	72.0	152.1	28.0	542.4			542.4	11
13	Mining of metal ores	63.4	18.2	284.5	81.8	347.8			347.8	15
14	Other mining and quarrying	206.4	23.4	674.7	76.6	881.1			881.1	9
15	Manufacture of food products and beverages	44.1	14.3	264.3	85.7	308.4			308.4	18
16	Manufacture of tobacco products	0.1	0.1	97.8	99.9	97.9			97.9	47
17	Manufacture of textiles	146.7	42.2	201.2	57.8	347.9			347.9	14
18	Manufacture of wearing apparel; dressing and dyeing of fur	6.9	3.5	188.6	96.5	195.5			195.5	32
19	Tanning and dressing of leather; manufacture of luggage, handbags, saddlery, harness and footwear	5.7	4.2	128.4	95.8	134.1			134.1	40
20	Manufacture of wood and of products of wood and cork, except furniture; manufacture of articles of straw and plaiting materials	12.2	4.7	249.6	95.3	261.8			261.8	23
21	Manufacture of pulp, paper and paper products	83.7	18.8	360.6	81.2	444.3			444.3	12
22	Publishing, printing and reproduction of recorded media	3.5	2.6	129.7	97.4	133.2			133.2	42
23	Manufacture of coke, refined petroleum products and nuclear fuel	694.4	58.6	38.6	3.3	732.9	451.6	38.1	1184.5	6
24	Manufacture of chemicals and chemical products	107.6	32.7	221.2	67.3	328.8			328.8	16
25	Manufacture of rubber and plastic products	10.6	4.6	222.0	95.4	232.6			232.6	24

26	Manufacture of other non-metallic mineral products	881.8	64.3	489.3	35.7	1371.1			1371.1	4
27	Manufacture of basic metals	67.1	22.4	232.6	77.6	299.7			299.7	19
28	Manufacture of fabricated metal products, except machinery and equipment	16.0	8.3	177.4	91.7	193.5			193.5	33
29	Manufacture of machinery and equipment n.e.c.	73.5	32.2	154.9	67.8	228.4			228.4	25
30	Manufacture of office machinery and computers	0.4	0.6	65.5	99.4	65.9			65.9	53
31	Manufacture of electrical machinery and apparatus n.e.c.	0.5	0.3	197.0	99.7	197.5			197.5	29
32	Manufacture of radio, television and communication equipment and apparatus	0.2	0.3	65.7	99.7	65.9			65.9	52
33	Manufacture of medical, precision and optical instruments, watches and clocks	0.6	0.5	142.6	99.5	143.2			143.2	39
34	Manufacture of motor vehicles, trailers and semi-trailers	0.4	0.4	103.2	99.6	103.6			103.6	45
35	Manufacture of other transport equipment	0.6	0.6	99.3	99.4	99.9			99.9	46
36	Manufacture of furniture; manufacturing n.e.c.	19.5	9.2	193.9	90.8	213.5			213.5	27
37	Recycling	2.4	0.8	297.0	99.2	299.4			299.4	20
40101A	Production of electricity from fossil fuels	5096.5	97.7	119.2	2.3	5215.7			5215.7	1
40101B	Production of electricity from renewable sources			39.4	100.0	39.4			39.4	58
40102	Distribution and trade of Electricity			2709.2	100.0	2709.2			2709.2	3
402	Manufacture, Distribution and trade of gas	76.6	13.6	125.7	22.3	202.2	361.4	64.1	563.6	10
41	Collection, purification and distribution of water			195.9	100.0	195.9			195.9	31
45	Construction	29.8	10.2	261.2	89.8	291.0			291.0	21
50	Sale, maintenance and repair of motor vehicles and motorcycles; retail sale of automotive fuel	18.4	11.6	140.9	88.4	159.4			159.4	37
51	Wholesale trade and commission trade, except of motor vehicles and motorcycles	44.0	15.7	236.5	84.3	280.4			280.4	22
52	Retail trade, except of motor vehicles and motorcycles; repair of personal and household goods	18.2	8.2	202.2	91.8	220.4			220.4	26
55	Hotels and restaurants	19.0	10.0	171.8	90.0	190.8			190.8	34
601	Transport via railways	499.6	38.8	789.4	61.2	1289.0			1289.0	5
602	Other land transport	3738.6	86.0	607.0	14.0	4345.6			4345.6	2
603	Transport via pipelines			44.0	100.0	44.0			44.0	56

61	Water transport	812.2	79.5	209.9	20.5	1022.1			1022.1	7
62	Air transport	776.8	81.7	174.0	18.3	950.8			950.8	8
63	Supporting and auxiliary transport activities; activities of travel agencies	40.7	20.7	155.5	79.3	196.1			196.1	30
64	Post and telecommunications	4.0	5.3	70.6	94.7	74.6			74.6	51
65	Financial intermediation, except insurance and pension funding	0.1	0.3	46.7	99.7	46.8			46.8	55
66	Insurance and pension funding, except compulsory social security	1.3	4.9	24.5	95.1	25.8			25.8	60
67	Activities auxiliary to financial intermediation	0.2	0.6	33.5	99.4	33.7			33.7	59
70	Real estate activities	3.2	7.5	39.1	92.5	42.2			42.2	57
71	Renting of machinery and equipment without operator and of personal and household goods	29.9	28.6	74.8	71.4	104.7			104.7	44
72	Computer and related activities	6.9	8.3	76.3	91.7	83.2			83.2	49
73	Research and development	110.2	68.2	51.5	31.8	161.8			161.8	36
74	Other business activities	11.9	14.8	68.3	85.2	80.2			80.2	50
75	Public administration and defence; compulsory social security	30.4	22.8	103.1	77.2	133.6			133.6	41
80	Education	8.8	14.0	54.1	86.0	62.9			62.9	54
85	Health and social work	69.2	45.1	84.1	54.9	153.3			153.3	38
90	Sewage and refuse disposal, sanitation and similar activities	52.5	24.7	160.2	75.3	212.7			212.7	28
91	Activities of membership organizations n.e.c.	52.4	13.0	349.1	87.0	401.5			401.5	13
92	Recreational, cultural and sporting activities	10.4	8.9	106.1	91.1	116.5			116.5	43
93	Other service activities	75.4	45.0	92.3	55.0	167.6			167.6	35
95	Activities of households as employers of domestic staff									61

Table 4: CO_2 Emissions corresponding to domestic consumption

Table 4. CO_2 Emissions corresponding to domestic consumption		**Corresponding to Direct Prod. Demand**	+	**Corresponding to Indirect Prod. Demand**	=	**Corresponding to Total Prod. Demand**	**Corresponding to Direct Cons. Demand**	=	**Corresponding to Final Demand**	**Tt. CO_2 Emiss.' Ranking**	**% Distrib. of CO_2 Emiss. by Ind.**
(y_{dom} = Final consumption of households + Collective consumption + Gross fixed capital formation + Change in stocks)		**$e'C\,y_{dom}$**		**$e'C\,(A+A^2+\ldots)\,y_{dom}$**		**$e'C(I-A)^{-1}y_{dom}$**	**$e'PZ\,y_{dom}$**		**Total CO_2 emissions**		
	unit: *10^3 tonnes of CO_2*	**(1)**	**(1)/(5) %**	**(2)=(3)-(1)**	**(2)/(5) %**	**(3)**	**(4)**	**(4)/(5) %**	**(5)=(3)+(4)**		
01	Agriculture, hunting and related service activities	143.6	32.7	296.2	67.3	439.8	0.0		439.8	15	1.3
02	Forestry, logging and related service activities	3.6	65.5	1.9	34.5	5.4			5.4	52	0.0
05	Fishing, fish farming and related service activities	135.3	72.0	52.7	28.0	188.0			188.0	23	0.6
13	Mining of metal ores									56	
14	Other mining and quarrying	0.3	23.4	1.0	76.6	1.3			1.3	54	0.0
15	Manufacture of food products and beverages	274.4	14.3	1644.6	85.7	1919.0			1919.0	5	5.7
16	Manufacture of tobacco products	0.0	0.1	26.2	99.9	26.2			26.2	47	0.1
17	Manufacture of textiles	54.5	42.2	74.8	57.8	129.3			129.3	28	0.4
18	Manufacture of wearing apparel; dressing and dyeing of fur	9.4	3.5	255.4	96.5	264.8			264.8	18	0.8
19	Tanning and dressing of leather; manufacture of luggage, handbags, saddlery, harness and footwear	2.8	4.2	63.4	95.8	66.2			66.2	37	0.2
20	Manufacture of wood and of products of wood and cork, except furniture; manufacture of articles of straw and plaiting materials	0.9	4.7	18.9	95.3	19.8			19.8	49	0.1
21	Manufacture of pulp, paper and paper products	7.6	18.8	32.7	81.2	40.2			40.2	40	0.1
22	Publishing, printing and reproduction of recorded media	2.2	2.6	81.7	97.4	83.9			83.9	33	0.2
23	Manufacture of coke, refined petroleum products and nuclear fuel	670.1	57.6	37.2	3.2	707.3	456.9	39.2	1164.1	10	3.4
24	Manufacture of chemicals and chemical products	93.5	32.7	192.2	67.3	285.7			285.7	17	0.8
25	Manufacture of rubber and plastic products	2.4	4.6	49.8	95.4	52.2			52.2	38	0.2
26	Manufacture of other non-metallic mineral products	119.8	64.3	66.5	35.7	186.3			186.3	24	0.5
27	Manufacture of basic metals									56	
28	Manufacture of fabricated metal products, except machinery and equipment	6.7	8.3	73.6	91.7	80.2			80.2	34	0.2
29	Manufacture of machinery and equipment n.e.c.	70.1	32.2	147.6	67.8	217.7			217.7	21	0.6
30	Manufacture of office machinery and computers	0.1	0.6	12.6	99.4	12.7			12.7	51	0.0
31	Manufacture of electrical machinery and apparatus n.e.c.	0.1	0.3	23.0	99.7	23.1			23.1	48	0.1

32	Manufacture of radio, television and communication equipment and apparatus	0.1	0.3	15.7	99.7	15.8			15.8	50	0.0
33	Manufacture of medical, precision and optical instruments, watches and clocks	0.2	0.5	34.2	99.5	34.4			34.4	41	0.1
34	Manufacture of motor vehicles, trailers and semi-trailers	0.1	0.4	27.6	99.6	27.7			27.7	46	0.1
35	Manufacture of other transport equipment	0.2	0.6	30.8	99.4	31.0			31.0	43	0.1
36	Manufacture of furniture; manufacturing n.e.c.	24.2	9.2	240.0	90.8	264.1			264.1	19	0.8
37	Recycling									56	
40101A	Production of electricity from fossil fuels									56	
40101B	Production of electricity from renewable sources									56	
40102	Distribution and trade of Electricity			4973.5	100.0	4973.5			4973.5	1	14.7
402	Manufacture, Distribution and trade of gas	21.2	13.6	34.8	22.3	56.0	100.0	64.1	156.0	26	0.5
41	Collection, purification and distribution of water			68.2	100.0	68.2			68.2	36	0.2
45	Construction	505.8	10.2	4430.4	89.8	4936.2			4936.2	2	14.6
50	Sale, maintenance and repair of motor vehicles and motorcycles; retail sale of automotive fuel	77.0	11.6	588.8	88.4	665.8			665.8	12	2.0
51	Wholesale trade and commission trade, except of motor vehicles and motorcycles	290.8	15.7	1563.8	84.3	1854.6			1854.6	8	5.5
52	Retail trade, except of motor vehicles and motorcycles; repair of personal and household goods	153.6	8.2	1708.9	91.8	1862.5			1862.5	7	5.5
55	Hotels and restaurants	171.6	10.0	1547.6	90.0	1719.2			1719.2	9	5.1
601	Transport via railways	37.1	38.8	58.6	61.2	95.8			95.8	32	0.3
602	Other land transport	3923.3	86.0	637.0	14.0	4560.3			4560.3	3	13.4
603	Transport via pipelines			0.0	100.0	0.0			0.0	55	0.0
61	Water transport	23.8	79.5	6.1	20.5	29.9			29.9	45	0.1
62	Air transport	245.7	81.7	55.0	18.3	300.7			300.7	16	0.9
63	Supporting and auxiliary transport activities; activities of travel agencies	35.9	20.7	137.1	79.3	173.0			173.0	25	0.5
64	Post and telecommunications	11.0	5.3	194.8	94.7	205.7			205.7	22	0.6
65	Financial intermediation, except insurance and pension funding	0.3	0.3	110.3	99.7	110.6			110.6	29	0.3
66	Insurance and pension funding, except compulsory social security	1.6	4.9	31.4	95.1	33.0			33.0	42	0.1
67	Activities auxiliary to financial intermediation	0.0	0.6	2.0	99.4	2.0			2.0	53	0.0
70	Real estate activities	37.0	7.5	457.7	92.5	494.7			494.7	14	1.5
71	Renting of machinery and equipment without operator and of personal and household goods	8.7	28.6	21.9	71.4	30.6			30.6	44	0.1
72	Computer and related activities	6.6	8.3	72.9	91.7	79.5			79.5	35	0.2

73	Research and development	30.1	68.2	14.1	31.8	44.1			44.1	39	0.1
74	Other business activities	15.9	14.8	91.4	85.2	107.3			107.3	30	0.3
75	Public administration and defence; compulsory social security	426.5	22.8	1445.0	77.2	1871.5			1871.5	6	5.5
80	Education	89.9	14.0	551.9	86.0	641.8			641.8	13	1.9
85	Health and social work	919.1	45.1	1116.9	54.9	2036.1			2036.1	4	6.0
90	Sewage and refuse disposal, sanitation and similar activities	25.7	24.7	78.4	75.3	104.2			104.2	31	0.3
91	Activities of membership organizations n.e.c.	100.7	13.0	671.3	87.0	772.0			772.0	11	2.3
92	Recreational, cultural and sporting activities	23.1	8.9	236.7	91.1	259.8			259.8	20	0.8
93	Other service activities	64.5	45.0	79.0	55.0	143.5			143.5	27	0.4
95	Activities of households as employers of domestic staff									56	
	Total	8,868.4	26.2	24,485.6	72.2	33,354.0	556.9	1.6	33,910.9		100

Table 5: Energy and CO_2 'embodied' in Portuguese international trade

Table 5. Energy and CO_2 'embodied' in Portuguese iInternational trade		Primary Energy Requirements						CO_2 Emissions						
		Exports		Imports		Exports - Imports		Exports			Imports			Exp - Imp
(y_{dom} = FCH + CC + GFCF + CS) (y_{exp} = Exports of G&S); (y_{imp} = Imports of G&S)		Total Primary Energy 'embodied' in Exports		Total Primary Energy 'embodied' in imports		Total Primary Energy Trade Balance		Corresp. to Direct Prod. Demand	Corresp to Ind. Prod. Demand	Tt. CO_2 em. corresp. to Port. exports	Corresp. to Imports for use in Prod.	Corresp to Imp. for use by final cons.	Tt. CO_2 em. corresp. to Port. Imports	Tt. CO_2 emis. Trade Balance
	unit for primary energy requirements: *10^3 toe*	$C(I-A)^{-1} y_{exp}$		$C(I-A)^{-1} B(I-A)_{-1} y_{dom} + C(I-A)^{-1} y_{imp}$		$f_{tb}=f_{exp}-f_{imp}$		$e'C\, y_{exp}$	$e'C(A+A^2+\ldots)y_{exp}$	$e'C(I-A)^{-1} y_{exp}$	$e'C(I-A)^{-1}B\,(I-A)^{-1}y_{dom}$	$e'C(I-A)^{-1}\, y_{imp}$	$e'C\ldots y_{dom}+ e'C(I-A)^{-1}y_{imp}$	$c_{tb}=c_{exp}-c_{imp}$
	unit for CO_2 emissions: *10^3 tonnes of CO_2*	(1) Oil	(2) Natural gas	(3) Oil	(4) Natural gas	(5) Oil	(6) Natural gas	(7)	(8)	(9)=(7)+(8)	(10)	(11)	(12)=(10)+(11)	(13)=(9)-(12)
01	Agriculture, hunting and related service activities	27.4	5.6	56.6	8.1	-29.2	-2.6	31.4	64.8	96.3	64.0	136.9	200.9	-104.6
02	Forestry, logging and related service activities	2.4	0.2	13.9	0.1	-11.5	0.0	5.1	2.7	7.7	2.8	0.1	2.9	4.9
05	Fishing, fish farming and related service activities	13.9	0.8	32.9	1.5	-19.0	-0.7	31.7	12.4	44.1	15.9	43.4	59.4	-15.3
13	Mining of metal ores	21.8	11.7	20.2	0.3	1.5	11.4	17.1	76.5	93.6				93.6
14	Other mining and quarrying	20.6	2.6	25.8	0.4	-5.2	2.2	16.1	52.5	68.6	0.1	0.6	0.7	68.0
15	Manufacture of food products and beverages	169.7	31.4	241.4	39.1	-71.8	-7.8	84.2	504.8	589.0	286.1	748.0	1034.1	-445.1
16	Manufacture of tobacco products	3.0	0.6	34.5	0.7	-31.5	-0.1	0.0	10.6	10.6	12.3	23.1	35.4	-24.8
17	Manufacture of textiles	136.8	110.9	69.9	21.5	66.9	89.4	284.6	390.4	675.0	17.1	116.0	133.1	541.9
18	Manufacture of wearing apparel;	98.2	45.5	86.7	20.0	11.5	25.6	14.3	390.7	405.0	62.3	273.3	335.6	69.4

	dressing and dyeing of fur													
19	Tanning and dressing of leather; manufacture of luggage, handbags, saddlery, harness and footwear	47.4	13.9	44.9	4.6	2.5	9.2	7.5	169.0	176.5	22.7	115.8	138.5	38.0
20	Manufacture of wood and of products of wood and cork, except furniture; manufacture of articles of straw and plaiting materials	94.4	16.4	41.6	0.7	52.8	15.7	15.2	310.2	325.3	3.5	4.9	8.4	316.9
21	Manufacture of pulp, paper and paper products	149.5	62.1	44.9	3.1	104.6	59.0	112.9	486.7	599.7	4.2	18.8	22.9	576.8
22	Publishing, printing and reproduction of recorded media	2.4	0.7	50.1	2.4	-47.8	-1.7	0.2	8.7	8.9	29.0	50.4	79.4	-70.5
23	Manufacture of coke, refined petroleum products and nuclear fuel	268.1	1.2	101.2	0.7	166.9	0.5	774.8	43.0	817.8	44.4	94.3	138.7	679.1
24	Manufacture of chemicals and chemical products	192.3	46.7	497.2	35.6	-304.9	11.1	227.1	466.7	693.9	40.0	503.8	543.8	150.1
25	Manufacture of rubber and plastic products	73.1	27.5	99.6	4.3	-26.5	23.2	13.1	273.4	286.5	10.3	51.5	61.8	224.7
26	Manufacture of other non-metallic mineral products	408.5	188.6	71.6	6.1	336.9	182.4	1082.0	600.3	1682.3	6.2	11.0	17.2	1665.1
27	Manufacture of basic metals	64.8	40.1	44.8	0.9	19.9	39.2	65.0	225.4	290.4		0.9	0.9	289.5
28	Manufacture of fabricated metal products, except machinery and equipment	57.7	19.8	66.6	3.0	-8.9	16.8	18.4	203.3	221.7	19.1	30.1	49.1	172.5
29	Manufacture of machinery and equipment n.e.c.	88.6	46.9	59.3	11.8	29.4	35.1	122.0	256.9	378.9	43.8	123.4	167.2	211.7
30	Manufacture of office machinery and computers	12.9	3.4	35.2	1.1	-22.3	2.4	0.3	46.9	47.2	8.9	25.6	34.5	12.7
31	Manufacture of electrical machinery and apparatus n.e.c.	72.6	11.8	33.3	1.1	39.3	10.8	0.7	247.7	248.4	5.4	24.4	29.8	218.6
32	Manufacture of radio, television and communication equipment and apparatus	35.7	7.6	48.2	2.1	-12.5	5.5	0.4	125.9	126.3	11.0	111.4	122.4	3.9
33	Manufacture of medical, precision and optical instruments, watches and clocks	10.1	2.1	52.4	2.8	-42.3	-0.8	0.2	35.3	35.5	11.0	90.0	101.1	-65.6
34	Manufacture of motor vehicles, trailers and semi-trailers	108.6	32.1	105.0	22.5	3.6	9.7	1.5	403.8	405.4	12.3	849.2	861.5	-456.1
35	Manufacture of other transport equipment	13.9	4.9	47.7	1.6	-33.8	3.4	0.3	53.5	53.8	14.2	29.8	44.0	9.8
36	Manufacture of furniture; manufacturing n.e.c.	53.2	16.2	68.5	10.1	-15.3	6.1	18.3	181.3	199.6	56.9	172.5	229.4	-29.8
37	Recycling			41.3	0.7	-41.3	-0.7							
40101A	Production of electricity from fossil fuels			47.0	1.0	-47.0	-1.0							
40101B	Production of electricity from renewable sources			159.9	3.4	-159.9	-3.4							

40102	Distribution and trade of Electricity	46.5	47.3	121.2	4.8	-74.7	42.5		251.9	251.9	84.4	0.4	84.8	167.2
402	Manufacture, Distribution and trade of gas	0.0	0.0	3.3	0.0	-3.3	0.0	0.0	0.0	0.0	12.7	0.0	12.7	-12.7
41	Collection, purification and distribution of water	0.0	0.0	47.7	1.8	-47.7	-1.7		0.1	0.1	16.0	0.1	16.1	-16.0
45	Construction	0.0	0.0	26.2	0.4	-26.2	-0.4	0.0	0.0	0.1	780.1	0.0	780.1	-780.0
50	Sale, maintenance and repair of motor vehicles and motorcycles; retail sale of automotive fuel	0.4	0.1	21.6	0.3	-21.2	-0.3	0.2	1.2	1.4	192.1	0.3	192.4	-191.0
51	Wholesale trade and commission trade, except of motor vehicles and motorcycles	87.5	8.8	18.3	0.3	69.2	8.6	44.9	241.6	286.6	304.1		304.1	-17.5
52	Retail trade, except of motor vehicles and motorcycles; repair of personal and household goods	9.8	3.1	15.5	0.3	-5.7	2.9	3.1	34.1	37.2	388.6	0.0	388.6	-351.5
55	Hotels and restaurants	19.7	8.9	29.6	6.7	-9.9	2.2	8.0	72.4	80.4	414.2	97.1	511.3	-430.8
601	Transport via railways	4.5	1.8	69.3	1.4	-64.7	0.3	6.9	10.9	17.8	3.4	0.2	3.6	14.2
602	Other land transport	1488.9	8.2	22.2	0.2	1466.7	8.0	3910.0	634.9	4544.9	48.3	2.4	50.6	4494.3
603	Transport via pipelines	0.1	0.0	13.9	0.1	-13.9	-0.1		0.3	0.3	0.0		0.0	0.3
61	Water transport	97.4	2.1	22.4	0.2	74.9	1.9	239.2	61.8	301.0	1.3	1.4	2.7	298.2
62	Air transport	363.9	13.0	120.6	3.5	243.2	9.6	928.5	208.0	1136.5	14.5	94.4	108.9	1027.6
63	Supporting and auxiliary transport activities; activities of travel agencies	28.8	7.8	52.0	1.1	-23.2	6.7	21.9	83.7	105.6	40.6	16.3	56.8	48.8
64	Post and telecommunications	9.4	2.6	15.8	0.8	-6.4	1.9	1.9	32.9	34.8	126.8	35.3	162.2	-127.4
65	Financial intermediation, except insurance and pension funding	1.5	0.6	9.0	0.8	-7.5	-0.2	0.0	5.9	5.9	108.6	46.0	154.6	-148.7
66	Insurance and pension funding, except compulsory social security	0.4	0.1	3.7	0.2	-3.4	0.0	0.1	1.4	1.5	58.9	15.5	74.4	-73.0
67	Activities auxiliary to financial intermediation	1.3	0.4	5.0	0.1	-3.8	0.3	0.0	4.7	4.8	2.7	3.7	6.4	-1.6
70	Real estate activities	0.0	0.0	4.3	0.1	-4.3	-0.1	0.0	0.2	0.2	538.5	1.2	539.7	-539.5
71	Renting of machinery and equipment without operator and of personal and household goods	1.8	0.2	6.4	0.1	-4.5	0.1	1.7	4.3	6.0	13.4	0.9	14.4	-8.3
72	Computer and related activities	2.6	1.0	9.7	0.2	-7.1	0.9	0.8	9.3	10.2	44.0	0.2	44.2	-34.0
73	Research and development	0.5	1.4	7.5	0.1	-7.0	1.3	3.2	1.5	4.7	12.5		12.5	-7.8
74	Other business activities	24.7	6.0	13.1	0.5	11.7	5.5	13.2	76.0	89.2	61.5	22.0	83.5	5.7
75	Public administration and defence; compulsory social security	0.0	0.0	9.2	0.2	-9.2	-0.1	0.0	0.0	0.0	644.2	0.0	644.2	-644.2
80	Education	0.0	0.0	6.4	0.1	-6.3	-0.1	0.0	0.1	0.1	469.0	0.5	469.5	-469.5
85	Health and social work	0.2	0.0	13.2	0.2	-13.0	-0.2	0.4	0.4	0.8	610.8	6.3	617.1	-616.3
90	Sewage and refuse disposal, sanitation and similar activities	0.2	0.0	18.7	0.3	-18.5	-0.3	0.1	0.4	0.6	22.5	1.2	23.7	-23.1

91	Activities of membership organizations n.e.c.	0.0	0.0	19.9	0.4	-19.9	-0.4	0.0	0.0	0.0	88.4		88.4	-88.4
92	Recreational, cultural and sporting activities	5.3	2.5	22.3	1.4	-17.0	1.1	1.9	19.9	21.8	102.6	28.6	131.2	-109.4
93	Other service activities	0.0	0.1	15.2	0.2	-15.2	-0.2	0.1	0.1	0.3	39.4	0.3	39.7	-39.4
95	Activities of households as employers of domestic staff			7.0	0.1	-7.0	-0.1				45.6	0.1	45.8	-45.8
	Total	4,442.9	867.7	3,112.4	238.3	1330.5	629.4	8,130.6	7,401.9	15,532.5	6,093.3	4,023.8	10,117.1	5,415.4

Table 6: Portuguese 'responsibility' for CO_2 emissions versus CO_2 emissions produced by the Portuguese economy

Table 6. Portuguese 'responsibility' for CO_2 emissions *versus* CO_2 emissions produced by the Portuguese economy		**Corresponding to domestic consumption**	+	**Corresponding to Portuguese imports**	=	**Portuguese 'responsibility' for CO_2 emiss.**		**Corresponding to domestic consumption**	+	**Corresponding to Portuguese exports**	=	**CO_2 emissions produced by the Port. Econ.**	
(y_{dom} = FCH + CC + GFCF + CS) (y_{exp} = Exports of G&S); (y_{imp} = Imports of G&S)		**$e'C(I-A)^{-1} y_{dom} + e'PZy_{dom}$**		**$e'C(I-A)^{-1}B(I-A)^{-1} y_{dom} + e'C(I-A)^{-1} y_{dom}$**		**$c_{resp} = c_{dom} + c_{imp}$**	**Portug. 'resp.' for CO_2 Emis.' Rank.**	**$e'C(I-A)^{-1} y_{dom} + e'PZy_{dom}$**		**$e'C(I-A)^{-1} y_{exp}$**		**$c_{emis} = c_{dom} + c_{exp}$**	**CO_2 by the Portug. Economy's Rank.**
	unit: *10^3 tonnes of CO_2*	**(1)**	**(1)/(3) %**	**(2)**	**(2)/(3) %**	**(3)=(1)+(2)**		**(4)**	**(4)/(6) %**	**(5)**	**(5)/(6) %**	**(6)=(4)+(5)**	
01	Agriculture, hunting and related service activities	439.8	68.6	200.9	31.4	640.7	17	439.8	82.0	96.3	18.0	536.1	21
02	Forestry, logging and related service activities	5.4	65.4	2.9	34.6	8.3	54	5.4	41.2	7.7	58.8	13.2	55
05	Fishing, fish farming and related service activities	188.0	76.0	59.4	24.0	247.4	26	188.0	81.0	44.1	19.0	232.1	35
13	Mining of metal ores						58			93.6	100.0	93.6	43
14	Other mining and quarrying	1.3	66.8	0.7	33.2	2.0	55	1.3	1.9	68.6	98.1	69.9	47
15	Manufacture of food products and beverages	1919.0	65.0	1034.1	35.0	2953.1	4	1919.0	76.5	589.0	23.5	2508.0	4
16	Manufacture of tobacco products	26.2	42.5	35.4	57.5	61.6	45	26.2	71.1	10.6	28.9	36.8	52
17	Manufacture of textiles	129.3	49.3	133.1	50.7	262.3	25	129.3	16.1	675.0	83.9	804.3	14
18	Manufacture of wearing apparel; dressing and dyeing of fur	264.8	44.1	335.6	55.9	600.4	18	264.8	39.5	405.0	60.5	669.8	16
19	Tanning and dressing of leather; manufacture of luggage, handbags, saddlery, harness and footwear	66.2	32.3	138.5	67.7	204.7	28	66.2	27.3	176.5	72.7	242.6	33
20	Manufacture of wood and of products of wood and cork, except furniture; manufacture of articles of straw and plaiting materials	19.8	70.2	8.4	29.8	28.2	52	19.8	5.7	325.3	94.3	345.1	25
21	Manufacture of pulp, paper and paper products	40.2	63.7	22.9	36.3	63.2	44	40.2	6.3	599.7	93.7	639.9	19

22	Publishing, printing and reproduction of recorded media	83.9	51.4	79.4	48.6	163.3	33	83.9	90.4	8.9	9.6	92.8	44
23	Manufacture of coke, refined petroleum products and nuclear fuel	1164.1	89.4	138.7	10.6	1302.8	10	1164.1	58.7	817.8	41.3	1981.9	7
24	Manufacture of chemicals and chemical products	285.7	34.4	543.8	65.6	829.5	16	285.7	29.2	693.9	70.8	979.6	13
25	Manufacture of rubber and plastic products	52.2	45.8	61.8	54.2	114.0	39	52.2	15.4	286.5	84.6	338.7	26
26	Manufacture of other non-metallic mineral products	186.3	91.5	17.2	8.5	203.6	29	186.3	10.0	1682.3	90.0	1868.6	10
27	Manufacture of basic metals			0.9	100.0	0.9	56			290.4	100.0	290.4	29
28	Manufacture of fabricated metal products, except machinery and equipment	80.2	62.0	49.1	38.0	129.4	36	80.2	26.6	221.7	73.4	301.9	28
29	Manufacture of machinery and equipment n.e.c.	217.7	56.6	167.2	43.4	385.0	22	217.7	36.5	378.9	63.5	596.6	20
30	Manufacture of office machinery and computers	12.7	26.9	34.5	73.1	47.2	48	12.7	21.2	47.2	78.8	59.9	50
31	Manufacture of electrical machinery and apparatus n.e.c.	23.1	43.7	29.8	56.3	52.9	47	23.1	8.5	248.4	91.5	271.5	32
32	Manufacture of radio, television and communication equipment and apparatus	15.8	11.4	122.4	88.6	138.2	34	15.8	11.1	126.3	88.9	142.1	39
33	Manufacture of medical, precision and optical instruments, watches and clocks	34.4	25.4	101.1	74.6	135.4	35	34.4	49.2	35.5	50.8	69.9	48
34	Manufacture of motor vehicles, trailers and semi-trailers	27.7	3.1	861.5	96.9	889.1	13	27.7	6.4	405.4	93.6	433.1	24
35	Manufacture of other transport equipment	31.0	41.3	44.0	58.7	75.0	43	31.0	36.5	53.8	63.5	84.8	46
36	Manufacture of furniture; manufacturing n.e.c.	264.1	53.5	229.4	46.5	493.5	19	264.1	57.0	199.6	43.0	463.7	23
37	Recycling						58						58
40101A	Production of electricity from fossil fuels						58						58
40101B	Production of electricity from renewable sources						58						58
40102	Distribution and trade of Electricity	4973.5	98.3	84.8	1.7	5058.2	2	4973.5	95.2	251.9	4.8	5225.4	2
402	Manufacture, Distribution and trade of gas	156.0	92.4	12.7	7.6	168.8	32	156.0	100.0	0.0	0.0	156.1	37
41	Collection, purification and distribution of water	68.2	80.9	16.1	19.1	84.4	42	68.2	99.8	0.1	0.2	68.3	49
45	Construction	4936.2	86.4	780.1	13.6	5716.3	1	4936.2	100.0	0.1	0.0	4936.2	3

50	Sale, maintenance and repair of motor vehicles and motorcycles; retail sale of automotive fuel	665.8	77.6	192.4	22.4	858.2	15	665.8	99.8	1.4	0.2	667.2	17
51	Wholesale trade and commission trade, except of motor vehicles and motorcycles	1854.6	85.9	304.1	14.1	2158.7	9	1854.6	86.6	286.6	13.4	2141.2	5
52	Retail trade, except of motor vehicles and motorcycles; repair of personal and household goods	1862.5	82.7	388.6	17.3	2251.1	7	1862.5	98.0	37.2	2.0	1899.6	8
55	Hotels and restaurants	1719.2	77.1	511.3	22.9	2230.5	8	1719.2	95.5	80.4	4.5	1799.6	11
601	Transport via railways	95.8	96.4	3.6	3.6	99.4	41	95.8	84.3	17.8	15.7	113.6	41
602	Other land transport	4560.3	98.9	50.6	1.1	4610.9	3	4560.3	50.1	4544.9	49.9	9105.2	1
603	Transport via pipelines	0.0	48.9	0.0	51.1	0.0	57	0.0	0.5	0.3	99.5	0.3	57
61	Water transport	29.9	91.6	2.7	8.4	32.7	51	29.9	9.0	301.0	91.0	330.9	27
62	Air transport	300.7	73.4	108.9	26.6	409.6	20	300.7	20.9	1136.5	79.1	1437.2	12
63	Supporting and auxiliary transport activities; activities of travel agencies	173.0	75.3	56.8	24.7	229.8	27	173.0	62.1	105.6	37.9	278.6	31
64	Post and telecommunications	205.7	55.9	162.2	44.1	367.9	23	205.7	85.5	34.8	14.5	240.5	34
65	Financial intermediation, except insurance and pension funding	110.6	41.7	154.6	58.3	265.3	24	110.6	94.9	5.9	5.1	116.5	40
66	Insurance and pension funding, except compulsory social security	33.0	30.7	74.4	69.3	107.5	40	33.0	95.7	1.5	4.3	34.5	54
67	Activities auxiliary to financial intermediation	2.0	23.7	6.4	76.3	8.4	53	2.0	29.4	4.8	70.6	6.7	56
70	Real estate activities	494.7	47.8	539.7	52.2	1034.4	12	494.7	100.0	0.2	0.0	494.8	22
71	Renting of machinery and equipment without operator and of personal and household goods	30.6	68.1	14.4	31.9	44.9	50	30.6	83.6	6.0	16.4	36.6	53
72	Computer and related activities	79.5	64.3	44.2	35.7	123.7	38	79.5	88.7	10.2	11.3	89.7	45
73	Research and development	44.1	77.9	12.5	22.1	56.7	46	44.1	90.4	4.7	9.6	48.8	51
74	Other business activities	107.3	56.2	83.5	43.8	190.8	30	107.3	54.6	89.2	45.4	196.5	36
75	Public administration and defence; compulsory social security	1871.5	74.4	644.2	25.6	2515.7	6	1871.5	100.0	0.0	0.0	1871.5	9
80	Education	641.8	57.8	469.5	42.2	1111.4	11	641.8	100.0	0.1	0.0	641.9	18
85	Health and social work	2036.1	76.7	617.1	23.3	2653.2	5	2036.1	100.0	0.8	0.0	2036.9	6
90	Sewage and refuse disposal, sanitation and similar activities	104.2	81.5	23.7	18.5	127.8	37	104.2	99.4	0.6	0.6	104.7	42
91	Activities of membership organizations n.e.c.	772.0	89.7	88.4	10.3	860.4	14	772.0	100.0	0.0	0.0	772.0	15

92	Recreational, cultural and sporting activities	259.8	66.4	131.2	33.6	391.1	21	259.8	92.3	21.8	7.7	281.6	30
93	Other service activities	143.5	78.3	39.7	21.7	183.2	31	143.5	99.8	0.3	0.2	143.8	38
95	Activities of households as employers of domestic staff			45.8	100.0	45.8	49						58
	Total	33,910.9	77.0	10,117.1	23.0	44,028.0		33,910.9	68.6	15,532.5	31.4	4,443.4	

CHAPTER 6

Compilation of Greek Regional Nameas and Emission Intensities for the Year 2005

Charalambos Economidis[a*], Nikos Stromplos[b] and Athanasios Sfetsos[c]

[a]Department of Public Administration, Panteion University,136 Syngrou Av., Athens 176 71, Greece; [b]Director of National Accounts, National Statistical Service of Greece and [c]Environmental Research Laboratory, INT-RP, NCSR Demokritos

Abstract: The aim of this paper is to compile and examine regional NAMEA tables for the Greek economy and for the year 2005. The five main regions of Greece have been determined in accordance with the National Strategic Reference Framework (NSRF) approved by the European Commission for the period 2007-2013.The present work utilizes basic data on air emissions derived from the Greek Ministry of the Environment, Physical Planning and Public Works. The economic data are from the 2005 Input-Output regional tables for the Greek economy produced by the National Statistical Service of Greece, the Greek Academy and the single NAMEA Table for 2005. The derived regional NAMEA tables are a valuable tool for examining regional variations by using a series of environmental-economic indices such as the direct emission intensity coefficient, the direct and indirect emission intensity coefficients and each emission factor intensity on each component of final demand of the Greek economy. The paper also aims to establish in which regions there is an accumulation of emissions (particularly CO_2) so that an anti-pollution policy can be formulated along with possible policies for substituting polluting production methods.

Keywords: NAMEA Tables; Regional Input-Output Tables; Environmentally Extended Input-Output Tables.

INTRODUCTION

The EU's Sixth Environment Action Programme (EAP), "Environment 2010: Our future, Our choice"(European Commission, 2002), sets Environment & Health as one of the four main target areas requiring greater effort – and air pollution is one of the key issues highlighted in this area. Air pollution is of major interest both at a national and an international level. In the European Union, member states are required to comply with the Clean Air for Europe (CAFE) objectives and new directives on air quality. Underlying trends in the allocation of GDP and consumption patterns are important in the context of attaining certain environmental goals (European Environmental Agency, 2003).

The National Accounting Matrix including Environmental Accounts (NAMEA) is a statistical information system that links regular national accounts with environmental accounts. The NAMEA system has been identified by the European Union as a relevant part of the framework for environmental satellite accounts of the national accounts (Commission for the European Communities, 1994).

The aim of this paper is to construct NAMEA tables at a regional level for the year 2005 with the use of the single NAMEA table (Economidis, et al., 2008). The five main regions of Greece have been determined in accordance with the National Strategic Reference Framework (NSRF) approved by the European Commission for the period 2007-2013.

The paper also aims to establish a guide for those regions in which high air emissions are produced, thus setting a generalized framework to propose a sustainable economic development plan with lower air emissions.

The first part of the paper focuses on the theoretic background of the NAMEA framework, the second on the environmental data used for this study, the third on the construction of Regional Input-Output Tables, the fourth on the calculation of eco-indicators and more specifically, methodology and results, while the fifth and final part presents the conclusions.

*Address correspondence to Charalambos Economidis:** Department of Public Administration, Panteion University,136 Syngrou Av., Athens 176 71, Greece. Phone +30 210 6921760 E-mail:checonom@panteion.gr

Maria Llop (Ed)

NAMEA TABLE: THEORETICAL FRAMEWORK

Economic Data

Accounting for sustainable development requires a broadening of scope of the conventional System of National Accounts (United Nations, *et al.,* 1993). This wider perspective is necessary to account for the priceless environmental and social externalities, which are important in a sustainable development context. The environmental accounts show the interactions between producer and consumer (household) activities and the natural environment. These interrelationships occur as a consequence of the environmental requirements of these activities: natural resource inputs and residual outputs. These requirements are appointed to these activities when and where they actually take place. This direct recording is consistent with prevailing national accounting practices. By providing economic and environmental data in a consistent Leontief-type framework, the NAMEA is particularly suited for analytical purposes (De Haan, M., 1996).

Definition of NAMEA

According to the Eurostat (Eurostat, 2001) the National Accounting Matrix including Environmental Accounts (NAMEA) constitutes a framework in which various types of statistical data have been consistently organized in such a way as to bring together economic and environmental information that originate from different parts of the statistical system. The core of this framework is a set of tables containing economic data and form a National Accounting Matrix (NAM) compiled for National Accounts. The Environmental Accounts (EA) consists of tables containing data that are often denominated in physical units. The types of physical environmental data taken into consideration in the NAMEA accounting framework include specific air emissions in particular, but also emissions of waste, wastewater and water use. The Energy Balance shows the supply and use of energy and stock data on subsoil and in forests assets. The NAM also provides possibilities to present environmental taxes, expenditures and other economic data.

<table>
<tr><td colspan="4">Ordinary National Account</td><td>Physical data</td></tr>
<tr><td></td><td colspan="3">Supply</td><td></td></tr>
<tr><td rowspan="3">Use</td><td>Trade Margins</td><td>Intermediate consumption</td><td>Final uses</td><td>Household emissions</td></tr>
<tr><td>Output</td><td></td><td></td><td>Emissions from industries & services</td></tr>
<tr><td>Imports</td><td>Value Added</td><td></td><td></td></tr>
<tr><td></td><td colspan="4">Employment energy and physical data</td></tr>
</table>

Source: Eurostat, 2001.

Figure 1: Schematic description of a NAMEA framework for air emissions.

Fig. **1.** shows how National Accounting Tables of Supply & Use and Environmental Accounts (emissions) can be expanded in the context of a NAMEA. Here, the NAM is made up of the Supply & Use Tables of ordinary National Accounts, to which are added household consumption according to purpose. As can be seen on the right side of the figure, the production activities of industries result in emissions, as well as in goods and services that are included in regular National Accounts. The consumption of Households and the corresponding emissions are displayed separately. Below the Supply & Use Tables it is also possible to present in physical units the industry use of labor, energy and other materials. Of course the NAM can also include other National Account Matrices, e.g. showing income, saving and financial flows. As an alternative, the NAM could include Input-Output Symmetric Tables.

The NAMEA Classification for Air Emissions

According to Eurostat (Eurostat, 2001) a classification for NAMEA based on NACE Rev. 1 (Statistical classification of economic activities in the European Community, Eurostat 1996) has been proposed as a common starting point for pilot studies. The classification proposed for NAMEA takes into consideration special environmental aspects focusing on industries active in manufacturing but also in transport and energy. In the case of service industries, less detail is requested.

In addition, a separate breakdown is proposed for NACE industries 26 and 27. Additional breakdowns should also be made for NACE industry 40 (Electricity, gas and water supply). It may be expedient in particular to isolate the production and distribution of electricity (40.1). An additional breakdown has been proposed for NACE industries 60 and 61 with the aim of distinguishing each type of transport included in these industries. Households are also taken into consideration in the NAMEA classification

The air emissions produced by households may be divided into emissions from transport, heating and other purposes. Transport emissions are allocated to households when the latter use their private automobiles or motorcycles. Emissions caused by public transport are attributed to the corresponding transport industry. Heating emissions are allocated to households when the latter use combustible material. Emissions from the production of electricity for households are not allocated to the latter but to electricity producers.

Table 1: NACE* Activities according to the 2005 Greek Input-Output Table (26 industries)

Code	NACE Activity Rev. 1	Code	NACE Activity Rev. 1
01 & 02	Agriculture	37	Recycling
5	Fisheries	40-41	Electricity, gas and water supply
10,11&12 / 13-14	Mining and quarrying	45	Construction
15-16	Manufacture of food products, beverages and tobacco	50-52	Wholesale and retail trade; repair of motor vehicles, motorcycles and personal and household goods
17-19	Manufacture of textiles and textile products	55	Hotels and restaurants
20A	Manufacture of wood and wood products	60-64	Transport, storage and communication
21-22	Manufacture of pulp, paper and paper products; publishing and printing	65-67	Financial intermediation
23	Manufacture of coke, refined petroleum products and nuclear fuel	70-74	Real estate, renting and business activities
24-25	Manufacture of chemicals, chemical products and man-made fibres	75&90	Public administration and defence; Sewage and refuse disposal
26	Manufacture of other non-metallic mineral products	80-84	Education
27	Manufacture of basic metals and fabricated metal products	85	Health and social work
28	Manufacture of fabricated metal products, except machinery and equipment	91	Activities of membership organizations n.e.c.
29-36	Manufacture of machinery and equipment	92, 93, 95 & 99	Recreational, cultural and sporting activities; Activities of households; Extra-territorial organizations

Nomenclature statistique des activités économiques dans la communauté européenne.

Differences Between NAMEA and other Statistics on Air Emissions

Data in the NAMEA must be comparable with the activities covered by National Accounts. However, according to Eurostat (Eurostat 2001) data on air emissions are in certain cases presented in a different way than in traditional emission statistics such as, for example, CORINAIR (CORe INventory of AIR emissions) and Intergovernmental Panel on Climate Change (IPCC) statistics because of different definitions of the activities covered by national accounts. National accounts include only emissions that can be traced to economic activities and further activities of the national economy rather than activities that take place on national territory. Moreover, emissions must be allocated to the various industries in the same way that economic data are allocated. It does not include emissions from non-economic agents (e.g. nature). Furthermore, the absorption of substances by nature is not taken into consideration in the NAMEA emission accounts; e.g. carbon storage should not be deducted from CO_2 emissions of forests. At the same time, the emissions must correspond to those activities that are carried out in the framework of the national economy rather than on national territory. Emissions caused abroad from national economy units, including tourism and transport activities, should be included in the accounts of the domestic industries and domestic household consumption. These differences modify the emissions data significantly, particularly in the case of industries that provide transport services. IPCC and CORINAIR statistics include only a limited part of the emissions connected with international transport services. In the context of the NAMEA, these emissions must be allocated to the economic activities that cause them.

All the emissions connected to the activity of an industry must be allocated to that industry. NACE Rev.1 identifies separate industries for land transport, water transport, air transport and supporting activities (NACE 60-63). In NAMEA only the emissions connected to regular transport services are allocated to these industries. Emissions from sectors that produce energy, especially power generation, should be allocated among the producers and not the users of the marketed energy. The NAMEA takes into account only emissions from primary energy use. When economic data are available, emissions from electricity production are allocated to NACE industry 40.1.

NAMEA – Possibilities for Analysis

The development of the NAMEA framework is aimed at analyzing the interrelationship between the economy and the environment. It makes it possible to assess both the impacts of economic aspects in environmental policy and the environmental factor in economic policy, with the help of an Input-Output analysis. Input-Output models can be developed with the NAMEA framework, which offers the possibility of evaluating policy measures (e.g. tax rate policies, reduction of emissions) in a given structure of the economy. Also, when combined with time series, the NAMEA can be used for the decomposition of the series, making it possible to identify underlying economic forces which affect the level of the environmental impact of economic activities.

According to Eurostat (Eurostat, 2001) in a NAMEA-based Input-Output model, the annual change in pollution can be a tool for analyzing topics as efficiency gains or losses in pollution per monetary unit of output, changes in the structure of economic production, composition and size of final demand. The NAMEA framework also makes it possible to calculate the cumulative environmental pressure of the final demand of goods and services, by calculating the indirect emissions corresponding to other economic industries whose products are used as intermediate consumption.

A NAMEA Pilot Study for Greece

The report "Natural resource accounts and environmental Input-Output Tables 1988-1998" (Mylonas, *et.al.,* 2000) was a first systematic attempt to develop a consistent NAMEA for Greece. In this study the environmental accounts showing air emissions (which include Energy & Material Balances, accounts for water, wood and fish) cover the period 1988-1996. The air emission accounts take into consideration seven pollutants (CO_2, N_2O, CH_4, SO_2, NO_X, CO and NMVOC) included in CORINAIR. The emissions are shown in accounts in accordance with a classification that is comparable with NACE Rev. 1. In the study (Mylonas *et.al* 2000) the calculation of the air emission data is based on CORINAIR data available according to the Selected Nomenclature for Sources of Air Pollution (SNAP) 1994. They are allocated to a 25 industries-level classification. Household emissions are taken into account since 1990, while the relation between transport and heating is not shown. In the tables displaying air emission data, the outputs of the aforementioned 25 industries are presented in values at current prices. The NAM is based on symmetric Input-Output Tables with homogeneous industries, in which intermediate consumption is valued at basic prices. The full Greek NAMEA is presented for 1994.

The compilation of NAMEA time series is presented (Mylonas, *et.al.,* 2000) as a database for an Input-Output Analysis of the economy-environment relationship. In addition to the direct emissions of industries which are given in the NAMEA, the analysis is developed with the Leontief inverse matrix model, which leads to the calculation of emissions indirectly generated by each industry and how all these emissions (direct and indirect) are allocated back to the components of final demand.

ENVIRONMENTAL DATA USED FOR THIS STUDY

The air emissions data are estimated using the so-called 'air emissions inventory first approach' which is mainly based on the allocation of energy balance data to NACE categories (Eurostat, 2007). At present, international agreements on air emissions include the CLRTAP (Convention on Long-Range Transboundary Air Pollution) with reporting to UNECE/EMEP and the UNFCCC (United Nations Framework Convention on Climate Change), with reporting based on the UNFCCC CRF (Common Reporting Format). The UNFCCC CRF covers 6 categories of greenhouse gases (CO_2, N_2 O, CH_4, HFCs, PFCs and SF6) plus 4 indirect greenhouse gases (NOx, CO, NMVOC, SO_2). The UNECE/EMEP reporting includes only NOx, CO, NMVOC and SO2 plus NH3 plus 9 heavy metals as well as 17 POPs (persistent organic pollutants).

The data utilized for this study are based on the official data reported by the Greek Ministry for the Environment Physical Planning and Public Works. The data are based on the CORINAIR methodology and classified according to the Selected Nomenclature for sources of Air Pollution (SNAP). The original data were processed by deriving a NAMEA-consistent total and arranging process-oriented data in order to make them fit into the NACE-based classification, presently adopted for NAMEA. A hybrid approach was followed to attribute the SNAP-classified emissions to NACE-based economic activities or household consumption functions: simple (direct) and complex allocations. With regard to the later, some SNAP process emissions had to be split into several NAMEA activities. These emissions were attributed to NACE codes or household consumption functions using fuel consumption data, technical data contained in CORINAIR, experts' knowledge or other data.

The air emissions have been further grouped and aggregated by three environmental pressure variables, namely Global Warming Potential (GWP), Acidification (ACID) and Tropospheric Ozone Forming Potential (TOFP), in addition to Particulate Matter (PM10) with diameter less than 10 mm, from the following set of equations:

$$GWP = CO_2 + 310 * N_2O + 21 * CH_4$$

$$ACID = SO_2 + 0.7 * NO_x + 1.9 * NH_3$$

$$TOFP = NMVOC + 1.22 * NO_x + 0.11 * CO + 0.014 * CH_4$$

The proposed grouping results from the combined effects that each primary pollutant has on ecosystems. GWP is a measure of climatic change, where ACID is primarily related to the effect of acid rain, eutrophication of ecosystems and cardiovascular diseases in humans. TOFP is related to the production of ozone in the lowest atmosphere and can be a major factor influencing the respiratory (e.g. asthma) and cardiovascular systems of humans. Both TOFP and ACID have been found to severely damage monuments of significant cultural heritage. PM10 is presently one of the most important pollutants associated with respiratory problems and carcinogenic potency. In a study conducted for 29 European cities (Katsouyanni *et al.*, 2001), the result for the city of Athens showed that an increase in daily PM10 levels by 10 mg/m3 results in an increase of the mortality rate by approximately 1.5%.

COMPILATION OF REGIONAL INPUT-OUTPUT TABLES FOR THE GREEK ECONOMY AND FOR THE YEAR 2005

According to Skountzos (Skountzos, *et al.*, 2007) the compilation of primary regional Input-Output tables is very costly and time-consuming and most countries prefer to adjust national tables to a regional level. In order to obtain an Input-Output table for a specific region from a national Input-Output table, the technique follows these steps:

a) Regionalization of national input-output coefficients.

b) Calculation of the quadrants of final demand, intermediate inputs and initial inputs of the regional Input-Output Tables.

Regionalization of National Input-Output Coefficients for the Greek Economy

In order to convert national input-output coefficients into regional coefficients according to Skountzos (Skountzos, *et al.*, 2007) we use the technique of adjusting national coefficients on the basis of the location quotients of a region. This requires the calculation of the Simple Location Quotient (*SLQ*) of an industry in a region and the Cross-Industry Location Quotient (*CILQ*) of an industry in a region.

The definition for *SLQ* of industry *i* in Region *R* is

$$SLQ_i^R = (X_i^R / X^R) / (X_i^N / X^N) = (X_i^R / X_i^N)(X^N / X^R) \quad \textbf{(1)}$$

X_i^R = Gross production (or employment) of industry *i* in region *R*

X^R = Gross production (or employment) of all industries in region *R*

X_i^N = Gross production (or employment) of industry i in the country as a whole

X^N = Gross production (or employment) of all industries in the country as a whole

The numerator in the equation (1) represents the participation of industry i of region R in the total production of the region. The denominator of the equation (1) represents the participation of total production of industry i of the country in the total production of the country. If industry i is less concentrated in region R than it is at a national level ($SLQ_i^R<1$) it is concluded that industry i is less capable of satisfying regional demand for its output and the direct input coefficient a_{ij}^{RR} (j=1,..., n) is estimated on the basis of the national input coefficients a_{ij}^N, by multiplying them with SLQ_i^R. If, however, industry i is more concentrated than at national level ($SLQ_i^R>1$) it is concluded that the national input coefficient a_{ij}^N, (j=1, ..., n) holds for the region and the 'surplus' of the output produced by industry i is exported to other regions. Thus, for row i in an estimated regional Input-Output table, the corresponding coefficients will be shaped as follows:

If $SLQ_i^R<1$, then $a_{ij}^{RR} = a_{ij}^N \cdot SLQ_i^R$, that is, the elements of row i of the coefficients of the national table are multiplied by SLQ_i^R.

If $SLQ_i^R>1$, then $a_{ij}^{RR} = a_{ij}^N$, that is, the elements of row i of the national table hold.

According to Skountzos (Skountzos, *et al.*, 2007) in equation (1) the fraction X_i^R/X_i^N represents the relative size of industry i, which supplies inputs to the industries that use its output, while the fraction X^R/X^N represents the relative size of the region. When industry i of region R is relatively small in comparison with industry j which uses the output of the former industry, then a part of inputs j must be imported by the region.

For the purpose of taking into consideration the relative size of industry j of region R, the national coefficients must also be modified with the Cross-Industry Location Quotient ($CILQ$), which is defined as:

$$CILQ_{ij}^R = (X_i^R/X_i^N) / (X_j^R/X_j^N) \quad \textbf{(2)}$$

The numerator of (2) represents the relative size of the industry in the region in comparison with the industry at a national level, while the denominator X_j^R / X_j^N represents the relative size of industry j of region R in comparison with industry j at a national level.

When $CILQ_{ij}^R<1$, industry i of the region is relatively small in comparison with industry j of the region that uses inputs of industry i. In such a case, part of the inputs of industry j must be imported, while when $CILQ_{ij}^R>1$, all the needs of industry j in terms of the output of industry i can be satisfied from within the region.

The coefficients along the diagonal of the national table of coefficients are multiplied by the corresponding SLQ, while elements outside the diagonal are modified as follows:

$$\text{If } CILQ_{ij}^R<1, \text{ then } a_{ij}^R = a_{ij}^N \cdot CILQ_{ij}^R$$

$$\text{If } CILQ_{ij}^R>1, \text{ then } a_{ij}^R = a_{ij}^N$$

Quadrant of Intermediate Consumption and Value Added for the Greek Economy

Having determined the regional input-output coefficients for each region, the next step is according to Skountzos (Skountzos, *et al.*, 2007) to estimate the quadrants of the Input-Output tables for that region.

The intermediate inputs of product i which are used in production in industry j of region R are given by the relationship:

$$Q_{ij}^R = a_{ij}^R Q_j^R \quad \textbf{(3)}$$

Q_{ij}^R = Input value of product i in the production of industry j of region R estimated at basic prices

Q_j^R = Gross value of production of product j of region R estimated at basic prices.

The regional coefficients a_{ij}^R are determined in a previous stage; if the value of production Q_j^R of industry j is known, then the intermediate inputs Q_{ij}^R can be calculated by relationship (3).

Final Demand Quadrant for the Greek Economy and for the Year 2005

The final demand quadrant consists of the vectors of private consumption, of government consumption, of investments and of net exports.

In accordance with Skountzos (Skountzos, *et al.*, 2007) the regionalization of the corresponding vectors of the national table is carried out as follows:

a) Private consumption is regionalized by using the data of the most recent Survey of Family Budgets of the National Statistical Service of Greece.

b) Government consumption is by definition equal to the aggregate of the salaries of public servants and the intermediate consumption required to produce public goods.

For the purpose of regionalizing the national magnitude, the number of public servants by industry (health, education, etc.) and region is used, as provided by the National Statistical Service of Greece.

c) Regional data by industry pertaining to investments are available in the publication 'Regional Accounts' of the National Statistical Service of Greece (NSSG, 2007).

d) Regional data on net exports may be obtained by deducting the regionalized magnitudes of users of each product (intermediate consumption, private consumption, government consumption, investments) from the estimated gross value of production by industry.

Regional Environmental Data

The air emissions data set, on a country level, were further attributed to a regional level, using the following approach:

- Obtain emissions data from the European Pollutant Emission Register database (EPER) and assign the facility on the corresponding region and NACE code.
- For each economic activity, which contains large point sources (LPS), deduce the LPS total from the country total.
- The remain from the previous step was assigned to each region using ancillary data, such as the number of enterprises, gross value added, and gross domestic product of the region, depending on the economic activity level.
- The finally estimated air emissions for each region were estimated as the sum of the previously estimated quantity and the total of LPS for each activity code.

CALCULATION OF ECO-INDICATORS

Methodology

The methodology of Miller and Blair (2009) has been followed to calculate emission multipliers. The total emission coefficient per production unit in each economic sector, as well as for final demand categories, has been estimated on the basis of input-output modelling in a number of recent studies including Cadarso & Fernandez-Bolanos (2002), Braibant (2002), Mylonas N. *et al.* (2000) and Belegri-Roboli A., Tsolas I. (2005). Input-output analysis is used in this paper for the calculation of emission multipliers for the various industries and pollutant types. The pollution indicators have been constructed using the following methodology:

We can express the input-output model in matrix terms:

$$X= AX+Y \quad (4)$$

Matrix A is known as the matrix of the technical coefficients, X the vector of total resources of the sector and Y the vector of final use of the products. Solving the equation (4) for X, we obtain:

$$X= (I-A)^{-1} Y \quad (5)$$

Where $(I-A)^{-1}$ is often referred to as the Leontief inverse. We applied a domestic oriented model, starting from final demand and quantifying the direct and indirect effects on production and emissions activated by final demand. The results can be presented as a re-attribution of the domestic production, which is derived from the basic Leontief model:

$$(I - A^{d)} X = (F^{t} - M) \quad (6)$$

A^d matrix of the domestic technical coefficients ($A^{t} = A^d + A^{m}$),

F^t vector of total (domestic + imported) final demand by industry,

M the import vector by industry, which is subtracted from total final demand.

The direct emission intensity coefficients a_{kj}^{e} of the k type of emission by industry j are defined by:

$$a_{kj}^{e} = E_{kj}/X_j \; j=1,\ldots, n \quad (7)$$

E_{kj} quantity of emission k by industry j (components of vector E)

X_j domestic value of output of industry j.

The coefficients a_{kj}^{e} show the extent to which each industry generates a certain direct emission intensity factor and describe the physical quantity of emission directly caused by the production of goods as a ratio of the value of domestic production at basic prices. We also compute the total environmental dependencies:

$$\varepsilon_{kj} = \hat{\mathbf{a}}_{kj}^{e} (\mathbf{I} - \mathbf{A}^{d})^{-1} \quad (8)$$

where ε_{kj} is the matrix of induced emission coefficients showing the emission intensity, including the induced emission in other industries indirectly affected by a change in final demand of a given industry (Mylonas, *et al.*, 2000).

The elasticity of emissions intensity with respect to final consumption e_j^c is estimated as the row sum of ε_{kj}, $e_j^c = \sum \varepsilon_{kj}$, including direct and indirect emissions for the j-th industry. These emissions are produced in the whole economy after the increase of a unitary expansion of the final demand of the specific industry.

The column sum of ε_{kj}, $e_k^p = \sum \varepsilon_{kj}$ is an estimate of the total emissions of the pollutants in the whole economy owing to a one unit increase of a given industry's production, termed as the elasticity of the emissions intensity with respect to production.

The direct and indirect emission intensity per unit of final demand categories is computed by the following operation:

$$\varepsilon^{d} = \hat{\boldsymbol{\varepsilon}}_{kj} \boldsymbol{F}^{t} \quad (9)$$

Where ε^d is the industry's extent of each emission factor intensity on each final demand component of the Greek economy for the year 2005.

Results

Tables **2a** – **6b**. (See Appendix) show the estimated coefficients by industry for the environmental stressors examined at regional level.

Regarding the direct emission intensity coefficient a_{kj}, the most important environmental stressor appears to be GWP and in particular CO_2, which dominates the emissions in this category.

At a regional level the highest direct emission intensity coefficient a_{kj} are in Central, Western & Eastern Macedonia and Thrace, followed by Attica, Western Greece, Peloponnese & the Ionian Islands, Southern & Northern Aegean and Crete, Thessaly, Epirus and Central Greece.

According to Ministry for the Environment Physical Planning and Public Works, (Ministry for the Environment Physical Planning and Public Works, 2008) electricity in Greece is produced by conventional energy sources, in which lignite is a important part. It is remarkable that two of the electricity generation facilities of the Public Power Corporation SA (one in Macedonia- Ptolemaida and one in Peloponnese-Megalopoly) are two of the most polluting production plants in Creece.

Furthermore, in NAMEA framework can be investigated the possibility of substituting lignite with solar energy for the production of electricity, and specifically the use of photovoltaic technology with the aim of reducing emissions and particularly CO_2, which is the majority of all greenhouse gas emissions and thus considered to be primarily responsible for climate change.

At regional level the highest direct emission intensity coefficients appear in: Attica in the NACE industries 23 and 37.Southern & Northern Aegean and Crete in the NACE industries 26 and 40-41 .Western Greece, Peloponnese & the Ionian Islands in the NACE industries 23 and 40-41. Thessaly, Epirus and Central Greece in the NACE industries 26 and 40-41.Central, Western & Eastern Macedonia and Thrace in the NACE industries 37 and 40-41

As expected, the energy production sector (NACE 40-41) exhibits the highest direct emission intensity coefficient, which is in line with similar studies (Tarancon Moran, 2008).

Other significant parameters are found in the manufacture of coke, refined petroleum products and nuclear fuel (NACE 23) manufacture of other non-metallic mineral products sectors (NACE 26) and recycling (NACE 37).

Of the other stressors, TOFP, ACID and PM10 exhibit lower values mainly in Attica in the NACE industry 23, Southern & Northern Aegean and Crete in the industry NACE 26 and Western Greece, Peloponnese & the Ionian Islands in the NACE industry 23.

The quantity e_k^p represents the total emission intensity of the industry induced directly and indirectly by the increase of 1000 units of final demand in all industries. As for a_{kj}^e, GWP appears to be the most important stressor. The highest values are found in: Central, Western & Eastern Macedonia and Thrace in the NACE industries 37 and 40-41. Attica in the NACE industries 23 and 37. Thessaly, Epirus and Central Greece in the NACE industry 26 .Western Greece, Peloponnese & the Ionian Islands in the NACE industries 23 and 40-41. Southern & Northern Aegean and Crete in the NACE industries 26 and 40-41.

Of the other stressors, TOFP, ACID and PM10 exhibit lower values.

The quantity e_j^c represents the total emission intensity of the industry induced directly and indirectly by the increase of 1000 units of final demand in all industries. The results are in accordance with the other indices estimated previously, with only GWP having an impact on the economy in the same industries and in the same regions but in different order: Attica, Central, Western & Eastern Macedonia and Thrace, Western Greece, Peloponnese & the Ionian Islands Thessaly, Epirus and Central Greece, Southern & Northern Aegean and Crete.

Tables **2b, 3b, 4b, 5b** and **6b** (See Appendix) present e^{d}, which is the industry's extent of direct and indirect emissions intensity factors per 1000 units on each of the final demand components. Household final consumption is the major category in all air emissions, followed by investment with the exception PM10.A general observation is the negative net exports in final demand; which means a great part of the emissions from other regions move to the region. (Regarding net exports, see p.8)

This finding suggests that any significant effort to reduce air emissions in Greece must seriously take into account demand side management and energy efficiency measures.

CONCLUSIONS

This paper discussed the construction NAMEA tables at a regional level for the year 2005.

The tables were constructed using estimations of emission inventories prepared by the Greek Ministry of the Environment and Public Works and economic activity data from the 2005 regional Input-Output Tables for the Greek economy. The five main regions of Greece have been determined in accordance with the National Strategic Reference Framework (NSRF) approved by the European Commission for the period 2007-2013.

The calculated indicators include the direct emission intensity coefficient, the direct and indirect emission intensity coefficients and the emission factors intensity on the components of final demand.

The analysis of the results showed that from a production perspective the most important environmental stressor in economic terms appears to be Global Warming Potential, which is directly related to CO_2.

At regional level the highest direct emission intensity coefficients a_{kj}^{e} are met in Central, Western & Eastern Macedonia and Thrace, followed by Attica, Western Greece, Peloponnese & the Ionian Islands, Southern & Northern Aegean and Crete, Thessaly, Epirus and Central Greece.

As for a_{kj}^{e}, in e_k^{p} GWP appears to be the most important stressor. The highest values of this stressor are found in: Central, Western & Eastern Macedonia and Thrace in the NACE industries 37 and 40-41. Attica, in the NACE industries 23 and 37 .Thessaly, Epirus and Central Greece in the NACE industry 26 .Western Greece, Peloponnese & the Ionian Islands in the NACE industries 23 and 40-41. Southern & Northern Aegean and Crete in the NACE industries 26 and 40-41

Of the other stressors, TOFP, ACID and PM10 exhibit lower values.

Regarding the e_j^{c} the results are in accordance with the other indices estimated previously, with only GWP impacting on the economy in the same industries and in the same regions but in different order: Attica, Central, Western & Eastern Macedonia and Thrace, Western Greece, Peloponnese & the Ionian Islands Thessaly, Epirus and Central Greece, Southern & Northern Aegean and Crete.

An in-depth analysis of economic activity found that the worse emitting industries are energy producing ones NACE 40-41 and the industries NACE 37, 26, 23.

Household consumption appeared to have the highest impact on air emissions from a demand perspective, which may point to the need for a more rational distribution of energy production. A general observation is the negative net exports in final demand; which means a great part of the emissions from other regions move to the region.

This finding suggests that any significant effort to reduce air emissions in Greece must seriously take into account demand side management and energy efficiency measures.

REFERENCES

Braibant, M. (2002). Environmental Accounts in France: NAMEA pilot study for France. *Fourteenth International Conference on Input- Output Techniques,* from http//www.iioa.org

Belegri- Roboli, A. and Tsolas, I. (2005). Estimation of intensity coefficients of total emissions in Greece (1988-96): An environmental input-output analysis. Proceedings of the 9th International Conference on Environmental Science and Technology, Rhodes Island, Greece 1-3 September 2005, pp. A-166-172.

Cadarso, A. and Fernández-Bolanos, A.F. (2002). Patterns of growth and consumption and their influence on the environment in Spain. *Fourteenth International Conference on Input-Output Techniques,* from http//www.iioa.org

Commission of the European Communities (1994). Direction for the EU on Environmental Indicators and Green National Accounting. The Integration of Environmental and Economic Information Systems. Brussels.

De Haan, M. and Keuning, J. S. (1996). Taking the Environment into Account: The NAMEA Approach. *The Review of Income and Wealth. Series 42, No. 2, June 199,* pp.131-148.

De Haan, M. and Kee, P. (2004). Accounting for sustainable Development. The NAMEA-based approach. Statistics Netherlands, OECD.

Economidis, Ch., Keramidas, D., Demertzi, A., Stromplos, N. and Vlachogianni, D. (2008). The compilation of a Greek environmental Input-Output Table for 2005. *International Input-Output meeting on managing environment. Seville, 2008. International Input-Output Association,* from http//www.iioa.org European Pollutant Emission Register (EPER) from http://www.eper.ec.europa.eu/eper/

Eurostat (1996). NACE Rev.1 Statistical classification of economic activities in the *European Community*. Luxemburg.

Eurostat (2001). NAMEA for air emissions Results of pilot studies, Theme 2 Economy *and finance.* European Commission, from http://epp.eurostat.ec.europa.eu

European Environmental Agency (2003). Europe's Environment: The Third Assessment. Environmental assessment report, No 10, European Environmental Agency, Copenhagen.

European Environmental Agency (2006). *Environmental Input-Output Analyses based on NAMEA data*. European Environmental Agency.

European Commission (2002). The Sixth Environment Action Programme of the European Community 2002-2012, Environment 2010: Our future, our choice. European Community, Luxemburg.

Eurostat (2007). NAMEA for Air Emissions. Compilation Guide. Preliminary Draft Version to be discussed and further developed by the ESTAT NAMEA TF, European Community.

Leontief, W. (1970). Environmental repercussion and the economic structure: an Input-output approach. *Review of Economics and Statistics, V. 52, n. 3,* pp. 262-271.

Leontief, W. and Ford, D. (1972). Air Pollution and the economic structure: empirical results of input-output computations. *In Input-Output Techniques, Eds. A. Brody and A. Carter. New York: American Elsevie*, pp .9-30.

Katsouyanni, K., Touloumi, G. and Samoli, E. (2001). Confounding and effect modification in the short-term effects of ambient particles on total mortality: Results from 29 European cities within the APHEA2 project. *Epidemiology 12*, pp. 521-531.

Medina, S., Plasencia, A., Ballester, F., Mücke, H.G. and Schwartz J. (2004). Apheis: public health impact of PM10 in 19 European cities. *J. Epidemiol. Community Health 58b,* pp. 831-836.

Miller, E.R. and Blair, P.D. (2009). *Input–Output Analysis Foundation and Extensions*. Cambridge University Press, 2nd revised edition.

Ministry for the Environment Physical Planning and Public Works. (2008). Annual inventory submission under the convention and the Kyoto protocol for greenhouse *and other cases for the years 1990-2006.* Ministry for the environment physical planning and public works.

Mylonas, N., Economakou, M., Frankopoulos, N., Krasadakis, A., Molfetas, K. Stromplos, N. and Vlachos, P. (2000). *Natural Resource and Environmental Input-Output Tables for Greece, 1988-98.* Eurostat and Institute of Computer and Communications Systems (ICCS) of National Technical University of Athens National Statistical Service of Greece (2005). *Input-Output Table for 2005.* Piraeus, mimeo.

National Statistical Service of Greece (2007). *Regional Accounts 2003-2005*. Piraeus. ECMT/OECD (1995). *Urban Travel and Sustainable Development*. OECD, Paris.

ECMT/OECD (2002). Implementing Sustainable Urban Travel Policies Final Report. OECD.

Skountzos, Th. (2007). *Inter-industry Relations in the Greek economy at National and Regional Level.* Academy of Athens. Studies: No 7 (in Greek).

Tarancon Moran, M.A., Del Rio, P. and Callejas Albinana, F. (2008). Tracking the genealogy of CO_2 emissions in the electricity sector: An intersectoral approach applied to the Spanish case. *Energy Policy*, 36, pp. 1915-1925.

United Nations (2000). Handbook of national accounting, integrated environmental and economic accounting. *An operational manual.* Series F, No. 78, New York.

United Nations (1993). *Handbook of National Accounting. Integrated Environmental and Economic Accounting.* Series F, No 61, New York.

APPENDIX

All environmental pressure variables are estimated in k Tonnes.

Table 2a: Emission intensity coefficients by industry and pollutant in Attica region

	GWP			TOFP			ACID			PM10		
	a_{kj}^e	e_k^p	e_j^c	a_{kj}	e_k^p	e_j^c	a_{kj}^e	e_k^p	e_j^c	a_{kj}^e	e_k^p	e_j^c
01 & 02	1.4632	3.8036	1.8355	0.0100	0.0286	0.0126	0.0127	0.0305	0.0159	0.0004	0.0007	0.0005
5	0.2509	2.3121	0.2544	0.0072	0.0249	0.0073	0.0026	0.0181	0.0026	0.0007	0.0008	0.0007
10,11&12 / 13-14	1.5482	3.8467	1.9000	0.0248	0.0413	0.0304	0.0076	0.0237	0.0093	0.0020	0.0023	0.0025
15-16	0.0996	0.6186	0.1366	0.0022	0.0063	0.0029	0.0004	0.0042	0.0005	0.0000	0.0001	0.0000
17-19	0.0825	1.5352	0.0939	0.0099	0.0217	0.0113	-0.0001	0.0105	-0.0001	0.0001	0.0003	0.0001
20A	0.0119	1.0309	0.0133	0.0032	0.0112	0.0036	0.0001	0.0076	0.0001	0.0000	0.0002	0.0000
21-22	0.0504	0.7292	0.0713	0.0013	0.0055	0.0018	0.0003	0.0043	0.0004	0.0004	0.0005	0.0005
23	23.0982	23.4637	43.5326	0.1973	0.2007	0.3717	0.1741	0.1764	0.3282	0.0018	0.0019	0.0033
24-25	0.9405	1.8885	1.5604	0.0067	0.0137	0.0112	0.0095	0.0161	0.0157	0.0004	0.0005	0.0007
26	2.7673	6.8020	3.4134	0.0214	0.0433	0.0264	0.0267	0.0474	0.0329	0.0027	0.0033	0.0034
27	0.7926	4.0253	1.1119	0.0069	0.0191	0.0097	0.0104	0.0224	0.0146	0.0023	0.0025	0.0032
28	0.4004	1.7362	0.5800	0.0010	0.0078	0.0014	0.0024	0.0097	0.0034	0.0001	0.0005	0.0001
29-36	1.2516	3.2304	1.8673	0.0025	0.0097	0.0037	0.0090	0.0160	0.0135	0.0000	0.0003	0.0001
37	28.2377	28.6769	34.5765	0.0396	0.0429	0.0485	0.0309	0.0340	0.0379	0.0007	0.0008	0.0009
40-41	5.2786	7.9223	8.1275	0.0101	0.0302	0.0156	0.0288	0.0476	0.0443	0.0003	0.0005	0.0004
45	0.0124	1.5739	0.0142	0.0024	0.0124	0.0027	0.0004	0.0108	0.0004	0.0001	0.0006	0.0001
50-52	0.0114	0.7003	0.0262	0.0004	0.0060	0.0010	0.0001	0.0052	0.0001	0.0000	0.0001	0.0000
55	0.0127	0.6196	0.0132	0.0004	0.0051	0.0004	0.0001	0.0045	0.0001	0.0000	0.0001	0.0000
60-64	0.2212	2.2674	0.3674	0.0059	0.0230	0.0098	0.0041	0.0194	0.0068	0.0001	0.0003	0.0001
65-67	0.0015	0.5253	0.0029	0.0002	0.0045	0.0003	0.0000	0.0039	0.0001	0.0000	0.0001	0.0000
70-74	0.0022	0.1636	0.0053	0.0001	0.0012	0.0001	0.0000	0.0011	0.0000	0.0000	0.0000	0.0000
75&90	0.1659	1.0654	0.1659	0.0010	0.0061	0.0010	0.0004	0.0059	0.0004	0.0001	0.0002	0.0001
80-84	0.0294	0.2995	0.0297	0.0007	0.0027	0.0007	0.0003	0.0022	0.0003	0.0000	0.0000	0.0000
85	0.0154	0.5210	0.0156	0.0005	0.0040	0.0005	0.0001	0.0038	0.0001	0.0000	0.0001	0.0000
91	0.0160	0.3773	0.0199	0.0000	0.0028	0.0000	0.0000	0.0027	0.0000	0.0000	0.0001	0.0000
92, 93, 95 & 99	0.0731	0.0731	0.0731	0.0104	0.0104	0.0103	0.0014	0.0014	0.0014	0.0001	0.0001	0.0001

Table 2b: Percentage attribution of final demand in Attica region

	Final consumption of Households	**Final consumption of non-profit organizations**	**Final consumption of Government**	**Gross fixed capital investment**	**Changes in inventories**	**Exports**
GWP	81.5144	0.6418	75.6050	141.8555	0.1794	-199.7961
TOFP	60.1291	0.4250	41.0602	72.2965	0.2393	-74.1500
ACID	72.2682	0.5515	54.2443	105.2822	0.3189	-132.6651
PM10	24.3809	0.1943	26.7905	82.1990	0.2158	-33.7806

Table 3a: Emission intensity coefficients by industry and pollutant in Southern & Northern Aegean and Crete region

	GWP			TOFP			ACID			PM10		
	a_{kj}^{e}	e_{k}^{p}	e_{j}^{c}	a_{kj}	e_{k}^{p}	e_{j}^{c}	a_{kj}^{e}	e_{k}^{p}	e_{j}^{c}	a_{kj}^{e}	e_{k}^{p}	e_{j}^{c}
01 & 02	1.4457	2.3699	2.7499	0.0100	0.0188	0.0382	0.0127	0.0230	0.0483	0.0004	0.0007	0.0008
5	0.3201	0.3543	0.3302	0.0092	0.0096	0.0191	0.0033	0.0036	0.0068	0.0008	0.0009	0.0009
10,11& 12 / 13-14	1.5482	2.2394	2.2184	0.0248	0.0311	0.0710	0.0076	0.0173	0.0218	0.0020	0.0022	0.0029
15-16	1.5932	2.7952	2.0221	0.0304	0.0423	0.0771	0.0041	0.0151	0.0104	0.0002	0.0006	0.0002
17-19	1.0624	2.4230	1.1605	0.1279	0.1516	0.2794	-0.0013	0.0148	-0.0029	0.0008	0.0015	0.0008
20A	1.1463	2.1519	1.2082	0.3068	0.3288	0.6468	0.0064	0.0183	0.0137	0.0022	0.0028	0.0023
21-22	0.7029	1.2079	0.7899	0.0174	0.0221	0.0392	0.0036	0.0101	0.0081	0.0054	0.0056	0.0060
23	0	0.0000	0.0000	0	0.0000	0.0000	0	0.0000	0.0000	0	0.0000	0.0000
24-25	3.4573	4.0947	5.5099	0.0234	0.0303	0.0748	0.0341	0.0433	0.1087	0.0014	0.0018	0.0023
26	11.0371	12.9362	12.7424	0.2113	0.2411	0.4878	0.3340	0.3815	0.7827	0.0384	0.0423	0.0444
27	3.5126	4.7284	4.7626	0.0307	0.0429	0.0832	0.0460	0.0639	0.1248	0.0100	0.0107	0.0136
28	3.2059	4.5036	4.5240	0.0077	0.0181	0.0216	0.0189	0.0350	0.0535	0.0007	0.0026	0.0010
29-36	5.5873	6.2294	7.9471	0.0112	0.0175	0.0319	0.0403	0.0485	0.1148	0.0002	0.0010	0.0003
37	0	0.0000	0.0000	0	0.0000	0.0000	0	0.0000	0.0000	0	0.0000	0.0000
40-41	7.9675	9.0355	12.6354	0.1078	0.1216	0.3418	0.1583	0.1743	0.5020	0.0007	0.0011	0.0011
45	0.0174	0.9612	0.0206	0.0033	0.0155	0.0078	0.0005	0.0185	0.0012	0.0001	0.0020	0.0001
50-52	0.0222	0.3763	0.0492	0.0009	0.0040	0.0039	0.0001	0.0042	0.0005	0.0000	0.0002	0.0000
55	0.0127	0.2180	0.0135	0.0004	0.0033	0.0008	0.0001	0.0026	0.0003	0.0001	0.0001	0.0000
60-64	0.2212	0.4622	0.3466	0.0059	0.0083	0.0184	0.0041	0.0072	0.0128	0.0001	0.0002	0.0002
65-67	0.0015	0.1535	0.0026	0.0002	0.0021	0.0006	0.0000	0.0024	0.0001	0.0000	0.0001	0.0000
70-74	0.0022	0.1527	0.0044	0.0001	0.0018	0.0002	0.0000	0.0024	0.0000	0.0000	0.0002	0.0000
75&90	0.1671	1.0809	0.1671	0.0011	0.0057	0.0022	0.0004	0.0090	0.0008	0.0000	0.0004	0.0001
80-84	0.0299	0.1514	0.0302	0.0007	0.0019	0.0015	0.0003	0.0020	0.0005	0.0000	0.0001	0.0000
85	0.0156	0.5013	0.0158	0.0005	0.0043	0.0010	0.0001	0.0057	0.0003	0.0000	0.0002	0.0000
91	0.0096	0.1355	0.0118	0.0000	0.0014	0.0000	0.0000	0.0019	0.0000	0.0000	0.0001	0.0000
92, 93, 95 & 99	0.1653	0.1653	0.1653	0.0235	0.0235	0.0469	0.0031	0.0031	0.0062	0.0001	0.0001	0.0001

Table 3b: Percentage attribution of final demand in Southern & Northern Aegean and Crete region

	Final consumption of Households	Final consumption of non-profit organizations	Final consumption of Government	Gross fixed capital investment	Changes in inventories	Exports
GWP	461.3812	0.0989	23.0957	118.7791	0.0156	-503.3704
TOFP	512.4911	0.0739	9.3386	53.8672	0.0340	-475.8048
ACID	340.3206	0.0923	13.5719	86.0828	0.0248	-340.0925
PM10	605.9192	0.0951	19.5321	190.6996	0.0641	-716.3102

Table 4a: Emission intensity coefficients by industry and pollutant in West Creece, Peloponnese and the Ionian islands region

	GWP			TOFP			ACID			PM10		
	a_{kj}^{e}	e_{k}^{p}	e_{j}^{c}	a_{kj}^{e}	e_{k}^{p}	e_{j}^{c}	a_{kj}^{e}	e_{k}^{p}	e_{j}^{c}	a_{kj}^{e}	e_{k}^{p}	e_{j}^{c}
01 & 02	1.4336	2.4229	3.1149	0.0100	0.0148	0.0218	0.0125	0.0263	0.0272	0.0004	0.0006	0.0009
5	0.2982	0.6994	0.3079	0.0086	0.0104	0.0089	0.0031	0.0081	0.0032	0.0008	0.0008	0.0008
10,11& 12 / 13-14	1.5482	2.8662	2.6904	0.0248	0.0288	0.0431	0.0076	0.0359	0.0132	0.0020	0.0024	0.0035
15-16	0.1147	1.5158	0.1477	0.0022	0.0103	0.0028	0.0005	0.0179	0.0006	0.0000	0.0004	0.0000
17-19	0.0215	1.3073	0.0242	0.0026	0.0080	0.0029	0.0000	0.0255	0.0000	0.0000	0.0004	0.0000

20A	0.0396	1.0181	0.0425	0.0106	0.0149	0.0114	0.0002	0.0180	0.0002	0.0001	0.0003	0.0001
21-22	0.0605	0.5994	0.0659	0.0015	0.0034	0.0016	0.0003	0.0110	0.0003	0.0005	0.0006	0.0005
23	11.0507	11.7230	17.5415	0.0401	0.0465	0.0637	0.1321	0.1412	0.2096	0.0001	0.0006	0.0001
24-25	0.5475	1.3658	0.7841	0.0037	0.0066	0.0053	0.0054	0.0228	0.0077	0.0002	0.0005	0.0003
26	3.0280	4.7486	3.6877	0.0172	0.0248	0.0209	0.0151	0.0454	0.0184	0.0016	0.0022	0.0019
27	0.5355	1.7919	0.7616	0.0047	0.0087	0.0067	0.0070	0.0352	0.0100	0.0015	0.0020	0.0022
28	0.5538	1.3598	0.7392	0.0013	0.0047	0.0018	0.0033	0.0189	0.0044	0.0001	0.0007	0.0002
29-36	0.5990	1.0244	0.8322	0.0012	0.0030	0.0017	0.0043	0.0128	0.0060	0.0000	0.0002	0.0000
37	0.0000	0.0000	0.0000	0.0000	0.0000	0.0000	0.0000	0.0000	0.0000	0.0000	0.0000	0.0000
40-41	10.1381	11.9516	16.4469	0.0137	0.0213	0.0223	0.3297	0.3678	0.5349	0.0042	0.0049	0.0069
45	0.0162	0.6336	0.0191	0.0031	0.0062	0.0036	0.0005	0.0081	0.0006	0.0001	0.0004	0.0001
50-52	0.0148	0.2535	0.0322	0.0006	0.0020	0.0013	0.0001	0.0044	0.0001	0.0000	0.0001	0.0000
55	0.0127	0.4133	0.0135	0.0004	0.0024	0.0004	0.0001	0.0079	0.0001	0.0000	0.0001	0.0000
60-64	0.2212	0.8018	0.3444	0.0059	0.0082	0.0092	0.0041	0.0135	0.0064	0.0001	0.0002	0.0002
65-67	0.0015	0.2411	0.0025	0.0002	0.0012	0.0003	0.0000	0.0050	0.0001	0.0000	0.0001	0.0000
70-74	0.0022	0.0877	0.0043	0.0001	0.0006	0.0001	0.0000	0.0014	0.0000	0.0000	0.0000	0.0000
75&90	0.1709	0.5028	0.1709	0.0011	0.0024	0.0011	0.0004	0.0065	0.0004	0.0001	0.0002	0.0001
80-84	0.0304	0.1312	0.0307	0.0007	0.0011	0.0008	0.0003	0.0026	0.0003	0.0000	0.0001	0.0000
85	0.0164	0.2230	0.0166	0.0005	0.0013	0.0005	0.0001	0.0043	0.0001	0.0000	0.0001	0.0000
91	0.0607	0.2138	0.0749	0.0001	0.0006	0.0001	0.0001	0.0033	0.0001	0.0000	0.0001	0.0001
92, 93, 95 & 99	0.0794	0.0794	0.0794	0.0113	0.0113	0.0113	0.0015	0.0015	0.0015	0.0001	0.0001	0.0001

Table 4b: Percentage attribution of final demand in West Creece, Peloponnese and the Ionian islands region

	Final consumption of Households	Final consumption of non-profit organizations	Final consumption of Government	Gross fixed capital investment	Changes in inventories	Exports
GWP	176.2458	0.0900	7.1104	26.2549	0.0485	-109.7496
TOFP	161.6324	0.0481	6.6992	31.9071	0.0621	-100.3489
ACID	146.7202	0.0684	4.9443	16.4191	0.0493	-68.2013
PM10	118.2216	0.0945	5.7650	28.2851	0.0578	-52.4240

Table 5a: Emission intensity coefficients by industry and pollutant in Thessaly, Epirus and Central Creece region

	GWP			TOFP			ACID			PM10		
	a_{kj}^e	e_k^p	e_j^c	a_{kj}^e	e_k^p	e_j^c	a_{kj}^e	e_k^p	e_j^c	a_{kj}^e	e_k^p	e_j^c
01 & 02	1.4363	1.8661	3.16148	0.0100	0.0130	0.02209	0.0126	0.0164	0.02766	0.0004	0.0006	0.00096
5	0.3007	0.3316	0.30904	0.0087	0.0091	0.00892	0.0031	0.0035	0.00320	0.0008	0.0008	0.00082
10,11& 12 / 13-14	1.5482	1.7304	2.09289	0.0248	0.0256	0.03350	0.0076	0.0094	0.01026	0.0020	0.0021	0.00276
15-16	0.0643	1.0060	0.08619	0.0012	0.0078	0.00164	0.0003	0.0086	0.00035	0.0000	0.0003	0.00001
17-19	0.0149	0.4850	0.01668	0.0018	0.0051	0.00201	0.0000	0.0046	-0.00002	0.0000	0.0002	0.00001
20A	0.0237	0.2886	0.02551	0.0064	0.0082	0.00683	0.0001	0.0027	0.00014	0.0000	0.0001	0.00005
21-22	0.0611	0.1797	0.06459	0.0015	0.0022	0.00160	0.0029	0.0041	0.00307	0.0005	0.0005	0.00049
23	0.0000	0.0000	0.00000	0.0000	0.0000	0.00000	0.0000	0.0000	0.00000	0.0000	0.0000	0.00000

24-25	0.3656	0.5592	0.52975	0.0025	0.0037	0.00360	0.0036	0.0054	0.00523	0.0002	0.0002	0.00022
26	12.6650	14.0202	15.61357	0.0404	0.0467	0.04986	0.0276	0.0320	0.03404	0.0030	0.0035	0.00371
27	1.8800	2.0302	2.84944	0.0041	0.0048	0.00619	0.0186	0.0195	0.02814	0.0009	0.0010	0.00137
28	0.2579	0.8502	0.33519	0.0006	0.0023	0.00080	0.0015	0.0068	0.00198	0.0001	0.0003	0.00008
29-36	0.3276	0.5980	0.44564	0.0007	0.0016	0.00089	0.0024	0.0046	0.00322	0.0000	0.0001	0.00002
37	0.0000	0.0000	0.00000	0.0000	0.0000	0.00000	0.0000	0.0000	0.00000	0.0000	0.0000	0.00000
40-41	2.2842	2.7252	3.31924	0.0066	0.0108	0.00962	0.0306	0.0344	0.04448	0.0003	0.0006	0.00040
45	0.0144	1.4871	0.01703	0.0027	0.0078	0.00324	0.0004	0.0052	0.00052	0.0001	0.0005	0.00011
50-52	0.0157	0.1014	0.03206	0.0006	0.0015	0.00126	0.0001	0.0009	0.00015	0.0000	0.0000	0.00000
55	0.0127	0.2340	0.01351	0.0004	0.0020	0.00039	0.0001	0.0021	0.00014	0.0000	0.0001	0.00001
60-64	0.2212	0.2930	0.32910	0.0059	0.0065	0.00876	0.0041	0.0049	0.00607	0.0001	0.0001	0.00014
65-67	0.0015	0.0604	0.00242	0.0002	0.0007	0.00026	0.0000	0.0006	0.00005	0.0000	0.0000	0.00000
70-74	0.0022	0.1097	0.00455	0.0001	0.0006	0.00011	0.0000	0.0005	0.00002	0.0000	0.0000	0.00000
75&90	0.1766	0.3158	0.17658	0.0012	0.0019	0.00117	0.0004	0.0015	0.00041	0.0001	0.0001	0.00006
80-84	0.0305	0.0599	0.03079	0.0007	0.0009	0.00075	0.0003	0.0005	0.00027	0.0000	0.0000	0.00002
85	0.0165	0.0999	0.01667	0.0005	0.0009	0.00051	0.0001	0.0008	0.00015	0.0000	0.0000	0.00001
91	0.0299	0.0769	0.03661	0.0000	0.0003	0.00005	0.0000	0.0005	0.00004	0.0000	0.0000	0.00003
92, 93, 95 & 99	0.0602	0.0602	0.06024	0.0085	0.0085	0.00855	0.0011	0.0011	0.00113	0.0000	0.0000	0.00004

Table 5b: Percentage attribution of final demand in Thessaly, Epirus and Central Creece region

	Final consumption of Households	Final consumption of non-profit organizations	Final consumption of Government	Gross fixed capital investment	Changes in inventories	Exports
GWP	64.55398	0.02702	4.84844	41.63966	0.01075	-11.07985
TOFP	78.06469	0.01949	5.16460	32.29733	0.05045	-15.59655
ACID	82.40453	0.02545	3.99693	28.56046	0.03208	-15.01944
PM10	64.40921	0.03957	5.05590	39.65493	0.05011	-9.20972

Table 6a: Emission intensity coefficients by industry and pollutant in Central, Western & Eastern Macedonia and Thrace region

	GWP			TOFP			ACID			PM10		
	a_{kj}^e	e_k^p	e_j^c	a_{kj}^e	e_k^p	e_j^c	a_{kj}^e	e_k^p	e_j^c	a_{kj}^e	e_k^p	e_j^c
01 & 02	1.43568	2.3463	3.19008	0.01004	0.0154	0.02230	0.01257	0.0186	0.02794	0.00044	0.0007	0.00097
5	0.26159	0.6831	0.26831	0.00755	0.0122	0.00775	0.00271	0.0067	0.00278	0.00069	0.0008	0.00071
10,11& 12 / 13-14	1.54822	2.4532	3.60163	0.02478	0.0276	0.05765	0.00759	0.0110	0.01766	0.00204	0.0024	0.00475
15-16	0.05917	1.4760	0.08001	0.00116	0.0101	0.00157	0.00036	0.0107	0.00049	0.00001	0.0005	0.00001
17-19	0.07204	1.5226	0.08216	0.00867	0.0159	0.00989	0.00166	0.0094	0.00189	0.00005	0.0006	0.00006
20A	0.04292	1.3557	0.04567	0.01149	0.0173	0.01222	0.00024	0.0066	0.00026	0.00008	0.0006	0.00009
21-22	0.15296	1.0972	0.16297	0.00380	0.0070	0.00404	0.00431	0.0081	0.00460	0.00117	0.0015	0.00124
23	3.13995	4.6469	5.08522	0.04289	0.0582	0.06946	0.04278	0.0493	0.06928	0.00024	0.0016	0.00039
24-25	1.30015	2.5756	1.90779	0.00712	0.0116	0.01044	0.01228	0.0174	0.01801	0.00035	0.0008	0.00051
26	2.12009	5.1728	2.58591	0.01411	0.0257	0.01720	0.01454	0.0246	0.01773	0.00158	0.0025	0.00193
27	0.88503	4.1796	1.38276	0.00479	0.0125	0.00748	0.00718	0.0152	0.01122	0.00156	0.0023	0.00244
28	0.39094	2.2304	0.53531	0.00093	0.0065	0.00128	0.00231	0.0089	0.00316	0.00009	0.0009	0.00012
29-36	0.93444	2.8295	1.29353	0.00187	0.0065	0.00259	0.00675	0.0115	0.00934	0.00004	0.0004	0.00005

37	30.25363	30.6672	36.07678	0.04248	0.0443	0.05065	0.03315	0.0352	0.03953	0.00076	0.0009	0.00090
40-41	28.06876	30.8521	41.75841	0.04611	0.0565	0.06860	0.07794	0.0877	0.11596	0.01015	0.0114	0.01511
45	0.01459	0.9352	0.01728	0.00278	0.0071	0.00329	0.00044	0.0048	0.00052	0.00010	0.0005	0.00012
50-52	0.01530	0.3086	0.03731	0.00060	0.0025	0.00146	0.00007	0.0018	0.00017	0.00000	0.0001	0.00000
55	0.01273	0.6253	0.01353	0.00037	0.0034	0.00039	0.00013	0.0033	0.00014	0.00001	0.0002	0.00001
60-64	0.22124	0.8131	0.35271	0.00589	0.0104	0.00939	0.00408	0.0083	0.00651	0.00010	0.0003	0.00015
65-67	0.00150	0.3236	0.00275	0.00016	0.0019	0.00030	0.00003	0.0017	0.00006	0.00000	0.0001	0.00000
70-74	0.00224	0.1120	0.00507	0.00005	0.0006	0.00012	0.00001	0.0005	0.00002	0.00000	0.0000	0.00000
75&90	0.34404	0.9781	0.34404	0.00120	0.0035	0.00120	0.00042	0.0032	0.00042	0.00006	0.0002	0.00006
80-84	0.03025	0.1733	0.03064	0.00074	0.0013	0.00075	0.00027	0.0009	0.00027	0.00002	0.0001	0.00002
85	0.01624	0.3309	0.01649	0.00049	0.0018	0.00050	0.00014	0.0017	0.00015	0.00001	0.0001	0.00001
91	0.02344	0.2176	0.02946	0.00003	0.0009	0.00004	0.00003	0.0009	0.00004	0.00002	0.0001	0.00002
92, 93, 95 & 99	0.09560	0.0956	0.09560	0.01357	0.0136	0.01357	0.00180	0.0018	0.00180	0.00007	0.0001	0.00007

Table 6b: Percentage attribution of final demand in Central, Western & Eastern Macedonia and Thrace region

	Final consumption of Households	Final consumption of non-profit organizations	Final consumption of Government	Gross fixed capital investment	Changes in inventories	Exports
GWP	71.73475	0.05835	8.46336	29.98982	0.04077	-10.28705
TOFP	93.45004	0.05805	8.37127	32.44700	0.09243	-34.41878
ACID	89.48951	0.05851	7.14906	31.55078	0.11355	-28.36141
PM10	65.27124	0.05992	5.66153	22.96123	0.06896	5.97712

CHAPTER 7

An Analysis of Primary Energy Requirements and Emission Levels Using the Structural Decomposition Approach: The Spanish Case

Ana-Isabel Guerra[a*] and Ferran Sancho[b]

[a]Department of Applied Economics, Universitat Autònoma de Barcelona, 08193-Bellaterra, Spain and [b]Department of Economics, Universitat Autònoma de Barcelona, 08193-Bellaterra, Spain

Abstract: Primary energy use in economic activities and emission of contaminants caused by physicochemical reactions in the use of energy goods go hand in hand. Using Spanish data for 1995, 2000, and 2004 we have implemented a version of the Structural Decomposition Analysis to compute the contributions coming from changes in efficiency gains, in final demand, direct and indirect input/output requirements in energy use and emissions. Additionally, we have also analysed the combined effect of these contributions over the multiplier effects. According to our findings, in both pairs of years, large contributions coming from energy efficiency gains occurred among the most energy intensive sectors. This is due not only to the observed decline in their effective consumption of primary energy use but also because of their role as "key forward sectors" that made these energy efficiency gains more effective. However, the remarkable final demand growth that has taken place during these years has increased the strength of their push effects, offsetting the contribution of these energy efficiency improvements. Finally, we show that the contribution of indirect requirements dominates the contribution of direct requirements in the majority of Energy sectors but for energy intensive sectors the opposite is found. Our findings could be useful as the basis for designing recommendations that may make energy efficiency policies more effective in themselves as well as promoting fewer emissions in relative terms.

Keywords: Structural Decomposition Analysis, Input-Output Analysis, Primary Energy Use, Emissions levels, Structural Change, Technological change, Multiplier Effects.

INTRODUCTION

The Input-Output (IO) framework (Leontief, 1941) can be seen as an adaptation of general equilibrium analysis that captures the existing quantitative interdependences between interrelated economic activities and does so in an easily described way using a set of linear equations. The quantitative information used in this type of analysis comes from the well-known Input-Output tables that are assembled by Statistical offices. These tables supply detailed data on the transactions of good and services divided into intermediate and final demand, as well as the structure of production costs in terms of intermediate costs and value-added. However, they only contain information about the net income generated in each production sector, but not about its owners. This implies that the circular flow of income cannot be fully reflected in Input-Output analysis since the existing income-expenditure interactions are neither incorporated nor considered.

In order to include these interactions, Input-Output tables are extended with additional information that fills the aforementioned gaps and leads to the construction of so-called Social Accounting Matrices (SAMs). SAMs are very useful as the numerical backbone for the implementation of Computational General Equilibrium (CGE) models (Scarf, 1967; Shoven and Whalley, 1984). These models combine the theoretical Arrow-Debreu framework (1954) with the statistical information contained in a given SAM, creating a micro-consistent approach in which all the market interactions are price-dependent. The numerical implementation is referred in the literature as calibration (Mansur and Whalley, 1984).

In fact, both IO and CGE frameworks are useful to guide specific policy decisions and can be used to analyse a large variety of economy-wide issues: these include trade policies, fiscal reforms, environmental policies and technological change, among others. According to the definitions above, Input-Output analysis is more limited than CGE models and it can be considered as a simplified version of the former (i.e. in CGE models quantities and prices

*Address correspondence to Ana-Isabel Guerra Department of Applied Economics, Universitat Autònoma de Barcelona, 08193-Bellaterra, Spain Tel.: +34 935811757; fax: +34 935812012.Email: aigh79@gmail.com

Maria Llop (Ed)

are inter-connected to changes while in Leontief's model these two set of variables are independent of each other and a version of the classical dichotomy applies). The simplicity of IO analysis,

however, has the benefit that it allows us to isolate the role of specific interactions in the economy, i.e. inter-industrial linkages. Thus, as a first approximation, it provides a simpler understanding of these particular interactions within the more complex ones as are those captured by the CGE framework where prices and quantities are mutually inter-connected.

When dealing with the derived economy-wide effects of efficiency changes, for instance, IO analysis is quite useful since it provides a simple but clear-cut mechanism to ascertain how efficiency improvements taking place in a specific sector spread throughout the economy and, thanks to the existing interactions among sectors, end up influencing the rest of sectors.

Data on intermediate input efficiency or productivity stems from input/output proportions that are obtained from IO tables. These proportions are known as Leontief direct input-output coefficients and are contained in the structural matrix. They can be constructed at the firm level or at the industry level. Clearly, the more disaggregate the data on input-output requirements and activity measures, the more accurate the efficiency analysis will be[1]. A more comprehensive analysis could be undertaken if detailed data were collected at the firm level. Unfortunately this kind of data is not commonly available and the analysis is usually based on sectoral fixed coefficients, rather than firm level ones. When dealing with production efficiency this is not the best option but in most cases, and because of data availability, this is more often than not the only available option.

The analysis of changes in technical coefficients across periods can provide useful information about actual and potential sources of efficiency (Gowdy and Miller, 1987; Rose and Chen, 1991; Casler and Hadlock, 1997; Oosterhaven and Van der Linden, 1997). In fact, the Leontief input-output coefficients are considered as one of the economy "key parameters" in IO analysis. Thus, studies on the comparative static change of these coefficients, together with changes in final demand, are often used to analyse the determinants of the variation in the production level across time. The comparative static technique that uses and compares data from different temporal input-output tables is known as Structural Decomposition Analysis (SDA) and it was first proposed by Carter (1970) to analyse variations in the Input-Output Tables for the USA economy across time[2]. Despite having some limitations[3], structural decomposition analysis has been applied to explain changes in a wide variety of economic variables: technology (Wolff, 1985, Sanchez-Chóliz and Duarte, 2006), primary inputs or net output (Oosterhaven *et al*, 1995) and especially during last decades, energy use (Gowdy and Miller, 1987; Howarth *et al.* 1991) and emissions levels (Alcántara and Roca, 1995; Casler and Rose, 1998; Liaskas *et al.* 2000).

The analysis of changes in the degree of energy use in an economy has gained increasing attention ever since the two oil crises of the seventies. At the beginning this interest was due to "humanity's overdependence" on limited fossil energy resources. Later on, the preoccupation with the degree of energy use went along with the concept of Sustainability—this being defined as the capability to produce goods and services in an economy while causing minimal environmental degradation. This explain why many researchers have applied the SDA when seeking the actual and past economic determinants of changes in the level of energy use and its derived by-products, i.e. the level of emissions of contaminants associated with the use of energy goods (Casler and Hannon, 1989; Rose and Chen, 1991; Lin and Polenske, 1995; Casler and Hadlock, 1997; Wier, 1998; Alcántara and Duarte, 2004, Llop, 2007). When the SDA is applied to explain changes in energy use, in addition to changes in input-output requirements and in final demand, it also includes as explanatory variable the change in the energy intensities of sectors. The latter is usually attributed to energy efficiency gains or losses. Although it is true that energy efficiency is related to the inverse of energy intensity, they are not exactly equivalent since the former measures a pure technological factor whereas the latter collects and aggregates influences from different causes, technological and otherwise (Shipper, 2000). Therefore, energy efficiency is defined in the present analysis as an attribution, rather than as a pure isolated property of technology.

---

[1] Input-output coefficients at the industry level should be rather interpreted as average input/output proportions but not minimal proportions that would provide better measures for the analysis of changes in productivity or efficiency (Raa and Mohnen, 2002, and Raa, 2007).

[2] See Rose and Casler (1996) for a review of the history of SDA.

[3] This approach only allows an additive decomposition while the alternative method, the Index Decomposition Analysis (I.D.A) makes possible a multiplicative decomposition (Hoekstra and Van der Berg, 2003).

There is a direct technological relationship between energy use and emissions of contaminants that is based on the chemical properties of combustion. We use this emissions technology to transform results based on primary energy use into emissions. The type of emissions that we consider includes carbon dioxide CO_2, nitrogen oxide NO_x and sulphur dioxide SO_2. The estimates we use are based on emissions data constructed by the INE (Instituto Nacional de Estadística). The transformation will allow us to visualize and quantify the implications of structural change in the Spanish economy as far as emissions are concerned. The time framework that we consider includes three reference years: 1995, 2000, and 2004. For the implementation of the SDA analysis these periods have been paired as (1995, 2000) and (2000, 2004).

The way we implement the SDA decomposition has a couple of novel features in relation to the standard approach. Firstly, it permits us to isolate the contribution on the level of primary energy use, hence on emissions too, stemming from final demand and intermediate input requirements (direct and indirect). This distinction is useful for the assessment of the relevance of changes in the value of the multiplier effects. Secondly, and similar to the analysis proposed by Casler and Hannon (1989), we have also distinguished variations in energy use and emissions coming from changes in direct intermediate input/output requirements from those that can be traced to changes in the indirect ones. These two decompositions, the process of disaggregating the contribution of the multiplier effects as well as those coming from the Leontief's inverse, provide a more thorough analysis of the determinants that explain changes in primary energy use and thus in emissions. In fact, we show that this more detailed SDA is especially useful for capturing the role of the changes in the strength of sectors' forward effects on energy use and their determinants. The interest on these effects stems from their relevance in transferring efficiency changes and for this reason this information is helpful for the design of those policies that aim at improving energy efficiency in the production process.

The rest of this study is organized as follows. In the next Section 2 we present the modified SDA methodology. Section 3 briefly discusses the data. In Section 4 we present and discuss the main results of the analysis. Section 5 concludes with a summary and possible future research lines.

THE SDA AND A MORE DETAILED DISAGGREGATION OF KEY PARAMETER CONTRIBUTIONS

Our point of departure for this analysis is sectors' primary energy intensity. We will denote it by a row vector ε defined as the ratio of total energy use in physical terms, $[E]_j$, to the output value, $[X]_j$. In matrix notation:

$$\varepsilon = E \cdot \hat{X}^{-1} \tag{1}$$

Total primary energy use can therefore be rewritten as:

$$E = \hat{\varepsilon} \cdot X \tag{2}$$

where the symbol '^' stands for the diagonalised matrix version of the corresponding vectors.Following Leontief's input-output model, we substitute total output by its equilibrium value in terms of technology (A) and final demand (f):

$$E = \hat{\varepsilon} \cdot (I - A)^{-1} \cdot f \tag{3}$$

According to expression (3), there is a functional relationship that links energy use to energy intensities, direct and indirect input/output requirements and final demand. Due to the special properties of A (see Henryk, 1988), i.e. the matrix *(I-A)* is non-singular, invertible, and the productivity of matrix A with respect to all column vectors $f \geq 0$ at the limit the power series approximation equals the inverse matrix[4] and thus:

$$E = \hat{\varepsilon} \cdot f + \hat{\varepsilon} \cdot A \cdot f + \hat{\varepsilon} \cdot \left[\sum_{h=2}^{\infty} A^h \right] \cdot f \tag{4}$$

[4] This result in matrix notation states:

$$(I - A)^{-1} = \sum_{h=0}^{\infty} A^h$$

Expression (4) above establishes a more disaggregate functional relationship than (3). It indicates that, in equilibrium, aggregate energy use by industry can be decomposed into three different components: a first one induced by final consumption, a second one coming from the direct input requirements of each sector to satisfy final demand, and a last and third one that captures all indirect energy requirements that originate from "down-the-line" production chains.

Similarly, expression (4) might be re-written in terms of emissions levels of those pollutants (G_p) that are linked with the combustion of energy, i.e. for index $p = CO_2$, NO_x and SO_2.

$$G_p = \hat{g}_p \cdot \hat{\varepsilon} \cdot (I - A)^{-1} \cdot f \tag{5}$$

In expression (5) g_p stands for the technological coefficients linking primary energy use with emissions' generation and it is computed as the ratio of total emission levels of pollutant p generated by sector j, $\left[G_p\right]_j$, over its total primary energy use, $\left[E\right]_j$. Again in matrix notation, this reads as:

$$g_p = G_p \hat{E}^{-1} \tag{6}$$

When comparing changes in energy use between two periods, from period t to period s, and using expression (3) above, the discrete approximation of the total differential of this expression can be seen to be given by:

$$\Delta E \approx \Delta\hat{\varepsilon} \cdot (I - A)^{-1} \cdot f + \hat{\varepsilon} \cdot \Delta(I - A)^{-1} \cdot f + \hat{\varepsilon} \cdot (I - A)^{-1} \cdot \Delta f \tag{7}$$

Using expression (7) we see that the variation in primary energy use is explained by three components: the contribution of changes in energy intensity, the contribution related to changes in the Leontief inverse and, finally, the contribution of changes in final demand.

If, instead, we are interested in analysing changes in air pollutants between period t and s, from expression (5) we derive the discrete approximation of the total differential for emissions, similarly to the previous expression (7), as:

$$\Delta G_p \approx \Delta\hat{g} \cdot \hat{\varepsilon} \cdot (I - A)^{-1} \cdot f + \hat{g} \cdot \Delta\hat{\varepsilon} \cdot (I - A)^{-1} \cdot f + \hat{g} \cdot \hat{\varepsilon} \cdot \Delta(I - A)^{-1} \cdot f + \hat{g} \cdot \hat{\varepsilon} \cdot (I - A)^{-1} \cdot \Delta f \tag{8}$$

Differently to expression (7) above, expression (8) includes an additional component, the contribution of changes in the technical emission coefficients related to the combustion of energy. These coefficients are closely related to the final energy technology that throughout the combustion of some primary energy resources, i.e. the combustion of fossil fuels, generate emissions that damage the natural environment.

In empirical research, the discrete approximate decomposition in expressions (7) and (8) are often based on base period weights (w_t), last period weights (w_s) or mid-point weights (μ). As an illustrative example, the alternative discrete approximate decomposition of (7) would be given by:

$$\Delta E_{w_t} = \Delta\hat{\varepsilon} \cdot (I - A_t)^{-1} \cdot f_t + \hat{\varepsilon}_t \cdot \Delta(I - A)^{-1} \cdot f_t + \hat{\varepsilon}_t \cdot (I - A_t)^{-1} \cdot \Delta f + \phi_t \tag{9}$$

$$\Delta E_{w_s} = \Delta\hat{\varepsilon} \cdot (I - A_s)^{-1} \cdot f_s + \hat{\varepsilon}_s \cdot \Delta(I - A)^{-1} \cdot f_s + \hat{\varepsilon}_s \cdot (I - A_s)^{-1} \cdot \Delta f + \phi_s \tag{10}$$

$$\Delta E_{\mu} = \Delta\hat{\varepsilon} \cdot (I - A_{\mu})^{-1} \cdot f_{\mu} + \hat{\varepsilon}_{\mu} \cdot \Delta(I - A)^{-1} \cdot f_{\mu} + \hat{\varepsilon}_{\mu} \cdot (I - A_{\mu})^{-1} \cdot \Delta f + \phi_{\mu} \tag{11}$$

where ϕ is a residual term that refers to the interaction of simultaneous effects. Expressions (9)-(11) are in fact the three most widely used types of weighted decompositions. It is precisely because of the non-uniqueness of the solution to the structural decomposition problem, that there are large differences between them when computing the contribution of each determinant. Additionally, Dietzenbacher and Los (1998) argue that some of the *ad-hoc* solutions, i.e. taking the average of (9) and (10), or using (11) appear unsatisfactory. Consequently, these authors suggest computing average parameter contributions overall possible decompositions reporting their range and variance. Following their recommendation, we proceed to compute the average and the variance of each component over the six possible decompositions:

$$\begin{aligned}\Delta E &= \Delta\hat{\varepsilon}\cdot(I-A_t)^{-1}\cdot f_t + \hat{\varepsilon}_s\cdot\Delta(I-A)^{-1}\cdot f_t + \hat{\varepsilon}_s\cdot(I-A_s)^{-1}\cdot\Delta f \\ &= \Delta\hat{\varepsilon}\cdot(I-A_s)^{-1}\cdot f_s + \hat{\varepsilon}_t\cdot\Delta(I-A)^{-1}\cdot f_t + \hat{\varepsilon}_t\cdot(I-A_s)^{-1}\cdot\Delta f \\ &= \Delta\hat{\varepsilon}\cdot(I-A_t)^{-1}\cdot f_s + \hat{\varepsilon}_s\cdot\Delta(I-A)^{-1}\cdot f_s + \hat{\varepsilon}_t\cdot(I-A_t)^{-1}\cdot\Delta f \\ &= \Delta\hat{\varepsilon}\cdot(I-A_s)^{-1}\cdot f_s + \hat{\varepsilon}_t\cdot\Delta(I-A)^{-1}\cdot f_s + \hat{\varepsilon}_t\cdot(I-A_t)^{-1}\cdot\Delta f \\ &= \Delta\hat{\varepsilon}\cdot(I-A_t)^{-1}\cdot f_t + \hat{\varepsilon}_s\cdot\Delta(I-A)^{-1}\cdot f_s + \hat{\varepsilon}_s\cdot(I-A_t)^{-1}\cdot\Delta f \\ &= \Delta\hat{\varepsilon}\cdot(I-A_s)^{-1}\cdot f_t + \hat{\varepsilon}_t\cdot\Delta(I-A)^{-1}\cdot f_t + \hat{\varepsilon}_s\cdot(I-A_s)^{-1}\cdot\Delta f\end{aligned} \quad \textbf{(12)}$$

Notice that we actually have the option of using a more disaggregated decomposition if, instead of working from expression (3), we use the approximation from the total differential of expression (4):

$$\begin{aligned}\Delta E \approx &\left[\Delta\hat{\varepsilon}\cdot f + \hat{\varepsilon}\cdot\Delta f\right] + \left[\Delta\hat{\varepsilon}\cdot A\cdot f + \hat{\varepsilon}\cdot\Delta A\cdot f + \hat{\varepsilon}\cdot A\cdot\Delta f\right] + \\ &+\left[\Delta\hat{\varepsilon}\cdot\sum_{h=2}^{\infty}A^h\cdot f + \hat{\varepsilon}\cdot\Delta\sum_{h=2}^{\infty}A^h\cdot f + \hat{\varepsilon}\cdot\sum_{h=2}^{\infty}A^h\cdot\Delta f\right]\end{aligned} \quad \textbf{(13)}$$

The first term in (13) refers to the changes in energy to fulfil final consumption requirements that depend on the changes of sectors' energy efficiency gains (loses) and those coming from changes in final demand. The second component picks up those contributions needed to satisfy direct intermediate input/output demand. In addition to the contribution of energy efficiency and final use changes, this second term also includes the contribution coming from the variations in the structural coefficients. Lastly, the third component captures the contributions generated by indirect intermediate requirements. Observe that, in fact, the contribution of the changes in the Leontief inverse presented in (13) is similar to the additive decomposition approach proposed by Casler and Hannon (1989). However, in our analysis these contributions are in terms of physical primary energy use:

$$\begin{aligned}&\hat{\varepsilon}\cdot\Delta(I-A)^{-1}\cdot f = \hat{\varepsilon}\cdot\Delta A\cdot f + \hat{\varepsilon}\cdot\left[\left[\left(I-A_s\right)^{-1}-I\right]\cdot A_s - \left[\left(I-A_t\right)^{-1}-I\right]\cdot A_t\right]\cdot f = \\ &\hat{\varepsilon}\cdot\Delta A\cdot f + \hat{\varepsilon}\cdot\left[\sum_{h=2}^{\infty}\Delta A^h\right]\cdot f\end{aligned} \quad \textbf{(14)}$$

The decomposition laid out in expression (13) allows us to analyse and quantify in a more detailed way the contribution of the changes in sectors' forward effects over their primary energy use. Variations in the strength of these "push" effects might be due to structural changes (i.e. changes in direct and indirect input/output requirements) or to the combination of several effects (i.e. demand growth together with changes in direct or/and indirect input/output requirements). To this extent, expression (13) isolates the contributions of the changes in direct and indirect input/output requirements while the more standard expression (7) quantifies the relevance of the combined effects.

The above decompositions can be transferred into emissions applying the technological coefficients that link energy use with emissions' generation. However in this case since we have four components, we calculate the average and the variance of the contribution of each component over twenty-four possible decompositions.

THE DATA

We perform an empirical application of the methodological procedure outlined above to data from the Spanish economy. Using a comparative static approach, we start by examining variations in energy use for three periods: 1995, 2000, and 2004. For 1995 and 2000 we use the symmetric input-output tables compiled by the Spanish National Institute of Statistics. The symmetric input-output table corresponding to the last period, 2004, has been constructed by the authors from the published make and use tables for the year. In doing so, we have applied the industry-technology assumption as outlined in ESA-95[5]. Formal details of the application can be found in (Ten Raa, 1995). Previous to the application of the present analysis, we have transformed all the input-output value flows to 1995 base prices using price indexes. This makes the comparison homogeneous and independent of the accumulated price changes over these periods.

---

[5] This acronym refers to the European Systems of Accounts (EUROSTAT, 1995).

The information about physical primary energy used (in *ktoes*—kilotons oil equivalent) at the sectoral level has been taken from the energy balances that are annually compiled by the International Energy Agency (IEA). In distributing this physical primary energy use, we have also taken into account the energy consumption used in the transformation process from primary to secondary energy and the energy losses due to transportation from the production points to the end-use locations. The latter has been assigned proportionally to the volume of demand in each energy sector.

The data on emissions levels of the air pollutants that are related to the use of primary energy, i.e. CO_2 *NOx* and SO_2, has been taken directly from the information, expressed in tonnes, that is annually compiled by the INE (Instituto Nacional de Estadística) for two of the periods we analyse here, 1995 and 2000. Detail information about the Environmental Satellite Accounts was not available for the period 2004. Consequently, using data on total emissions levels of the aforementioned pollutants published by the INE for the period 2004 and applying the RAS method (Bacharach, 1971), we have updated the available 2003 environmental accounts data to this year.

DETERMINANTS OF CHANGES IN PRIMARY ENERGY USE AND THE DERIVED EMISSIONS LEVELS

"A First Glance": Trends in Sectoral Energy Intensities and Emissions Levels

Our analysis distinguishes 15 non-energy sectors and 4 distinct energy sectors (see sectoral details in Table **1**). This level of aggregation is the result of linking primary energy use accounts in physical units with input-output tables in value terms. Before explaining the main determinants of the changes in the degree of primary energy use and its associated negative sub-products, which contribute to climate change in the Spanish economy, we will first examine the trends in sectoral energy intensities and its derived emissions levels.

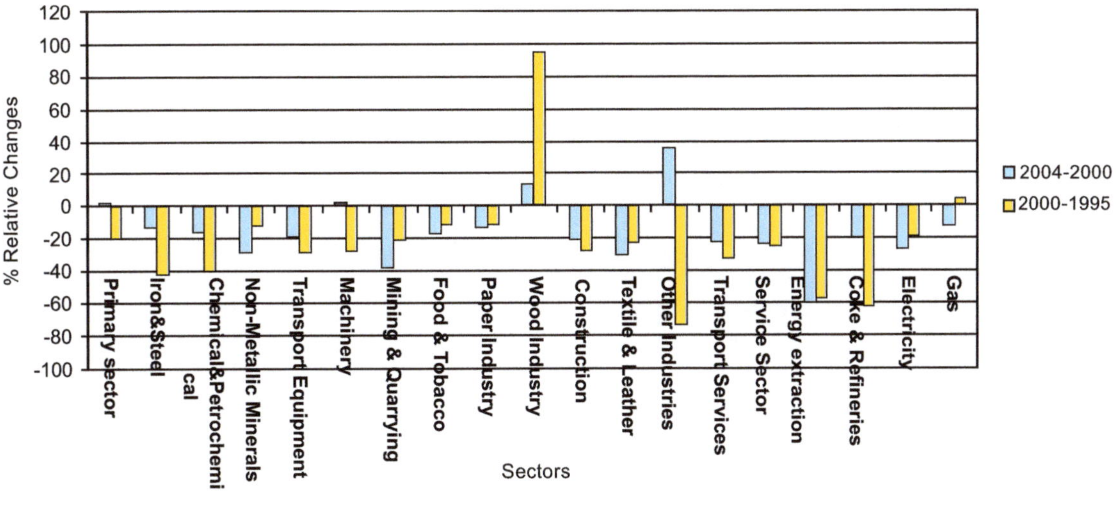

Graph 1: Trends in Sectoral Energy Intensities for Spain (*ktoes*/output in value terms). % Relative Changes for each pair of years (1995-2000, 2000-2004).

Graph **1** depicts relative variations in energy intensities per industry for each of the two pair of years here considered. From 1995 to 2000, we observe that all the specified sectors reduced their effective energy consumption with the exception of the *Wood Industry* and *Gas* sectors. During these years, and among the specified sectors, the highest changes in energy intensities as measured in this analysis, i.e. ratio of sectoral physical energy use in *ktoes* to total output in value terms, occurred in two of the Energy sectors: *Coke & Refineries* followed by the *Energy Extraction* sector. The decline in energy intensity in these sectors of the energy block might well be explained by the substantial decrease in the intermediate and final consumption of coal. From 1995 to 2000 the overall consumption in *ktoes* units of coal experienced a reduction of 6.12 percentage points, whereas the fall from 2000 to 2004[6] was of 5.8 percentage points. Lastly, among the Non-Energy sectors and during the same periods, there was a remarkable decline in energy intensity levels in the *Iron & Steel* sector as well as in the *Chemical & Petrochemical* industry.

[6] Energy Book of Spain (2000 and 2004).

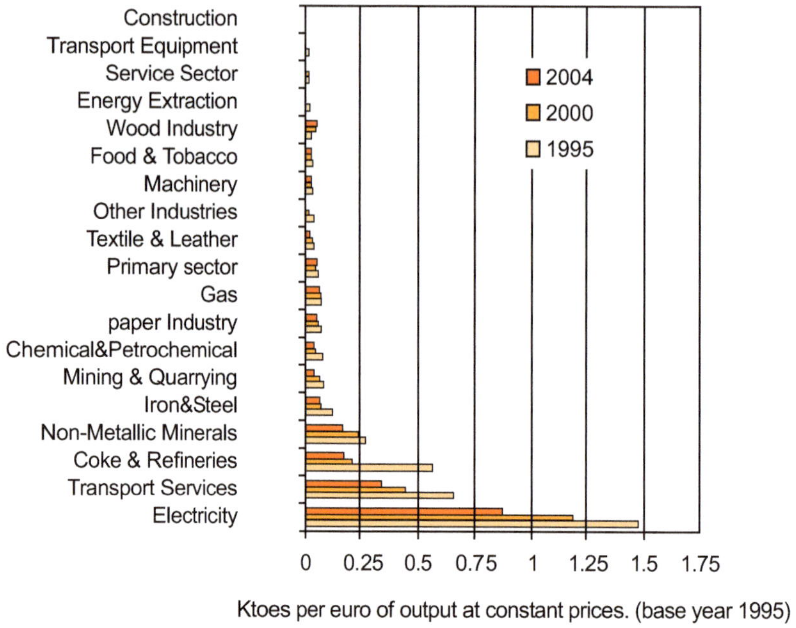

Graph 2: Sectoral Energy Intensities in the Spanish Economy 1995-2000-2004

During the last pair of years compared, from 2000 to 2004, we find that the *Wood Industry*, once again, together with the *Machinery*, *Transport Equipment*, and *Primary* sectors presented an increase in their level of energy intensity. For these periods, the highest decline in the energy intensity ratio also took place in the *Energy Extraction* sector followed in this case by the *Mining & Quarrying* and *Non-Metallic Minerals* sectors. These sectors also rank among the most energy intensive sectors for the three years considered. This is shown in Graph **2** that depicts, from highest to lowest, sectoral energy intensity ratios for the Spanish economy.

It seems then that the strongest decline in energy intensities have occurred among the most energy intensive sectors in both pair of years. There are two reasons that might explain these findings. Firstly, in the input-output approach changes in sectoral energy intensive ratios are very often ascribed to energy efficiency improvements. According to this definition of energy efficiency, since energy input costs constitute a relevant share in the cost structure of these sectors, they might have more incentives to adapt technology to promote a more efficient use of this input, i.e. the *Iron & Steel* industry has been increasingly using electric ovens[7]. Secondly, these industries produce a large number and variety of products whose energy composites are substantially different. Therefore, it is also plausible that during a given period the share of products that present low energy content was much larger than that during the reference period. The case of the *Chemical & Petrochemical* industry can be used as an illustrative example. According to the Annual Reports of the Spanish Industry published by the Ministry of Industry and Energy, the production of soaps and detergents has been increasing remarkably from 1995 to 2004. Apart from kerosene and lubricants, among others, these products are also manufactured by the *Chemical & Petrochemical* industry. However, their production requires a lower amount of energy inputs than those of the other products of this industry.

As can be asserted from Graph **2**, the *Electricity* and *Transport Services* sectors present the highest degree of dependency from energy resources. Nonetheless, these two sectors have experienced slight relative changes in their degree of energy intensive (see Graph **1**), although in absolute terms their variation in energy intensiveness have appeared to be the strongest among all productive units. This is not a surprising result since the higher the initial dependency of these sectors, the more difficult and costly is to adapt the technology to reduce it. These results show, to a certain extent, that there is a lack of incentives in these sectors for adopting energy reducing technologies. Therefore, government intervention may be needed in order to speed up their technological adaption. These figures also indicate, by the way, the so-far limited capacity of the current Spanish regulatory actions in actually achieving a reduction in primary energy use and thus in the derived emission levels. In practice, environmental regulations (especially since the approval of the first environmental directive in 1967) have stemmed from the Common

[7] Annual Reports of the Spanish Industry (Spanish Ministry of Industry and Energy).

Environmental Policy of the European Union. These regulations have included fiscal incentives in the corporate tax (*Ley 43/1995; Real Decreto, 2/2003*), emission controls *(Ley 16/2002),* subsidies to improve energy efficiency (*Directive E4-2004-2012*) and the promotion of renewables with direct subsidies for investment and operation costs (*Plan of 1999 for the Promotion of Renewables*). In sharp contrast, Spain has made little use of one of the most efficient environmental policy instruments, namely, the so-called Ecotaxes[8]. An indication of this lack of fiscal action is the fact that the final prices of energy in Spain have been lower than the average prices of energy vis à vis those of other European countries (according to the IEA reports; see for example World Energy Outlook, 2000).

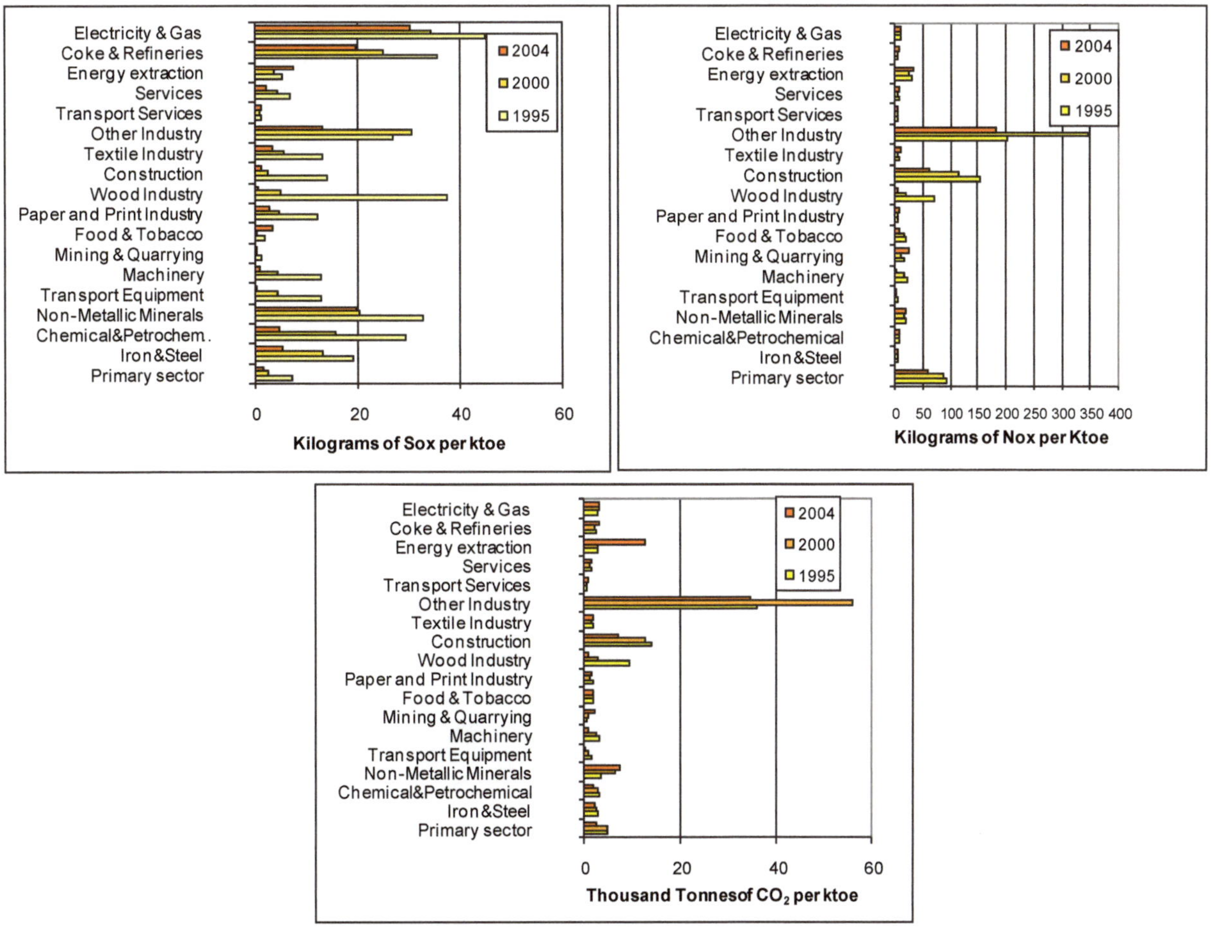

Graph 3: Sectoral Energy-Emissions Intensities. 1995-2000-2004

In terms of emissions levels originated by energy use, results and thus the conclusions are not much different (see Graph **3** above). As mentioned in the previous section, a huge amount of man-made emissions of CO_2, NO_x and SO_2 is related to the combustion of fossil fuels, with the exception of natural gas. The combustion of natural gas generates a small amount of CO_2 plus water vapour. In fact, these air emissions constitute exactly the same compounds that we exhale when we breathe. As can be asserted from Graph **3**, the most remarkable changes have been occurring in the SO_2 emission intensity ratio. In absolute terms and differently to the remaining air pollutants here considered, i.e. the CO_2 and NO_x, the amount of SO_2 emission levels was in 2004 about 24 percent below the levels of 1995.

Additionally, this unbalanced situation between low/medium energy prices and the set of existing environmental regulations might also explain why primary energy use and emissions levels has increased over time despite observed energy intensity gains. Thus, from 1995 to 2000 primary-energy use increased by 20 percentage points while, on average, sectors' energy intensities felt by 22 percentage points. Similarly, when comparing the last two pair of years 2004-2000,

[8] Ecotaxes are defined as taxes levied on the degree of energy use and other natural resources taking into account the capacity of the environment to absorb pollution and waste.

total primary energy use went up by 13 percentage points and energy efficiency gains accounted for about 23 percentage points. The SDA approach should be helpful in unveiling the main determinants explaining the increase in the level or primary energy use and their derived emission levels that have offset the energy efficiency improvements.

A More Detailed Analysis: Attributing Changes in Primary Energy use and Emissions Levels

We have implemented the SDA decomposition shown in expressions (7) and (8) above separately for each pair of years: first from 1995 to 2000 and then, from 2000 to 2004. As outlined in section II above when attributing variations in primary energy use we have also computed the average (μ) and the standard deviation (σ) for the contributions of the three determinants among the 3! possible decompositions presented in (12). According to expression (7) these determinants are: energy efficiency changes ($\Delta\varepsilon$), variation in direct and indirect input/output requirements ($\Delta(I-A)^{-1}$) and variations in final demand (Δf). For each pair of years, these results for the Non-Energy and the Energy sectors are reported respectively in Table ***1a*** and Table **2**. For ease of presentation and explanation, Table ***1a*** only depicts the results for some of the most energy intensive sectors within the Non-Energy block (See Graph **2** above): *Transport Services*, *Iron & Steel,, Non-Metallic Minerals*, and *Mining & Quarrying*. The results of the remaining sectors included in this group are depicted in Table **1b** in the Annex.

When looking at the changes in sectors' primary energy use during the first time frame analysed (2000-1995), among the Non-Energy Sectors (See first half of Table 1a), we can firstly observe that Transport Services, followed by the Chemical & Petrochemical sector, has shown the largest contribution in each of three determinants. The average contribution of each determinant in the Transport Services sector in relative terms is remarkably above the average of the Non-Energy sectors' block. The negative sign of the contributions of the first two determinants indicates that changes in both energy intensity and direct and indirect input-output requirements have favoured the decrease in the primary energy use of this sector. However, the large and positive contribution from final demand changes has offset the latter effects. This result has been a common pattern in the majority of the sectors (see Table 1b) even if they are relatively less dependent on energy inputs than those reported in Table 1a). Secondly, and provided that changes in the energy-output coefficient are attributed to changes in energy efficiency, other energy intensive sectors such as the Iron & Steel industry and the Chemical & Petrochemical sector have also experienced above average energy efficiency contributions.

However, they appear to be much lower than those of the Transport Services sector. This difference stems from the higher forward linkage effects of the Transport Services sector compared to other production units. This therefore demonstrates a point already mentioned in the introduction: large forward effects might make, ceteris paribus, energy efficiency gains to be more effective. Nevertheless, if large push effects are accompanied with a considerable demand growth, this might lead to the opposite effect.

With respect to the Energy Sectors, from 1995 to 2000 (see first half of Table 2) the Coke & Refineries industry followed by the Electricity sector have had the largest contribution coming from variations in the energy technical coefficients. Again, if variations in these coefficients stems from technical change in energy inputs, these findings might be also explained through the existing sectoral differences in terms of their "push" effects. Lastly, and similar to the case of the Non-Energy sectors, the contribution of final demand has also offset the contribution of the other two determinants in most Energy sectors.

Comparing average contributions from Energy and Non-Energy sectors, those coming from energy efficiency improvements and final demand changes are much larger in Energy sectors than in Non-Energy sectors. The relevant role of the former as sellers of energy inputs to the other productive units and the strong interdependencies among them justify these findings (Guerra & Sancho, 2010). Concerning the contribution of the changes in input-output coefficients, they will be explained in more detail in the next section following the alternative decomposition stated in expression (13).

When analyzing changes in primary energy use from 2000 to 2004, the results are similar to those obtained under first sub-period. Among the Non-Energy sectors, once again The *Transport Services* sector has shown the strongest contribution explained by the decline in the energy intensity coefficient although far below the previous sub-period value, from 1995 to 2000. Similar conclusions are drawn with respect to this determinant in the case the *Iron & Steel* and the *Chemical & Petrochemical* industries. Among the Energy sectors, and also during this second sub-period, the *Electricity* sector has presented the largest negative contribution coming from the energy intensity determinant. This might be explained by the strong relative decline of this coefficient observed from 2000 to 2004 (see Graph **1**).

The explanation for these findings might be two-fold. On the one hand, as long as changes in the energy-output coefficients are closely related to technological change (Hicks neutral or non-neutral technological change), strong energy efficiency gains between 2000 and 2004 might be behind these results. On the other hand, these findings might be traced to the increasing use of renewables in the production of electricity (See the Energy Book of Spain, 2000; 2004). That is to say, they might be also justified not by technological change as such, i.e. using the same energy input in a more efficient way, but rather by the substitution of energy inputs themselves: the use of renewables in Spain has been growing across time to such a point that renewables use in electricity generation almost doubled from 1990 to 2004 (from 5983 ktoes to 9124 ktoes).

Following the same methodology and using expression (8), we have also analysed changes in the by-products derived from energy use. In fact, the contributors of the variations in primary energy use constitute a sub-set of those that determine changes in their derived emissions levels. Apart from variations in final demand, vertical integration and energy intensiveness, increases or declines in emissions levels are also explained by changes in the emission-energy technical coefficients, i.e. Δg_p. Variations in emission levels, in other words, also stem from changes in the degree of environmental efficiency of energy inputs themselves. Environmental efficiency of energy inputs is mainly explained by the so-called "energy-mix". Sectoral efficiency in these terms is stronger, the lower the sectoral emission-energy coefficient is. Consequently, the energy coefficient gives us information about the energy-output technology while the emission-energy coefficient refers to the primary energy production process, i.e. solar, wind, fossil fuels, marine and biodiesels.

Graph **4a-b** depicts separately for each period and for each pollutant the average relative contribution of each of the four determinants outlined in expression (8) derived from energy use. As it is common in most SDA analysis, the most relevant contributor to the changes in emissions levels was the variation in final demand, for both periods. From 1995 to 2000, changes in final demand have contributed on average to increase absolute sectoral emissions levels by almost 48 thousand tonnes in the case of CO_2, 257 thousand kilograms of NO_x and 281 thousand kilograms of SO_2. Similar results were obtained when for the subsequent time-frame, i.e. 2004-2000.

From 1995 to 2000, for most productions units and for the three pollutants considered, the second most relevant contributor has turned out to be the variation in emission-energy coefficients. However, the sign of this determinant has differed remarkably among sectors and among pollutants: changes in environmental energy efficiency have contributed to the decrease of SO_2 emissions while in the case of CO_2 we have found the opposite result. Since SO_2 is mainly derived from the combustion of fossil fuels, these results indicate that the share of renewables in the composition of primary energy has been increasing over time in the Spanish economy. This has been specially the case of those sectors included in the Energy block, i.e. the *Electricity and Gas* sectors. Although more smoothy than those of the previous period, we have found similar patterns when analysing sectoral variations in emissions levels from 2000 to 2004. A noteworthy result was the weak contribution of sectoral inter-dependencies. In fact, this is not a surprising result for developed economies such as Spain. For economies of this type, the strong changes in sectoral vertical integration have already occurred, i.e. in the case of Spain from 1986 till 1993 and this explains the marginal role played by this determinant.

Table 1a: Determinants Contributions to the variations in primary energy use in the Non-Energy block for the Spanish economy according to expression (7). 1995-2000/2000-2004

Sector	*Determinant*	*Maximum*	*Minimum*	□	*□Relative Average Contribution**		*Maximum*	*Minimum*	□	*Relative Average Contribution**	□
				2000-1995					*2004-2000*		
Transport Services	$\Delta\varepsilon$	-7728.17	-14379.3	**-10820.77**	**-157.23 %**	3498.193	-7278.05	-10856.2	**-9050.77**	**-163.54 %**	1853.606
	$\Delta(I-A)^{-1}$	-794.881	-2128.26	**-1369.615**	**-19.90%**	481.223	1590.793	898.4973	**1211.968**	**21.90%**	285.539
	Δf	22831.67	15405.06	**19072.38**	**277.13%**	3764.528	15230.32	11580.65	**13372.81**	**241.64%**	1731.549
Iron & Steel	$\Delta\varepsilon$	-1937.27	-3669	**-2807.08**	**-551.83%**	993.762	-685.938	-1010.22	-846.668	**-58.75%**	167.5355
	$\Delta(I-A)^{-1}$	44.49	3.719	**21.47**	**4.22%**	19.695	255.309	166.082	207.8781	**14.42%**	38.52502
	Δf	4172.647	2421.214	**3294.296**	**647.60%**	948.3958	2259.812	1905.404	2079.79	**144.32%**	153.672
Chemical & Petrochemical	$\Delta\varepsilon$	-1377.64	-2571.61	**-1964.01**	**-960.57%**	655.99	-568.767	-905.357	-730.926	**-107.64%**	153.123
	$\Delta(I-A)^{-1}$	-57.84	-202.724	**-116.13**	**56.79%**	48.507	-188.645	-339.281	-257.827	**37.97%**	66.403
	Δf	2901.586	1681.768	**2284.601**	**1117.37%**	638.5677	1869.098	1472.545	1667.754	**245.61%**	186.89
Non-Metallic Minerals	$\Delta\varepsilon$	-523.22	-940.462	**-729.583**	**-33.85%**	234.217	-1735.99	-2948.37	-2311.55	**-467.92%**	570.681
	$\Delta(I-A)^{-1}$	-49.438	-127.352	**-85.383**	**-3.96%**	34.7	-217.07	-623.098	-389.45	**-78.87%**	176.993
	Δf	3207.535	2735.903	**2970.214**	**137.81%**	236.6582	3885.199	2535.428	3194.997	**646.76%**	655.712
Mining & Quarrying	$\Delta\varepsilon$	-52.136	-104.147	**-77.235**	**-88.06%**	26.643	-132.945	-210.562	-170.893	**-19.72%**	39.411
	$\Delta(I-A)^{-1}$	-16.626	-38.109	**-26.159**	**-29.82%**	7.909	-4.869	-14.618	-8.883	**-0.10%**	4.072
	Δf	222.1084	161.2855	**191.0925**	**217.89%**	28.87819	1145.101	947.877	1046.276	**120.74%**	105.516
Average Non-Energy Sectors' Contribution	$\Delta\varepsilon$	**220.895**	**-10820.7**	**-1469.306**	**-83.03%**	**2742.041**	444.483	**-9050.77**	-1074.98	**-130.30%**	2335.639
	$\Delta(I-A)^{-1}$	**143.011**	**-1369.61**	**-126.844**	**-7.16%**	**370.233**	**1211.968**	-389.45	23.605	**-2.86%**	369.528
	Δf	**19072.384**	**131.451**	**3365.580**	**190.20%**	**5891.834**	**13372.81**	153.7771	1876.335	**227.44%**	3341.808

Relative Average Contribution represents the ratio of average determinant contribution to overall energy changes in percentages. For this reason, their sum equals 100 percent

Table 2: Determinants Contributions to the variations in primary energy use in the Energy block for the Spanish economy according to expression (7). 1995-2000/2000-2004

Sector	*Determinant*	*Maximum*	*Minimum*	□	□*Relative Average Contribution**	□	*Maximum*	*Minimum*		*Relative Average Contribution**	□
		2000-1995					*2004-2000*				
Energy Extraction Sector	$\Delta\varepsilon$	-97.468	-259.352	-173.809	**-755.68%**	76.230	-97.9009	-164.924	-128.683	**126.15%**	23.43593
	$\Delta(I-A)^{-1}$	102.4282	23.159	53.592	**233.00%**	26.486	-12.1693	-44.2363	-25.4731	**24.97%**	14.33738
	Δf	228.0718	76.76614	143.2173	**622.67%**	60.87034	80.48363	26.55767	52.1558	**-51.13%**	26.61325
Coke & Refineries	$\Delta\varepsilon$	-3643.45	-11037.9	-7122.281	**-774.34%**	3454.526	-1206.07	-1847.25	-1505.93	**3621.67%**	247.804
	$\Delta(I-A)^{-1}$	4634.353	959.991	2360.437	**256.63%**	1255.449	-537.212	-985.234	-740.492	**1780.84%**	190.559
	Δf	9442.04	2794.684	5681.626	**617.71%**	2702.021	2597.48	1832.934	2204.841	**-5302.52%**	347.6997
Electricity Sector	$\Delta\varepsilon$	-4537.07	-7323.34	-5660.838	**-131.52%**	1365.027	-7385.31	-11197.9	-9275.96	**-440.51%**	1995.516
	$\Delta(I-A)^{-1}$	-1232.04	-3403.94	-2196.779	**-51.03%**	880.959	-283.566	-562.077	-407.191	**-19.33%**	114.8401
	Δf	14371.5	10073.28	12161.79	**282.55%**	1945.944	13713.72	9879.67	11788.88	**559.84%**	2046.727
Gas Sector	$\Delta\varepsilon$	12.359	4.595	8.260	**3.93%**	3.569	-40.3211	-65.6573	-52.9163	**-37.83%**	13.44892
	$\Delta(I-A)^{-1}$	88.317	51.842	69.862	**33.26%**	19.050	11.62511	7.077971	9.205577	**6.58%**	2.051865
	Δf	151.574	112.7096	131.925	**62.80%**	19.612	197.436	169.9812	183.5626	**131.25%**	12.7211
Average Energy Sectors' Contribution	$\Delta\varepsilon$	8.2602	-7122.28	-3237.167	**-237.28%**	3691.668	-52.9163	-9275.96	-2740.87	**-521.57%**	4407.612
	$\Delta(I-A)^{-1}$	2360.436	-2196.77	71.778	**5.26%**	1860.523	9.205577	-740.492	-290.988	**-55.37%**	354.1052
	Δf	12161.787	131.925	4529.638	**332.02%**	5720.062	11788.88	52.1558	3557.36	**676.94%**	5575.429

Relative Average Contribution represents the ratio of average determinant contribution to overall energy changes in percentages. For this reason, their sum equals 100 percent

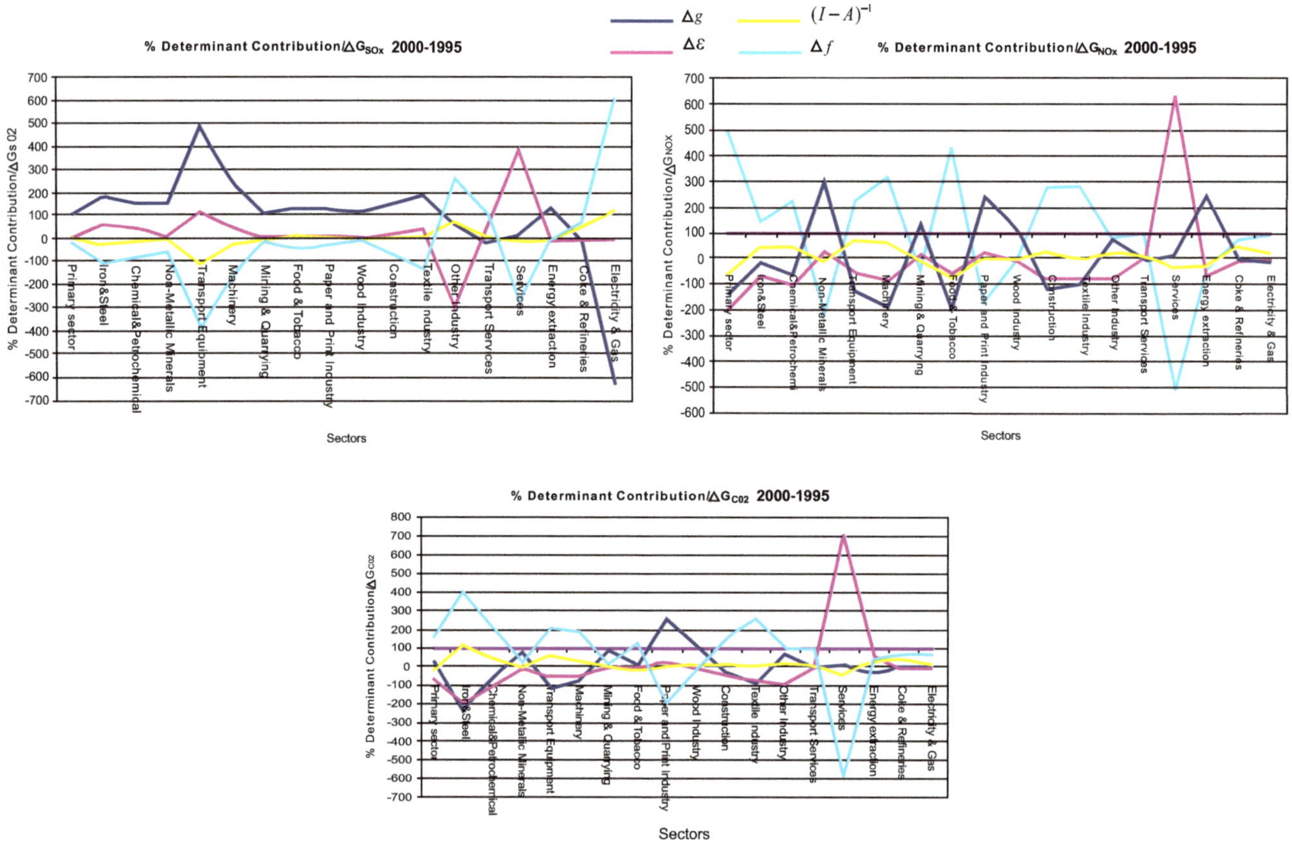

Graph 4a: Determinant Contributions Relative to Overall Change in Emissions levels. 2000-1995.

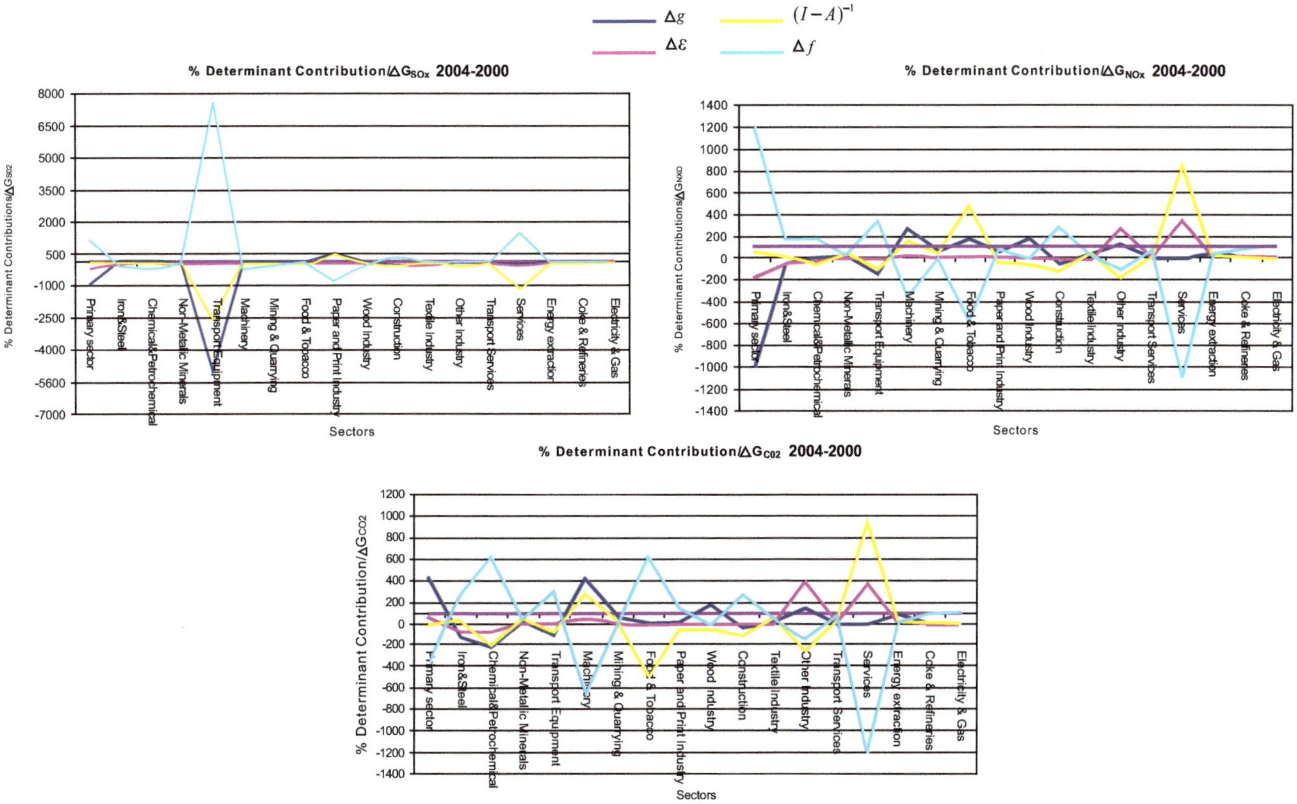

Graph 4b: Determinant Contributions Relative to Overall Change in Emissions levels. 2004-2000. Determinants of the Changes in Energy use According to the Typology of Multiplier Effects

Expression (13) in section II shows that it is possible to derive a more disaggregated and detailed decomposition than that provided from expression (7). Using (13) then we can classify changes in sectors' primary energy use according to the three types of multiplier effects already presented in section II: variations in the strength of multiplier effects coming from final demand, from direct input-output requirements and from indirect sectors interdependencies. We consider that the information provided by our proposed decomposition of the variations in sectoral energy use is useful for a better understanding of the role played by vertical integration in determining the overall degree of dependence from this input in the Spanish economy.

Table 3: Determinants Contributions to the Variations in sectors' Primary Energy use for the Spanish economy according to expression (13). 1995-2000/2000-2004

Sectors	$\Delta\hat{\varepsilon} f + \hat{\varepsilon}\Delta f$		$\left[\Delta\hat{\varepsilon} A f + \hat{\varepsilon}\, \Delta A f + \hat{\varepsilon}\, A\, \Delta f\right]$		$\left[\Delta\hat{\varepsilon}\sum_{h=2}^{\infty} A^h f + \hat{\varepsilon}\Delta\sum_{h=2}^{\infty}(A)^h f + \hat{\varepsilon}\sum_{h=2}^{\infty} A^h \Delta f\right]$	
	2000-1995	***2004-2000***	***2000-1995***	***2004-2000***	***2000-1995***	***2004-2000***
Energy Extraction Sector	*3.98*	*1.44*	*18.62*	*35.01*	*77.38*	*63.54*
Coke and Refineries	*17.38*	*-56.12*	*30.73*	*131.25*	*51.87*	*24.86*
Production of Electricity	*-7.87*	*37.88*	*37.28*	*39.76*	*70.58*	*22.34*
Production of Gas	*21.24*	*36.53*	*28.78*	*18.59*	*49.97*	*44.86*
Average Contribution in Energy Sectors	***8.68***	***4.93***	***28.85***	***56.15***	***62.45***	***38.90***
Primary sector	*71.65*	*33.12*	*31.88*	*36.81*	*-3.54*	*30.06*
Iron&Steel	*16.07*	*11.46*	*35.00*	*31.18*	*48.92*	*57.35*
Chemical& Petrochemical	*45.63*	*59.04*	*10.80*	*23.75*	*43.55*	*17.20*
Non-Metallic Minerals	*17.749*	*-25.02*	*44.64*	*1.11*	*37.60*	*123.90*
Transport Equipment	*67.27*	*58.25*	*21.18*	*20.31*	*11.54*	*21.42*
Machinery	*66.569*	*36.46*	*20.32*	*26.81*	*13.11*	*36.72*
Mining & Quarrying	*19.18*	*20.83*	*36.02*	*66.56*	*44.78*	*12.60*
Food & Tobacco	*74.75*	*52.98*	*17.14*	*26.92*	*8.09*	*20.10*
Paper and Print Industry	*11.30*	*35.11*	*49.38*	*50.75*	*39.31*	*14.13*
Wood Industry	*10.71*	*13.13*	*37.28*	*33.73*	*52.00*	*53.13*
Construction Sector	*55.69*	*45.70*	*26.70*	*28.69*	*17.60*	*25.60*
Textile Industry	*77.28*	*63.23*	*20.23*	*24.54*	*2.48*	*12.21*
Other Industry	*68.38*	*47.36*	*18.34*	*26.65*	*13.27*	*25.98*
Transport Services	*57.37*	*20.98*	*8.16*	*38.64*	*34.45*	*40.36*
Service Sector	*74.88*	*55.82*	*14.31*	*22.57*	*10.80*	*21.60*
Average Contribution in Non-Energy Sectors	***48.97***	***35.23***	***26.09***	***30.60***	***24.93***	***34.16***

The results for each sector as well as average determinant contributions for both Energy and Non-energy blocks are summarised in Table **3** above. From the information in this table we can conclude that the average impact of total intermediate consumption, direct and indirect, was much larger in the Energy block than in the Non-Energy one. The opposite occurs with respect to the multiplier effects that can be traced throughout final demand requirements.

This finding is common to the two time frames considered here. The most energy intensive sectors within the Non-Energy block, such as the *Transport Services* sector, the *Iron & Steel* sector and the *Mining & Quarrying* industry, though still far below the Energy sectors' levels, have shown higher contributions coming from intermediate demand than those that stem from final requirements. Two main conclusions can be drawn. Firstly, the strength of sectoral interdependencies appears to be relevant for determining the degree of energy use not only in energy intensive sectors but also in the overall economy. This is especially so in the case of the Energy sectors since they are located 'down-the-line' in the production chains. In the case of the other energy intensive sectors included in the Non-Energy block, these findings might be justified by the strong interdependencies with the Energy sectors. Secondly, these results also convey the idea that despite the dominant contribution of the changes in final demand, the strength of the multiplicative effects that stem from sectoral interdependencies should be also taken into account. Our proposed decomposition of the changes in primary energy use suggest that from a structural point of view, inter-industrial linkages have been more relevant than final demand in explaining the size of these variations. This is because multiplier effects from sectoral interdependencies remarkably increase the strength of "push effects".

In terms of policy recommendations, our findings indicate that in order to reduce overall energy use, an effective option could be constructed taking into account the set of market interdependencies. In this line it would be advisable to raise the amount of resources devoted to energy efficiency policies. However, under the scenario whereby there is a pronounced increase in final demand, energy efficiency improvements might be partially or even fully offset by the dominant positive contribution of this determinant. In short, energy efficiency policies might be more effective if combined with policies specially orientated to reduce energy use in final demand requirements.

CONCLUSIONS

In this study, we have implemented a variation of the SDA to analyse the determinants of the changes in primary energy use and associated emission levels for the Spanish case and for two pair of years: firstly from 1995 to 2000 and then from 2000 to 2004. According to this methodology, there are tree basic determinants: changes in final demand, in energy intensity and in direct and indirect input-output requirements. Combining data from input-output tables with sectors' primary energy use in physical units, we have shown that despite the remarkable decline in sectors' energy intensity levels (on average, from 1995 to 2000 there is a reduction of 22 percentage points while from 2000 to 2004 is of 23 percentage points), primary energy use has been increasing basically due to demand growth.

Final demand growth has therefore been the driving force that explains the increase in primary energy use offsetting contributions arising from the other two determinants. The specific way in which demand growth took place during these periods has even favoured more economy-wide energy use. Just consider, in this line of reasoning, that the Construction and Services sectors absorb, together, almost 80 percent of this final consumption growth. Both sectors are relevant in energy paths and the Construction sector is in fact a "key backward" sector. Additionally, we have shown that the largest contributions coming from final demand and energy efficiency improvements occurred in the Energy sectors and in those with high energy intensity. Since these two production blocks stand out from their large forward effects, these results stress the role that these impacts have in making energy efficiency policies more effective.

Apart from analysing and separately comparing the contributions of these three determinants in primary energy use, we have also computed their combined contributions in the multiplier effects. Through the application of this novel decomposition, our results indicate that for both pair of years, the effects coming from direct and indirect intermediate consumption were observed to be the highest in the Energy sectors themselves followed by other energy intensive sectors included in the Non-Energy block. These findings have not only therefore highlighted once again the relevance of these sectors as transferors of the energy efficiency improvements; they again illustrate the need to combine this knowledge with policies that tackle final use.

Lastly, when analysing the determinants of the changes in emissions levels closely related to energy use, our results indicate the relevant contribution of the changes in the "energy-mix" that suggest a remarkable success of policies that pursue an increase in the use of renewables.

One of the limitations of the current analysis is that the way in which we have defined energy efficiency changes is rather an attribution and hence their indirect effects cannot be quantified (i.e. Rebound or Backfire effects). Therefore, a more sound analysis of energy efficiency changes and policies should perhaps be undertaken using a CGE framework.

ACKNOWLEDGEMENTS

We are very grateful to Dra Maria Llop and Dr. Rutger Hoekstra for their comments and suggestions on the earlier draft. All errors and shortcomings are the sole responsibility of the authors.

REFERENCES

Alcántara, V. and Duarte, R. (2004). "Comparison of energy intensities in European Union Countries. Results of a Structural Decomposition Approach". *Energy Policy*, 32, 177-189.

Alcántara, V. and Roca, J. (1995). "Energy and CO2 in Spain. Methodology of Analysis and Some Results". *Energy Economics*, 17, 221-230.

Arrow, K.J and Debreu, G. (1954). "Existence of Equilibrium for a Competitive Economy". *Econometrica*, 22, 265-290.

Bacharach, M. (1971). *Biproportional Matrices and Input-Output Change.* Cambridge: Cambrigde University Press.

Brookes, L. (1990). "The Greenhouse Effect, the Fallacies in the Energy Efficiency Solution". *Energy Policy*, 18, 199-201.

Carter, A. (1970). *Structural Change in the American Economy.* Cambridge, MA: Harvard University Press

Casler, S.D. and Hannon, B. (1989). "Readjustment potentials in industrial energy Efficiency and Structure". *Journal of Environmental Economics and Management.* 17, 93-108.

Casler, S.D and Hadlock, D. (1997). "Contributions to Change in the Input-Output Model: the Search for Inverse Important Coefficients". *Journal of Regional Science*, 37, 175-193.

Casler, S.D. and Rose, A. (1998). "Carbon dioxide emissions in the U.S. Economy: a Structural Decomposition Analysis". *Environmental and Resource Economics*, 11, 349-363.

Dietzenbacher, E. and Los, B. (1998). "Structural Decomposition Techniques: Sense and Sensitivity". *Economic Systems Research*, 10, 307-323.

EUROSTAT, (1995). *European system of national and regional accounts ESA 1995*, Brussels.

Gowdy, J. M. and Miller, J.L. (1987). "Technological and Demand Change in Energy use: Input-Output Analysis". *Environmental and Planning A,* 19, 1387-1398.

Guerra, A.I. and Sancho, F. (2009). "Measuring Energy Linkages with the Hypothetical Extraction Method: the case of Spain". Forthcoming in *Energy Economics*.

Hoekstra, R. and Van der Berg, J. (2003). "Comparing Structural and Index Decomposition Analysis". *Energy Economics*, 25, 39-64.

Howarth, R.B., Schipper, L., Duerr, P.A. and Strom, S. (1991). "Manufacturing Energy use in eight OECD countries: Decomposing the Impacts of changes in Output, Industry Structure and Energy Intensity". *Energy Economics*, 13, 135-142.

Khazooms, J.D. (1980). "Economic Implications of Mandated Efficiency Standards for Household Appliances". *The Energy Journal*, 4, 21-40.

Leontief, W.W. (1941). *The Structure of the American Economy*, New York: Oxford University Press.

Liaskas, K., Mavrotas, G.,Mandaraka, M. and Diakoulaki, D. (2000). "Decomposition of industrial CO2 emissions. The case of European Union". *Energy Economics*, 22, 383-394

Lin, X. and Polenske, K. R. (1995). "Input-Output Anatomy of China's Energy Use Changes in the 1980s". *Economic Systems Research*, 7, 67-84.

Llop, M. (2007). "Economic structure and pollution intensity within the environmental input–output framework", *Energy Policy* 35, 3410–3417.

Mansur, A. and Whalley, J. (1984). "Numerical specification of applied general equilibrium models: estimation, calibration and data". In Scarf, H. & Shoven, J. (Eds.), *Applied General Equilibrium Analysis.* New York: Cambridge University Press.

Oosterhaven, J. and Van der Linden, J.A. (1997). "European Technology and Income Changes for 1975-85: An inter-country Input-Output Decomposition". *Economic System Research*, 9, 393-412.

Oosterhaven, J., Hoen, A. R. and Van der Linden, J. A. (1995). "Technology, trade and real value added growth of EC countries, 1975-1985", paper presented at the 11th International Conference on Input-Output Techniques, New Delhi.

Raa, T.T. (1995). *Linear Analysis of Competitive Economies.* London: Harvester-Wheatsheaf, LSE Handbooks in Economics.

Raa, T.T and Mohnen, P. (2002)."Neoclassical Growth Accounting and Frontier Analysis: A Synthesis". *Journal of Productivity Analysis*, 18, 111-128.

Raa, T.T (2007). "The Extraction of Technical Coefficients from Input-Output Data", *Economics System Research*, 19, 453-459.

Rose, A and Chen, C.Y. (1991). "Sources of Change in Energy Use in the US Economy, 1972-1982: a Structural Analysis". *Resources and Energy*, 13,1-21.

Rose, A. and Casler, S. (1996). "Input-Output Structural Decomposition Analysis: A Critical Appraisal". *Economic Systems Research*, 8, 33-62.

Sánchez-Chóliz, J. and Duarte, R. (2006). "The Effect of the Structural Change on the Self-Reliance and Interdependence of Aggregate Sectors: the case of Spain". *Structural Change and Economic Dynamics,* 17, 27-45.

Scarf, H.E. (1967). On the Computation of Equilibrium Prices. In Fellner, W.J. (Ed), *Ten Economic Studies in the Tradition of Irving Fisher*. New York: John Wiley & Sons.

Schipper, L. (2000). "On the rebound: the interaction of energy efficiency, energy use and economic activity. An introduction". *Energy Policy*, 28, 351-353.

Shoven, J.B. and Whalley, J. (1984). "Applied General Equilibrium Models of Taxation and Trade: An Introduction nd Survey". *Journal of Economic Literature*, 22, 1007-1051.

Wier, M. (1998). "Sources of Change in Emissions from Energy: A Structural Decomposition Analysis". *Economic Systems Research*, 10, pp. 99-111.

Wolff, E.N. (1995). "Industrial composition, inter-industry effects, and the U.S. productivity slowdown". *Review of Economics and Statistics*, 67, 268-277.

STATISTICAL SOURCES

From the Annual reports of the Ministry of Industry, Tourisms and Commerce:

- Energy Book of Spain, 2000.
- Energy Book of Spain, 2004.
- Chemistry industry in Spain (several years)
- Industrial sector in Spain (several years)

From the OCDE-IEA reports:

- World Energy Outlook, 2000.

Table 1b: Determinants Contributions to the variations in primary energy use in the Non-Energy block for the Spanish economy according to expression (7). 1995-2000/2000-2004

Sector	Determinant	Maximum	Minimum	□	□Relative Average Contribution*	□	Maximum	Minimum	□	Relative Average Contribution*	□
		2000-1995					2004-2000				
Primary Sector	$\Delta\varepsilon$	-386.04	-741.65	-553.94	**-149.03%**	167.584	62.60	42.20	51.94	**6.74%**	8.53
	$\Delta(I-A)^{-1}$	-227.03	-482.58	-341.60	**-91.90%**	93.60	-187.36	-270.14	-228.53	**-29.67%**	43.94
	Δf	1503.18	1044.49	1267.23	**340.93%**	207.81	994.66	899.41	946.58	**122.93%**	41.05
Service Sector	$\Delta\varepsilon$	-1194.10	-2255.62	-1724.12	**-11.82%**	574.76	-1636.04	-2548.85	-2088.64	**-173.28%**	478.47
	$\Delta(I-A)^{-1}$	189.40	99.58	143.01	**0.98%**	36.99	135.84	175.02	161.81	**13.42%**	3509.26
	Δf	22752.44	3946.21	16161.18	**110.84%**	6714.21	924.89	3207.59	3132.18	**259.85%**	506.58
Transport Equipment	$\Delta\varepsilon$	-170.28	-376.01	-271.78	**-80.30%**	114.51	-177.54	-243.36	-210.28	**-208.21%**	35.14
	$\Delta(I-A)^{-1}$	35.70	11.91	21.98	**6.49%**	8.58	15.95	8.48	11.87	**11.75%**	3.22
	Δf	697.28	482.87	588.25	**173.80%**	105.92	333.87	265.63	299.40	**296.46%**	33.85
Machinery	$\Delta\varepsilon$	-192.72	-398.72	-295.36	**-86.33%**	116.48	30.71	23.01	26.83	**7.11%**	3.99
	$\Delta(I-A)^{-1}$	17.96	9.26	13.14	**3.84%**	2.77	34.23	24.21	29.18	**7.74%**	5.42
	Δf	727.88	521.75	624.34	**182.49%**	109.69	329.23	312.79	320.97	**85.14%**	7.38
Food &Tobacco	$\Delta\varepsilon$	-209.51	-383.46	-291.11	**-56.94%**	81.71	-434.75	-628.99	-531.76	**141.61%**	106.21
	$\Delta(I-A)^{-1}$	-209.27	-423.08	-309.01	**-60.44%**	91.61	4.66	0.74	2.49	**-0.66%**	2.02
	Δf	1270.72	959.10	1111.32	**217.39%**	140.04	193.54	114.86	153.77	**-40.95%**	41.22
Paper & Print Industry	$\Delta\varepsilon$	-165.21	-277.16	-219.67	**-32.23%**	60.35	-235.83	-389.30	-307.21	**-154.36%**	57.74
	$\Delta(I-A)^{-1}$	92.14	35.70	61.91	**9.084%**	25.62	-230.19	-388.95	-304.21	**-152.86%**	71.77
	Δf	917.73	764.83	839.26	**123.14%**	54.37	927.15	699.06	810.43	**407.23%**	102.10
Wood Industry	$\Delta\varepsilon$	292.82	152.52	220.89	**50.27%**	73.31	117.10	67.50	90.21	**34.04%**	18.48
	$\Delta(I-A)^{-1}$	36.30	11.12	22.53	**5.12%**	11.44	-83.28	-148.44	-114.81	**-43.32%**	30.66
	Δf	265.73	128.59	195.98	**44.60%**	71.34	335.05	248.33	289.60	**109.28%**	28.34
Textile Industry	$\Delta\varepsilon$	-210.07	-385.35	-294.80	**-135.83%**	89.51	-358.07	-460.32	-408.97	**199.50%**	46.32
	$\Delta(I-A)^{-1}$	-54.26	-121.37	-83.93	**-38.67%**	23.83	-30.84	-46.74	-38.56	**18.81%**	8.18
	Δf	697.00	498.40	595.76	**274.50%**	95.22	287.68	197.62	242.54	**-118.31%**	48.66
Construction Sector	$\Delta\varepsilon$	-51.92	-97.06	-73.99	**-106.98%**	24.01	-53.32	-109.91	-80.53	**-48.51%**	27.31
	$\Delta(I-A)^{-1}$	17.44	7.31	11.70	**16.91%**	3.45	75.55	34.92	53.07	**31.97%**	17.94
	Δf	156.02	108.21	131.45	**190.06%**	21.77	231.97	159.26	193.45	**116.54%**	24.13

	$\Delta\varepsilon$	-1411.46	-2908.8	-2137.02	**252.21%**	777.1	506.90	382.89	444.48	**51.86%**	66.02
	$\Delta(I-A)^{-1}$	285.41	42.98	133.39	**-15.74%**	88.14	25.30	11.67	18.07	**2.10%**	5.73
Other industries	Δf	1895.14	479.12	1156.33	**-136.47%**	718.3	458.29	331.41	394.43	**46.02%**	66.62

***Relative Average Contribution represents the ratio of average determinant contribution to overall energy changes in percentages. For this reason, their sum equals 100 percent**

CHAPTER 8

Measuring the Air Pollution of Tourism: An Input-Output Model for the Campania Region

Maria Llop[a] and Simona Sabena[b*]

[a]*Departament d'Economia, Universitat Rovira i Virgili,Avgda. Universitat n° 1, 43204 Reus, Spain and* [b]*Politecnico di Torino University*

Abstract: In recent decades, travel and tourism have come to represent a major economic growth sector. To better understand the impact of tourism activity, research on tourism development is undertaken in various fields, involving both theoretical and applied models. The aim of this chapter is to establish a method for analysing the impact of regional tourism development and the associated environmental consequences. The method employed here uses an input-output model with income generated by the tourism sector and emissions released into the atmosphere. The model is applied to the Italian region of Campania, an area with high cultural value, and is used to calculate the emission multipliers of regional activities and to simulate changes in tourist demand and its subsequent effects on regional income and regional emissions.

Keywords: air pollution, input-output model, tourism activity.

INTRODUCTION

Travel and tourism have become strategic activities for economic growth and economic development. Tourism development research comprises both theoretical and applied models, most of which only strive to understand some of the dimensions involved in the development of a tourist area. Indeed, although it is generally accepted that the assessment of tourism impact from an economic-financial point of view is not sufficient, there has been considerable progress in terms of "systemic" approaches to economic tourism analysis, for example through the construction of Tourism Satellite Accounts (TSA). On the other hand, some methodologies consider tourism without taking into account the interaction between tourism activity and the environment, thus disregarding the environmental impact associated with tourism and its implications at each site. Other methodologies, quantitative or qualitative, monetary or not monetary, are exclusively focused on the evaluation of the pressures generated on the environment without considering the risks that these pressures can pose to economic development. Our work aims to establish a method for analysing the impacts linked to regional tourism consumption and the subsequent environmental effects. Our method consists of an input-output model relating to income generated by the tourism sector and emissions released into the atmosphere. Specifically, we extend the conventional input-output model to account for the variation in emissions when there is a variation in tourism demand.

Several recent contributions have used the input-output model to account for the greenhouse emissions of production processes. Ostblom (1998) evaluated Swedish emissions of carbon dioxide, sulphur oxide and nitrogen oxide and analysed the results from the point of view of Sweden's environmental goals and medium-term projections for economic growth. Lenzen (2002) decomposed the Australian environmental input-output multipliers using structural path analysis. This decomposition revealed environmentally important input paths within pollution emissions, energy consumption and resource uses in the Australian production system. Lenzen *et al.* (2004) constructed a multi-region input-output model, which was used to calculate pollution generation and CO_2 multipliers for five European countries, taking into account the greenhouse gases involved in international trade operations. Alcántara and Roca (1995) presented an input-output model to analyse primary energy requirements and CO_2 emissions in Spain between 1980 and 1990. Cadarso and Fernández-Bolaños (2002) calculated the total emissions in Spain between 1980 and 1995. They included private consumption emissions in the matrix of emission multipliers, and considered consumption as another category of pollution commodities. Rodríguez *et al.* (2007) used a multi-sector model to conduct an environmental and economic analysis on the basis of a social accounting matrix for Spain, with

[*]**Address correspondence to Maria Llop:** Departament d'Economia, Universitat Rovira i Virgili,Avgda. Universitat n° 1, 43204 Reus, Spain. Email: maria.llop@urv.cat

data for the year 2000. Butnar and Llop (2007) defined a relative context of emissions in the input-output framework and applied it to the Spanish economy. Finally, Llop (2007) used a structural decomposition analysis to identify the economic effects and the pollution intensities within the total variation of the Spanish emission multipliers.

This chapter aims to apply the input-output emissions model to an area with a high cultural value: the Italian region of Campania. The statistical data used consisted of the supply and use table of the Campania Region, provided by the Istituto Regionale per la Programmazione Economica della Toscana (IRPET, 2004), to include the economic transactions between production sectors; the National Accounting Matrix with Environmental Accounts (NAMEA), provided by the Italian Statistics Institute (ISTAT, 2005), to include the emissions of activities by sector; and finally, statistics relating to tourism consumption and tourism characteristics, provided by the Tourism Department of Campania.

The method used here calculates the emission multipliers of regional activities. It is also used to simulate changes in the final demand of tourists and its subsequent effects on regional income and regional emissions. Finally, we analyse not only the total emissions caused by tourism in Campania and Italy but also and the importance of the emissions generated by regional tourists in the total national emissions.

The remainder of the chapter is organised as follows. The next section describes the tourism activity in the region and its effects on the region's economic activity. Section 3 presents the characteristics of tourism in Italy in general and in the Campania region in particular. Section 4 describes the input-output framework on which our work is based, and section 5 describes the databases used in our empirical application. Our results are presented in section 6 and our conclusions are discussed in section 7.

TOURISM: DEFINITIONS AND CONCEPTUALISATIONS

In the last few decades, tourism has become one of the fastest growing activities in the world. Tourism expenditure has significant implications both for countries of origin and destination, and it contributes to a worsening of the payment balance in the net tourism generating countries and an improvement in the net recipient countries. Therefore, tourism can raise or reduce a country's dependence on other countries and it can be very important in helping to develop countries whose economies, apart from tourism, are based on primary products.

At the same time, from a strictly economic point of view, tourism development is an outdated concept because natural capital, which allows for growth and development, is not an infinite resource. Therefore, in the long term, poor use of natural resources can adversely affect growth. Uncontrolled tourism practices in communities with particular ecological characteristics in which tourism is the primary resource puts pressure on ecosystems and tends to reduce biodiversity. We have to bear in mind that, in the short term, tourism is an immediate resource and, in the long term, extensive and sustained pressure on natural resources can destroy it. Therefore, the host community has to define strategies that reconcile economic, social and environmental issues.

The negative aspects related to tourism should not be used as justification for rejecting it, but as a motivation to solve environmental problems, through the definition and implementation of policies that take the interactions between population, environment and tourism into consideration.

The Economic Effects of Tourism: Income and Employment Multipliers

Tourism generates income and employment directly in the sectors in which tourist expenditure or tourism-related investment takes place, and it also induces further growth throughout the economy as those receiving higher incomes spend their earnings. Income and employment generation result not only from expenditure by foreign tourists, but also from domestic tourist spending, which often exceeds that of foreign tourists.

Moreover, changes in tourism demand that affect income and employment in the sectors related to tourism depend in part on the existence of the appropriate surplus resources within the economy. It is also important to determine whether there is a surplus linked to the evaluation of the potential growth in demand to raise output, and the way in which consumers and businesspeople formulate their expectations in order to determine whether an increase in demand results in higher output or inflation. If a surplus capacity is not available, this method provides spurious results, as demonstrated by Wanhill (1988). Therefore, capacity constraints must be introduced into the multiplier model in order to take this problem into account.

Two models can be used to estimate income and employment generation resulting from tourism: the Keynesian multiplier model and the input-output model. Both approaches permit the definition of multipliers, which are the ratios between the value of income or employment generated and the initial change in tourist spending or tourism-related investment.

The Keynesian income multiplier model involves the use of a range of equations to estimate the aggregate multiplier values associated with different types of tourist expenditure or investments. The alternative definitions of income can be measured in terms of gross domestic product (GDP) and gross national product (GNP).

Like the Keynesian income multipliers model, the input-output model can calculate the aggregate multiplier values for different definitions of income. It also provides multiplier values for different sectors of the economy and captures the interrelationships between these productive sectors at a given point in time.

Industrial Characteristics of Tourism Activity

The tourism industry is an increasingly important part of the economy and it helps to generate income and employment. It has become organised in highly dynamic spatial networks of production and consumption and it plays a role in several critical issues in modern economics, such as globalisation, deindustrialisation and regional economic restructuring, the spatial division of labour, urban revitalization and the evolution of services. Furthermore, tourism is typically conceived as any goods or services that are consumed by a tourist, and the travel and tourism industry is defined as a provider of tourist goods and services, or as a production system which facilitates access to fixed assets such as landscapes, ruins, museums, parks and monuments.

From a technical point of view, it is necessary to define the term "tourist". A "tourist" can be defined as any person who stays away at least one night from his or her place of permanent residence. Additionally, institutions such as the Committees on Statistics of the International Union of Official Tourism Organizations and the World Tourism Organization (UNWTO) have invested considerable energy in ensuring that this definition is applied universally so that data collected are comparable between countries and regions.

As travel and tourism are currently keys to economic growth, it is important to investigate the concept of tourism and its interaction with the environment in greater depth. The problematic nature of tourism as an industry can be seen in the definition proposed by Tucker and Sundberg (1988): "*... tourism is not an industry in the conventional sense as there is no single production process, no homogenous product, and no locally confined market....*" The implication is that the tourism industry does not need any special analysis or policy consideration per se because it does not exist. Thus, tourism-related sectors, such as transport, restaurants and accommodation are industries in the conventional sense, but tourism as a whole is not. Smith (1998) instead proposed what he called a supply-side definition of tourism: *"... tourism is the aggregate of all businesses that directly provide goods and services to facilitate business, pleasure, and leisure activities away from the home environment...."* Such a definition is fundamental for any consideration of tourism as an industry. Subsequently, Leiper (1990) suggested that tourism might be described as "partially industrialised" since visitors are served, as part of the tourism experience, both by firms that cater almost exclusively to visitors as well as by others for whom visitors are only a small part of their client base. These positions generated a discussion between Smith and Leiper. Smith claimed that while tourism is not a conventional industry, it can be measured and defined in a way that is consistent with other industries. Leiper countered that tourism can be understood as a mix of industries that are involved in the provision of services to visitors to varying degrees, and should not be characterised as a single industry, conventional or otherwise. One important barrier to the acceptance of tourism as an industry is linked to the fragmentation and credibility of tourism statistics. The fragmentation of statistics often occurs because the majority of tourism businesses in most destination regions are small or medium-sized enterprises with limited resources, often bound by family ties, and the statistics they produce are usually concerned with day-to-day operations. The latter is related to different units of measurement (where one organization includes only visiting friends and relatives, another includes both visiting friends and relatives and business travel and so on) and the quality of data sources. In other words, tourism is created by different types of industries and is not a single product but rather a wide range of goods and services that interact to provide an opportunity to satisfy a tourist experience that comprises both tangible and intangible aspects.

Tourism may not be a coherent industry since it does not produce a distinct product; it can therefore be defined as a complex production process that begins with a series of primary inputs or production factors. These primary inputs can be converted into intermediate inputs or tourist facilities (e.g. restaurants, airlines, hotels) that are further redefined by various intermediate outputs or tourist services (e.g. room services, meals, drinks). The result is a final output or tourist experience no matter what the individual motivation may be (e.g. for pleasure, business, visiting friends or relatives, etc).

Additionally, other important aspects linked to the definition of tourism are:

- *Visitors*. This concept consists of "tourists" who stay overnight in a destination, as opposed to "same day visitors" or excursionists who do not;
- *Tourism expenditure*. This is an important matter, which involves the money spent before, during and after a trip, for different categories of travellers, different reasons and different sub-sectors of the tourism industry. Moreover, it is important to mention that goods and services purchased by tourists can also be purchased by non-tourists;
- *Tourism industry*. This is defined by the set of industries identified by the national standard industrial classification system that would either cease to exist or would exist in a substantially reduced form in the absence of tourism, as most of their activities are directed towards satisfying tourist demand. Air transportation and food services are examples, respectively, of these conditions. Non-tourism industries include any other industry, such as groceries, or retail clothing. It should be recognised that some non-tourism industries could be considered tourism industries at a local or seasonal level. In order to explain the aspects concerning tourism and the travel industry it is necessary to consider Smith's (1998) definition in which the tourism industry is made up of industries that would cease to exist in the absence of tourism. The rule of thumb suggests that if the share of receipts generated by tourist demand exceeds 15% for an industry, then that industry should be included in the tourist industry.

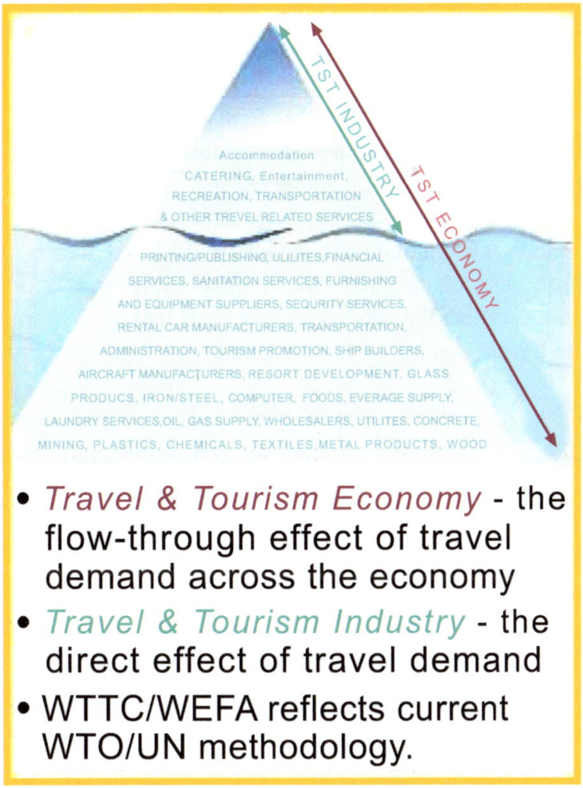

Source: World Travel and Tourism Council (WTTC).

Figure 1: Tourist industries and tourist economy

The World Travel and Tourism Council (WTTC) generated the definition in Fig. **1** in order to produce a statistical data set and reports according to the Tourist Satellite Accounts. They distinguish the "travel and tourist industry" as the industry that supplies goods and services to travellers, from the "travel and tourism economy" which groups together all the intermediate activities that provide the tourist and travel industry and are indirectly affected by tourist activities, such as hotels, transport, food, services, etc. Nevertheless, it is clear that tourism is a full-fledged sector, even though it may not be considered an industry because its peculiar features go beyond conventional definitions.

The nature of tourist commodities is also particular. Tourists consume a set of goods and services, so tourist products are "composite goods" because they involve transport, hotels, catering, handicrafts, entertainment and other services such as banking and travel intermediation (Economides and Salop, 1992; Campaner, 2000).

Finally, it is important to point out that the coordination of supply and demand in the tourist sector is an essential part of destination management. There are many different stakeholders involved in the tourism and travel sector and the complexity of their inter-relationships makes the strategies required to coordinate them difficult to devise.

CHARACTERISTICS OF ITALIAN TOURISM

Italy

The development of the tourism industry in Italy emphasises the two-speed dynamic of tourism depending on the region analysed. The regional distribution of tourist expenditure shows some clear territorial differences. On average, every euro spent on tourism activities in 2005 gave a value added equal to 79 cents, which is in line with the same value for 2004, because tourist behaviour was quite similar in different areas of the country. Instead, what makes a greater difference between regions is tourist expenditure and the share of the total effects that remains in each region.

In 2005, worldwide tourism results were excellent with a 5.5% increase in movement. This was mainly due to the Asian and American markets, because demand in Central Europe is still slow and is conditioned by the persistence of uncertain conditions.

The results for the Italian economy in 2005 indicate that total expenditure grew in nominal terms by 2%, and tourism helped to offset the negative effects of economic development. Also in 2005, Italian tourism maintained its positions on the market in terms of turnover and even witnessed significant recoveries.

An overview of the last decade shows that although Italian tourism achieved good results in 2000, it had to wait until 2004 and 2005 to come close to those results again, as the numbers of tourists visiting Italy decreased continuously from 2001 to 2004. These dynamics reflect the succession of events that have characterised the negative economic cycle in Europe, which has led to a reduction in consumption propensity and, consequently, in tourist spending.

In macroeconomic terms, Table **1** shows that in 2005 the 88.6 million euros of tourist consumption in Italy was shared out as follows: 29.1 million spent by foreign demand (32.9% of the total) and 59.4 million spent by domestic tourists (67.1% of the total).

Table 1: Total tourism expenditure in Italy (millions of euros)

	FOREIGN TOURIST CONSUMPTION		DOMESTIC TOURIST CONSUMPTION	
	2004	**2005**	**2004**	**2005**
AGRICULTURAL PRODUCTS	493	498	1.480	1.516
ENERGY PRODUCTS	1.299	1.313	2.817	2.885
FOOD AND BEVERAGE	1.826	1.845	5.514	5.649
TEXTILE AND LEATHER	1.222	1.235	2.433	2.491
OTHER INDUSTRY	2.754	2.785	6.445	6.600

CONSTRUCTION	44	44	156	160
BUSINESS	3.870	3.912	9.716	9.952
HOTELS AND RESTAURANTS	12.860	12.997	16.903	17.297
TRANSPORT	621	628	1.538	1.574
FINANCIAL INTERMEDIATION	50	51	106	109
BUILDING RENT	1.780	1.798	6.289	6.444
RECREATIONAL ACTIVITIES	1.840	1.860	4.320	4.424
OTHER SERVICES	145	146	336	345
TOTAL	28.804	29.111	58.051	59.445

Source: Regional Tourism Department of Campania.

Table **1** also shows the destination of tourism spending in Italy by sector and distinguishes between the tourist spending of Italian tourists and foreign tourists. In terms of the breakdown of tourist spending shown in Table **1**, the data on Italian visitors confirm some structural trends. In relative terms, they spend more than foreigners on car and flat rental, and less on accommodation and catering, while they buy larger quantities of goods in the "other industry" sector.

The Campania Region

In order to better understand the Campania region, it is important to point out that the "south of Italy" is defined as a strongly Mediterranean product and is an important resource within the framework of Italian tourism as a whole. Nevertheless, the development process in the south has been different to that in the rest of the country because of marked inequalities at a regional level and different historical and socio-economic aspects, which have led to the development of different categories of tourism.

The region of Campania is one the most important regions both in terms of European and Italian tourism, because it is characterised by many archaeological sites, islands, beaches and different cities with cultural heritage, history and traditions. Data concerning the total tourist flow published by the Italian Statistics Institute (ISTAT) show that there were 19.1 million stays (or days of stay) and 4.5 million arrivals in 2005 which represent a slight increase of 1.4% for stays and 0.1% for arrivals compared to the data from 2004.

Moreover, the period between 1995 and 2000 saw increases in the primary tourism indicators in Campania. However, in the 2000-2002 period the trend was inverted, due to the instability created by the events of September eleventh and by difficulties linked to the city of Naples and the surrounding area. Over the next two years, 2002-2004, new growth was experienced both in terms of stays and arrivals. The number of arrivals and stays for foreign tourists grew by 3.8% during this time, although this increase did not occur at a national level, where the change in the number of arrivals compared to the previous period was negative (-0.3%).

It is important to analyse the flow of foreign tourists because, as shown in Fig. **2**, the top twenty countries represent 88% of the total arrivals and stays. Fig. **2** also shows that the five countries with the highest number of arrivals are the United States, the United Kingdom, Germany, France and Japan. Apart from these countries, which are called "consolidated tradition countries", it is interesting to see the position of South Korea, which comes just after Japan, and which represents 3% of all foreign arrivals. There are also a limited number of countries representing the majority of foreign stays (Germany, the United Kingdom, France and the United States). The concentration of arrivals and stays in a reduced number of countries may indicate that tourism in Campania is vulnerable to a certain extent, in the sense that tourism expenditure depends on the response of a limited number of customers.

We can also analyse the data concerning stays and arrivals related to the 2000-2006 period provided by ISTAT. As shown in Table **2**, the total number of arrivals and stays is fairly stable, though the total number of arrivals of foreign tourists in 2006 slightly exceeded the 2000 figure. For Italian tourists, the trend oscillated between 2000 and 2003 and showed a continuous decrease during the 2003 to 2006 period. In terms of total arrivals and stays, there is a slight reduction in both during the period analysed.

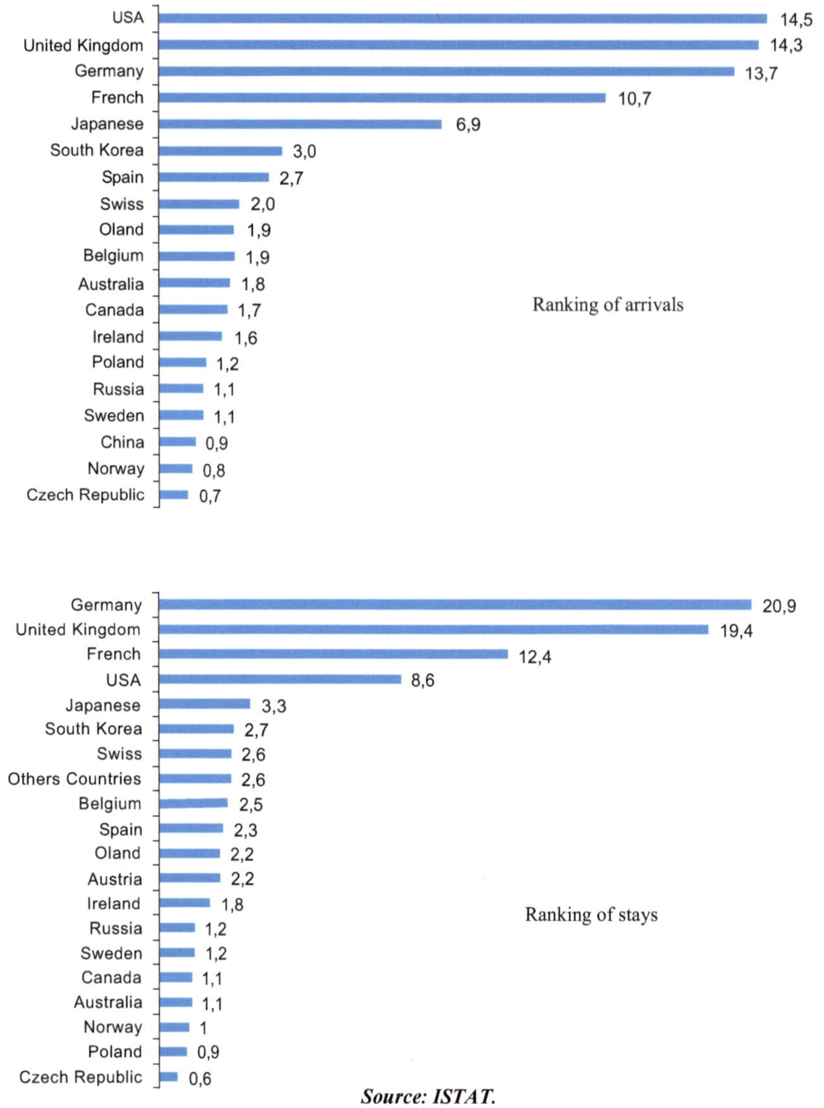

Source: ISTAT.

Figure 2: Ranking of tourist flows: top twenty countries (percentages), 2004

Table 2: Number of arrivals and stays in Campania

	ITALIAN		FOREIGN		TOTAL	
	ARRIVALS	STAYS	ARRIVALS	STAYS	ARRIVALS	STAYS
2000	2,765.317	11,642.757	1,801.052	9,056.208	4,566.369	20,698.695
2001	2,723.676	11,703.729	1,827.024	9,258.850	4,550.700	20,962.579
2002	2,777.419	11,681.368	1,775.399	8,641.845	4,552.818	20,323.213
2003	2,837.210	11,688.575	1,692.666	8,020.377	4,529.876	19,708.952
2004	2,795.356	11,674.982	1,742.351	8,232.532	4,537.707	19,907.514
2005	2,663.905	10,979.735	1,781.514	8,151.239	4,445.419	19,130.974
2006	2,656.816	10,990.060	1,805.062	8,155.823	4,506.878	19,145.883

Source: ISTAT.

Table **3** and Figs. **3** and **4** show the rates of variation compared to the previous year during the 2000-2006 period. In terms of arrivals, we can see that Italian and foreign tourists display the opposite behaviour in practically all the years. As a result, the total number of arrivals is fairly stable, showing variation near zero percent throughout the period.

Table 3: Variation of arrivals and stays in Campania (percentages)

	ITALIAN		FOREIGN		TOTAL	
	ARRIVALS	STAYS	ARRIVALS	STAYS	ARRIVALS	STAYS
2001	-1.5	0.5	1.4	2.2	-0.3	1.3
2002	2.0	-0.2	-2.8	-6.7	0.0	-3.1
2003	2.2	0.1	-4.7	-7.2	-0.5	-3.0
2004	-1.5	-0.1	2.9	2.6	0.2	1.0
2005	-4.7	-6.0	2.2	-1.0	-2.0	-3.9
2006	-0.3	0.1	3.8	0.1	1.4	0.1

Source: ISTAT.

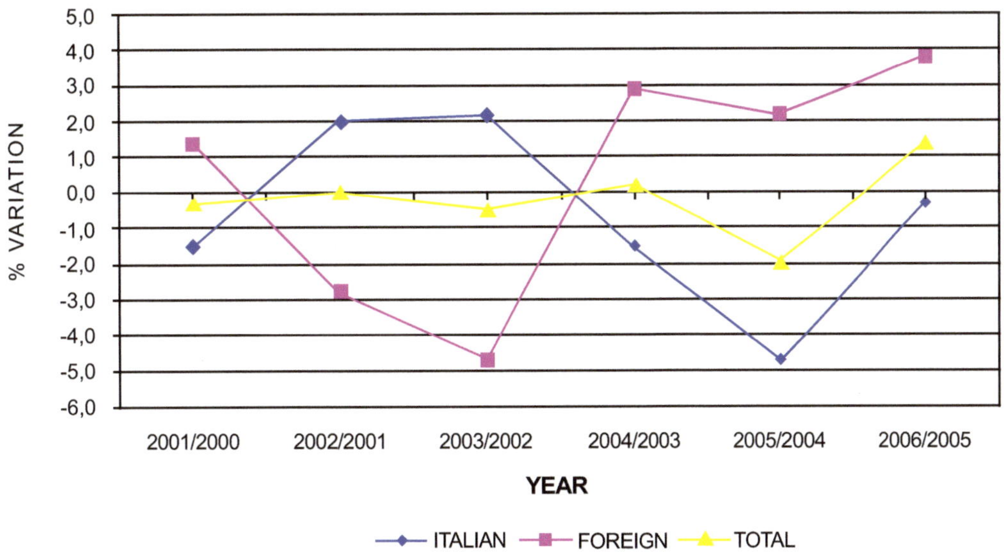

Source: ISTAT.

Figure 3: Annual variation of arrivals (%)

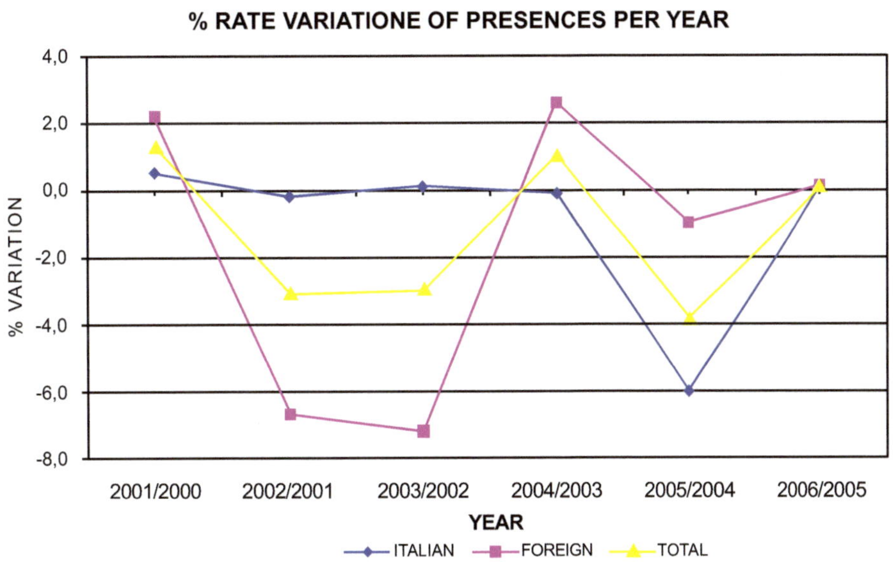

Source: ISTAT.

Figure 4: Annual variation of stays (%)

In conclusion, Italian tourism in Campania is more stable than foreign tourism. The total number of arrivals and stays, therefore, is comprised of different patterns in the two kinds of tourist analysed for the Campania region during the 2000 to 2006 period. This evidence suggests that interventions in these two different tourist markets should be individually defined in order to successfully meet their objectives. In other words, regional tourism in Campania should be analysed in terms of two different tourist markets: domestic and foreign

INPUT-OUTPUT ANALYSIS

The input-output analysis, which emphasises the interdependencies between industries and sectors, is used to estimate the environmental effects of changes in tourist demand. The main feature of the model is that it provides a very detailed picture of the structure of the economy at a particular point in time. This is achieved by categorising all the productive activities in the economy into industry sectors and documenting all the economic transactions (purchases and sales) that occur during a period of time (usually one year) between these sectors.

Our research involves using the classic input-output model to capture the interaction between the productive system and tourism, and the environmental damage caused by tourism. The standard representation input-output framework is described by the following matrix equation:

$$X = AX + Y \quad (1)$$

where X is the vector of the final production in each sector, A is the technical coefficients matrix calculated by dividing the intermediate consumption by the production in each activity, and Y is a vector of the final demand in each sector. Equation (1) can be written as:

$$X = (I - A)^{-1} Y \quad (2)$$

where $(I - A)^{-1}$ is the Leontief inverse matrix. This expression includes all the consequences activated in the production sphere when there is a modification in final demand. An increase in demand in one sector will generate an increase in its production to cover the new demand and, at same time, that sector will buy more input from the other sectors, and so on.

The model allows one to see the variations of output values when there is a change in final demand. In other words, it shows how sector production changes the economy when there is a change in tourism demand as follows:

$$\Delta X = (I - A)^{-1} \Delta Y \quad (3)$$

In this sense, the increase in demand for a specific sector generates an increase in production in that sector to satisfy the new demand. At the same time, this sector demands more input from other sectors and so on.

Additionally, our model is used to assess the emissions that are generated by tourism through the use of a matrix B that contains the impacts produced by sectors per unit of sector output which, in this case, are the emissions of pollutants (Butnar and Llop, 2007).

It is therefore possible to evaluate how the increase in demand in the tourism sector leads to a variation in final production and, additionally, how pollutant emissions increase. The impact generated on emissions as a function of final demand can be calculated through the transformation of equation (2) as follows:

$$F = B(I - A)^{1} Y \quad (4)$$

where F is the impact vector that, in our case, shows the emissions caused by each sector activity. For a more detailed assessment, it is possible to analyse the impacts in emissions based on the variation of final demand, as follows:

$$\Delta F = B(I - A)^{1} \Delta Y \quad (5)$$

where $B(I-A)^{-1}$ is the matrix of emission multipliers, which measures the amount of impact caused by an exogenous and unitary inflow in the final demand linked to sector j.

In order to empirically apply the model to a given area, the (non-symmetrical) supply and use tables of the region must be transformed into a symmetrical matrix (Miller and Blair, 2009). These matrices are used to obtain matrix A of the technical coefficients (symmetrical) through the following calculation:

$$A = D'*C \quad \textbf{(6)}$$

where C is defined by the shares of the elements of the use matrix divided by the domestic output that the domestic industry uses, and D' is the transpose of D, which is defined by the shares of each product compared to the final output.

DATABASE

The model described in the previous section was used to comprehensively evaluate the impact of tourism on economic activity and on the environment because it takes into account the interaction between economic sectors and the environment.

In order to empirically implement the model, we used the 2004 supply and use matrix for the region of Campania provided by the Istituto Regionale per la Programmazione Economica della Toscana (IRPET). These tables break down production by sector with 29 homogenous production activities and contain the information expressed in basic prices for the year 2004. The calculation of the direct structural coefficients or input-output coefficients matrix A follows expression (6) above (Miller and Blair, 2009).

The environmental data linked to the atmospheric emissions were obtained from the Italian Statistics Institute, which defined a National Accounting Matrix with Environmental Accounts for Italy in 2003. This matrix contains 29 production sectors. The data on pollution emissions are organised in matrix B. The NAMEA distinguishes different gas emissions, such as CO_2, NO_x, SO_x, N_2O, CO and others regulated by the Kyoto Protocol. Like the input-output coefficients matrix, the columns in B contain 29 different production activities.

Table 4: Production sectors and gases

SECTORS		GAS EMISSIONS (Kilotons)	
1	Agriculture, hunting and forestry	1	CO_2
2	Fishing	2	CO_2 from biomass
3	Mining and quarrying of energy-producing materials	3	N_2O
5	Mining and quarrying, non-energy-producing materials	4	CH_4
6	Food products, beverages and tobacco	5	NO_x
7	Textiles and textile products	6	SO_x
8	Leather and leather products	7	NH_3
9	Wood and wood products	8	NMVOC
10	Pulp, paper and paper products	9	CO
11	Coke, refined petroleum products and nuclear fuel	10	PM10
12	Chemicals, chemical products and man-made fibres	11	Pb (Kg)
13	Rubber and plastic products		
14	Other non-metallic mineral products		
15	Basic metals and fabricated metal products		
16	Machinery and equipment		
17	Electrical and optical equipment		
18	Transport equipment		
19	Other manufacturing		
20	Electricity, gas and water supply		
21	Construction		

22	Wholesale and retail trade		
23	Hotels and restaurants		
24	Transport, storage and communication		
25	Financial intermediation		
26	Public administration		
27	Education		
28	Health and social work		
29	Other community, social and personal service activities		

To better understand how tourism influences the environment, the vector of final demand linked to the tourism sector in Campania must be taken into account. The 2004 figures were obtained from IRPET.

Finally, to define the modification in the final demand vector it is necessary to simulate a variation of tourist consumption, that is, an increase or a decrease in tourism expenditures. In our analysis, the variation in the final demand vector, ΔY, should follow the same trend as the percentage of variation in tourist stays between the years 2000 and 2006 in the Campania region.

EMPIRICAL RESULTS

The goal of this research is to calculate the impact that tourists have on a regional system in terms of both the economic effects and the generation of gas emissions.

The analytical context used in this study shows how exogenous and unitary inflows to the final demand of tourists affect emissions. In other words, calculating the matrix of emission multipliers $B(I-A)^{-1}$ and vector F of total emissions provides a general representation of the ecologic-economic channels that exist in the production system and their links to tourism activity. This tells us how tourism affects emissions in terms of regional air pollution.

First, we focus on the emission multipliers that quantify the changes in the levels of emissions in response to unitary changes in the final demand of the economy, and second, we analyse the patterns that explain the changes in emissions due to changes in tourism consumption.

Emission Multipliers

Following the logic of the input-output representation of pollution processes, an exogenous increase in final demand should lead to an increase in production of all activities in order to cover the new demand and, as levels of pollution have a direct and fixed relationship with levels of production, this should also lead to an increase in emission levels.

This section quantifies the changes in the amount of gas emissions brought on by exogenous and unitary changes in the final demand of activities. From this perspective, it is possible to identify which production activities are responsible for the largest increases in the levels of pollution after an increase in their exogenous demand. These results are very valuable for designing abatement measures for industrial pollution.

Table **5** contains the elements of matrix $B(I-A)^{-1}$ corresponding to the emission multipliers. The elements in this table show the changes in Campania emissions when there is an exogenous and unitary inflow to all the activities. The sum of the rows shows the increase in the emissions of the corresponding pollutant gas when there is one unitary injection in the final demand of all the activities simultaneously. These total values therefore reflect the contaminating effects of each type of emission caused by joint inflows to all the production sectors.

From the information in Table **5** it is clear that some bilateral effects are very significant in terms of the generation of pollution, and this means that some activities have a significant influence on total gas emissions in the region of Campania. These results suggest that the inflows received from a reduced number of activities contribute to the generation of most of the pollution originating in the Campania production system. For instance, NH_3 emissions are mostly caused by agriculture, food, beverages and tobacco, and hotels and restaurants, with other activities contributing much less to the emission of this particular gas. The results in Table **5** indicate that emissions in

Campania are considerably asymmetrical by sector, and the effects of production activities on air pollution are very heterogeneous. These results show that an increase in emissions essentially depends on the activity that receives the exogenous inflow of the final demand.

Table 5: Emission multipliers ($B\ (I - A)^{-1}$). Campania, 2004, in kilotons

	AGRICULTURE, HUNTING AND FORESTRY	FISHING	MINING AND QUARRYING OF ENERGY MATERIALS	MINING AND QUARRYING, NON ENERGY MATERIALS	FOOD, BEVERAGES AND TOBACCO	TEXTILES AND TEXTILE PRODUCTS	LEATHER AND LEATHER PRODUCTS	WOOD AND WOOD PRODUCTS	PULP, PAPER AND PAPER PRODUCTS	COKE, REFINED PETROLEUM AND NUCLEAR FUEL
CO_2	2,616.2225055	3,844.0368587	13.7198834	6,443.3552990	2,809.9475554	3,291.5881792	1,692.1859036	2,921.4321051	4,497.2670463	12,310.8694551
CO_2 (from biomass)	130.2170510	118.3047985	0.3163231	224.1349094	78.6015082	127.4721709	52.3772351	75.2911983	91.7222131	24.4396188
N_2O	16.0764688	0.1953570	0.0012360	0.5273137	3.0917136	0.3302736	0.4123908	0.4249481	0.3319325	0.3336958
CH_4	169.4557641	2.9912683	6.0263016	4.7220086	36.3210382	5.0750492	6.9253334	5.0904617	6.5472967	7.7601707
NO_x	27.6764701	35.2087771	0.0713082	18.8271202	9.6679889	5.6609189	4.2487158	7.6296648	5.6652677	17.3129048
SO_x	1.6097978	2.6658958	0.0019016	8.4497588	2.8537261	3.1936983	1.8702356	2.9977450	2.8818344	54.0246953
NH_3	85.0184462	0.3250395	0.0010459	0.2070153	15.4792921	0.6877102	1.4365833	1.1293802	0.4529999	0.0945454
NMVOC	9.4372330	6.9935458	1.6660443	3.5181868	6.5350048	1.8988890	23.5718312	29.3464543	9.2903617	20.0926044
CO	80.3288290	20.5900678	0.1862570	8.4538992	17.1427979	3.3789109	3.8018889	6.0076352	3.4929099	4.7540195
PM10	6.9743545	3.9875404	0.0070357	2.2864254	1.7296885	0.6173046	0.5104325	0.8894667	0.5259156	1.3227587
Pb (Kg)	0.1573280	0.3553134	0.0000000	1.7297430	0.4706209	0.2769171	0.3562966	0.8352556	0.3950752	0.7376819
CO_2	5,297.4398917	3,574.5770560	18,161.3619515	5,552.8088183	2,547.7338999	1,950.5556267	2,276.9963417	1,806.7272320	51,621.6962396	2,119.3701139
CO_2 (from biomass)	77.5513195	93.1257518	88.5748196	43.5360019	89.7970713	48.5175131	56.2380777	48.7230644	1,599.1198179	27.5917210
N_2O	5.3788951	0.5932320	1.3688781	0.2496359	0.2134661	0.2001188	0.1925234	0.1889212	2.2841846	0.2005948
CH_4	10.4845473	5.7351951	6.2849158	4.6458752	2.9927688	3.0764992	3.1022304	2.5435979	91.3224072	2.4254843
NO_x	7.1764859	6.0596563	43.7301425	7.5247679	5.2130268	4.1381092	4.4817165	4.7714813	44.1921652	6.5242932
SO_x	6.2510214	3.3881951	22.6406250	5.6718778	2.3390704	2.0980817	2.1803867	1.8320165	64.1724896	2.4771757
NH_3	0.5523858	0.5742579	0.2581389	0.2866601	0.2522775	0.2461181	0.2424919	0.3021503	0.1847817	0.2015328
NMVOC	9.6025988	6.3499866	3.3922616	9.7802429	5.2080275	3.2141916	5.0193808	14.2748868	13.7364415	7.5787014
CO	7.1805007	5.0504720	21.2416524	68.7131866	10.1468562	5.2983270	8.1702989	7.1168554	15.0186511	6.0419859
PM10	0.7823956	0.6409053	6.4595705	3.9762813	0.8704059	0.5461581	0.6902131	0.7076962	2.7457802	1.1800131
Pb (Kg)	0.7124036	0.8312224	28.1195751	22.5610123	2.8105518	1.6872396	2.3175751	1.7755786	1.7510171	2.3594525
CO_2	2,110.2083298	1,892.4514505	3,816.8514432	664.3141579	726.0663530	1,022.8830228	419.2051845	1,020.2618759	1,806.9933753	148,829.1271555
CO_2 (from biomass)	40.7989451	55.1302356	38.9764074	13.0993840	14.1099988	32.8846632	11.1390689	27.3702563	396.1234464	3,725.2845902
N_2O	0.3264877	0.7227957	0.3180401	0.0625640	0.0834920	0.1113895	0.0316738	0.5114709	0.8071186	35.5708124
CH_4	4.7231106	9.2751344	2.8434076	1.0994511	1.2201201	3.2337129	0.6785606	2.7925449	90.6039729	499.9982285
NO_x	8.0260504	5.3905842	21.8432746	2.2806202	2.5497197	2.8185561	0.7517617	2.4047952	4.6319680	316.4783115
SO_x	1.9575728	1.9229925	6.7883829	0.7168842	0.7276199	1.1333774	0.4188669	1.0557327	1.3880530	209.7097110
NH_3	0.8631965	3.1188362	0.3830376	0.0830394	0.1506273	0.1073639	0.0230498	0.4915310	1.2354164	114.3889511
NMVOC	3.2064987	1.8419374	4.2021906	0.5951413	0.7097156	0.9969448	0.1969978	0.9391102	3.2290413	206.4244525
CO	5.1353684	5.1947836	12.3632431	1.3259242	1.5763584	5.1103734	0.3970688	1.8500696	2.4061405	337.4753314
PM10	0.8547552	0.6558639	1.6908336	0.2158630	0.2629574	0.2847283	0.0634268	0.2417751	0.4155322	42.1360774
Pb (Kg)	0.4113149	0.2490644	0.6861936	0.1056163	0.1445451	0.2309325	0.0362187	0.1882453	1.2456557	73.5376460

Final Demand Assumptions

Following the logic of the input-output model, vector F shows the gas emissions as a function of the final demand of each sector. Additionally, we can calculate the emissions caused by each component of final demand separately. That is, we can break down vector F into the emissions attributed to different items of final demand.

Table **6** divides vector F into two parts. The first takes into account the emissions caused by household consumption in the Campania region, and the second shows the emissions caused by Italian and foreign tourist expenditure in the region. Finally, we can calculate the emissions caused by total consumption as the sum of those two values.

Table 6: Emissions of households and tourists ($F = B(I - A)^{-1}Y$). Campania, 2004 (kilotons)

	HOUSEHOLD CONSUMPTION	ITALIAN AND FOREIGN TOURIST CONSUMPTION	TOTAL
CO_2	17,8469.47 (95.61%)	8,189.99 (4.39%)	186,659.47
CO_2 from biomass	6,566.28 (95.26%)	326.72 (4.74%)	6,893.00
N_2O	51.73 (94.79%)	2.84 (5.21%)	54.57
CH_4	1,175.63 (94.91%)	62.99 (5.09%)	1238.62
NO_x	447.29 (94.67%)	25.18 (5.33%)	472.47
SO_x	239.50 (96.08%)	9.75 (3.92%)	249.26
NH_3	181.87 (94.76%)	10.04 (5.24%)	191.92
NMVOC	224.32 (95.09%)	11.58 (4.91%)	235.90
CO	395.81 (94.79%)	21.76 (5.21%)	417.57
PM10	50.17 (94.69%)	2.81 (5.31%)	52.98
Pb (tons)	40.23 (95.60%)	1.85 (4.40%)	42.08

As Table **6** shows, greenhouse gases generated by household consumption is the predominant component in total emissions. In fact, the quantities of gas emissions produced by Italian and foreign tourism consumption range between 4.39% (for CO2) and 5.31% (for PM10). In other words, fewer emissions are caused by tourism than by the population that lives in the Campania Region, who generate between 94.69% (for PM10) and 95.61% (for CO2) of the total emissions.

We can also analyse the effects on regional emissions caused by a variation in final demand, the ΔF in the model. This simulation analysis considers two alternative scenarios. In the first, the reduction applied to total consumption was defined as equal to 1.267%, according to the average reduction in the total stays in the region during the 2000-2006 period. Second, we analysed an increase in tourist consumption of 5%, in accordance with the average growth of tourist stays worldwide, according to tourism reports of the Campania region.

The first column in Table **7** coincides with the emissions in Table **6** attributed to tourist emissions in the region of Campania. The second column illustrates that the reduction in regional emissions is very small for most gases. This result suggests that the reduction in the number of stays would have provoked an insignificant decrease in regional emissions.

The last column in Table **7** contains the emissions that a 5% increase in tourist expenditure would represent, in keeping with the worldwide trend. It is important to consider that tourism is represented by different production sectors, such as food and beverage, transport, and services and, in general, the transport and some of the services used by tourists release CO_2 into the atmosphere. Therefore, there is a linear consequence between an increase in arrivals (and in stays) and an increase in CO_2 emissions. In conclusion, although tourism is one of the greenest production sectors compared to other industrial activities, it seems clear that it is essential to pay attention to some critical activities involved in the tourism industry in order to reduce CO_2 emissions.

Table 7: Changes in emissions of households and tourists ($\Delta F = B(I - A)^{-1}\Delta Y$). Campania, 2004 (kilotons)

	Benchmark	Situation 1[a]	Situation 2[b]
CO_2	8,189.99	8,086.23	8,599.49
CO2 from biomass	326.72	322.58	343.06
N_2O	2.84	2.80	2.98
CH_4	62.99	62.19	66.14
NO_x	25.18	24.86	26.44
SO_x	9.75	9.63	10.24
NH_3	10.04	9.91	10.54
NMVOC	11.58	11.43	12.16
CO	21.76	21.48	22.85
PM10	2.81	2.78	2.95
Pb (tons)	1.85	1.83	1.94

a. **emissions of a 1.267% reduction in tourist consumption.**
b. **emissions of a 5% increase in tourist consumption.**

The input-output method provides interesting information about how the consumption generated by households and tourists can affect the pressure on the environment in terms of emissions. Another interesting piece of evidence is the comparison of air pollution levels in the Campania region with those at the national level. This comparison provides insight into the direction that environmental policies aimed at achieving the sustainable development of tourism in a region with a high cultural value should take.

Table **8** contains the emissions caused by total consumption in Italy and in Campania. It also shows the relative contribution of Campania emissions (of both total consumption and tourist consumption) to total Italian emissions. The values in Table **8** indicate that the emissions caused by consumption in Campania are high compared with the emissions at a national level. Regional emissions of CH_4 amount to approximately 75% of the Italian values, and regional emissions of SO_x amount to 48.35% of the national level. The values in Table **8** show that this region is responsible for a high level of emissions at a national level. This result suggests that environmental policies aimed at reducing total emissions in Italy should consider the region of Campania as one of the most polluting regions and therefore treat it as a priority area in which intervention is needed.

Table 8: Emissions in Italy and Campania, 2004 (kilotons)

	TOTAL CONSUMPTION EMISSIONS IN ITALY	TOTAL CONSUMPTION EMISSIONS IN CAMPANIA	CAMPANIA COMPARED TO ITALY (%)	TOURIST CONSUMPTION EMISSIONS IN CAMPANIA	CAMPANIA TOURISTS COMPARED TO ITALY (%)
CO_2	505,092.62	186,659.47	36.96%	8,189.99	1.62%
CO_2 from biomass	14,000.05	6,893.00	49.24%	326.72	2.33%
N_2O	136.55	54.57	39.96%	2.84	2.08%
CH_4	1,646.35	1,238.62	75.23%	62.99	3.83%
NO_x	1,277.27	472.47	36.99%	25.18	1.97%
SO_x	515.53	249.26	48.35%	9.75	1.89%
NH_3	423.41	191.92	45.33%	10.04	2.37%
NMVOC	1,303.69	235.90	18.09%	11.58	0.89%
CO	4,388.47	417.57	9.52%	21.76	0.50%
PM10	168.52	52.98	31.44%	2.81	1.67%

Pb (tons)	238.43	42.08	17.65%	1.85	0.78%

The last two columns of Table **8** show the emissions caused by tourist consumption in the region and their contribution to total Italian emissions. Once again, this table shows that tourism activity in Campania generates a very small quantity of emissions in Italy. In other words, it seems that regional tourism activity does not cause significant damage to national air quality.

Our empirical results suggest that tourism does not have a high impact on total greenhouse emissions. Therefore, tourist activity can be considered an important instrument for economic development in Campania and one in accordance with sustainable development goals.

In order to explain the environmental consequences of tourism activity, we require flexible analyses that deal with the economic and ecologic relationships that occur in pollution generation processes. The application shown in this chapter could be useful in defining and implementing policies focused on both pollution control and regional economic development.

CONCLUSIONS

Tourism development has become one of the world's most important industrial sectors over the last 30 years. This rapid development has been coupled with negative environmental impacts on the territories where tourism has developed most. In the last few years, economists, ecologists and geographers have studied the relationships between the economy and the environment, and more specifically, between the productive sectors, the consumption of natural resources and the associated pollution. This joint analysis has allowed guidelines to be defined that can improve not only the sustainability of tourism but also regional development strategies. Moreover, the complexity of demand and consumption and the subsequent creation of emissions by the tourism sector mean that policies are needed which involve different economic and environmental aspects.

The consequence of this complexity is that the end effects of all possible tourism regulations will essentially depend on the economic agents involved and the type of measures implemented. Tourism can be seen, at the same time, as a risk and an opportunity for sustainable development in a specific area.

In the short term, tourism can generate economic benefits for regional production and local employment. In the long term, however, tourism can be associated with an inappropriate use of natural resources and an unsuitable lifestyle for the local community. These negative externalities, problems, and costs can lead to the destruction of tourism itself in the long term.

Our empirical analysis of the Campania region has determined the emissions levels generated by private household consumption and tourism consumption. One important finding is that there are significant differences between the pollution generated by tourism and the pollution generated by regional consumption.

We also found that the contribution of regional emissions to those of the country as a whole is significant for most gases. In contrast, tourism consumption in the region of Campania contributes very little to total Italian emissions.

REFERENCES

Alcántara, V. and Roca, J. (1995). "Energy and CO_2 Emissions in Spain: Methodology of Analysis and Some Results for 1980-1990", *Energy Economics*, 17, 221-230.

Alcántara, V. (1995). *Economía y Contaminación Atmosférica: Hacia un Nuevo Enfoque desde el Análisis Input-Output.* Unpublished doctoral thesis, Universidad de Barcelona: Barcelona.

Aguilera Klink, F. (1992). La Preocupación por el Medio Ambiente en el Pensamiento Económico Actual. *Información Comercial Española, 711*, 209-216.

Azqueta, D. Y. and Ferreiro, A. (1994). *Análisis Económico y Gestión de Recursos Naturales.* Alianza Editorial: Madrid.

Butler, R. W. (1991). *Designing Organisations: a Decision-Making Perspective.* Routledge: London.

Butnar, I. and Llop, M. (2007). Composition of Greenhouse Gas Emissions in Spain: An Input-Output Analysis, *Ecological Economics*, 61, 388-395.

Cadarso, M. A. and Fernández-Bolaños, A. (2002). *Patterns of Growth and Consumption and their Influence on the Environment in Spain.* Fourteenth International Conference on Input-Output Techniques. Montreal. Canada.

Campaner, U. (2000). *Lezioni di Economia Industriale del Turismo.* DUET, Università Ca'Foscari Venezia.

Costantini, C. and Tudini, A. (2003). How to Develop an Accounting Framework for Ecologically Sustainable Tourism. In V. Kneese, and J.L. Sweeney, (Eds.). *Handbook for Natural Resource and Energy Economics*. Elsevier Publishing Co.: New York.

Duarte, R., Sánchez-Choliz, J. and Bielsa, J. (2002). "Water Use in the Spanish Economy: An Input-Output Approach", *Ecological Economics*, 43, 71-85.

Fletcher, J. E. (1989). Input-Output Analysis and Tourism Impact Studies. *Annals of Tourism Research*, 16, 514-529.

Førsund Finn, R. (1985). Input-Output Models, National Economic Models, and the Environment. In V. Kneese, and J.L. Sweeney, (Eds.). *Handbook for Natural Resource and Energy Economics.* Elsevier Publishing Co.: New York.

Fossati, A. and Panella, G. (2000). Tourism and Sustainable Development: a Theoretical Framework. In A. Fossati and G. Panella (Eds.). *Tourism and Sustainable Economic Development*, Kluwer: Dordrecht.

Ioannides, D. and Debbage, K. (1998). *The Economic Geography of the Tourist Industry. A Supply-side Analysis,* Routledge: London.

Istituto Regionale per la Programmazione Economica della Toscana (IRPET) (2004). *Campania Region Supply and Use Table of 2004*: Firenze.

Istituto Regionale per la Programmazione Economica della Toscana (IRPET) (2004). *Campania Region Vector of Consumptions of 2004*: Firenze.

Istituto Nazionale di Statistica (ISTAT) (2003). *NAMEA. Serie 1990–2003*: Roma.

Lahr, M. L. and Dietzenbacher, E. (2001). *Input-Output Analysis: Frontiers and Extensions*. Palgrave: New York.

Leiper, N. (1990). Tourist Attraction Systems. *Annals of Tourism Research,* 77, 367-384.

Leontief, W. (1936). "Quantitative Input-Output Relations in the Economic System of United States", *Review of Economics and Statistics, 18*, 104-132.

Leontief, W. (1970). "Environmental Repercussions and the Economic Structure: An Input-Output Approach", *Review of Economics and Statistics, 52*, 261-272.

Leontief, W. and Ford, D. (1972). Air Pollution and Economic Structure: Empirical Results of Input-Output Computations. In A. Broady and A.P. Carter (Eds.). *Input-Output Techniques.* North Holland Publishing Company: Amsterdam.

Leontief, W. (1966). *Input-Output Economics*. Oxford University Press: New York.

Lenzen, M. (2002). "A Guide for Compiling Inventories in Hybrid Life-Cycle Inventories: Some Australian Results", *Journal of Cleaner Production*, 10, 545-572.

Lenzen. M., Pade. L. L. and Munksgaard J. (2004). "CO_2 Multipliers in Multi-Region Input-Output Models", *Economic Systems Research*, 16, 391-412.

Llop, M. (2007). "Economic Structure and Pollution Intensity within the Environmental Input-Output Framework", *Energy Policy*, *35*, 3410-3417.

Llop, M. (2008). "Economic Impact of Alternative Water Policy Scenarios in the Spanish Production System: An Input-Output Analysis", *Ecological Economics*, *68*, 288-294.

Llop, M. and Pié, L. (2008). "Input-Output Analysis of Alternative Policies Implemented on the Energy Activities: An Application for Catalonia", *Energy Policy*, *36*, 1642-1648.

Miller R. E. and Blair P. D. (2009). *Input-Output Analysis: Foundations and Extensions*, 2nd Edition, (Cambridge University Press).

Ostblom, G. (1998). The Environmental Outcome of Emissions-Intensive Economic Growth: A Critical Look at Official Growth Projections for Sweden up to the Year 2000. *Economic Systems Research*, 10, 19-29.

Patterson, M.G. and McDonald, G. (2004). How Clean and Green is New Zealand Tourism? Lifecycle and Future Environmental Impacts. In M.G. Patterson and G. McDonald, (Eds.). *Landcare Research Science Series*, Manaaki Whenua Press, Lincoln: New Zealand.

Pearce, D. (1976). *Environmental Economics*. Logman: London.

Pearce, D.W. and Turner, R. K. (1991). *Economia delle Risorse Naturali e dell'ambiente.* Il Mulino: Bologna.

Proops, J. L. R. (1988). Energy Intensities, Input-Output Analysis and Economic Development. In M. Ciaschini, (Eds.). Input-Output Analysis. *Current Developments*, Chapman and Hall: New York.

Proops, J. L. R., Faber, M., Wagenhals, G. (1993). *Reducing CO_2 Emissions. A Comparative Input-Output Study for Germany and U.K.*. Springer-Verlag: New York.

Reea, T. T. (2005). *The Economics of Input-Output Analysis*. Cambridge: University, Cambridge.

Roca, J. and Serrano, M. (2007). "Income Growth and Atmospheric Pollution in Spain: an Input-Output Approach", *Ecological Economics, 63*, 230-242.

Rodríguez, C., Llanes, G. and Cardenete, M. A. (2007). "Economic and Environmental Efficiency using a Social Accounting Matrix". *Ecological Economics*, 60, 774-786.

Smith, S. L. J. (1998). Tourism as an Industry. In D. Ioannides and K. G. Debbage (Eds.). *The Economic Geography of the Tourism Industry*. Routledge: London and New York.

Tucker, K. and Sundberg, M. (1988). *International Trade in Servicies*. Routledge.

Wanhill, S. R. C. (1988) "Tourism Multipliers under capacity constraints", *Service Industries Journa,*. 8(2), 136-142.

World Travel and Tourism Committee (WTTC) (2000). *Tourism Satellite Accounts: Research Summary and Highlights, Year 2000*, from http://www.wttc.org.

CHAPTER 9

Input-Output Table for Environmental Analysis of Japan: Construction and Application Study to Solar Power Satellites

Satoshi Nakano[*,a] **and Keiichiro Asakura**[b]

[a]*The Japan Institute for Labour Policy and Training, Keio Economic Observatory, Keio University, Japan and* [b]*Faculty of Economics, Ryutsu Keizai University, Japan*

Abstract: This paper presents the construction method of the 2000 Input-Output Table for Environmental Analysis of Japan and its application study. The first half of the paper describes the construction of energy inputs and CO_2 emissions tables corresponding to the official Input-Output Table by the Ministry of Internal Affairs and Communications, using economic and energy statistics. The second half quantifies the CO_2 emission of new power generation technology; Solar Power Satellites (SPS) as one of the application study.

Keywords: CO_2 emission, Life Cycle Assessment, Solar Power Satellites.

INTRODUCTION

Greenhouse gas (GHG) reduction targets of developed countries, including Japan, are provided in the Kyoto Protocol that came into effect in February 2005. Although Japan is required to reduce GHG emissions by 6% from 1990 levels during the first commitment period (2008–2012), domestic emissions have gradually increased instead. Even so, Prime Minister Hatoyama pledged to reduce emissions by 25% from 1990 levels by 2020 at the UN Climate Change Summit in 2009.

After the third UNFCCC Conference of the Parties (COP3) in 1997, international discussion regarding measures against global warming has continued, and COP15 was held in 2009. COP15 introduced the Copenhagen Accord and outlined measures to be implemented after 2013. However, forging an international consensus is a challenging task.

Our research group of environmental issues at Keio Economic Observatory, Keio University, has tried to construct the Input-Output Table for Environmental Analysis (IOTEA) 1985 and has addressed global warming issues based on the database. We used officially published information as much as possible for constructing the IOTEA 1995 (Asakura *et al.* 2001) and enhanced the repeatability of constructing the database. The IOTEA 2000 (Nakano *et al.* 2008) was constructed using the 2000 Input-Output Table of Japan, and a framework for analyzing CO2 emission structures by economic activities was prepared.

The IOTEA is not only a basic reference for life cycle assessment (LCA) of technologies but also a database for scenario analysis of recycling processes and multi-sectoral economic models. If other countries construct the IOTEAs using common concepts and classifications and these tables are linked, the environmental impact of technology transfer and carbon leakage can be assessed.

This paper presents the construction method for the IOTEA 2000 of Japan and its application to case studies. The first half of the paper describes the construction of the table with energy inputs and CO2 emissions corresponding to the official 2000 Input-Output Table constructed by the Ministry of Internal Affairs and Communications using economic and energy statistics. The second half quantifies the CO2 emission of a new power generation technology as an application case study.

COMPOSITION OF IOTEA OF JAPAN

The IOTEA of Japan consists of six tables (Fig. **1**): (1) monetary inputs of raw materials, including the energy goods listed in Table **1**; (2) physical inputs of energy goods (original unit); (3) physical inputs of energy goods (calorie

[*]**Address correspondence to Satoshi Nakano:** The Japan Institute for Labour Policy and Training, 4-8-23 Kamishakujii, Nerimaku, Tokyo 177-8502, Japan. Tel: +81-3-5903-6223. Fax: +81-3-5903-6118. E-mail: nakano@sanken.keio.ac.jp (or) nakano@jil.go.jp.

Maria Llop (Ed)

basis); (4) physical inputs of energy goods (CO2 basis); (5) physical inputs of energy goods for non-energy use (CO2 basis); and (6) CO2 emissions.

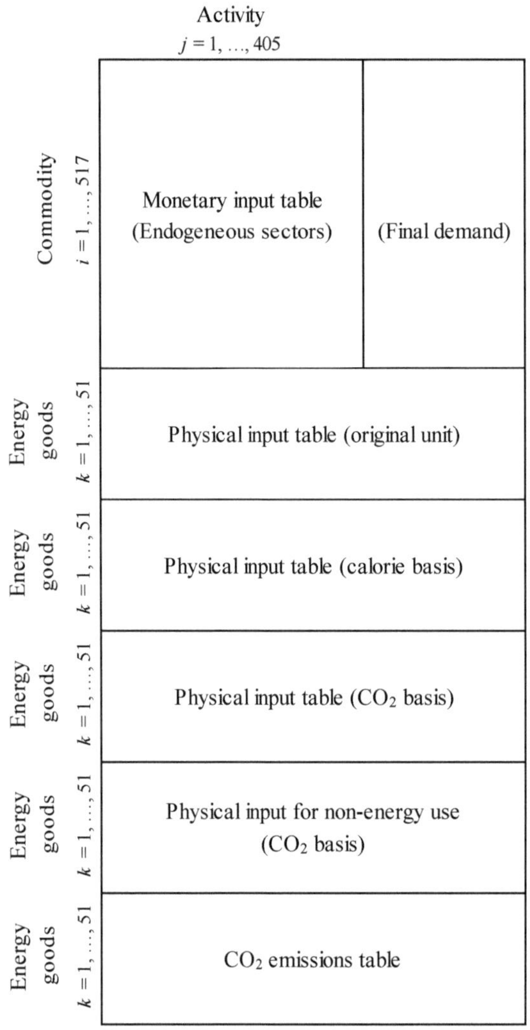

Figure 1: Composition of Input-Output Table for Environmental Analysis (IOTEA)

The monetary input table shows the monetary inputs of raw materials by activities valued at producer prices. We used the transaction table (basic sector classification: 405 column sectors, 517 row sectors) of the 2000 Input-Output Table as the monetary input table of the IOTEA. For analysis using the square table by sector aggregation, the following aggregation method is employed. First, row sectors are aggregated using six digits from the top of the seven-digit row code to reduce the number of row sectors to 401. Next, the square monetary input table (399 × 399) is derived by aggregating both column and row sectors based on Table

The physical input table (original unit) shows the physical inputs of energy goods listed in Table **1** for each activity, by weight or volume. These energy goods include limestone, iron, and steel. Limestone, pig iron, crude steel (converters and electric furnaces), iron scrap, and blast furnace dust are required to calculate the carbon balance. These goods also include substitutable goods such as fly ash, blast furnace slag, converter slag, and electric furnace slag for other inputs that contain carbon.

By using the heating value per weight or volume as listed in Table **1**, we can transform the physical input table (original unit) into the physical input table (calorie basis). Because the physical input table (calorie basis) shows the total heating value of energy inputs, we can identify energy-intensive sectors.

We can obtain the physical input table (CO2 basis) by using the carbon content per weight or calorie as well as the physical input table (calorie basis). The physical input table (CO2 basis) indicates that carbon in the inputs is fully emitted as CO2. However, there are energy inputs for non-energy use. Hence, carbon in inputs for non-energy use should be deducted from the physical input table (CO2 basis). This deduction is described in the physical input table of energy goods for non-energy use (CO2 basis). The CO2 emissions table is constructed by deducting the energy inputs for non-energy use from the energy inputs (CO2 basis).

Table 1: Energy goods in IOTEA

	Energy goods	**Original unit**	**Heating value per original unit**	**CO_2 emissions per heating value**	**Carbon content**
			MJ/Unit	**kg-CO_2/GJ**	**(ratio by weight)**
1	Limestone	t			0.120
2	Fly ash	t			
3	Blast furnace slag	t			
4	Converter slag	t			
5	Electric furnace slag	t			
6	Coking coal	t	31814	81.61	
7	Steam coal	t	25426	94.75	
8	Crude petroleum	kl	38721	67.64	
9	Natural gas	$1000m^3$	41023	50.81	
10	LNG	t	54418	49.57	
11	Gasoline	kl	35162	66.03	
12	Jet fuel oils	kl	36418	67.62	
13	Kerosene	kl	37255	66.82	
14	Light oils	kl	38511	68.01	
15	Heavy oil A	kl	38930	69.60	
16	Heavy oil B and C	kl	41023	72.68	
17	Naphtha	kl	33488	67.95	
18	LPG (liquefied petroleum gas)	t	50232	59.73	
19	Oil produced by conversion	kl	33488	70.45	
20	Hydrocarbon oil	t	41023	77.09	
21	Hydrocarbon gas	$1000m^3$	39348	59.41	
22	Petroleum coke	t	35581	93.18	
23	Coke	t	30139	107.66	
24	Coke oven gas	$1000m^3$	20093	42.36	
25	Blast furnace gas	$1000m^3$	3349	99.32	
26	Converter furnace gas	$1000m^3$	8372	141.44	
27	Electric furnace gas	$1000m^3$	8372	183.25	
28	Tar	t	32065	89.15	
29	Crude benzene	t			0.923
30	Pig iron	t			0.040
31	Crude steel (converters)	t			0.003
32	Crude steel (electric furnaces)	t			0.003
33	Pig iron scrap	t			0.040
34	Steel scrap	t			0.003

35	Electricity	million kWh	3599960		
36	Private power generation	million kWh	3599960		
37	Gas supply	$1000m^3$	41860	49.68	
38	Steam and hot water supply	GJ	1000		
39	Black liquor	bone-dry t	12558	94.17	
40	General waste	t	6614	84.40	
41	Scrap wood	bone-dry t	16744	76.99	
42	Animal and plant residues	t			
43	Paper scrap	t	18795	90.45	
44	Wood waste	t	17581	96.69	
45	Waste textile	t			
46	Waste oil	t	27000	108.10	
47	Waste plastic	t	32341	79.02	
48	Sludge	t	14651	75.08	
49	Waste tire	t	32341	54.31	
50	Blast furnace dust	t			0.300
51	Used paper	t			

Source) IOTEA 2000

Table 2: Sector aggregation for IOTEA

IOTEA		**official IO**	
Column sector			
011300	Vegetables	011301	Vegetables(outdoor)
		011302	Vegetables(under facilities)
031100	Marine fisheries(domestic)	031101	Coastal fisheries
		031102	Off-shore fisheries
		031103	Distant water fisheries
031200	Inland water fisheries and culture	031201	Inland water fisheries
		031202	Inland water culture
261101	Pig iron	261101	Pig iron
271109	Other non-ferrous metals	271109	Other non-ferrous metals
511100	Electricity	511101	Electricity(nuclear power)
		511102	Electricity(thermal power)
		511103	Electricity(water power, etc.)
Row sector			
011300	Vegetables	011300	Vegetables
031100	Marine fisheries(domestic)	031100	Marine fisheries(domestic)
031200	Inland water fisheries and culture	031200	Inland water fisheries and culture
261101	Pig iron	261101	Pig iron
		261201	Scrap iron
271109	Other non-ferrous metals	271109	Other non-ferrous metals
		271201	Non-ferrous metal scrap
511100	Electricity	511100	Electricity

ESTIMATION

First, we construct the table that shows the physical inputs of energy goods (original unit), using economic and energy statistics. Next, the energy input table (original units) is converted into tables that describe the physical inputs of energy goods (calorie basis and CO_2 basis) by per unit heat quantity and carbon content. Third, we estimate the energy inputs for non-energy use (CO_2 basis) from the information on energy consumption by usage. Finally, the CO_2 emissions table is built by deducting the energy inputs for non-energy use from the energy inputs (CO_2 basis).

Physical Input Table (Original Unit)

Physical Input Table of 2000 Input-Output Table

The physical inputs of coking coal, steam coal, crude petroleum, gasoline, jet fuel oils, kerosene, light oils, heavy oil A, heavy oil B and C, naphtha, Liquefied petroleum gas (LPG), coke, electricity, gas supply, and steam and hot water supply are based on the physical input table of the *2000 Input-Output Table.* Although the physical inputs of coal are available from the physical input table of the *2000 Input-Output Table,* we cannot divide it into coking and steam coal. Therefore, we divided coal inputs in the *2000 Input-Output Table* using the coking and steam coal shares in the physical input table of the *1995 Input-Output Table.*

Natural Gas and Liquid Natural Gas (LNG)

Natural gas and LNG consumption is estimated by the transaction table of the *2000 Input-Output Table* and *Japan Exports & Imports 2000.* The natural gas sector in the transaction table includes natural gas and LNG. The transaction table shows not only the monetary input of domestic natural gas but also the monetary input of imported natural gas. All LNG is imported, while all natural gas is domestically produced. Therefore, the domestic natural gas in the transaction table denotes so-called natural gas, and the imported gas denotes LNG. Natural gas and LNG consumption is estimated by dividing the monetary inputs of domestic and imported gas in the transaction table by the unit prices of natural gas and LNG, respectively. Table **3** shows the unit prices of these energy goods.

Table 3: Unit price of LNG and natural gas in 2000

	Unit	Price
LNG	yen/t	28,199
Natural gas	yen/1000m^3	31,494

Source: 2000 Input-Output Table and Japan Exports & Imports 2000.

By Product Gas and Other Energy Inputs

Mining and Manufacturing Sector

The consumption of oil produced by conversion, hydrocarbon oil, hydrocarbon gas, petroleum coke, coke oven gas, blast furnace gas, converter furnace gas, electric furnace gas, and waste tires in the mining and manufacturing sectors (excluding ten iron and steel sectors and the petroleum refinery products sector) is described in the *Structural Survey of Energy Consumption in Commerce and Manufacturing 2000.*

The industry classification in the *Structural Survey* is based on the classification in the *Census of Manufacturers 2000.* This classification is not consistent with the sector classification of the *2000 Input-Output Table.* Hence, we converted the energy consumption of the former into the latter using a bridge table between the *Census of Manufacturers* and the *Input-Output Table* that was included in the *2000 Input-Output Table.*

The energy consumption in the *Structural Survey* includes the consumption for boilers to obtain heat and electricity. The private power generation of each industry is reported in the private power generation sector of the *Input-Output Table.* Therefore, we divided the energy consumption for boilers into the consumptions for generating electricity and obtaining heat by using the amount of private power generation and the thermal efficiency for power generation (38.1%). The former was allocated to the private power generation sector of the *Input-Output Table.*

Ten Iron and Steel Sectors

The consumption of hydrocarbon oil, petroleum coke, coke oven gas, blast furnace gas, converter furnace gas, electric furnace gas, tar, and iron scraps in ten iron and steel sectors, including pig iron, ferroalloys, crude steel (converters and electric furnaces), hot-rolled steel, steel pipes and tubes, cold-finished steel, coated steel, cast and forged steel, and cast and forged materials (iron) was obtained from the *Yearbook of Iron and Steel Statistics 2000.* The byproduct gas yield is also available from this publication. The energy consumption for power generation and boilers in the iron and steel sectors is divided by the steam consumption for power generation and production process. Table **4** shows the corresponding relationship between the *Yearbook* and IOTEA. The energy consumption of ten iron and steel sectors (Table **5**) was estimated based in Table **4**.

Table 4: Bridge table between *Yearbook of Iron and Steel Statistics* and IOTEA

Yearbook of Iron and Steel Statistics	**IOTEA**
For sintering	Pig iron
For pellets	
For iron-making	
For ferro-alloys	Ferro alloys
For steel-making(LD converters)	Crude steel (converters)
For steel-making(electric furnaces)	Crude steel (electric furnaces)
For steel forgings	Cast and forged steel
For steel castings	
For rolled steel, and steel pipes and tubes	Hot rolled steel
	Steel pipes and tubes
	Cold-finished steel
Other iron and steel sector	Coated steel
For power generation, boiler and co-generation	Private power generation
	Ten iron and steel sectors
Coke production sector	Coal products

Table 5: Energy consumption of ten iron and steel sectors in 2000

	Coke oven gas	**Balst furnace gas**	**Converter furnace gas**	**Electric furnace gas**	**Hydrocar bon oil**	**Petroleu m coke**	**Tar**
	1000m^3	**1000m^3**	**1000m^3**	**1000m^3**	**kl**	**t**	**t**
Yearbook of Iron and Steel Statistics and Structural Survey of Energy Consumption in Commerce and Manufacturing							
For sintering	157,390	57,197	29,409	0	0	0	2,072
For pellets	52,235	0	0	0	0	0	0
For iron-making	1,533,700	31,657,698	1,097,780	0	0	601,745	42,759
For ferro-alloys	3,741	1,455	5,005	6,565	0	6,526	0
For steel-making(LD converters)	334,090	8,981	19,857	0	0	0	0
For steel-making(electric furnaces)	27,534	680	2,630	0	0	6,668	0
For steel forgings	38,447	2,002	7,799	0	0	0	0

For steel castings	2,654	0	0	0	0	0	0
For rolled steel, and steel pipes and tubes	4,166,929	1,342,584	1,517,728	0	0	0	0
For power generation, boiler and co-generation	1,555,768	34,648,421	2,245,809	0	0	0	25,339
Other iron and steel sector	380,777	1,559,431	34,686	0	0	54	0
Coke production sector	1,474,748	16,407,326	206,722	0	142,010	566,474	78,353
Cast and forged materials (iron)	53	0	0	0	0	0	0
Total	9,728,066	85,685,775	5,167,425	6,565	142,010	1,181,467	148,523
Input-Output Table for Environmental Analysis							
Pig iron	1,869,002	41,562,807	1,416,568	0	0	601,745	52,695
Ferro alloys	4,011	1,907	6,290	6,565	0	6,526	0
Crude steel (converters)	358,175	11,770	24,955	0	0	0	0
Crude steel (electric furnaces)	29,519	891	3,305	0	0	6,668	0
Hot rolled steel	2,597,832	1,023,167	1,109,170	0	0	0	0
Steel pipes and tubes	412,166	162,333	175,978	0	0	0	0
Cold-finished steel	1,457,328	573,975	622,220	0	0	0	0
Coated steel	408,227	2,043,656	43,591	0	0	54	0
Cast and forged steel	44,064	2,624	9,801	0	0	0	0
Cast and forged materials (iron)	57	0	0	0	0	0	0
Private power generation	1,072,937	23,895,320	1,548,825	0	0	0	17,475
Coal products	1,474,748	16,407,326	206,722	0	142,010	566,474	78,353
Total	9,728,066	85,685,775	5,167,425	6,565	142,010	1,181,467	148,523

Source: Input-Output Table 2000, Yearbook of Iron and Steel Statistics 2000, and Structural Survey of Energy Consumption in Commerce and Manufacturing 2000.

Three Pulp and Paper and Petroleum Refinery Products Sectors

The black liquor and scrap wood consumption of the pulp, paper, and paperboard sectors is included in the *Yearbook of the Current Survey of Energy Consumption in Manufacturing 2000*. The consumption of hydrocarbon oil, hydrocarbon gas, and petroleum coke in the petroleum refinery products sector is also included in this publication. The consumption for boilers of these sectors is divided into the consumption for private power generation and the production process by the steam consumption. Tables **6** and **7** show the black liquor and scrap wood consumption of the pulp and paper sectors, respectively. Table **8** shows the energy consumption of the petroleum refinery products sector.

Table 6: Black liquor consumption of three pulp and paper sectors in 2000 (Unit: bone-dry t)

	Consumption incl. private power generation use	**Share of private power generation**	**Consumption for private power generation**	**Consumption excl. private power generation use**
Pulp	5,933,778	0.463	2,750,183	3,183,595
Paper	7,898,600	0.463	3,660,837	4,237,763
Paperboard	762,188	0.463	353,258	408,930

Source: Yearbook of Current Survey of Energy Consumption in Manufacturing 2000.

Table 7: Scrap wood consumption of three pulp and paper sectors in 2000 (Unit: bone-dry t)

	Consumption incl. private power generation use	**Share of private power generation**	**Consumption for private power generation**	**Consumption excl. private power generation use**
Pulp	71,347	0.393	28,054	43,293
Paper	224,246	0.393	88,174	136,072
Paperboard	53,071	0.393	20,868	32,203

Source: Yearbook of Current Survey of Energy Consumption in Manufacturing 2000.

Table 8: Hydrocarbon oil, petroleum oil, and hydrocarbon gas consumption of petroleum refinery products sector in 2000.

	Unit	**Consumption incl. private power generation use**	**Share of private power generation**	**Consumption for private power generation**	**Consumption excl. private power generation use**
Hydrocarbon oil	kl	203,346	0.289	58,845	144,501
Petroleum coke	t	142,624	0.289	41,273	101,351
Hydrocarbon gas	$1000m^3$	8,848,048	0.043	382,927	8,465,121

Source: Yearbook of Current Survey of Energy Consumption in Manufacturing 2000.

Electricity (Thermal Power) Sector

The consumption of coke oven, blast furnace, and converter furnace gases in the thermal power electricity sector is described in the *Outline of Electricity Demand and Supply FY 1999 and 2000.* Table **9** shows the energy consumption of the electricity (thermal power) sector.

Table 9: Coke oven gas, blast furnace gas, and converter furnace gas of electricity (thermal) sector in 2000

	Unit	**Consumption**
Coke oven gas	$1000m^3$	2,350,952
Blast furnace gas	$1000m^3$	40,385,092
Converter furnace gas	$1000m^3$	1,477,861

Source: Outline of Electricity Demand and Supply 1999 and 2000.

Gas Supply Sector

The consumption of coke oven, hydrocarbon, and methane gases in the gas supply sector is based on the *Yearbook of the Gas Supply 2000.* We related the coal and off gases included in other gases to coke oven and hydrocarbon gases, respectively. Table **10** represents the energy consumption of the gas supply sector.

Table 10: Gas consumption of gas supply sector in 2000

	Unit	**Consumption**
Coke oven gas	$1000m^3$	218,209
Hydrocarbon gas	$1000m^3$	81,626
Methane gas	$1000m^3$	720
Digestion gas	$1000m^3$	391

Source: Yearbook of Gas Supply 2000.

General and Industrial Waste

The amount of incinerated general waste and industrial waste—including slag, metal scrap, animal excreta, construction and demolition waste, animal and plant residues, dust, paper scrap, glass and pottery waste, waste oil, combustion residue, animal carcass, wood waste, waste plastic, waste acid, waste textile, waste rubber, sludge, and waste alkali—is estimated using the *State of Discharge and Treatment of Industrial Waste* and the *State of Discharge and Treatment of Municipal Solid Waste* for FY 2000.

General waste management is allocated to the waste management service (public) sector in the *Input-Output Table*, and the incineration disposal amount of general waste is available from the report. Industrial waste management is allocated to the waste management services (private) sector. Because industrial waste is incinerated to reduce the volume in the intermediate process, we treat the reduced amount of incinerated waste such as paper scraps and wood waste as the incinerated amount. The incinerated amount of waste oil, waste plastic, and sludge is estimated using the ratio of the incinerated amount to the total amount in the *IOTEA 1990* (Ikeda *et al.* 1996). Table **11** shows the incinerated amount of general and industrial wastes in 2000.

Table 11: Incinerated waste in 2000

		Unit	Incinerated amount	IOTEA
General waste		t	40,304,000	Waste management services (public)
Industrial waste	paper scrap	t	898,413	Waste management services (private)
	wood waste	t	2,901,729	Waste management services (private)
	waste oil	t	921,106	Waste management services (private)
	waste plastic	t	1,005,945	Waste management services (private)
	sludge	t	5,340,089	Waste management services (private)

Source: State of Discharge and Treatment of Industrial Waste, State of Discharge and Treatment of Municipal Solid Waste and IOTEA 1990.

Slag of Blast Furnace, Converter and Electric Furnace, Dust of Blast Furnace and Fly Ash

The generation and utilization of blast furnace, converter, and electric furnace slag are obtained from the *Statistical Yearbook of Iron and Steel Slag*. The information on fly ash is based on a discussion with the Japan Fly Ash Association. The generation of blast furnace dust is estimated using the dust generation per unit production of pig iron in the *IOTEA 1990*.

Physical Input Table (Calorie Basis)

The physical input table (calorie basis) is converted from the physical input table (original unit) using the heating value per original unit (Table **1**). This table shows which sector is energy intensive.

Physical Input Table (CO_2 Basis), Physical Input Table for Non-Energy use (CO_2 Basis), and CO_2 Emission Table

The physical input table (CO_2 basis) is calculated by multiplying the physical input table (calorie basis) and CO_2 emissions per heating value listed in Table **1**. The physical input table for non-energy use (CO_2 basis) is estimated using the combustion ratio or carbon balance table methods. The CO_2 emissions table is then built by deducting the physical input table for non-energy use (CO_2 basis) from the physical input table (CO_2 basis).

The combustion ratio method for estimating the physical input table for non-energy use (CO_2 basis) calculates the combusted proportion of the total inputs of energy goods and removes the combustion amount from the total inputs. In contrast, the carbon balance table method estimates the carbon content of outputs and uses it as the physical input for non-energy use. We applied the carbon balance table method to five sectors, including the coal products, pig iron, crude steel (converters), crude steel (electric furnaces) and gas supply sectors. The combustion ratio method was applied to the rest of sectors.

Combustion Ratio Method (Structural Survey of Energy Consumption in Commerce and Manufacturing 2000)

We applied the combustion ratio method to 400 sectors in the IOTEA. The combustion ratio in nine petrochemical products and chemical fertilizer sectors is based on the *Yearbook of the Current Survey of Energy Consumption in Manufacturing 2000*, while the ratio in the petroleum refinery products sector is estimated from the *Yearbook of*

Production Supply and Demand of Petroleum, Coal and Coke 2000 and the *Structural Survey of Energy Consumption in Commerce and Manufacturing 2000*. We assumed that all combustion ratios of the primary and tertiary industry sectors in the other 389 sectors are equal to one. The combustion ratio of the secondary industry sector in 389 sectors is based on the *Structural Survey of Energy Consumption in Commerce and Manufacturing 2000*.

However, we have given the combustion rate of certain energy goods. We converted the classification of the *Structural Survey of Energy Consumption in Commerce and Manufacturing* into that of the *Input-Output Table* using only the corresponding relationship between the shipment of the former and production of the latter. Therefore, the converted energy consumption may be not consistent with the classifications of the *Input-Output Table*. We used the following assumptions to tackle the problem. All coke oven gas, blast furnace gas, converter furnace gas, electric converter gas, gasoline, light oils, jet fuel oil, black liquor, scrap wood, general waste, paper scrap, wood waste, waste oil, waste plastic, sludge and waste tire were burned for all cases (i.e., the combustion ratio of these energy goods was equal to one). All coking coal was combusted in the chemical fertilizer and ferroalloy sectors, which do not produce coke, while no coking coal was combusted in the other sectors.

The *Structural Survey of Energy Consumption in Commerce and Manufacturing* reports energy consumption as raw materials. The combustion amount is estimated by deducting the consumption as raw materials from the total consumption, and the combustion ratio is obtained by dividing the combustion amount by the total consumption.

Combustion Ratio Method (Year Book of the Current Survey of Energy Consumption in Manufacturing 2000)

The combustion ratios in nine petrochemical product sectors and the chemical fertilizer sector are based on the *Yearbook of the Current Survey of Energy Consumption in Manufacturing 2000*. The nine petrochemical product sectors include petrochemical basic products, petrochemical aromatic products, aliphatic intermediates, cyclic intermediates, synthetic rubber, thermo-setting resins, thermoplastics resins, high function resins, and other resins. We assumed the same combustion rate for the nine petrochemical products sectors. Tables 12 and 13 show the combustion ratios of energy goods in the nine petrochemical product sectors and the chemical fertilizer sector, respectively.

Table 12: Combustion share of nine petrochemical products sectors in 2000

	Unit	Consumption incl. non-energy use	Consumption for non-energy use	Combustion share
Kerosene	kl	1,094,258	992,762	0.093
Naphtha	kl	35,639,148	35,639,148	0.000
LPG	t	4,395,741	3,985,356	0.093
Oil produced by conversion	kl	16,823,249	16,823,249	0.000

Source: Yearbook of Current Survey of Energy Consumption in Manufacturing 2000.

Table 13: Combustion share of chemical fertilizer sector in 2000

	Unit	Consumption incl. non-energy use	Consumption for non-energy use	Combustion share
Natural gas	$1000m^3$	167,873	87,310	0.480
Naphtha	kl	483,224	453,264	0.062
LPG	t	30,309	6,949	0.771
Hydrocarbon gas	$1000m^3$	344,954	228,348	0.338

Source: Yearbook of Current Survey of Energy Consumption in Manufacturing 2000.

Combustion Ratio Method (Yearbook of Production Supply and Demand of Petroleum, Coal and Coke 2000)

The combustion ratio in the petroleum refinery product sector is calculated using the Yearbook of Production Supply and Demand of Petroleum, Coal and Coke 2000 and the Structural Survey of Energy Consumption in

Commerce and Manufacturing 2000. If the ratios obtained from the two sources were different, we selected the lower one. Table **14** represents the combustion ratio of energy goods in the petroleum refinery products sector.

Table 14: Combustion share of petroleum refinery products sector

	Unit	Consumption incl. non-energy use	Consumtion for combustion	Combustion share
Steam coal	t	198,399	195,869	0.98725
Kerosene	kl	92,073	41,455	0.45024
Light oils	kl	2,752	148	0.05378
Naphtha	kl	60,557	0.3	0.00001
Petroleum coke	t	1,965	1,872	0.95303
LPG	t	180,042	37,143	0.20630

Source: Yearbook of Production Supply and Demand of Petroleum, Coal and Coke 2000, and Structural Survey of Energy Consumption in Commerce and Manufacturing 2000.

Combustion Ratio of Limestone

Limestone initiates a chemical reaction when it is heated or added to acid and the CO2 is discharged. Most sectors consume limestone through the chemical reaction. However, the materials for ceramics sectors only crush the limestone, and the combustion ratio of limestone is equal to zero in this sector. The combustion ratio of limestone is estimated using information for 1995 from the Central Research Institute of Electric Power Industry (Hondo *et al.* 2002).

Physical Input of Gas Supply

The *Structural Survey of Energy Consumption in Commerce and Manufacturing 2000* reports LNG consumption of the chemical industries, while the *Input-Output Table 2000* reports LNG consumption of only three sectors: gas supply, electricity (thermal), and private power generation. The LNG data of the *Structural Survey* includes the LNG supplied by gas suppliers. On the other hand, the *Input-Output Table* reports the LNG supplied by gas suppliers in the gas supply sector.

The cyclic intermediates, synthetic dyes, and organic pigment manufacturing data of the *Structural Survey* consider LNG as a raw material. Therefore, if the sectors shown in the *Input-Output Table* in relation to these manufacturing sectors burn all of their gas supply, the CO_2 emissions might be overestimated. Hence, when calculating the combustion ratio of the gas supply, the combusted gas supply of the sectors that consume LNG as raw material is estimated by deducting the gas supply as raw material from total gas supply inputs.

Carbon Balance Table Method

We applied the carbon balance table method to the coal product, pig iron, crude steel (converters), crude steel (electric furnaces), and gas supply sectors. The carbon balance table shows the carbon content of inputs and outputs like a balance sheet. CO_2 emissions are calculated by deducting the total carbon content of inputs from the total carbon content of outputs.

We developed a material balance table that shows the physical inputs and outputs (original unit) and then converted the physical quantity (original unit) of the material balance table into carbon using the information listed in Table **1**. Tables **15**–**19** show the material balance table of the pig iron, crude steel (converters), crude steel (electric furnaces), and gas supply sectors. Tables **20**–**24** show the carbon balance table based on Tables **15**–**19**.

Table 15: Material balance table of coal products sector in 2000

	Unit	Input	Output
Coking coal	t	67,858,120	
Steam coal	t	60,000	
Gasoline	kl	56	

Kerosene	kl	8,069	
Light oils	kl	260	
Heavy oil A	kl	1,670	
Heavy oil B and C	kl	383	
Hydrocarbon oil	t	142,092	
Hydrocarbon gas	$1000m^3$	356	
Petroleum coke	t	566,672	
Coke	t		38,562,016
Coke oven gas	$1000m^3$		13,994,001
Blast furnace gas	$1000m^3$	18,904,221	
Converter furnace gas	$1000m^3$	363,916	
Tar	t		1,561,026
Crude benzene	t		519,867
Gas supply	$1000m^3$	605	

Source: IOTEA 2000.

Table 16: Material balance table of pig iron sector in 2000

	Unit	Input	Output
Limestone	t	17,753,143	
Coking coal	t	397,518	
Steam coal	t	5,043,956	
Natural gas	$1000m^3$	1,334	
Kerosene	kl	75	
Heavy oil A	kl	1,507	
Heavy oil B and C	kl	33,958	
LPG	t	8,259	
Petroleum coke	t	601,745	
Coke	t	35,960,569	
Coke oven gas	$1000m^3$	2,379,125	
Blast furnace gas	$1000m^3$	41,562,807	132,380,518
Converter furnace gas	$1000m^3$	1,416,568	
Tar	t	52,695	
Pig iron	t		81,105,642
Pig iron scrap	t	2,488	
Gas supply	$1000m^3$	1,532	
Blast furnace dust	t		1,217,351

Source: IOTEA 2000.

Table 17: Material balance table of crude steel (converters) sector in 2000

	Unit	Input	Output
Limestone	t	17,794,346	
Steam coal	t	730	

Natural gas	1000m^3	222	
Kerosene	kl	9,711	
Heavy oil A	kl	18,488	
Heavy oil B and C	kl	2,473	
LPG	t	851	
Coke	t	96,054	
Coke oven gas	1000m^3	455,934	
Blast furnace gas	1000m^3	11,770	
Converter furnace gas	1000m^3	24,955	8,437,446
Pig iron	t	77,145,345	
Crude steel (converters)	t		75,793,461
Pig iron scrap	t	557,251	
Steel scrap	t	6,274,734	
Gas supply	1000m^3	15,057	

Source:IOTEA 2000.

Table 18: Material balance table of crude steel (electric furnaces) sector in 2000

	Unit	Input	Output
Limestone	t	1,003,835	
Steam coal	t	558	
Natural gas	1000m^3	1,048	
Kerosene	kl	9,002	
Heavy oil A	kl	10,466	
Heavy oil B and C	kl	2,002	
LPG	t	1,048	
Petroleum coke	t	6,668	
Coke	t	74,084	
Coke oven gas	1000m^3	37,576	
Blast furnace gas	1000m^3	891	
Converter furnace gas	1000m^3	3,305	
Electric furnace gas	1000m^3		98,148
Pig iron	t	1,780,351	
Crude steel (electric furnaces)	t		30,665,213
Pig iron scrap	t	742,014	
Steel scrap	t	30,028,684	
Gas supply	1000m^3	21,245	

Source: IOTEA 2000.

Table 19: Material balance table of gas supply sector in 2000

	Unit	Input	Output
Coking coal	t	40,298	
Steam coal	t	442	
Natural gas	1000m^3	1,397,788	
LNG	t	15,562,894	

Kerosene	kl	412	
Heavy oil B and C	kl	427	
Naphtha	kl	1,027,075	
LPG	t	1,808,427	
Hydrocarbon gas	$1000m^3$	408,377	
Coke oven gas	$1000m^3$	615,287	
Gas supply	$1000m^3$	305,972	25,734,147
Methane gas	$1000m^3$	720	

Source: IOTEA 2000.

Table 20: Carbon balance table of coal products sector in 2000 (Unit: t-C)

	Input	**Output**
Coking coal	48,046,942	
Steam coal	39,421	
Gasoline	35	
Kerosene	5,478	
Light oils	186	
Heavy oil A	1,234	
Heavy oil B and C	311	
Hydrocarbon oil	122,554	
Hydrocarbon gas	227	
Petroleum coke	512,407	
Coke		34,125,070
Coke oven gas		3,248,008
Blast furnace gas	1,714,726	
Converter furnace gas	117,525	
Tar		1,216,929
Crude benzene		479,837
Gas supply	343	
Total	50,561,390	39,069,844
CO_2		11,491,546

Source: IOTEA 2000.

Table 21: Carbon balance table of pig iron sector in 2000 (Unit: t-C)

	Input	**Output**
Limestone	2,130,377	
Coking coal	281,462	
Steam coal	3,313,980	
Natural gas	758	
Kerosene	51	
Heavy oil A	1,114	
Heavy oil B and C	27,613	
LPG	6,758	

Petroleum coke	544,122	
Coke	31,822,946	
Coke oven gas	552,195	
Blast furnace gas	3,769,996	12,007,707
Converter furnace gas	457,472	
Tar	41,079	
Pig iron		3,244,226
Pig iron scrap	100	
Gas supply	869	
Blast furnace dust		365,205
Total	42,950,892	15,617,138
CO_2		27,333,754

Source: IOTEA 2000.

Table 22: Carbon balance table of crude steel (converters) sector in 2000 (Unit: t-C)

	Input	**Output**
Limestone	2,135,322	
Steam coal	480	
Natural gas	126	
Kerosene	6,593	
Heavy oil A	13,662	
Heavy oil B and C	2,011	
LPG	696	
Coke	85,002	
Coke oven gas	105,822	
Blast furnace gas	1,068	
Converter furnace gas	8,059	2,724,823
Pig iron	3,085,814	
Crude steel (converters)		227,380
Pig iron scrap	22,290	
Steel scrap	18,824	
Gas supply	8,540	
Total	5,494,310	2,952,203
CO_2		2,542,107

Source: IOTEA 2000.

Table 23: Carbon balance table of crude steel (electric furnaces) sector in 2000 (Unit: t-C)

	Input	Output
Limestone	120,460	
Steam coal	367	
Natural gas	596	
Kerosene	6,112	
Heavy oil A	7,734	

Heavy oil B and C	1,628	
LPG	858	
Petroleum coke	6,029	
Coke	65,560	
Coke oven gas	8,721	
Blast furnace gas	81	
Converter furnace gas	1,067	
Electric furnace gas		41,067
Pig iron	71,214	
Crude steel (electric converters)		91,996
Pig iron scrap	29,681	
Steel scrap	90,086	
Gas supply	12,050	
Total	422,243	133,063
CO_2		289,181

Source: IOTEA 2000.

Table 24: Carbon balance table of gas supply sector in 2000 (Unit: t-C)

	Input	Output
Coking coal	28,533	
Steam coal	290	
Natural gas	794,656	
LNG	11,450,399	
Kerosene	280	
Heavy oil B and C	347	
Naphtha	637,423	
LPG	1,479,763	
Hydrocarbon gas	260,373	
Coke oven gas	142,808	
Gas supply	173,541	14,595,893
Methane gas	387	
Total	14,968,802	14,595,893
CO_2		372,909

Source: IOTEA 2000.

RESULTS

Table **25** shows the results obtained by aggregating the sector classifications. Japan's CO_2 emission in 2000 was approximately 1.354 billion tons CO_2, which represents an increase of 3.1% compared with 1995 emission levels. The National Institute for Environmental Studies estimate (Nansai and Moriguchi 2006) was 1.326 billion tons CO_2.

The top three sectors in terms of CO_2 emissions are as follows: the electricity, gas, and heat supply sector (0.393 billion tons CO_2); the transport sector (0.193 billion tons CO_2); and consumption expenditure (private, 0.174 billion tons CO_2), in that order. The emissions in the consumption expenditure (private, 24 million tons CO_2) and the electricity, gas, and heat supply sector (21 million tons CO_2) showed the largest increase.

The emissions for the communication and broadcasting, public administration, and electrical machinery have rapidly been increasing (57.6%, 47.8%, and 39.4%, respectively), while the emissions of textile products, consumption expenditure outside households, and petroleum and coal products have been considerably reduced (−30.7%, −25.5%, and −19.6%, respectively).

Table 25: CO_2 emissions by sector in 1995 and 2000

	1995		2000		Growth
	Emisssions	Share	Emissions	Share	1995-2000
	t-CO_2	%	t-CO_2	%	%
Agriculture, forestry and fishery	20,446,520	1.6	16,848,417	1.2	-17.6
Mining	770,861	0.1	763,409	0.1	-1.0
Foods	14,977,620	1.1	14,662,041	1.1	-2.1
Textile products	5,251,253	0.4	3,639,174	0.3	-30.7
Pulp, paper and wooden products	30,497,052	2.3	30,524,256	2.3	0.1
Chemical products	46,361,400	3.5	48,271,757	3.6	4.1
Petroleum and coal products	90,380,493	6.9	72,629,713	5.4	-19.6
Ceramic, stone and clay products	99,611,766	7.6	88,969,799	6.6	-10.7
Iron and steel	96,826,806	7.4	131,702,770	9.7	36.0
Non-ferrous metals	5,271,842	0.4	5,163,190	0.4	-2.1
Metal products	3,799,588	0.3	4,281,744	0.3	12.7
General machinery	3,007,966	0.2	3,734,340	0.3	24.1
Electrical machinery	3,949,852	0.3	5,505,275	0.4	39.4
Transportation equipment	4,896,870	0.4	5,706,417	0.4	16.5
Precision instruments	398,726	0.0	532,365	0.0	33.5
Miscellaneous manufacturing products	6,072,431	0.5	7,682,751	0.6	26.5
Construction	15,508,430	1.2	13,844,529	1.0	-10.7
Electricity, gas and heat supply	372,257,006	28.3	393,005,951	29.0	5.6
Water supply and waste management services	49,270,767	3.8	47,096,719	3.5	-4.4
Commerce	13,882,135	1.1	12,680,898	0.9	-8.7
Financial and insurance	1,109,870	0.1	1,220,418	0.1	10.0
Real estate	3,175,160	0.2	3,214,177	0.2	1.2
Transport	208,086,963	15.8	193,469,233	14.3	-7.0
Communication and broadcasting	1,017,307	0.1	1,602,811	0.1	57.6
Public administration	10,697,508	0.8	15,806,927	1.2	47.8
Education and research	9,951,649	0.8	11,387,279	0.8	14.4
Medical service, health and social security and nursing care	12,330,404	0.9	13,517,487	1.0	9.6
Other public services	1,199,628	0.1	1,196,242	0.1	-0.3
Business services	5,534,919	0.4	6,290,060	0.5	13.6
Personal services	22,118,376	1.7	21,720,041	1.6	-1.8
Office supplies	0	0.0	0	0.0	0.0
Activities not elsewhere classified	3,009,736	0.2	1,679,750	0.1	-44.2
Consumption expenditure outside households (column)	1,872,853	0.1	1,395,770	0.1	-25.5
Consumption expenditure (private)	149,812,625	11.4	174,168,007	12.9	16.3
Total emissions	1,313,356,384	100.0	1,353,913,717	100.0	3.1

Source: IOTEA 1995 and 2000.

APPLICATION

Introduction

For a case study application of the IOTEA, we focused on Solar Power Satellites (SPS) as a future alternative power generation technology. SPS technology involves a satellite carrying photovoltaic (PV) panels in geostationary orbit (GEO) that continuously generates electricity independent of the weather or time of day and transmits this power to the Earth's surface. This study measured the CO_2 emissions from the latest SPS technology — multi-bus tethered-SPS — which was presented by Sasaki (the Japan Aerospace Exploration Agency, JAXA) using the IOTEA; several previous types of SPS were included for comparison. The results revealed that the CO_2 emissions from multi-bus tethered SPS per unit of energy generated is a little more than that from a nuclear power system. However, the generated emissions are much less than an LNG-fired power system or a coal-fired energy system. Hence, we concluded that the latest SPS is currently one of the most effective alternative technologies for future CO_2 reduction in electric power generation.

Basic Concept of SPS

The PV cells have been receiving increasing attention as a means of electricity generation that produces no CO_2, NOx, or SOx pollution. However, because solar energy generation is impossible at night and the poor efficiency during cloudy weather, stable electricity generation is difficult. However, if solar panels are launched into space, they can produce continuous power independent of the weather or the day-and-night cycle. The solar power satellite (SPS) concept is very simple: a satellite carrying PV panels in GEO generates electricity and transmits it to the Earth's surface.

The basic concept of SPS was first published by Glaser (1968); the US Department of Energy (DOE), and the National Aeronautics and Space Administration (NASA) published a reference system in 1978, which is referred to as the "DOE/NASA reference system" in this paper. Although the reference system was published more than 30 years ago, no other equally detailed system including ground facilities and space transportation system has been proposed since then; therefore, it remains the representative plan for future SPS systems.

Fig. **2** shows the concept of the DOE/NASA reference system. The satellite is shown in the upper part: it has a rectangular structure 10 km long by 5 km wide and 300 m deep. It carries PV panels over its surface and transmits the generated power from the 1-km diameter antenna using high-frequency microwaves. The lower half shows the rectenna on the Earth, which receives and rectifies the microwaves from the satellite; it is elliptical in shape and has dimensions of 13 km by 10 km. Each satellite-rectenna pair has an output of 5 GW, and the reference system is comprised of 60 such satellites. The total annual output of electric energy has been estimated to be 2,628 billion kWh.

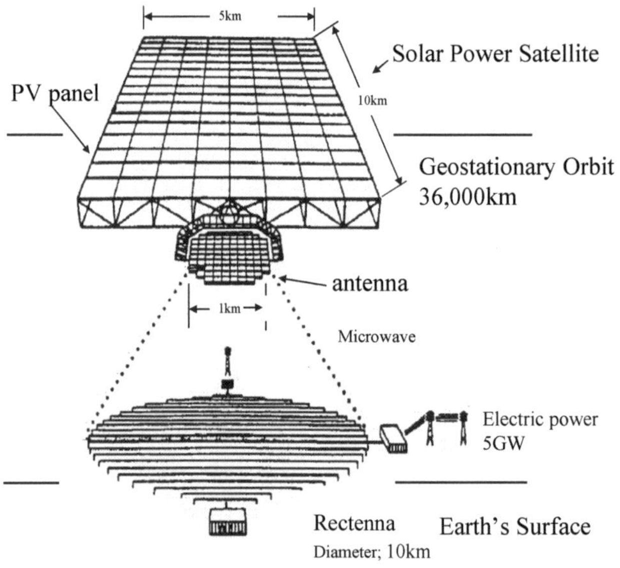

Source: DOE/NASA (1980) SPS-FY79 Program Summary.

Figure 2: DOE/NASA reference system

The SPS concept of the DOE/NASA reference system is very clear, but it may be too large in scale for construction; therefore, smaller types of SPS have been presented by the Institute for Unmanned Space Experiment Free Flyer (USEF), the New Energy and Industrial Technology Development Organization (NEDO) and JAXA that have relatively higher feasibility.[1] In this study, we focused on the new multi-bus tethered SPS that was developed by Sasaki (2006a, 2009).

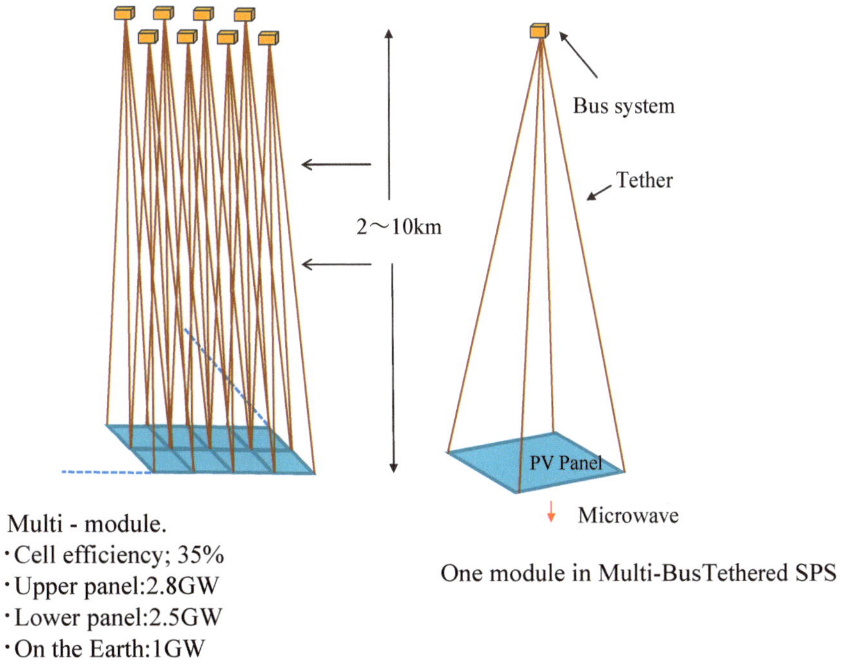

Note: This technology presented by Sasaki (2006a, 2009).

Figure 3: Features of multi-bus tethered satellite

Fig. **3** shows the satellite structure of the multi-bus tethered SPS; the new SPS system has two features. First, the satellite has a multi-module structure, and the tethers link the bus system with a PV panel in each module. Second, each module itself functions as an electric power generator. The attached PV panel has a high power conversion efficiency of 35%, and the total electric power generated by 625 modules is 2.8 GW in the upper panel and 2.5 GW in the lower one.[2] The generated electricity is charged by a battery, controlled to 1.36 GW and changed to microwave beams; the microwave is then transmitted to the rectenna, which receives and rectifies the microwaves and supplies 1 GW of electricity to industries and households.

We then proceed to the SPS construction process in Fig. **4**, which is deeply related to the calculation of the CO_2 emissions. First, the Reusable Launch Vehicle (RLV) carries the Orbital Transfer Vehicle (OTV) and satellite to low-earth-orbit; the OTV then carries the satellite to geostationary orbit; finally, the satellite deploys automatically, and the SPS satellite is completed when the 625 modules are connected to each other. We discuss the RLV and OTV structures in more detail here.

The total mass of the RLV is 2,000 tons; it is comprised of the payload (50 tons), structure (200 tons), liquid oxygen (LOX) (1,500 tons), and liquid hydrogen (LH_2) (250 tons); the latter two serve as propellants. Fourteen RLVs make 1,000 round trips in total.[3]

The OTV has 2,151 kW of PV panels which ionize liquid argon (LAr) for space propulsion. The total mass of the OTV is 145 tons, which is comprised of the payload (50 tons), structure (43 tons), PV panels (22 tons), and liquid argon (LAr) (30 tons). One hundred seventy-one OTVs make 600 round trips in total.

---

[1] See the New Energy and Industrial Technology Development Organization (1994), Sasaki *et al.* (2004, 2006a, b).

[2] The current conversion efficiency of space solar cells has not yet reached 35%.

[3] Total mass-payload ratio was assumed to be 2.5%, which is very high and a future target. The present ratio is about 1.5%.

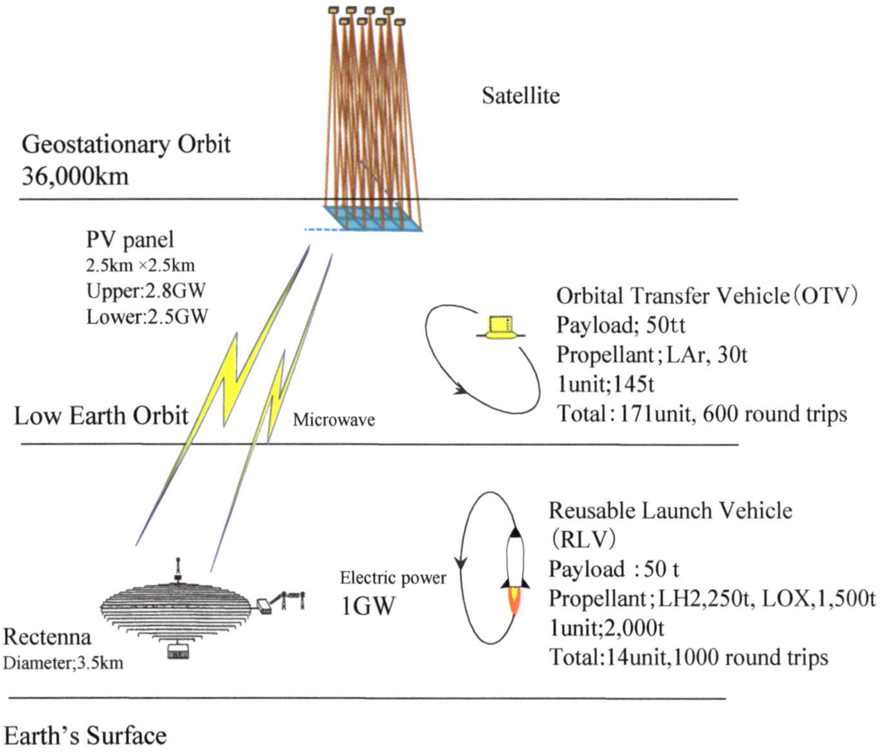

Note: This Picture was drowned by authors based on Sasaki (2006a, 2009) and the viewpoint of calculation of CO_2 emissions from SPS.

Figure 4: Construction on multi-bus tethered satellite- Key Items

The Model

The CO_2 emission that would be produced by constructing and operating the SPS system is estimated using the IOTEA 2000, which was presented in the first part of this paper. The input-output model for environmental analysis based on open input-output model is given by;

$$CO_2^k = C(I - A)^{-1} f^k \qquad \textbf{(1)}$$

C: CO_2 emission coefficient matrix (diagonal)

$(I - A)^{-1}$: Leontief inverse matrix

f^k: final demand (FD) vector of kth item of the SPS system

(e.g., $k = 1$, satellite; $k = 2$, OTV; $k = 3$, rectenna ;…)

$CO_2{}^k$: CO_2 emission of kth item of SPS system.

C on the right-hand side of equation (1) is derived in the first part of this paper, calculated by (CO_2 emission) /(domestic production) in each sector and $(I - A)^{-1}$ can be calculated from the official *2000 Input-Output Table*; therefore, we have to determine the FD vectors for each item such as the satellite, OTV, RLV, rectenna, propellant (LAr, LOX and LH_2), and PV panel, as shown in Fig. **4**, to solve for CO_2^k.

Fig. **5** shows the basic procedure for determining an FD vector, using the satellite as an example. First, the unit price and amounts of material inputs are gathered; second, these are linked according to the *Input-Output Table* classification; finally, the trade and transport margins are added.

①Material Input Information(e.g. Satellite)

Resource Requirements	Material Input	Unit Price
silicon transistor	a	p_a
silicon diode	b	p_b
CPU	c	p_c
DRAM	d	p_d
•	•	•
•	•	•
•	•	•

②I-O sector

I-O Classification	Prices
semiconductor devices	a×p_a
semiconductor devices	b×p_b
integrated circuits	c×p_c
integrated circuits	d×p_d
•	•
•	•
•	•

③Add Margin

I-O Classification	Prices
semiconductor devices	a×p_a
semiconductor devices	b×p_b
integrated circuits	c×p_c
integrated circuits	d×p_d
•	•
•	•
•	•
trade and transport margin	m1
	m2
	•
	•

Note: Main data source of FD vectors estimated are DOE/NASA (1980), Society of Chemical Engineers (1995), Yearbook Machinery Statistics, Unit price information in Input output databases, Naruo et al.(1996) and Sasaki(2006a,2009) etc.

Figure 5: Procedure to determine FD vectors

Here, we summarize the basic information to determine the FD vectors of the SPS total system.

Satellite: A satellite needs the following electronic components per square meter: 4 silicon transistors, 68 field-effect transistors, 4 diodes, 4 MUPs, 4 DRAMs, 8 chip resistors, 8 tantalum electrolytic capacitors, 1 m^2 multilayer printer boards, and 4 lithium ion batteries. Each satellite is comprised of 4,400 tons of rolled and drawn aluminum products and 45 tons of tether. Each unit price is from the *2000 Yearbook of Machinery Statistics* and the detailed domestic products table by sector and commodity of the *2000 Input-Output Table*.

OTV

The unit price of LAr in OTV is based on the annual average price in the Economic Research Association (2000). The OTV structure was estimated from Sasaki and Yamagiwa (2000), the cargo orbit transfer vehicle (COTV) developed by DOE/NASA (1980), the detailed domestic products table by sector and commodity, and the airplane activity vector in the *2000 Input-Output Table*.

RLV

The unit price of LH_2 is based on estimates from Naruo *et al.* (1996), and the price for LOX is from the *2000 Yearbook of Machinery Statistics*. The RLV structure was estimated from the heavy lift launch vehicle (HLLV) developed by DOE/NASA (1980), the detailed domestic products table by sector and commodity, and the airplane activity vector in the *2000 Input-Output Table*.

Rectenna

The rectenna cost structure, its installation cost, and the number of diodes and antennas are estimated based on another type of rectenna from DOE/NASA (1980), large-scale solar power systems on the ground (e.g., Society of Chemical Engineers 1995, Kato *et al.* 1994, Nomura *et al.* 1995), and the electric power facilities construction activity in the *2000 Input-Output Table*. Inverters and relay switches are estimated from work done by the Society of Chemical Engineers (1995), Kato *et al.* (1994) and Nomura *et al.* (1995)

PV

PV that are attached to the satellite and OTV are assumed to have high-conversion efficiency, be resistant to radiation, and workable except for the cover glass, which is similar to current copper indium gallium diselenide (CIGS) thin-film PV cells; however, it is difficult to obtain the structural information for this particular type. Therefore, we use recent solar cell activity estimated by Nakano (2006) under the strong assumption that solar cell activity does not change according to the conversion efficiency.

Overview of CO_2 Emissions

In this section, we describe the main results for estimates of CO_2 emissions from SPS construction. Table **26** shows that the released CO_2 would be 11 million tons. The largest amount is released from the production processes of LOX and LH_2 in RLV, which account for 60% of the total CO_2 emissions. The second largest amount comes from the PV attached to the satellite and the OTV in total, which account for 22% of the total emissions.

Table 26: CO_2 emissions from SPS by items

Item		**kiloton**	**share(%)**
Satellite	Structure	1116.9	10.4
	PV	2194.9	20.4
OTV	Structure	75.3	0.7
	LAr	61.0	0.6
	PV	152.3	1.4
RLV	Structure	47.0	0.4
	LOX, LH2	6406.9	59.6
Recttna		693.4	6.5
Total		10747.7	100.0

Note: OTV: Orbital Transfer Vehicle, RLV: Reusable Launch Vehicle, PV: Photovoltaic cell, LAr: Liquid argon, LH2: Liquid hydrogen, LOX: Liquid oxygen. Figures are calculated by eq. (1).

Table **27** shows the four highest-ranking sectors of CO_2 emissions in the SPS system. For LH_2 and LOX in RLV, which induced the largest emissions according to Table **26**, the production process of these propellants, such as compression and cooling, require large amounts of electricity; therefore, electricity-related sectors were ranked high as a result. In short, Table **27** shows that each item in the SPS system requires various kinds of materials directly, but direct and indirect CO_2 emissions are mainly induced by electrical power generation.

Table 27: CO_2 emissions from SPS by sectors

	(a) satellite (structure)	**Share(%)**	**(b) OTV (structure)**	**Share(%)**
1	electricity	35.4	electricity	32.7
2	private power generation	10.4	private power generation	13.0
3	pig iron	6.2	pig iron	6.5
4	coal product	5.5	coal product	5.7
	others	42.5	others	42.1

	total	100.0	total	100.0
	(1,117 kilotons)		(75 kilotons)	
	(C) OTV (LAr)	Share(%)	(d) RLV (structure)	Share(%)
1	electricity	73.1	electricity	30.9
2	compressed gas and liquefied gas	7.9	private power generation	15.1
3	private power generation	3.7	coal product	7.8
4	coal product	2.2	pig iron	7.7
	others	13.2	others	38.5
	total	100.0	total	100.0
	(61 kilotons)		(47 kilotons)	
	(e) RLV (LH2, LOX)	Share(%)	(g) Rectena	Share(%)
1	electricity	63.9	pig iron	24.0
2	road freight transport	7.5	electricity	23.2
3	compressed gas and liquefied gas	6.7	private power generation	8.7
4	private power generation	3.6	coal product	7.9
	others	18.3	others	36.2
	total	100.0	total	100.0
	(6,407 kilotons)		(693 kilotons)	
	(h) PV (satellte and OTV)	Share(%)	(i) SPS total	Share(%)
1	electricity	47.6	electricity	54.4
2	private power generation	10.7	private power generation	6.3
3	coal product	7.5	road freight transport	5.2
4	pig iron	4.7	coal product	4.1
	others	29.5	others	30.0
	total	100.0	total	100.0
	(2,347 kilotons)		(10,748 kilotons)	

Note: Figures are calculated by eq. (1).

Comparison of CO_2 Emission

Lastly, we compare the CO_2 emissions of the multi-bus tethered SPS system with different kinds of electricity generation systems.

First, the annual energy production of SPS can be calculated as:

$$1 \text{ GW} \times 24 \text{ h} \times 365 \text{ day} = 8{,}760 \text{ GWh}.$$

Furthermore, if we assume a lifetime is 40 years, and the CO_2 emissions from SPS construction is 10,748 kilotons, the CO_2 emission per kWh can be estimated as:

$$10{,}748 \text{ kilotons}/40 \text{ years}/8{,}760 \text{ GWh} \times 1000 = 30.7 \text{ g } CO_2/\text{kWh}.$$

In addition, the ratio of annual maintenance and repair, including current operations, is assumed to be 2.5%; therefore, the CO_2 emission per kWh can be calculated as:

$$30.7 \text{ g } CO_2/\text{kWh} \times 1.025 = 31.4 \text{ g } CO_2/\text{kWh}.$$

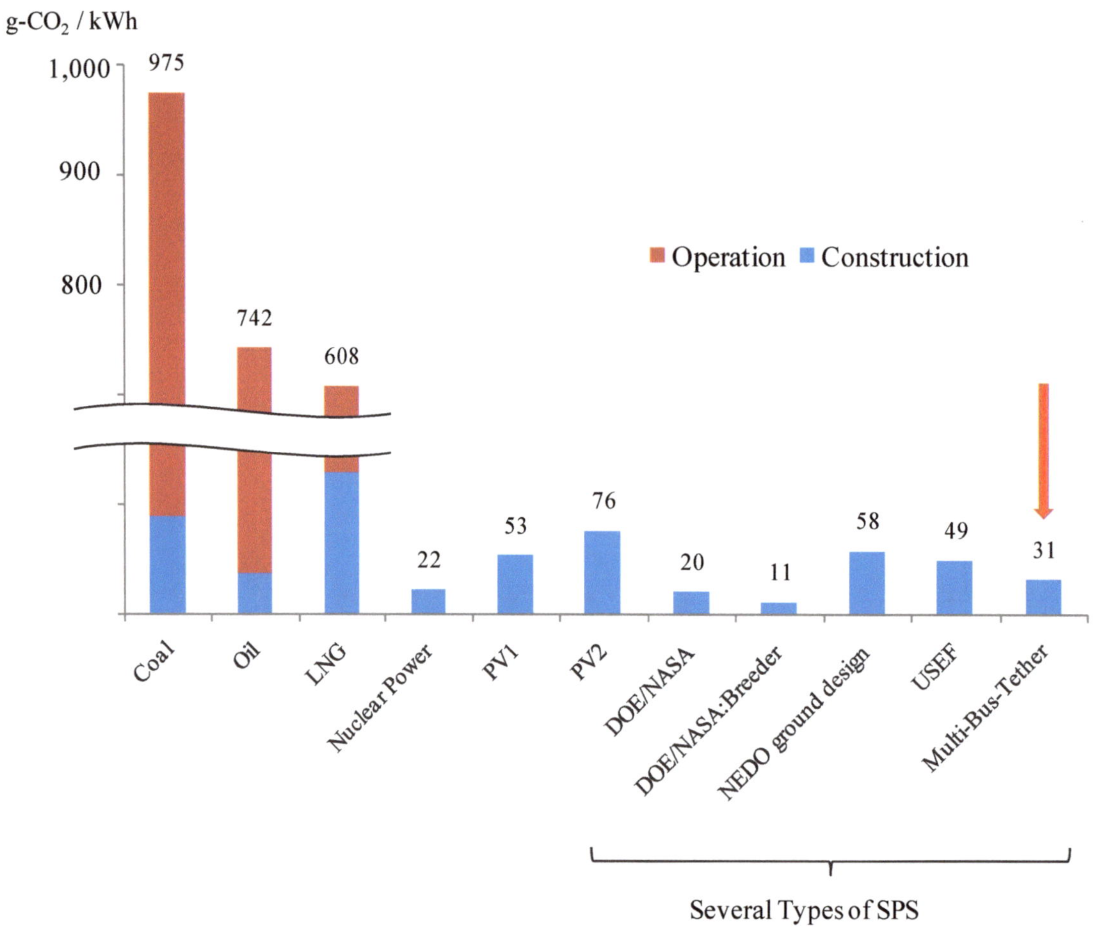

Notes: 1) Figures for Coal, Oil, LNG, Nuclear, and PV1 were estimated by Hondo (2000). 2) Figure for PV2 is a recalculation of Nakano (2006) using eq. (1). 3) Figures for several types of SPS are estimated by our group; DOE/NASA and DOE/NASA Breeder are from Asakura et al. (2002), NEDO from Ohashi et al. (2001), USEF from Asakura et al. (2003). 4) Lifetime assumption for multi-tethered satellite system: 40 years. 5) Total repair ratio of multi-tethered satellite system is assumed to be 2.5%.

Figure 6: CO_2 emissions per kWh of energy production

Fig. **6** compares the CO_2 emissions per kWh of electrical energy produced by several types of existing electric power generation systems and the SPS systems. When comparing SPS systems, the DOE/NASA reference system has the lowest CO_2 emissions per kWh, as it has a very efficient transport system; i.e., the total mass-payload ratio is relatively higher than those for NEDO, USEF, and multi-bus tether, which means relatively less propellant is needed.

When the CO_2 emissions of the multi-bus tethered SPS is compared with existing electric power generation systems, the SPS CO_2 emission is a little higher than that of nuclear power; however, it is much lower than that of fossil fuel electric power generation, 1/30 of coal, 1/24 of oil, and 1/20 of natural gas.

This study clearly shows that construction of the SPS system releases large amounts of CO_2; however, the CO_2 emissions per kWh for SPS are much lower than that of existing power plants. In addition, our recent calculations show that the CO_2 per kWh of SPS is in double digits even when the structures are different, such as DOE/NASA, NEDO, USEF, and multi-bus tether.

Further investigation is required on how to reduce CO_2 emissions by "solar breeding," in which installed SPS supplies electricity for producing further SPS or liquid fuel. This is a very challenging research target, and we will try to further develop the next stages.

CONCLUDING REMARKS

This paper is a report on the estimation method for the *IOTEA 2000* and its application study. Energy and economy statistics are considerably developed in Japan compared with other countries. This has led to the detailed estimation of the *Input-Output Table*. The amount of information for energy and environmental analyses is increasing. For instance, we can estimate the energy consumption for co-generation and the recycling sector in the *Input-Output Table*. However, at the same time, the *Structural Survey of Energy Consumption in Commerce and Manufacturing* has already become out of date.

The IOTEA provides information on the detailed structure of CO_2 emissions, which is necessary to assess ecofriendly technologies and to introduce measures against global warming. Hence, ensuring that the necessary statistics are up-to-date and continuously estimating the IOTEA is a major challenge. Effective utilization of the *Survey of Energy Consumption* and *Comprehensive Energy Statistics* should be discussed.

ACKNOWLEDGEMENTS

We thank Susumu Sasaki (Japan Aerospace Exploration Agency, JAXA) and Yoshihiro Naruo (JAXA) for providing us technical information on the SPS system. Our thanks are also due to Kanji Yoshioka (Keio University) and Hitoshi Hayami (Keio University) for many valuable comments and suggestions on this study. The authors are solely responsible for any errors.

REFERENCES

Asakura, K., H. Hayami, M. Mizoshita, M. Nakamura, S. Nakano, M. Shinozaki, A. Washizu & K. Yoshioka (2001). *The Input-Output Table for Environmental Analysis*, Keio University Press. (in Japanese)

Asakura, K., Collins, P., Nomura, K., Hayami, H. & Yoshioka, K. (2002). CO_2 Emission from Solar Power Satellite, *KEO Discussion Paper*, No.G-145, Keio Economic Observatory, Keio University. (in Japanese)

Asakura, K., Kobayashi, Y. & Yoshioka, K. (2003). CO_2 Emission from a New Solar Power Satellite System of USEF, *proceedings 6th SPS Symposium* 117-122. (in Japanese)

Department of Energy (DOE) and National Aeronautics and Space Administration (NASA), U.S. (1979). *Satellite Power System*, DOE/ER-0023.

(1980). *Preliminary Material Assessment for the Satellite Power System (SPS)*, DOE/ER-0038. Economic Research Association, Japan (2000). *Price Data for Construction Cost Estimating*, Economic Research Association. (in Japanese)

Electricity and Gas Industry Department, Agency for Natural Resources and Energy (2000). *Outline of Electricity Demand and Supply FY 1999*, Chuwa Printing Co., Ltd. (in Japanese)

Electricity and Gas Industry Department, Agency for Natural Resources and Energy (2001). *Outline of Electricity Demand and Supply FY 2000*, Chuwa Printing Co., Ltd. (in Japanese)

Gas Market Division, Electricity and Gas Industry Department, Agency for Natural Resources and Energy (2001). *Yearbook of the Gas Supply 2000*, The Japan Gas Association. (in Japanese)

General Policy Division, Director-General's Secretariat, Agency for Natural Resources and Energy (2002). *Comprehensive Energy Statistics FY 2001*, Tsusho Sangyo Kenkyusha. (in Japanese)

Glaser, P. E. (1968). Power from the sun, *Science*, 162, 857-861. Hondo, H., Uchiyama, Y. & Morizumi, Y. (2000). Evaluation of Power Generation Technologies based on Life Cycle CO_2 Emissions - Re-estimation using the Latest Data and Effects of the Difference of Conditions, *Socio-economic Research Center, Rep*, No.Y99009. (in Japanese)

Hondo, Y., Y. Moriizumi, Y. Tonooka & A. Kannari (2002). Estimation of Greenhouse Gas Emission Factors Using 1995 Japanese Economic Input-Output Table, *Journal of the Japan Institute of Energy*, 81(9), 828-844. (in Japanese)

Ikeda, A., M. Suga, M. Shinozaki, H. Hayami, K. Fujiwara & K. Yoshioka (1996). *The Input-Output Table for Environmental Analysis*, KEO Monograph Series No.7, Keio Economic Observatory, Keio University. (in Japanese)

Kato, K., Yamada, K., Inaba, A., Shimatani, T., Tabata, S., Kawamura, S., Shibuya, H., Iwase, Y., Kakumoto, T., Kojima, T. & H. Komiyama (1994). Cost Evaluation of Photovoltaic Energy System, *The Journal of Chemical Engineering of Japan*, 20(2), 261-267. (in Japanese)

Ministry of Finance (2001). *Japan Exports & Imports 2000*, Japan Tariff Association. (in Japanese) The English version of trade statistics is also available from http://www.customs.go.jp/toukei/info/index_e.htm.

Ministry of Internal Affairs and Communications (2004). *2000 Input-Output Table*, National Federation of Statistics Association. (in Japanese) The English version is also available from http://www.stat.go.jp/english/data/io/io00.htm.

Nakano, S., H. Hayami, M. Nakamura and M. Suzuki (2008). *The Input-Output Table for Environmental Analysis and its Application*, Keio University Press. (in Japanese)

Nakano, S. (2006). CO_2 Reduction Effect and User Cost of Residential Photovoltaic System, *KEO Discussion paper*, No.102, Keio Economic Observatory, Keio University. (in Japanese)

Nakano, S. (2009). The Input-Output Table for Environmental Analysis 2005: Estimation and Results, *KEO Discussion Paper* No.117, Keio Economic Observatory, Keio University. (in Japanese)

Nansai, K. and Y. Moriguchi (2006). Practical determination of sector environmental burdens applied to input-output analysis, *Journal of Life Cycle Assessment, Japan*, 2(1), 22-41. (in Japanese)

Naruo, Y., Inatani, Y. and T. Ota (1996). Regarding the fuel supply system for fully reusable rocket to achieve high-frequency operation, *Proceedings of Space Transportation Symposium*, ISAS, 82-85. (in Japanese)

New Energy and Industrial Technology Development Organization (1994). *New Sunshine Project*, NEDO. (in Japanese)

Nomura, N., Akai, M., Inaba, A., Yamada, K and H. Komiyama (1995). Estimation of Energy Payback Time of Solar Power Station based on Input-Output Analysis, *Energy and Resources*, 16(5), 57-64. (in Japanese)

Nippon Slag Association (2001). *Statistical Yearbook of Iron and Steel Slag FY2000*, Retrieved from http://www.slg.jp/. (in Japanese)

Ohashi, E., Matsuhashi, R., Ishitani, H., Yoshida, Y., Hikita, K. and K. Yoshioka (2001). CO_2 Emission from Solar Power Satellite-Reference System and New Concept, *KEO Discussion paper*, No.G-127, Keio Economic Observatory, Keio University. (in Japanese)

Research and Statistics Department, Economic and Industrial Policy Bureau, Ministry of Economy, Trade and Industry (2001a). *Structural Survey of Energy Consumption in Commerce and Manufacturing 2000*, Economy, Trade and Industry Statistics Association. (in Japanese)

Research and Statistics Department, Economic and Industrial Policy Bureau, Ministry of Economy, Trade and Industry (2001b). *Yearbook of Iron and Steel Statistics 2000*, Research Institute of Economy, Trade and Industry. (in Japanese)

Research and Statistics Department, Economic and Industrial Policy Bureau, Ministry of Economy, Trade and Industry (2001c). *Yearbook of Production Supply and Demand of Petroleum, Coal and Coke 2000*, Research Institute of Economy, Trade and Industry. (in Japanese)

Research and Statistics Department, Economic and Industrial Policy Bureau, Ministry of Economy, Trade and Industry (2001d). *Yearbook of the Current Survey of Energy Consumption in Manufacturing 2000*, Economy, Trade and Industry Statistics Association. (in Japanese)

Research and Statistics Department, Economic and Industrial Policy Bureau, Ministry of Economy, Trade and Industry (2001e). *2000 Yearbook of Machinery Statistics*, Research Institute of Economy, Trade and Industry. (in Japanese and English) (2002). *Census of Manufactures 2000*, Printing Bureau, Ministry of Finance. (in Japanese) The English outline is available from http://www.meti.go.jp/english/statistics/tyo/kougyo/index.html.

Sasaki, S. and Y. Yamagiwa (2000). Transportation by Ion Thruster OTV, mimeo.

Sasaki, S., Tanaka, K, Kawasaki, S., Shinohara, N., Higuchi, K., Okuizumi, N., Senda, K. and the USEF SSPS Study Team (2004). Conceptual Study of SSPS. Demonstration Experiment, *Radio Science Bulletin*, 310, 9-14.

Sasaki, S., Tanaka, K., Higuchi, K., Okuizumi, N., Kawasaki, S., Shinohara, M. and K. Ishimura (2006a). Engineering Research for New Tethered Solar Power Satellite, *Proceedings of 25th ISTS*, 780-785.

Sasaki, S., Tanaka, K., Higuchi, K., Okuizumi, N., Kawasaki, S., Shinohara, M. and K. Ishimura (2006b). A new concept of solar power satellite: Tetherd-SPS, *Acta Astronautica*, 60, 153-165.

Sasaki, S. (2009). The SPS design and system technology, In Yoshioka, K. Matsuoka, H. & H. Hayami (Eds.), *Essays on the Solar Power Satellite : An Interdisciplinary Study of Space Industry and the Future of Society* (pp. 45-59), Keio University Press. (in Japanese)

Science Applications International Corporation and NASA (1997). Space Solar Power – A fresh Look at the Feasibility of Generating Solar Power in Space for Use on Earth, Report Number SAIC-97/1005.

Society of Chemical Engineers, Japan (1995). *Evaluation of Solar Photovoltaic Technology II.* (in Japanese)

Waste Management and Recycling Department, Ministry's Secretariat, Ministry of Environment (2002a). *State of Discharge and Treatment of Industrial Waste FY 2000*, Retrieved from http://www.env.go.jp. (in Japanese)

Waste Management and Recycling Department, Ministry's Secretariat, Ministry of Environment (2002b). *State of Discharge and Treatment of Municipal Solid Waste FY 2000*, Retrieved from http://www.env.go.jp. (in Japanese)

Yoshioka, K., Suga, M., Nomura, K. and K. Asakura (1998). An Application of the Input-Output Table for Environmental Analysis (9) –CO_2 Emission from Solar Power Satellite, *Business Journal PAPAIOS*, Pan Pacific Association of Input-Output Studies, 8(2), 28-44. (in Japanese).

Subject Index

A

Air pollution 132
Atmospheric emissions 31

C

CO_2 Emissions 1-46-65-149
CO_2 Responsibility 65

E

Emissions levels 112
Energy 46
Energy intensities 65
Environmentally extended input-output tables 96

G

GHGs emissions 13
Greece 96

H

Hybrid I-O analysis 65

I

Input-Output 1
Input-Output analysis 31-112
Input-Output model 132
Italy 132

J

Japan 149

K

Key sectors in emission 1
Kyoto protocol and natural gas substitution 13

L

Life cycle assessment 149

M

Multipliers, demand and supply 1
Multiplier effects 112
Multipliers decomposition methodology 46

N

NAMEA tables 96

P

Portugal 65
Primary energy Use 112

R

Regional input-output tables 96

S

Social accounting matrices 46
Solar power satellites 149
Spain 1-31-46-112
Structural change 112
Structural decomposition analysis 112
Structural path analysis 31
Subsystems analysis 46

T

Technological change 112
Tourism activity 132
Turkey 13

www.ingramcontent.com/pod-product-compliance
Lightning Source LLC
LaVergne TN
LVHW070951210926
848482LV00002B/184

* 9 7 8 1 6 0 8 0 5 5 8 2 1 *